Beyond Filial Piety

Life Course, Culture and Aging: Global Transformations
General Editor: Jay Sokolovsky, University of South Florida St. Petersburg

Published by Berghahn Books under the auspices of the Association for Anthropology and Gerontology (AAGE) and the American Anthropological Association Interest Group on Aging and the Life Course.

The consequences of aging will influence most areas of contemporary life around the globe: the makeup of households and communities; systems of care; generational exchange and kinship; the cultural construction of the life cycle; symbolic representations of midlife, elderhood, and old age; and attitudes toward health, disability, and life's end. This series will publish monographs and collected works that examine these widespread transformations with a perspective on the entire life course as well as mid/late adulthood, engaging a cross-cultural framework. It will explore the role of older adults in changing cultural spaces and how this evolves in our rapidly globalizing planet.

BEYOND FILIAL PIETY

Rethinking Aging and Caregiving in Contemporary East Asian Societies

Edited by

Jeanne Shea, Katrina Moore, and Hong Zhang

berghahn
NEW YORK • OXFORD
www.berghahnbooks.com

First published in 2020 by
Berghahn Books
www.berghahnbooks.com

Library of Congress Cataloging-in-Publication Data

A C.I.P. cataloging record is available from the Library of Congress
Library of Congress Cataloging in Publication Control Number:
2020937014

British Library Cataloguing in Publication Data

A catalogue record for this book is available from the British Library.

ISBN 978-1-78920-788-0 hardback
ISBN 978-1-80073-447-0 paperback
ISBN 978-1-78920-789-7 ebook

For our parents, our families, our teachers, and our research participants

CONTENTS

PART II. Aging and Caregiving in Japanese Contexts

PART III. Aging and Caregiving in Korean Contexts

ILLUSTRATIONS

TABLES

ACKNOWLEDGMENTS

WE WISH TO EXPRESS OUR deepest gratitude to the many people who helped us to bring this edited volume to life. Marion Berghahn and the Association for Anthropology and Gerontology (AAGE) and the American Anthropological Association Interest Group on Aging and the Life Course led the way in supporting Berghahn Books' Life Course, Culture, and Aging: Global Transformations series, of which this volume is a part. Series Editor Jay Sokolovsky gave us steady encouragement and sage advice throughout the process of writing the book; his wise mentorship was critical to bringing this complex multi-authored work to fruition. The three anonymous reviewers shared astute direction for revision that greatly enhanced the manuscript, especially with regard to further situating our research within the broader scholarly literature. Berghahn Assistant Editor Tom Bonnington provided us with adept editorial guidance, and Elizabeth Martinez and her staff and copy editor Alison Hope took meticulous care in the book production process. David Prout provided excellent professional indexing for the volume, for which the Anthropology Department, Asian Studies Program, and Office of the Vice President for Research at the University of Vermont and the Provost's Office at Colby College provided funding. University of Vermont student Lauren Rigney provided some very helpful volume-related research assistance. A generous grant from the Chiang Ching-kuo Foundation helped to support the paperback edition of the book, which Berghahn Production Editors Keara Hagerty and Caroline Kuhtz prepared for publication. We are also grateful to our families who supported the countless hours that it took to complete this labor.

NOTES ON TEXT AND TRANSLITERATION

- Acronyms and abbreviations are defined on first instance in each chapter.

- In addition to the English language, other languages appearing in this volume include instances of Chinese, Japanese, Korean, and Russian.

- Non-English words have been translated from the original language into American English.

- Important non-English words have been included in the body of chapters, as well as in a glossary at the end of each chapter.

- On first use of a non-English word in a chapter, the English is given first, followed by the transliteration of that word provided in parentheses. From then on, the transliteration is used on its own in that chapter.

- Readers can look back to earlier in the chapters or to the glossary at the end of each chapter for a refresher if they forget the translation. In addition, the chapter glossaries include terms in Chinese, Japanese, or Korean, as the case may be.

- The Chinese language consists of many different spoken dialects united by written Chinese characters. As a result, Chinese characters for all Chinese words are included in chapter glossaries. For the sake of consistency across chapters, most Chinese transliterations are given in the official Mandarin dialect of China using the pinyin phonetic system. It should be noted, however, that the Hong Kong research in this volume was largely done in Cantonese, the dominant dialect for that Special Administrative Region.

- For Japanese, the Hepburn system of transliteration was used. Material in Japanese script is also included in chapter glossaries. For transliterated material, macrons are used to indicate long vowels in Japanese. For example, Hōkyōji reads as long vowels with circumflexes on both o's.

- For Korean, the form of Korean found in South Korea, Hanguk Eo, is used. For the most part, romanization of Korean words follows the McCune-Reischauer system, although chapter 10 uses the system of the National Institute of Korean Language. Korean script is also provided in chapter glossaries.

- Romanization of Russian words follows the Library of Congress system, with the exception of some commonly accepted alternative spellings.

INTRODUCTION

Jeanne Shea, Katrina Moore, and Hong Zhang

Introduction

IN THIS VOLUME WE EXPLORE aging and caregiving in contemporary East Asian societies with Chinese, Japanese, or Korean cultural roots. Aging, caregiving, and their intersections have long been a key concern in East Asian societies, largely from the perspective of support and care for the elderly. This focus has stemmed from centuries-old Confucian ideals involving filial piety, a major component of which has asked adult children to fulfill obligations to respect, obey, support, and care for their elderly parents. Recent research shows that this traditional ideal has become more difficult to realize in practice today, given the demographic and social transformations sweeping East Asia in the past two decades. At the same time, evidence is emerging of evolution in cultural values such that seniors taking care of themselves and each other and/or continuing to take care of children or grandchildren far into their later years is more socially expected and intensively practiced than in the past. As such, this book brings together examinations of social support for, and productive aging by, the elderly.

Within the next three decades, the elderly proportion of the world's population will rise markedly, and East Asian societies will be among those locales at the forefront of this unprecedented demographic change. While East Asia is not the only place facing a high degree of population aging, the speed of its population aging and its Confucian tradition make it distinctive regarding how related issues and strategies are viewed and manifested.

This book is designed for students, faculty, researchers, and practitioners in the fields of social gerontology, Asian studies, anthropology, sociology, social work, public health, and policy studies. It shows how in order to understand and address issues of aging and caregiving in East Asia, we need to go beyond romanticism about traditional respect for the elderly and familial eldercare in Confucian cultures (on such Orientalism, see Buch 2015: 278) to examine the complex patterns of social change transforming those societies. It also shows how lived experience is far more complex than the stark images of catastrophic futures inexorably linked to population aging and perceived decline in traditional Confucian values. In this vein, it illustrates some of the ways in which governments, communities, families, and individuals are taking the challenge of an aging society as an opportunity for social innovation, collaboration, and productive aging, not just as a demographic crisis (HelpAge International 2015).[1] Finally, it shows how similar demographic and social changes may meet varied interpretations, responses, and consequences in different geopolitical locales, despite all having Confucian roots.

This volume was written in dialogue with Charlotte Ikels's (2004) classic collection on *Filial Piety*, noting changes as well as continuities in discourse and practice over the decade and a half since its publication. East Asian populations are much older today, and much has changed in demographic, social, and public policy terms. In order to promote comparison over time, our volume engages some of the same themes that Ikels's volume did. These include the ways in which demographic change, "modernization," and the state are affecting support and care for the aged, as well as how communities, families, and individuals are changing in terms of discourse and practice apropos filial piety and old-age support and care. Our volume also extends anew or more deeply into certain thematic areas, and adds updated ethnographic material and geographic locations. It adds material on the compression of modernization and speed of population aging. It does more to balance content on care done both for the aged and *by* the aged. It also contains more content on emerging social innovations, interaction of familial and nonfamilial options, the role of community, social stratification, productive aging, caregiving, death and dying, and imagined futures.

Origin and Development of this Volume

This edited volume began with chapters by several of the authors who were involved in ongoing dialogue about aging and caregiving in East Asia. These initial chapters included those by Shea (chap. 2), Kim (chap. 8), Long and Campbell (chap. 9), Lee and Chee (chap. 10), and Han and Shea (chap. 12). A major theme that emerged from our dialogue was how meanings and dynamics of aging and caregiving no longer fit neatly into a traditional Confucian lens of filial respect, obedience, support, and care for elders. In line with that theme, coeditors Jeanne Shea and Hong Zhang sought other authors, striving for thematic interplay across chapters and inclusion of other geocultural areas including Hong Kong, Taiwan, and Singapore, which have also seen rapid aging and social transformation in recent decades. This brought chapters by Tang and Shea (chap. 1), M. Zhang (chap. 3), Shum and Lum (chap. 4), Thang and Mehta (chap. 5), Sun (chap. 6), Moore (chap. 7), and Szawarska (chap. 11). Later, chapter author Moore joined Shea and Zhang as coeditor. Our book contains three chapters on mainland China (chaps. 1–3); one each on Hong Kong (chap. 4), Singapore (chap. 5), and Taiwan (chap. 6); three on Japan (chaps. 7–9); and three on South Korea (chaps. 10–12).

Our aim has been to produce a collection that analyzes rich qualitative data gathered in the past decade on aging and caregiving in East Asian communities, while placing that data into larger demographic, cultural, and sociohistorical context. A second aim has been to draw clear analytical connections and distinctions across chapters in order to promote cross-site comparison within East Asia. Of course, as with any edited volume, the chapters here cannot represent all of East Asia or all aging-related and caregiving-related trends therein. Nonetheless, what we hope to have achieved is an interconnected body of scholarship that addresses emerging themes in aging and caregiving in East Asia, going beyond a simple focus on traditional forms of filial piety.

The contributors to this volume are rooted in a range of academic disciplines, including anthropology, sociology, social work, and social gerontology. The authors come from a wide variety of institutional home bases, including Australia, China, Hong Kong, Israel, Japan, Poland, Singapore, South Korea, Taiwan, and the United States. A serendipitous collaboration, the authors also hail from many different countries of origin, including all of the above with one exception: Japan. In joining this array of disciplinary, institutional, and geocultural perspectives, we hope to deliver material that will enrich future comparative research on aging and caregiving in East Asian societies.

Defining Our Focus: What We Mean by Aging, Caregiving, and Filial Piety

This volume chronicles some of the emerging views and responses regarding the aging of persons and societies, and the caregiving practices in East Asia today. We should define what we mean by aging and caregiving, and then filial piety. In referring to aging, we mean a number of things. We mean population aging and aging societies as discussed earlier. We also mean aging as an experience, a life-course process, a generational or intergenerational process, and a sociocultural notion. We include notions of "good aging" or "aging well," social expectations for treatment of the aged, social roles of older adults, social images of aging, and local responses to aging-related policy and programs. The term "caregiving" here means material support, affective caring about, respectful treatment of, interpersonal gestures of caring for, taking care of someone, nursing through sickness, assisting in disability or frailness, helping with instrumental activities of daily living (IADLs) like housework or grocery shopping, and helping with activities of daily living (ADLs) like bathing, dressing, eating, transferring, and toileting. In addition to eldercare, we also mean caregiving done *by* seniors for other elders or for their adult children or grandchildren. Being a caregiver or the recipient of caregiving are not mutually exclusive. Eldercare can come from a variety of social actors, including various family members, old or young, community members, government programs, hired helpers, contract services, nonprofits, or community programs. Such resources are often combined and complementary, rather than mutually exclusive.

One major theme in this volume is how contemporary East Asian societies are engaging with, but also moving beyond, filial piety in terms of the meanings and social patterns surrounding aging and caregiving in daily life. Thus, it is important to begin with a clear definition in cultural and historical context. The notion of filial piety comes from a set of philosophical teachings originating from the scholar Confucius (551–479 BCE) in China in the sixth century BCE. Confucian teachings concern themselves heavily with proper roles and behaviors within the family and on the part of rulers. Over time, these teachings were transferred to Japan, Korea, Hong Kong, Taiwan, Singapore, and other sites.

As Ikels (2004) explained, the term "filial piety" is represented in Chinese by the character 孝, which is written phonetically as *xiao* (pronounced see-ow) in standard Mandarin Chinese. In Japanese and Korean, the term "filial piety" is written using the same character. In its most common definition, filial piety is a traditional Confucian value that calls on adult children to fulfill obligations to respect, obey, support, and care for elderly parents, as seen in the character itself. As Ikels (2004) wrote: The character *xiao* is composed from two other characters: the top half of the character *lao* [old] and the bottom half of the character *zi* ["son" or child] (2–3). "When combined to constitute *xiao*, the element derived from the *lao* rests on top of the character *zi*, that is, the 'elder' is on top of the 'son.' This ideograph communicates multiple messages of which the officially preferred one is that the old are supported by the young(er) generation" (3).

Historically, the character has been most frequently read as the young or *zi* (子) respecting, obeying, supporting, or taking care of the old or *lao* (老). However, it also contains another meaning of the continuation of the family line, since in Confucian tradition fathers were expected to produce sons (子) in order to carry on the family name as a duty to their parents and ancestors (Ikels 2004: 2). All of these elements of meaning have shown themselves in both the classic Confucian texts and in government decrees and popular thought documented over the centuries in China, Japan, and Korea (2–3).

The concrete meaning of filiality was recorded in the *Classic of Filial Piety:* "In serving his parents, a filial son reveres them in daily life; he makes them happy when he nourishes them; he takes anxious care of them in sickness; he shows great sorrow over their death; and he sacrifices to them with solemnity" (Confucius quoted in Chai and Chai 1965: 331). Here, in the word "son" we see the patrilineal patriarchal foundation of traditional Chinese, Japanese, and Korean families, since it was sons and their wives who were expected to carry out filial duties to the elders. This was because traditionally daughters left their family of origin and shifted their allegiance to their husband's family after marriage.

The presence of a Confucian ideal for filial piety, however, of course, does not mean that everyone in ancient times put these ideals into practice, as Confucius and his successor Mencius (372–289 BCE) themselves bemoaned (Legge 1933: 16, 725). According to Mencius, failure to carry on the family line was the worst of all unfilial acts (725) since "it affects not only one's parents but the entire ancestral line" (Ikels 2004: 3). Close behind, though, in Mencius's list of unfilial acts, were various ways of failing to support and protect one's aging parents. These included actions related to laziness, avarice, and/or being "selfishly attached to" one's own wife and children (Legge 1933: 763–64). The latter indicates traditional ideals privileging relationships between aging parents and adult children over conjugal relationships or young nuclear families.

Beneath this plain surface lies a world of complexity in which various individuals, families, communities, and polities in different times, places, and situations have constructed different spins on filial piety. Ikels (2004) argues that the precise take on filial piety has depended on demographic, economic, social, and historical factors, as well as personal circumstances related to wealth, gender, exposure to competing value systems, and other considerations. This means that, although filial piety is a powerful point of common reference, it is also subject to dispute and reinterpretation (2).

Dialogue with Classic Collection on Filial Piety

As mentioned, this volume has been developed in dialogue with Ikels's (2004) classic collection on *Filial Piety.* Here we join that volume in examining the complexities of aging and eldercare in East Asian societies beyond a shared traditional discourse on filial obligations. Although our edited collection is entitled *Beyond Filial Piety*, we share a central aim with Ikels's volume to go beyond traditional ideals of filial piety to examine contemporary discourse and practice. Along those lines, Ikels's volume showed how both discourse and practice related to filial piety were evolving away from classic prescription, with many traditional manifestations of filial piety no longer desirable or tenable and new interpretations and practices emerging in the wake of demographic aging, modernization, and social change. It also showed how state policy may variously play a role of "supporting or undercutting the practice of filial piety" (12).

Building on this common core, our book goes beyond Ikels's classic in the sense of time, space, and some aspects of thematic focus. Much has changed in East Asian societies over the fifteen years since Ikels's volume was published, while at the same time, some continuities remain. We update the demographic and policy context, while bringing in fresh case material. We have also been able to expand in geographical coverage to include Hong Kong, Taiwan, and Singapore, in addition to China, South Korea and Japan. This allows us to cast a wider net in exploring commonalities and differences across East Asian societies regarding approaches to aging and caregiving. We also bring new themes to the table, as well as fresh perspectives on old themes. Our volume includes chapters focusing on caregiving by elders themselves, whether for themselves, their spouses, or their children or grandchildren. We also have a chapter that goes beyond adult children to examine filiality in grandchildren. Finally, as nonfamilial alternatives have rapidly grown despite still being inadequate, we expand on the theme of increasing eldercare options from government, community, or the market. While much work has taken the perspective of adult children facing related caregiving demands, our volume also highlights perspectives of seniors on meanings of aging and caregiving and related strategies in regard to not only being cared for but also caring for themselves and fellow oldsters and for younger generations.

Contribution with Respect to Other Edited Volumes on Aging in East Asia

A review of recent social research books published in English covering aging in more than one nation or territory of East Asia shows that many are focused on macro demographic, survey-based, policy-focused, or economic aspects of population aging.[2] Such works involve varying geographical clusters, including East Asia (Higo and Klassen 2015; Langsdorf, Traub-Merz, and Ding 2010; Suzuki 2014), Asia overall (Asia Development Bank [ADB] 2017; Eggleston and Tuljapurkar 2010; Goodman and Harper

2008; Walker and Aspalter 2014), or the World Bank's East Asia & Pacific region (World Bank 2016). Many focus on aging in general (Arifin 2007; Fu and Hughes 2009; Harper 2014), on health or well-being in old age (Hermalin 2002), or on health and financial issues (Powell and Cook 2009), rather than on caregiving in particular. A large number of works, including most of the aforementioned, are based on quantitative research on large data sets (see also Smith and Majmundar 2012). Others using a more qualitative or mixed methods approach are focused on topics such as successful aging (Cheng et al. 2015) or women as resources (Mehta 2005).

The current volume makes a contribution to the fields of anthropology, sociology, social gerontology, social work, policy studies, and Asian studies by providing an interdisciplinary collection of chapters analyzing contemporary aging and caregiving in East Asia. In doing so, it accomplishes some things that other books on aging in Asia do not. It contains chapters on nearly all East Asian societies, defined as those nations or territories in the geographic area of East Asia, or in Southeast Asia but heavily influenced historically by Confucianism.[3] The book also provides more focus than aging in general by centering on the connections, dynamics, and tensions between aging and caregiving. While many previous volumes are on either social support for the aged or productive aging, this collection brings both themes to the table, exploring not only support and care of the elderly, but also seniors' agency and contribution to the support and care of themselves and others. Written by seasoned researchers with extensive experience in their countries of focus, each chapter draws connections to other parts of the volume, generating interdisciplinary and cross-regional dialogue. We examine recent interpretations of and responses to the traditional ideal of filial piety, contemporary familial patterns of care of and by elders, emerging forms of nonfamilial care for the aged, social stratification in relation to aging and care, productive aging, caregiving, death and dying, and imagined futures. We also include a glossary of non-English words within each chapter to help area experts to better assess our work and to guide readers who are new to a culture or topic.

Literature Review on Modernization, Social Change, and Filial Piety

Some early scholarly works presented a romantic view of aging in East Asia, arguing for a relatively timeless tradition of filial respect, support, and care for elders. For example, in studying Japan, Palmore (1975) and Palmore and Maeda (1985) argued that the "Oriental" tradition of cultural respect for the elderly, including filial piety, could stave off the ill effects of modernization on the social status of the aged. In doing so, they argued against the idea that modernization and industrialization would inevitably lead to a cultural convergence toward the same kind of devaluation and social isolation of the aged as had developed in Western nations.

Recent scholarship has shown that social change associated with rapid modernization in East Asian societies has, in fact, presented some serious challenges to traditional forms of filial piety (Cai et al. 2012; Chen and Powell 2012; Ikels 2004; Janelli and Yim 2004; Kaneda and Raymo 2003; Raymo and Kaneda 2003; Shea and Zhang 2016; Traphagan and Knight 2003; Wang 2004; Zhang 2009). Such scholarship has shown how multiple dimensions of modernization have made it more difficult to carry out conventional filial piety than was the case in the past. Such dimensions of modernization have included swift industrialization, increased wage labor outside the home, expanded female labor participation, and increasing importance of wage labor relative to domestic subsistence activities. It is important to note the rapid speed of such changes. Whereas many Western nations launched industrialization in the late 1800s or early 1900s, East Asian societies underwent a compressed industrial modernization in the space of mere decades, primarily during post–World War II reconstruction, although China had a second spike after the 1978 reforms. While it took place later for China than for the others, such modernization has also included rapid urbanization, increased youth migration, marketization, Westernization, and globalization. It has also involved reduced family size, decline in intergenerational coresidence, attenuated intergenerational relations, falling status of the elderly, privileging of the nuclear family, rising individualism, and escalating life aspirations among younger cohorts.[4] All these trends have made traditional filial ideals and familial support and care for elders much more difficult than in the past in many contexts. Whereas these trends were present prior to 2000 (Ikels 2004), they have picked up speed and depth in the past two decades, causing additional difficulties in maintaining former normative expectations for respect, support, or care of senior family members.

Still, as other elements of recent research show, filial piety remains an important touchstone in East Asian societies for both governments and ordinary folks, while at the same time changing over time in relative emphasis (Ikels 2004; Janelli and Yim 2004; Long and Littleton 2003; Sorensen and Kim 2004; Sun 2017; Traphagan and Knight 2003; Zhang 2017). Over the past half century, East Asian governments have moved away from some traditional elements of filial piety such as an emphasis on the continuation of the family line through descendants and total obedience from the young toward the old. Instead, post–World War II efforts focused on building modern societies that provided mass education to both genders and privileged governmental authority and population control over traditional lineages and parental power. This meant that meanings of filial piety associated with respect, support, and care for the elderly were foregrounded, while messages about obedience to older family members and continuance of the family line were sidelined (see also Ikels 2004: 12). As Danely (2014) notes, while modernization may lead to cultural change and weakening of traditional forms of filial piety, it does not translate into wholesale "deculturation" or abandonment of filial piety as a value (17).

Some recent studies have indicated an increasing tendency for ordinary folks' orientation to filial piety to be focused on positive affective bonds and warm interpersonal interactions (e.g., Shi 2009; Yan 2016, 2018). This has developed in tandem with improvements in youth education and parental investment in youths and the rise in pensions and health insurance for the elderly. Given that pensions have gained a more prominent role in old-age support in East Asian locales over time, there has also been declining attention to financial support for, instrumental assistance to, and direct care of aging parents, although such facets still play a role. Given the "4-2-1" problem with declining fertility leading to four grandparents and two parents but just one grandchild in many East Asian families, the situation today often involves parents and grandparents forming an alliance to cultivate the youngest generation to compete in today's hypercompetitive environment. Yan (2016, 2018) has called this "descending familism" (or neofamilism) as family attention is focused downward onto the youngest living generation, rather than on elders. Filial piety survives in an altered form, with cultivation of youths foremost.

With growing aspirations for gender equity, the contemporary practice of filial piety in East Asian societies is increasingly viewed as more gender neutral and within a context of bilateral rather than merely patrilineal kinship patterns (e.g., Shi 2009; Traphagan and Knight 2003). Modern campaigns for gender equality together with declining fertility have meant that for a large swath of East Asian families today, women and girls are often included in the family line (Fong 2004) rather than viewed as pure outsiders (Wolf 1972). In sum, while difficult to realize, variegated, disputed, and changing, filial piety as a multivocal symbol remains a central point of reference in the lives and governance of East Asia.

Methodological Approach

Methodologically, chapters in this volume focus on ethnographic, qualitative, or mixed methods. The reason for this methodological focus is that so much research on aging and eldercare today is on a macro demographic or policy level, which often lacks sufficient linkages with lived experiences of daily life, all too often leading to broad assumptions about older people being overwhelmingly dependent (Shea 2018). Similar to Traphagan and Knight (2003) and others before us, we aim to bring together the macro demographics with the micro of qualitative research. Grounding analysis in a review of relevant social science literature, each of the chapters draws on original data stemming from participant observation (chaps. 1–9, 11–12), interviews (chaps. 1–3, 5–12), and/or popular media representations (chaps. 5, 8, 10). Each of the chapters also incorporates secondary data on demographics and policy context. One chapter (chap. 1) includes and another (chap. 9) refers to original community survey data. Compared with the other chapters, chapter 4 is the most applied and policy-oriented chapter.

Theoretical Perspectives

Implicitly or explicitly, the chapters in this volume use a variety of theoretical perspectives. In an anthropological and sociological sense, these perspectives include practice theory, interpretivism, critical theory, globalization theory, and social constructionism. Articulated by Bourdieu (1977), practice theory focuses on the embodied views and practices of social actors as influenced by social structures while at the same time involving personal agency. Practice theory centers on interactions between macro social structures and micro personal practices through the strategies people use to make their way through life. All chapters use practice theory in examining the interactive relationship between the social structure of normative ideas and values and institutional forms surrounding aging and caregiving and the strategies and behavior of individuals in situational context. Developed by Geertz (1973), interpretivism is a theoretical lens that focuses on the "native point of view," that is, the viewpoints of insiders to a culture. It emphasizes looking at the meanings of things from the perspective of local people and showing how people view and interact with their world in ways that are in dialogue with their culture. This perspective is found in most chapters, especially chapters 2–9 and 11–12. Critical theory incorporates two main strands. One strand headed by Foucault (1984) focuses on "bio power," or the way in which agents of power shape authorized knowledge and social institutions in ways that affect people's everyday lives, often in ways they do not realize. This involves control over people's bodies through modern governmental, bureaucratic, medical, and scientific management of populations. The second strand, sometimes referred to as a political economy approach, involves attention to social inequalities related to resources, status, or power in a population (e.g., Singer and Baer 1995). We see a critical theory approach in chapters 1, 4, and 10–12. Globalization theory focuses on social change over time and global flows of ideas, ideals, people, things, models for doing things, and ways of living (e.g., Appadurai 1996). To some extent, we see globalization theory at play across the volume in terms of evolving global flows of ideas about and models for what constitutes good aging and appropriate care, but most notably in chapters 6–7 and 11–12. Social constructionism (Berger and Luckmann 1966) states that social groups perceive, interpret, and build their worlds using cultural or subcultural lenses that define for them what exists and what things mean. Here, we often treat tradition, modernity, Eastern, or Western as imagined realities that may or may not map onto actual social change or locales.

The chapters also variously incorporate theoretical approaches best defined for our purposes within the interdisciplinary field of social gerontology (Bengtson and Settersten 2016), including a life-course perspective, age stratification theory, social exchange theory, and feminist approaches. The life-course perspective (e.g., Elder 1974/1999) examines how earlier physical, cultural, and social experiences can affect older people's outlooks, health, social situations, and fortunes in life. This perspective can be deployed at the level of individuals or of generational cohorts, or both. We find this framework used to some extent in all of the chapters but most prominently in chapters 1–3, 9, and 11. Age stratification theory (e.g., Riley 1974) examines how the hierarchical power balance among the generations depends on demographics, policies, culture, and generational histories and how the societal age structure affects people's roles, self-concept, and life satisfaction at different stages of their life. In most chapters, we see the theme of today's older generations having lower social status in relation to younger generations than in the past (chaps. 1–3, 6, 8, 10). Social exchange theory (Dowd 1975) sees personal status of the elderly in society as defined by the balance between people's contributions to society and the costs of supporting them. In this volume, we read of policy concerns about demographic "old-age dependency" ratios, and we witness seniors as not only receiving social support but also as helping themselves and others within and across generations. In many chapters seniors express worries about being perceived as a drain on others and voice a strong commitment to remaining productive contributors to family, community, and/or society for as long as possible (chaps. 1–3, 8–9, 11). Finally, in alliance with feminist approaches (e.g., Calasanti 2008; Lamb 2000), some chapters introduce analyses related to gender roles and changes therein (chaps. 2, 5, 7, 9–11). A common theme is the trend in many contemporary East Asian contexts toward increasing gender equity or gender neutrality (e.g., chaps. 2–3; on gender neutrality, see also Zhang 2017).

Demographic and Sociohistorical Context
of Aging in East Asian Societies

East Asian societies are now home to a very large and rising number of old people and to some of the oldest and most rapidly aging populations on earth. Demographically, East Asia may offer a glimpse of global demographic futures. As the elderly proportion of the world's population rises sharply over the next three decades, East Asian societies will be among those at the forefront of this unprecedented demographic change. This section examines the demographic and sociohistorical contexts of aging in East Asian societies, which will serve as important background for understanding the content of the chapters to follow.

Population aging is a global issue but with local variation not just demographically, but also in terms of definitions. Worldwide, there are presently two common formal benchmarks for old age: age sixty, often used by the United Nations' (UN's) World Health Organization (WHO) and developing countries like China; and age sixty-five, generally used by Western nations like France, Western-dominated organizations like the Organisation for Economic Co-operation and Development (OECD), and high-income countries outside the West like Japan. Culturally, age sixty was also the traditional benchmark for old age in China and its historical area of influence. As population aging sweeps the world over the next several decades, we expect that, of the rival measures, age sixty-five will eventually become the global standard. Therefore, for the sake of consistency, in this volume's Introduction and Conclusion at least, we use age sixty-five as the starting point to define old age.

In this section we draw on comparative data from the World Population Prospects database available online from the Population Division of the UN Department of Economic and Social Affairs (UN 2017). We begin with raw numbers, then move on to degree of population aging, and culminate with speed of population aging. On each of these measures, East Asia overall, or some part of it, is remarkable in terms of the scale, degree, and speed of aging.

According to UN figures (UN 2017), given its enormous population of 1.4 billion, China has the largest raw number of old people on earth. As of 2015, the most recent year with comparative UN data, with a population of 1.4 billion China had 135.2 million people age sixty-five and above, equal to over 40 percent of the total U.S. population. With much smaller populations, our other East Asian locales trail in raw numbers. With 122 million people overall, Japan was second, with just under 32.3 million seniors that year. Then South Korea had just over 6.5 million out of 51 million, Taiwan just under 2.9 million out of 23.49 million, Hong Kong 1.1 million out of

7.3 million, and Singapore 648,000 out of 5.5 million. Still, with China's size, together East Asian elders represent almost 30 percent of the world's nearly 612 million old folks. Since World War II East Asian societies have undergone a large increase in the raw number of seniors. China and Japan saw the most-dramatic rise, with China skyrocketing from just over 41 million seniors in 1950 to more than 214 million at present and Japan rising from a little over 6 million seniors in 1950 to more than 41 million today.

Degree of Population Aging in East Asian Societies in 2015

Beyond raw numbers, East Asian societies have a high degree of population aging. Measured as the ratio of those aged sixty-five and above in the total population, Japan has the most extreme degree of population aging in the world today. Again, drawing on UN figures (UN 2017), 26 percent of Japan's population was age sixty-five and above in 2015, significantly higher than the global high-income country average of 17.0 percent for that year. In comparison, the most aged Western societies had a lower degree of population aging than Japan.[5] The other four high-income East Asian societies under comparison, often called the "four tigers" for their economic ascent following Japan, also currently have a relatively high degree of population aging in global perspective, although not yet as high as the most aged Western countries. In 2015 Hong Kong was 15.2 percent elderly, South Korea 13.0 percent, Taiwan 12.3 percent, and Singapore 11.7 percent, all above the world average of 8.3 percent elderly, although a bit lower than the 17.0 percent high-income country average.[6] The only middle-income country in our East Asia comparison group, China, was 9.7 percent elderly in 2015, which is high for its income level, above the 7.0 percent average for middle-income nations that year.[7]

Trends over Time in Degree of Population Aging in East Asia: Past and Projected

In terms of trends over time, following World War II the elderly proportion of the population has been consistently rising in East Asian locales, starting from a low baseline (see figure 0.1). In 1950 East Asian societies had a low proportion of seniors in their population relative to other parts of the world. Drawing on UN figures (UN 2017), in 1950 they ranged from Japan at the top of the group with 4.9 percent of its population aged sixty-five and above, then China at 4.4 percent, down to Korea at 2.9 percent, Hong Kong at 2.5 percent, Singapore at 2.4 percent, and Taiwan at 2.2 percent (see figure 0.1). By comparison, 5.1 percent of the world's population as of 1950 was elderly, higher than the East Asian locales for that period. At that time, emerging from previously low levels of modernization and the ravages of war, levels of economic development across these sites were still relatively low, with none yet considered high-income countries/territories. As of 1950, in degree of population aging Japan and China were a little above the middle-income country average of 4.1 percent elderly, but the other four areas under analysis fell below the low-income average of 3.1 percent elderly for that period.[8]

Japan began a rapid ascent in population aging in the 1970s, just before it gained high-income country status in the late 1970s (World Bank 2019). Using UN figures (UN 2017), Japan rose from 6.9 percent elderly in 1970, to over 14 percent in 1995, and over 21 percent by 2010. The other five East Asian locales also rose in degree of population aging over that period, but not at the same level. After Japan, Hong Kong was the most aged of these sites over that period, rising from 4.1 percent elderly in 1970 to 10 percent in 1995 and 13 percent in 2010. By 1995 Japan surpassed the average percent elderly for high-income countries, with the oldest population in the world, as also reported in Ikels's (2004) edited volume. According to current UN data (UN 2017), Japan's populace is predicted to retain

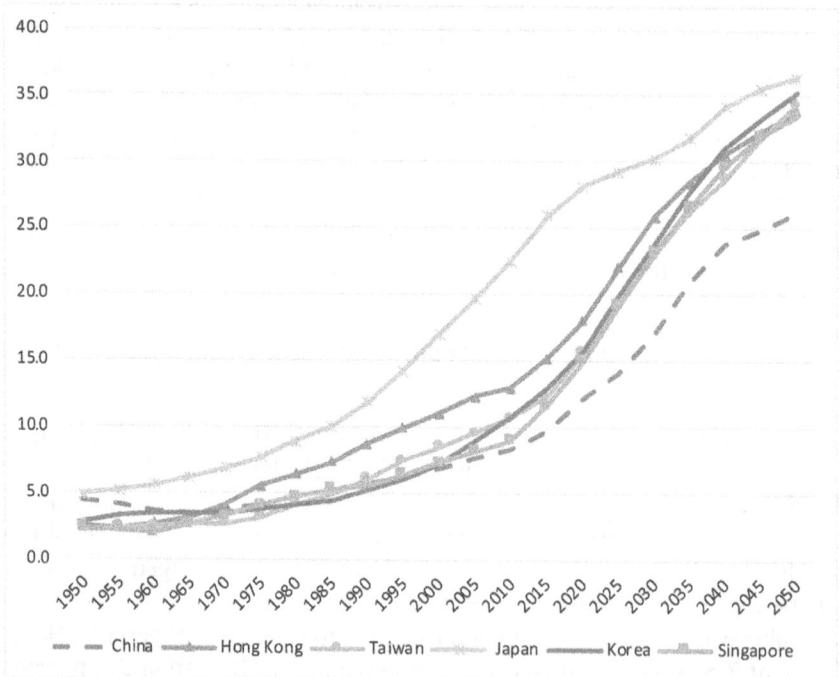

FIGURE 0.1. Percentage of Population Age Sixty-Five and Above, 1950–2050, for Selected East Asian Societies. Source: UN 2017. Created by the authors.

most-aged status through 2050 when projections peg it at 36.4 percent elderly.[9]

Since 2010 the other five East Asian locales began a steep ascent in population aging, with Hong Kong, Korea, Singapore, and Taiwan in the middle, and China at the low end of the group. This followed on the heels of economic development as the four tigers gained high-income status in the 1980s (World Bank 2019), and China moved from being a low-income to a middle-income country in 2008 (Zhang 2009) after three decades of market reforms.[10] UN data (UN 2017) shows how, beginning in 2010, all of the four tigers plus China began a rapid rise in population aging, but with China rising at a slightly slower rate than the others. The rapidity of their ascent is remarkable. UN (2017) data show that from 2010 to 2015 alone Hong Kong went from 13.0 percent to 15.2 percent elderly, Korea from 10.7 percent to 13.0 percent, Taiwan 10.7 percent to 12.3 percent, Singapore 9.0 percent to 11.7 percent, and China 8.4 percent to 9.7 percent.

Even more notable are current predictions for the aging of East Asian societies in the decades leading up to 2050, a time span beyond that dealt with in Ikels (2004).[11] According to the UN (2017), after 2010 the four tigers are expected to begin to age more rapidly than Japan such that by 2050 they will approach its level, with Korea at 35.3 percent elderly, Taiwan 34.5 percent, Hong Kong 33.9 percent, and Singapore 33.6 percent. China, the one middle-income country in the set, is expected to rise a little less rapidly than the four tigers, but still fast enough to reach 26.3 percent elderly by 2050. All six locales are projected to be above the predicted 2050 average for their income class, slated at 26.8 percent elderly for high-income and 15.9 percent for middle-income countries.[12] Although the four tigers did not top the high-income category for degree of population aging in 2015, by 2050, they are anticipated to do so.[13] Although the assumptions of these projections may not pan out, experts consider this scenario extremely likely. Such a high degree of population aging was not anticipated in Ikels (2004), at which time a projected 27 percent for Japan by 2025 was considered colossal (8).

Speed of Population Aging in East Asia over Time

Another important dimension is the speed of population aging, and these East Asian societies are remarkable in their rapidity therein. The UN (2017) defines an "aging society" as having more than 7 percent of the population age sixty-five and above, an "aged society" as more than 14 percent in that age range, and a "super-aging society" as more than 21 percent age sixty-five and above (see also Coulmas 2007). The time lapse from 7 percent to

14 percent, or from 14 percent to 21 percent, is used to measure the speed of population aging (Kinsella 2009). In both journeys, East Asia is experiencing extreme time compression in its population aging, a compression that has been intensifying over the decade and a half since 2004.

Aging to Aged Society

East Asian populations have been aging at a more rapid pace than most Western societies and are expected to maintain an even quicker ascent in the near future (2020–50). In terms of going from an aging to an aged society, while most Western countries took as much as 115 years to rise from 7 percent to 14 percent elderly (Kinsella 2009), East Asian societies took a far shorter time, with Japan and China taking about twenty-six years, Singapore and South Korea nineteen years, and Hong Kong eighteen years (figure 0.2). While having different historical timing by place for reaching aging or aged society status, these societies show similarly rapid paces for going from one echelon to the next.

Again using UN data (UN 2017), in terms of becoming an aging society or 7 percent elderly, Japan became an aging society in the early 1970s, Hong Kong in the early 1980s, Taiwan the early 1990s, and Korea and

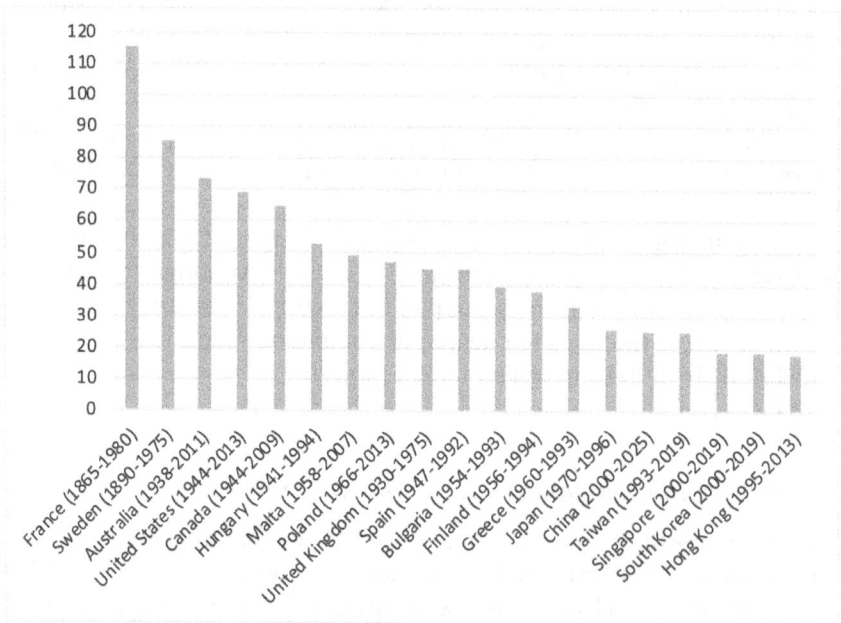

FIGURE 0.2. Speed of Population Aging in Selected Societies to Go from Aging to Aged Society. Sources: Estimates calculated from Kinsella 2009; UN 2017. Created by the authors.

Singapore the late 1990s. China reached 7 percent in the early 2000s (see figure 0.2), with its late entry related to its lower level of economic development and large rural population. China was one of the first developing countries to become an aging society, and, as a result, it is often referred to as a society that "has gotten old before getting rich." As to entering the ranks of aged societies or 14 percent elderly, Japan became aged in the early 1990s, and was the only aged East Asian society at the time the Ikels (2004) volume was published. Hong Kong became aged next in the early 2010s, and then Taiwan, Korea, and Singapore in the late 2010s. China is not there yet, but is projected to get there in the mid-2020s, again being one of the first developing countries to reach that level. This means that in moving from an aging to an aged society, Japan and the four tigers took, and China is expected to take, only about two to two and a half decades, ranging from eighteen years for Hong Kong to twenty-six years for Japan and China, with the others in between (UN 2017). This is far less time than Western nations took (Kinsella 2009; UN 2017).

Aged to Super-Aging Society

With respect to going from an aged (14 percent elderly) to a super-aging (21 percent elderly) society, East Asia's pace is even more rapid. In 2004 no society worldwide had yet reached the super-aging level. UN (2017) data show that it was in 2008 that Japan became the world's first super-aging society, going from 14 percent to 21 percent elderly in roughly twelve years. By contrast, it took Germany, the first major Western country crossing the 21 percent threshold, about forty-two years to make this journey (see figure 0.3). This was well ahead of Western countries, among which only a few like Germany, Italy, Greece, Finland, and Portugal had reached super-aging level as of 2019.[14] For the rest of the East Asian countries we are examining, the four tigers are expected to become super-aging societies in the mid to late 2020s, with Hong Kong in 2024, Korea 2027, and Singapore and Taiwan 2028. China is projected to reach 21 percent elderly, or super-aging status, in about 2036.[15]

The speed of moving from an aged to a super-aging society in East Asia is impressive. Whereas for most Western nations it took, or is expected to take, twenty to fifty-five years to go from 14 percent to 21 percent of the population aged sixty-five and above, in the East Asian locales it has taken, or is slated to take, eight to seventeen years. Of these locales, Hong Kong is at the slower end, expected to take seventeen years. Projected to take just eight years to cross this threshold, South Korea is the fastest aging society on earth today. In between those two ends of the spectrum, there is Japan which took twelve years, China projected to take ten years, and Singapore and Taiwan both slated for nine years.

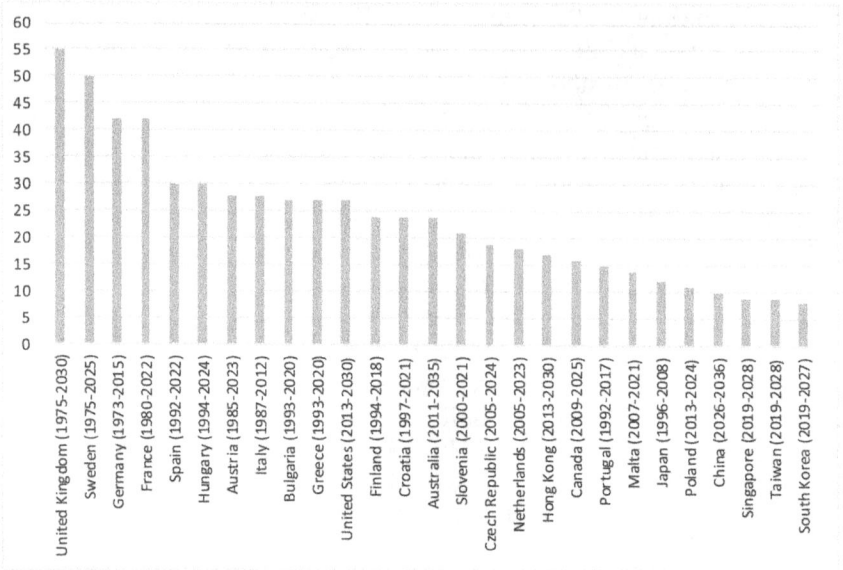

FIGURE 0.3. Speed of Population Aging in Selected Societies to Go from Aged to Super-Aging Society. Sources: Estimates calculated from UN 2017; Kinsella 2009. Created by the authors.

Reasons for Rapid Population Aging in East Asian Societies

Demographically, population aging generally involves some combination of declining fertility and rising life expectancy, both of which factors East Asian societies exhibit. In some cases, immigration and emigration also play a role, but other than a blip around the 1997 turnover of Hong Kong back to China, age-related population in-flows and out-flows have not played a significant role thus far in the population aging of the societies under consideration.

Declining and sustained low fertility has played a large role in population aging in East Asian societies. Overall the total fertility rate, defined as the average number of children per woman of childbearing age, has fallen sharply in East Asian societies since World War II (see figure 0.4). Referencing UN (2017) data, in the 1950–55 period, the total fertility rate was high in all six societies under review, at 6.72 in Taiwan, 6.61 in China, 6.02 in Singapore, 5.65 in Korea, 4.44 in Hong Kong, and 2.96 in Japan (see figure 0.4).[16]

By the 1990–95 period, as noted in Ikels (2004), all six societies had fallen below 2.0 children per woman, or replacement level.[17] Japan and Singapore dipped below replacement level earliest of the six, in the 1975–80 period. Hong Kong followed in 1980–85 and South Korea and Taiwan in

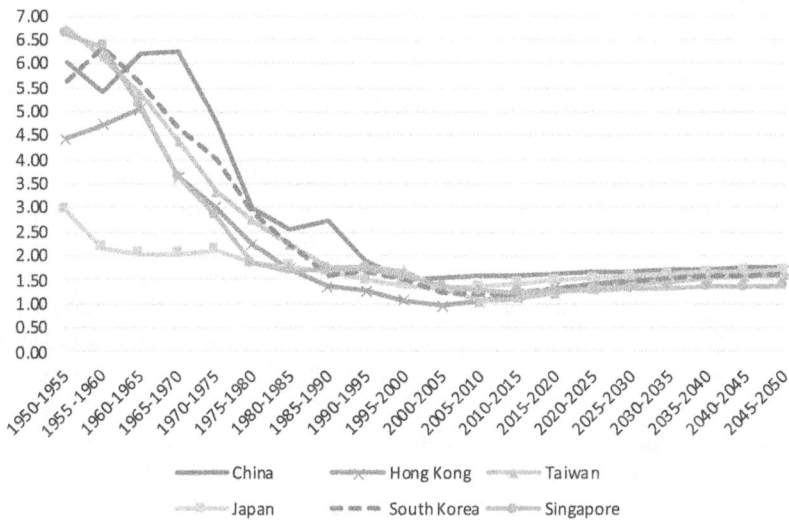

FIGURE 0.4. Total Fertility Level, 1950–2050. Source: UN 2017. Created by the authors.

1985–90. By 1990–95 China had joined them. From 1990 onward, with slight ups-and-downs here and there, overall fertility levels in these societies continued to fall. In 2001 South Korea hit a total fertility rate thought at the time to be the lowest low fertility level until it dipped to 1.08 in 2005 (Eun 2007: 52). By the 2010–15 period, total fertility rates had fallen to 1.11 for Taiwan, 1.20 for Hong Kong, 1.23 for South Korea and Singapore, 1.41 for Japan, and 1.60 for China (UN 2017). These low fertility levels have resulted in a reduced proportion of young people in these settings and contributed to the rapid pace of population aging therein. In all six settings, the proportion of young people aged fourteen and younger is now lower than the elderly proportion of the population (UN 2017).

Across all six locales, a number of factors contributed to the sharp and sustained fertility decline. These include economic development, increasing female education, rising gender equity in labor participation, and improved contraceptive access. More women have been prioritizing earning wages and self-actualization over marriage or raising large families, fearing that raising many children will make their own lives more difficult. In China the fertility decline is also linked with the state-instituted Single Child Family Policy (Ikels 2004), which from the 1980s to 2015 permitted one child per couple in urban areas and two in rural areas if the first child was disabled or a girl.[18] In each of these places in response to the portents of extreme population aging and concerns about future pensions and care, each site has made some recent efforts to encourage childbearing to boost fertility rates, but with little success thus far. For Japan, population decline has already begun, and is expected to also significantly affect South Korea and Taiwan over the coming decades (UN 2017), raising concerns about future workforce numbers and tax revenue (chaps. 7–11).

Rising life expectancy is the second main contributor to the high degree of population aging we see in East Asia today and into the future. UN (2017) figures show that in 1950 life expectancies at birth in these societies ranged from a little over forty-three and forty-seven years in China and Korea, respectively, to fifty-eight to sixty-two years in the other four (see figure 0.5). Life expectancy in these societies rose quite steadily from that time through the present. In the early to mid-2000s life expectancy at birth for both sexes reached seventy-three to eighty-two years, ranging from Japan with almost eighty-two years at the high end, to Hong Kong with almost eighty-one and a half years, Singapore seventy-nine years, Korea and Taiwan about seventy-seven years, to China with seventy-three years at the low end (UN 2017).[19] At that time, life expectancy in only three East Asian sites topped the U.S. rate of seventy-seven years. By 2018 life expectancy at

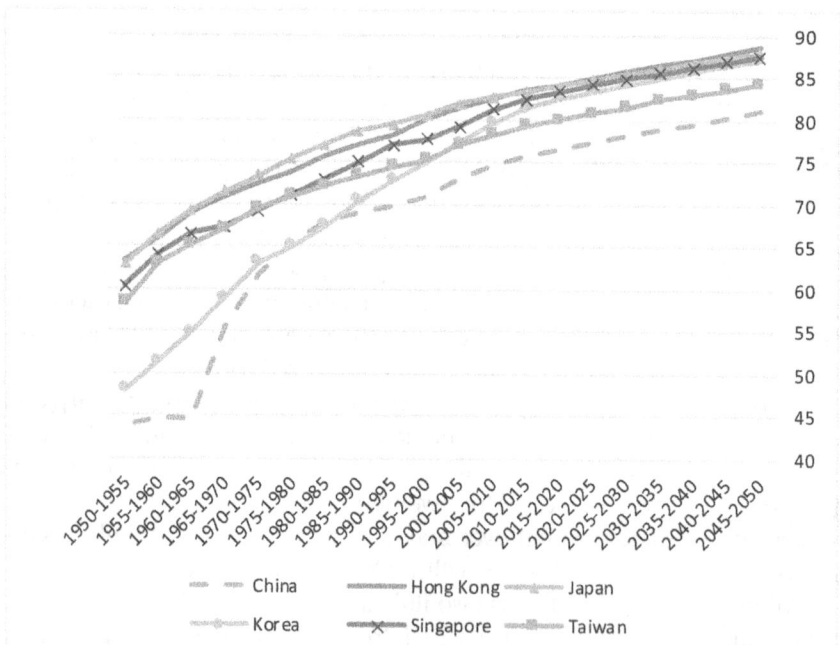

FIGURE 0.5. Life Expectancy at Birth, Both Sexes, Selected East Asian Societies, 1950–2050. Sources: National Statistics Republic of China (Taiwan) 2018; UN 2017; U.S. Census Bureau 2017. Created by the authors.

birth in five of the six sites were higher than life expectancy in the United States, with the exception being China, which was already not far behind. Hong Kong, Japan, and Singapore were at the top with 84.16, 83.98, and 83.30 years, respectively. Next were South Korea and Taiwan at 82.44 and 80.4 years. While lowest for these groups, at 76.48 years, China's life expectancy is outstanding for a middle-income country and only three years behind the United States (UN 2019a).

These life expectancies were already higher than ever before recorded for these sites, and they are projected to rise to even higher levels in the coming decades. By 2050, at the high and low ends for our six sites, life expectancy in Hong Kong is predicted to reach about eighty-nine years, and in China almost eighty-two years. In the middle, we have Taiwan around eighty-five years and Japan, Korea, and Singapore around eighty-eight years. By that time, U.S. life expectancy, at 84.74 years, is expected to be below all of these areas but China.

In addition to life expectancy at birth, life expectancy at age sixty-five has also been increasing steadily (UN 2017). As of the 2015–20 period, after reaching the age of sixty-five people are expected on average to live an additional twenty-two years in Japan and Hong Kong, twenty-one in South Korea and Singapore, twenty years in Taiwan, and sixteen years in China (UN 2019a). Many elderly in East Asia today live well beyond the national life expectancy at birth, into their nineties and beyond. Each of these nations has a growing number of centenarians, with Japan having the largest number at more than 70,000 as of 2019. Japan is also currently home to the oldest living person, a 116-year-old woman ("Ahead of Respect for the Aged Day" 2019). On the one hand, this is the embodiment of good fortune to be able to achieve such longevity, but, on the other hand, it also means that some need to manage long periods of chronic illness, sometimes requiring decades of intensive eldercare.

Reasons for rising life expectancies in these East Asian societies are multiple. They include economic development, improved living conditions, better nutrition, and preventive measures throughout the life course and in later life, and advances in medical technology, medicine, and treatment. Together, climbing life expectancies and declining fertility have generated the population aging that is happening now.

In Chinese these two demographic trends in combination are called the "population-aging plus fertility-decline" transformation (*laoling shaozi hua*). This term encapsulates the situation of aging societies today, involving unprecedented and increasing numbers of elderly people living longer and in potential need of care for longer than ever before, at the same time that there are fewer children being born to help support and take care of the elderly.

Crosscutting Themes

Overall, this volume examines the changing social expectations that exist with regard to familial support in later life and with respect to caregiving of and by the elderly in contemporary East Asian societies. It explores the emerging cultural meanings of and social responses to population aging, with a focus on sociocultural phenomena that include, but also go beyond, attention to the presence or absence of traditional forms of filial piety. Collectively, the contributors explore the question of how the relationship between aging and caregiving is being transformed in terms of contemporary cultural meanings, social practices, and everyday experiences. Our chapters show how these broad demographic and social changes are playing out on the ground in local context, with both similarities and differences across sites. The authors show how elders, families, communities, and societies are responding to the new and changing circumstances. In doing so, they explore not only how social change has brought about some unwelcome challenges with respect to eldercare, but also how it has also opened up some new opportunities both for providing support and care for elders and for living a productive and/or meaningful later life.

This volume engages a variety of crosscutting themes that will be of significance to those with interests in aging, life course, caregiving, culture, society, kinship, family, intergenerational issues, aging societies, and/or social change.[20] Described below, these themes fall into several major categories in relation to the nexus of aging and caregiving. As alluded to earlier in the chapter, these themes include traditional ideals versus contemporary realities and competing values, the role of the state and public policy, contemporary patterns of familial and nonfamilial care, social stratification issues, senior agency and productive aging, intersections of caregiving and death, and imagined futures. While not every chapter picks up every one of these themes, each chapter engages several. Running through the volume there is also a tension between the notion of population aging as a problem or a crisis versus a blessing or an opportunity for innovation.

Traditional Ideals versus Contemporary Realities and Values

Like Ikels's (2004) volume before us, our edited collection focuses heavily on the theme of discourse versus practice; and the tensions between traditional ideals and present realities, as well as among coexisting competing values. In many contexts, East Asian cultures are known for respecting and taking care of their elders. This is a common generalization both inside and outside East Asia. In China, people making a comparison between China and the West often say, "Chinese people do not throw their old people into a nursing home unlike in the West." Likewise, people in Western contexts often romanticize Asia as a place where the wisdom and experience of the elders are held in high esteem and old folks are taken care of at home until death by their families "unlike in the West." These generalizations often neglect the distance between traditional ideals and modern realities and serve to stereotype both Eastern and Western societies, an oversight that this edited collection seeks to join other scholars in addressing.

As in Ikels's volume, our focus is on what ordinary people in East Asian contexts say and do, rather than on seeking orthodoxy in classic texts or governmental pronouncements. In doing so, we also attend to emerging ways of talking about and "doing" aging and caregiving and to gaps between discourse and reality. We also explore the creative ways in which people are reinterpreting the meanings of aging and caregiving and developing new social arrangements involving elders and care by and/or for them. Our chapters show how ordinary people in East Asia today are making sense of the evolving relationship between aging and caregiving in their everyday lives, and how they are assessing what constitutes proper reciprocity and care in life-course and generational perspective. Each chapter engages in some way with the theme of the mismatch between traditional cultural ideals and present realities or competing values, together with social responses to those gaps.

In our edited collection, we show how such mismatches and tensions have been heightened since the 1980s and 1990s, during which time most of the research for the Ikels volume was conducted. Our volume also demonstrates the expanded ways in which folks are reinterpreting filial piety and what counts as filial piety therein. The chapters show what ordinary people in East Asian contexts are saying and doing with respect to aging and caregiving, and how they are negotiating filial expectations against a backdrop of accelerating demographic and social change. Contributors examine changing social realities and social expectations as to intergenerational versus intragenerational closeness and the reciprocity equation across generations in the latter half of the life course. We explore the attenuation of intergenerational ties and filial obligations of adult children and their relation to changing societal age structure, social values, political/economic circumstances, residential patterns, geographic distance, and/or social context, and the ways in which families and communities are adapting to these changes. We also examine competing values such as senior self-reliance or independence, or seniors continuing to make contributions to family or society into later life. Overall, we examine East Asian people's continuing moral, cultural, and practical adaptability apropos aging and caregiving and who should provide care to whom and how, in the face of deepening population aging and compression of modernization.

Role of the State and Public Policy

The role of the state and public policy is another important crosscutting theme that was examined in Ikels's (2004) volume; like filial piety, this theme is found in all of the chapters in our present volume. Like in many other aging societies, East Asian governments have been part of both the problem and the solution in relation to population aging and care (12). Government policies encouraging economic development, industrialization, modernization, female education, women's participation in paid employment, migration, and family planning have contributed to fertility decline. Likewise, policies facilitating economic development, medical advancements, and public health measures have contributed to greater longevity. The combined effects of these state policies have inadvertently contributed to the "problem" of population aging.[21] Concerned about potential for further population aging and growing needs for pensions and long-term care to negatively affect economic development and national strength, governments have also inserted themselves as an intended part of the solution by generating policies that address issues of support and care for the aged and productive aging.

Ikels (2004) noted how East Asian states have not just supported filial piety, but rather in some ways have also undercut it as a value or practice (12). She also pointed out how the dimensions of filial piety supported by contemporary East Asian states constitute a "much reduced" version of it (12). Namely, instead of the traditional emphasis on obedience to aging parents and "production of descendants" as key "signifiers of filial piety," governments today focus on support for and care of aging parents by adult children. The authors thus further pointed out how while some state policies supported certain aspects of filial piety, other state policies undermined some dimensions of it. The present edited collection further examines these themes, taking an updated look at a wider range of East Asian states and their most recent related public policies.

Policies related to governmental support of the elderly in East Asia have undergone considerable change since 2004 and vary widely, as described by Tham et al. (2018) and Yeh, Cheng, and Shi (2018). The forerunner for generous policy is Japan. In the vanguard of population aging, Japan established universal pension coverage and universal health care through mandatory insurance in 1961, and it established universal long-term care insurance in 2000. Korea, which largely modeled its system after Japan, comes next in terms of earliness and generosity. Korea established a national pension scheme in 1988, national health insurance in 1989, and long-term care insurance in 2008. In this regard, Taiwan is next with national health insurance established in 1995, a national pension program in 2008, and publicly funded tax-based long-term care insurance in 2000. Interestingly, while policies such as these are supportive of the elderly, some argue that they may perversely reduce filial piety through state displacement of familial support.

In terms of aging-related policy in Singapore and Hong Kong, although both of these locales are known for excellent health care, they are also more prone to leaving old-age support to individuals and families. Instead of defined-benefits, both have mandatory defined-contribution pension systems, with Singapore's starting in 1955 and Hong Kong's beginning in 2000. As of 2015 Singapore established universal health insurance coverage with MediShield Life. Although Hong Kong does not have universal health insurance coverage, it has a public health-care system with very low fees to promote affordability. As of 2018 Hong Kong was starting a voluntary health insurance scheme. Neither Singapore nor Hong Kong has universal long-term care insurance, but Singapore has a national ElderShield program for severe disability and Hong Kong has a mandatory provident fund based on defined-contribution. Both places share concern that too much government support may reduce familial contributions.

China's aging-related policies lag behind the other locales and show considerable regional unevenness. As the only middle-income, rather than high-income, area of the bunch, China is aiming for universal pension and universal health insurance coverage by sometime in 2020, and it is well on its way to that goal. However, both pension amounts and health insurance coverage levels vary widely between rural and urban and between poor and wealthy areas of China, since both these programs are decentralized with respect to level of benefits. Benefits in poor rural areas are very low. China currently does not have universal long-term care insurance, although since 2016 China has begun to pilot long-term care insurance in selected cities. While China is known for its Law for the Protection of the Rights and Interests of the Elderly of 2013, updated from 1996, which emphasizes family first for old-age support and care, it is more moral admonition than effectual policy.

Aging-related public policy across East Asian polities varies in other respects as well, along with sharing some commonalities. Degree of market involvement for pension provision, health-care services, long-term care services, and insurance products varies, with Japan and Korea at the lower end. Coverage of hospice services as inpatient or home-based services varies from site to site, with Japan at the forefront and Korea just having started inpatient hospice coverage. Each of the six locales has some form of policy advocating healthy, successful, or productive aging, although details vary. In each place, governmental provisions for the elderly have been improving, but they are still insufficient to meet current and especially future needs. Our volume examines how policy impacts aging and care and filial piety in each of the locales examined.

Contemporary Patterns of Familial Care

All of the chapters in this volume deal with the issues of sociodemographic change and contemporary patterns of familial care. They trace shifts in the locus of familial responsibility and changes in the balance of who is expected to take care of whom, how, and where. Chapters include discussion on issues of monetary support (chaps. 1–4, 6, 8–11), housing (chaps. 1–6, 8, 10–11), instrumental assistance (chaps. 1–12), direct familial care (chaps. 2–12), domestic helper provision (chaps. 2, 4–6, 10), and emotional support (chaps. 2, 5–7, 9–10, 12). In general, we see a shift toward more situational flexibility in kinship roles (chap. 10) and more plasticity in spatial arrangements of kin (chaps. 3, 6, 11). Whoever is most able to step forward to provide care does so, and caregivers or recipients move to wherever care is needed or available.

While increased flexibility was noted in Ikels (2004), such flexibility has expanded in scope in terms of who values or practices it and in relation to what. Coresidence of elders with adult children has become less and less common over time. Among adult children, there is increased individual flexibility as to whether son(s) or daughter(s) or some combination therein intervenes if elder support or care is needed. The traditional patrilineal pattern of care by sons and their wives remains in some areas, but is combined with growing bilateral kin care tendencies. We also observe how, with expanding longevity, many adult child caregivers for aging parents are now themselves old, rather than middle-aged as life expectancy continues to rise. In addition, several chapters examine elder caregiving by familial caregivers other than adult children, including senior self-care or spousal care (chaps. 2, 9) or caring by grandchildren (chap. 5).

As mentioned, many chapters note the shift to a more gender-neutral approach to support and care for aging parents related to modernization campaigns to promote gender equity and dilute patrilineal traditions (chaps. 2, 5, 7, 9–11).[22] Mentioned as rising in some East Asian settings in Ikels (2004; Janelli and Yim 2004: 143; Miller 2004), the idea that daughters may be filial and provide eldercare has since deepened. In some areas it has even become common to insist that daughters provide as good or even better eldercare than sons or daughters-in-laws, despite, or perhaps because of (see also Miller 2004: 52) how traditionally such care was not expected of them (chaps. 2, 9–10).

Three chapters engage population movement and its relation to intergenerational care (chaps. 3, 5, 11), as opposed to the traditional ideal of fixed coresidence. Over the past several decades, there has been a flood of domestic rural-to-urban migration within East Asian countries, focused on youths seeking opportunities in the cities. In most such cases, parents migrate from the countryside, leaving grandparents behind to take care of grandchildren; in a growing number of situations, however, older parents are following their children to the city to help with housework and child-care there (chap. 3). In a smaller but rising number of cases, young adults from East Asian societies are also moving internationally, generally leaving their parents behind (chap. 6), although sometimes inviting their parents to visit their new home abroad.

Contemporary Patterns of Nonfamilial Care

Another theme in this volume is that nonfamilial forms of eldercare are growing and shifting, including in-home, community-based, and institutional care provided as supplements and/or alternatives to familial care (see also Hinton and Chen 2016; Shea and Zhang 2016). Growing in availability first in Japan, then in the four tigers, then in China, such options have expanded rapidly across East Asian sites over the past decades. Chapters examine new social balances being forged between traditional dependence on family versus reliance on nonfamilial options for support or care (chaps. 2, 4, 6–7, 10–12). As the locus of responsibility widens beyond the family, nonfamilial options are emerging from a variety of sources, including government, community, nonprofit, and market sources (chaps. 1, 4, 6, 11–12).

Market Options

Similar to government forces, market forces are both producing the problems posed by and generating various solutions for aging societies. The lower fertility and higher longevity that define aging societies are in part created by the kind of rapid economic development sought by market economies. The focus on work outside the home and labor mobility, both of which make caregiving a challenge, is also part of the marketization of economies. At the same time, however, producers and consumers are using market forces to make and consume new products, services, and technologies for ailing seniors and their caregivers. Some chapters raise the concept of the "outsourcing" of care or filial piety from the family to the market (chaps. 3, 6–7).

Public, Nonprofit, or Community Options

It is difficult to isolate private market-based solutions from public nonprofit ones, since they are often intermingled. Similarly, drawing a line between government and civil society is also tough, as is making a clear separation between familial and nonfamilial or between government and market. Nonetheless, these distinctions do get made. Observations on community-based elder support or care are present in most of the chapters, where community means various things, ranging from a neighborhood, a village, volunteers, age peers, a nunnery, or a coop.

Combinations

Of course, familial and nonfamilial care are not necessarily mutually exclusive, and nonfamilial support is often needed so that familial care can be successful (Sokolovsky 2009, 2020). Some chapters provide observations on how different kinds of nonfamilial and/or familial sources of support or assistance are combined (chaps. 1–2, 4, 6–7, 9–12), as well as how different combinations of family members and government, community, and/or market strategies are assembled. In a positive light, this means many potential choices, possibility for tailoring to individual preferences, and diversification of risk. Likewise, many chapters note how there are fewer set norms of engagement and more of a situational negotiation of whatever works best in aging and caregiving today (chaps. 2–3, 6–7, 9–11), together with a shifting from one assemblage of strategies to the next in caregiving as circumstances change over time. In a negative light, however, many "options" are not available to all, coordination across actors can be challenging, and some wonder if so many players are needed just so that they can pass the buck from one to the next.

Social Stratification Issues

Social stratification within and across generations and issues of equity are another important theme in some chapters. Some share how filial ideals may be more difficult for those in lower social echelons to achieve (chaps. 2, 4), although one chapter cites literature that showed income as unrelated to level of filial piety, probably due to how it was operationalized (chap. 10). In terms of stratification across generations, many chapters mention issues of expanding intergenerational inequity in which resources and care are funneled toward younger generations (chaps. 2–3, 7–8, 10). Several chapters show how seniors may fare very differently, depending on socioeconomic status in their ability to access forms of support and/or familial or nonfamilial care (chaps. 1–2, 4, 8, 10, 12). Such class stratification in access to support and services is found in all of the societies under investigation but varies by region in its extent and impact.

Senior Voices, Agency, and Productive Aging

One central aim of our volume is to illustrate senior voices, agency, and forms of productive aging. Many of our chapters feature the viewpoints of elderly persons (chaps. 2–3, 6–7, 9, 11). Most of our chapters show how elders are not just dependents, but are also active contributors to society, families, and communities (chaps. 1–3, 6–9, 11), taking care of themselves, elderly spouses (chaps. 2, 9), and/or other elderly people (chap. 9). Other chapters examine intensification of continued care by elders for younger generations (chaps. 1, 5), a phenomenon made possible by increased prosperity, improved disease prevention and treatment, increased longevity, and more state support for seniors through pensions and other benefits.

Intersection of Aging, Caregiving, Life Courses, Dying, and Death

Caregiving is patterned not just cross-sectionally, but also longitudinally over the time frame of intersecting life courses, illness trajectories, and caregiving journeys. One chapter in this volume examines in-depth how the ways in which family caregivers view and manage caregiving tasks change over time as the care recipient's illness progresses (chap. 9). This and other chapters strive to bring together two themes often separated in social gerontology as well as in Asian studies: caregiving in later life, and death and dying (chaps. 2, 8–9, 12). These chapters illustrate continuity experienced by many caregivers and elders in East Asian settings between long-term eldercare, end-of-life care, and care for or neglect of the dead. In China and Japan concerns over seniors dying alone have attracted media attention and spurred changes in policies and programs (chaps. 2, 8). Several chapters also explore older adults' perspectives on continuities between caregiving in life and death or between caregiving and mourning (chaps. 2, 9, 12), as well as between definitions of a good life and a good death (chaps. 2, 12). These chapters reveal tensions between impetuses to expand longevity versus compress morbidity (chaps. 2, 9, 12). Two chapters include widows' ideas about caregiving that extend to the living from the dying or the dead (chaps. 2, 9).

Organization of Volume

Between the introductory and concluding chapters, the book is divided into three sections by cultural area. Each of these sections examines intersections of aging and caregiving. Part I examines the Chinese contexts of China, Hong Kong, Singapore, and Taiwan; part II examines Japanese contexts; and part III brings the analysis to Korean settings.

In part I, Aging and Caregiving in Chinese Contexts, chapter 1 by Youcai Tang and Jeanne Shea reviews old-age support in rural China and examines the potential of a recent model village experiment providing collectively financed community-based support for village seniors to enhance filial relations. Chapter 2 by Jeanne Shea explores the meanings of spousal eldercare for dementia caregivers in the context of both life and death in Shanghai. In chapter 3 Min Zhang investigates the experiences of migrant grandparents moving domestically from lower-tier to top-tier cities in China to help their adult children, who migrated for work, with housework and childcare. Chapter 4 by Michelle Shum and Terry Lum traces the reasons for the high institutionalization rate of elders in Hong Kong and lays out a new community-based approach to aging in place that aims to provide better support for family caregivers. In chapter 5, Leng Leng Thang and Kalyani Mehta examine interviews with grandchildren in response to a short state-sponsored film promoting filial piety in Singapore, showing a gap between the desire and the ability to act in a filial manner. In chapter 6, Ken Chih-Yan Sun explores interview data on how Taiwanese immigrants to the United States work to construct transnational networks of emotional and practical care for their aging parents back home in Taiwan. He explores how these immigrants and their left-behind parents feel about these arrangements and the parents' experience of aging apart.

In part II, Aging and Caregiving in Japanese Contexts, chapter 7 by Katrina Moore opens with a discussion of how Japanese elders negotiate personhood within kin-based and non-kin-based care relationships. She focuses on independence and self-reliance as key new values, which are in frequent conflict with older values of dependence and interdependence. In chapter 8, Heekyoung Kim explores the social context behind the recent case of "missing centenarians" in Japan whose deaths went unreported due to familial neglect or financial embezzlement of pension checks, and how community volunteers may be able to help. In chapter 9, Susan Long and Ruth Campbell analyze longitudinal ethnographic data on the familial caregiving careers of spousal caregivers and adult children and daughters-in-law taking care of elderly family members in Japan through years of sickness and into dying and death.

In part III, Aging and Caregiving in Korean Contexts, Hyun Ji Lee and Kyong Hee Chee open with chapter 10 on the meaning of filial piety and good-enough care in contemporary Korean families, examining how the government's long-term care policy is shifting the locus of responsibility from families onto society. In chapter 11, Dorota Szawarska analyzes longitudinal data on the complex trade-offs of a South Korean program offering to repatriate seniors forcibly conscripted to Sakhalin by the Japanese during World War II but without including those seniors' adult children or intensive caregiving provisions in the offer. In chapter 12, Sooyoun Han and Jeanne Shea describe new biopolitical challenges that are arising for the family caregivers of Korean elders related to end-of-life care and decision-making in an era of increasingly complex biomedical practices and hospice as a new and not well-understood option.

Finally, the concluding chapter draws together our findings, thinks further about population projections and imagined futures, and considers implications for future policy and research. Although our focus is on East Asian societies, we invite the reader to compare with other cultural communities. Today humanity is facing the question of how populations can enjoy unprecedented longevity in a way that is compatible with the flourishing of society overall, or, as a recent World Bank (2016) publication put it, how we can both "live long and prosper" (1). This volume offers some East Asian responses to that question at the nexus of aging and care.

Acknowledgments

We wish to acknowledge series editor Jay Sokolovsky for his guidance and assistant editor Tom Bonnington for his support. We are also grateful to the anonymous reviewers for their valuable suggestions for streamlining this chapter.

Jeanne Shea (邵镜虹) is associate professor of anthropology and director of the Health and Society Program at the University of Vermont in Burlington, Vermont, USA. Recipient of two Fulbright Awards, she has published on menopause and midlife, marital relationships, the family, spousal caregiving, senior volunteering, evidence-based medicine, and community supports for aging in place in China. Most recently, she has published several research articles in *Ageing International* (2016, 2017, 2018) and a chapter on China's Senior Companions Program for *The Cultural Context of Aging: Worldwide Perspectives* (Sokolovsky 2020).

Katrina Moore is an honorary associate in Japanese Studies, Faculty of Arts and Social Sciences, the University of Sydney. She is the author of *Joy of Noh: Embodied Learning and Discipline in Urban Japan* (SUNY Press 2014). She contributed chapters to Vera Mackie and Mark McLelland (eds.), *Routledge Handbook of Sexuality Studies in East Asia* (Routledge 2015); Maren Godzik (ed.), *Altern in Japan* (Verlag 2009); and articles in *Aging and Anthropology* (2017), *Japanese Studies* (2013), *Asian Anthropology* (2010), and *Journal of Cross-Cultural Gerontology* (2010). She currently researches conservation practices as well as family and household relationships.

Hong Zhang is associate professor of East Asian Studies at Colby College in Waterville, Maine, USA. Dr. Zhang's research interests include family and marriage, one-child policy, intergenerational relations, population aging, new eldercare patterns, urbanization, and rural-urban migration in contemporary China. Dr. Zhang has published in numerous edited volumes, including recent chapters in *Transformation of Chinese Patriarchy* (Santos and Harrell 2017) and *Cultural Context of Aging: Worldwide Perspectives* (Sokolovsky 2020). Her work has also appeared in academic journals such as *Ageing International, Journal of Contemporary China, China Quarterly, Signs,* the *China Journal,* and *Asian Anthropology.*

Glossary

xiao	孝	Filial piety.
lao	老	Old.
laoling shaozi hua	老龄少子化	The transformation entailed in a confluence of population aging and fertility decline.
zi	子	Son or child.

Notes

1. "Silver tsunami" is a crisis-oriented term for population aging used in some media and policy discourse to conjure an overwhelming surge of old or "silver-haired" people, which calls up the image of a tidal wave threatening to drown society.
2. Special journal issues on aging in Asia are beyond the scope of this review.
3. Exceptions include Macau, Mongolia, North Korea, and Vietnam.
4. Many of these trends also exist in other parts of the world (Danely and Lynch 2015), but their expressions vary, and here we focus on manifestations in East Asian contexts.
5. The 2015 figures for the elderly proportion of the most aged European populations included Italy with 22.4 percent elderly, Germany with 21.1 percent, Portugal with 20.7 percent, Finland with 20.3 percent, Bulgaria with 20.1 percent, Greece with 19.9 percent, Sweden with 19.6 percent, and France and Croatia with 18.9 percent each, all below Japan.
6. Some other more moderately aged Western societies come closer to the four tigers in 2015, such as the United Kingdom at 18.1 percent elderly, Canada at 16.1 percent, Australia at 15 percent, and the United States at 14.6 percent elderly.
7. The degree of population aging in East Asian societies today is much higher than that reported in the Ikels (2004) volume. Based on 1999 U.S. Census Bureau figures, that volume reported for that time the proportion of elderly in the popula-

tion to be 16 percent for Japan, 8.2 percent for Taiwan, 6.6 percent for China, and 6.4 percent for Korea (Ikels 2004: 8).

8. In 1950 high-income countries averaged 7.9 percent elderly.

9. Projections have risen since Ikels's volume was published. At that time, 1999 U.S. Census Bureau figures projected Japan's elderly to reach 27 percent of the population by 2025 (Ikels 2004: 8). Current UN (2017) estimates are 29.3 percent by 2025.

10. Initially, Hong Kong had begun in the 1970s to track the slope of Japan's ascent, rising by 1995 to 2.5 percentage points higher than the other tigers. However, Hong Kong decelerated to the pace of the other tigers around the 1997 return of Hong Kong from the British to China, due to an outflow of older wealthy residents and an inflow of younger Chinese workers.

11. Recent UN (2017) projections for the elderly proportion of the population expected for 2025 outstrip the 1999 U.S. Census Bureau projections given for 2025 in the areas covered by Ikels (2004: 8). This includes Japan projected now for 29.3 percent elderly by 2025 versus a 27 percent projection back then for 2025, Korea 19.9 percent versus 16 percent, Taiwan 19.3 percent versus 16 percent, and China 14.2 percent versus 13 percent.

12. Worldwide, 15.8 percent of the world's population is expected to be age sixty-five and above by 2050; for comparison, low-income countries are projected to reach 5.3 percent elderly at that time (UN 2017).

13. Furthermore, UN (2017) projections show that beyond 2050 two of the tigers are projected to overtake Japan in degree of population aging, Korea from 2060 onward and Singapore from 2065 onward.

14. For degree of population aging and projections therein, World Bank (2017) data are slightly different from the UN (2017) data presented here with regard to exact percentages and dates. For example, the World Bank states that Italy reached 23 percent age sixty-five and above, Germany reached 21 percent, and France and Sweden reached 20 percent in 2017. Discrepancies arise from methodological differences. To maintain consistency, this chapter sticks with UN data. While details vary, rough rankings, timing, and trends over time in the two data sets are consonant.

15. For other points of reference, Canada, the United States, and Australia are projected to hit super-aging status by 2025, 2030, and 2035, respectively (UN 2017).

16. In 1950 five of our six East Asian locales were tracking the low- and middle-income country average for total fertility rate of 6.39 and 5.64, while Japan was near the high-income country rate of 2.98.

17. Replacement level is the number of children needed to replace a married couple, i.e., two children.

18. There is a debate about the degree to which the Single Child Family Policy, versus socioeconomic development and maternal education and employment, are responsible for China's 1980–2015 fertility decline (especially as Korea's fertility levels plummeted without such policy). In 2015 the Single Child Family Policy was lifted due to concern about population aging and a Comprehensive Three-Child Policy is now in place.

19. Due to incomplete data, the Taiwan line from 2020 onward in this graph has been extrapolated based on pattern of other lines.

20. These notations of the appearance of various crosscutting themes in chapters are not meant to be exhaustive. Readers will undoubtedly find additional tie-ins not found in this overview.
21. Some feminist scholars have argued that East Asian national economic development has rested on the backs of unpaid care provided by family members, especially women, raising concerns that governmental calls for filial piety are also a modern neoliberal devolution of state responsibility.
22. Implicitly, we see that care by grandparents for grandchildren has also become more gender-balanced with grandmothers and grandfathers providing intimate and pragmatic care (M. Zhang in chapter 3). In spousal eldercare more men are rising to the challenge (Shea in chapter 2, Long and Campbell in chapter 9), although still less often than women. In addition, men continue to be seen as less capable than women in caregiving.

References

"Ahead of Respect for the Aged Day, Number of Centenarians in Japan Tops 70,000." 2019. *Japan Times*, 13 September. Retrieved 1 March 2020 from https://www.japantimes.co.jp/news/2019/09/13/national/japan-centenarians-top-70000/#.XjdJz2hKiUk.

Appadurai, Arjun. 1996. *Modernity at Large: The Cultural Dimensions of Globalization*. Minneapolis: University of Minnesota Press.

Arifin, Evi N. 2007. "Special Issue: Growing Old in Asia: Implications and Challenges." *Asia-Pacific Population Journal* 21 (3): 1–144.

Asia Development Bank (ADB). 2017. "Population and Aging in Asia." Retrieved 20 March 2019 from https.adb.org/features/asia-s-growing-elderly-population-adb-s-take.

Bengtson, Vern L., and Richard Settersten. 2016. *Handbook of Theories of Aging*, 3rd ed. New York: Springer.

Berger, Peter L., and Thomas Luckmann. 1966. *The Social Construction of Reality: A Treatise in the Sociology of Knowledge*. Garden City, NY: Anchor Books.

Bourdieu, Pierre. 1977. *Outline of a Theory of Practice*. Cambridge, UK: Cambridge University Press.

Buch, Elana. 2015. "Anthropology of Aging and Care." *Annual Review of Anthropology* 44: 277–93.

Cai, Fang, John Giles, Philip O'Keefe, and Dewen Wang. 2012. *The Elderly and Old Age Support in Rural China: Challenges and Prospects*. Washington, DC: International Bank for Reconstruction and Development.

Calasanti, Toni. 2008. "Theorizing Feminist Gerontology, Sexuality and Beyond: An Intersectional Approach." In *Handbook of Theories of Aging*, 2nd ed., ed. Vern Bengtson, Daphna Gans, Norella Putney, and Merril Silverstein, 471–86. New York: Springer.

Chai, Ch'u, and Winberg Chai. 1965. *The Sacred Books of Confucius and Other Confucian Classics*. New Hyde Park, NY: University Books.

Chen, Sheying, and Jason L. Powell, eds. 2012. *Aging in China: Implications to Social Policy of a Changing Economic State*. New York: Springer.

Cheng, Sheung-Tak, Iris Chi, Helene H. Fung, Lydia W. Li, and Jean Woo. 2015. *Successful Aging: Asian Perspectives.* New York: Springer.

Coulmas, Florian. 2007. "Facts and Discourses." In *Population Decline and Ageing in Japan: The Social Consequences, Florian Coulmas,* 1–16. New York: Routledge.

Danely, Jason. 2014. *Aging and Loss: Mourning and Maturity in Contemporary Japan.* New Brunswick, NJ: Rutgers University Press.

Danely, Jason, and Caitrin Lynch. 2015. "Introduction: Transitions and Transformations: Paradigms, Perspectives, and Possibilities." In *Transitions and Transformations: Cultural Perspectives on Aging and the Lifecourse,* ed. Caitrin Lynch and Jason Danely, 3–20. New York: Berghahn.

Dowd, J. J. 1975. "Aging as Exchange: A Preface to Theory." *Journal of Gerontology* 30 (5): 584–94.

Eggleston, Karen, and Shripad Tuljapurkar, eds. 2010. *Aging Asia: The Economic and Social Implications of Rapid Demographic Change in China, Japan and South Korea.* Stanford, CA: Shorenstein Asia-Pacific Research Center.

Elder, Glen H. Jr. 1974/1999. *Children of the Great Depression: Social Change in Life Experience,* 25th anniversary ed. Boulder, CO: Westview Press.

Eun, Ki-Soo. 2007. "Lowest Low Fertility in the Republic of Korea: Causes, Consequences, and Policy Responses." *Asia-Pacific Population Journal* 22 (2): 51–72.

Fong, Vanessa. 2004. *Only Hope: Coming of Age under China's One-Child Policy.* Stanford, CA: Stanford University Press.

Foucault, Michel, with ed. Paul Rabinow. 1984. *The Foucault Reader.* New York: Pantheon.

Fu, Tsung-hsi Fu, and Rhidian Hughes, eds. 2009. *Ageing in East Asia. Challenges and Policies for the Twenty-First Century.* New York: Routledge.

Geertz, Clifford. 1973. *The Interpretation of Cultures.* New York: Basic Books.

Goodman, Roger, and Sarah Harper, eds. 2008. *Ageing in Asia: Asia's Position in the New Global Demography.* New York: Routledge.

Harper, Sarah, ed. 2014. *Critical Readings on Ageing in East Asia.* Leiden, Netherlands: Brill.

HelpAge International. 2015. "Older People in Ageing Societies: Burden or Resource?" In *HelpAge Network Asia/ Pacific Regional Conference 2014,* 1–20. Retrieved 24 March 2020 from http://envejecimiento.csic.es/documentos/documentos/HelpAge-personasmayores-sociedadesenvejecen-Carga-recursos-05-2015.pdf.

Hermalin, Albert I., ed. 2002. *The Well-Being of Elderly in Asia: A Four-Country Comparative Study.* Ann Arbor: University of Michigan Press.

Higo, Masa, and Thomas R. Klassen. 2015. *Retirement in Japan and South Korea: The Past, the Present and the Future of Mandatory Retirement.* New York: Routledge.

Hinton, Ladson, and Hongtu Chen. 2016. "Eldercare in Asia: A Call for Policy Development Beyond Traditional Family Care" *Ageing International* 41 (4): 331–34.

Ikels, Charlotte, ed. 2004. *Filial Piety: Practice and Discourse in Contemporary East Asia.* Stanford, CA: Stanford University Press.

Janelli, Rogers, and Dawnhee Yim. 2004. "The Transformation of Filial Piety in Contemporary South Korea." In Ikels, *Filial Piety,* 128–152.

Kaneda, Toshiko, and James M. Raymo. 2003. "Trends in the Quantity and Quality of Life at Older Ages in Japan." In Traphagan and Knight, *Demographic Change,* 147–75.

Kinsella, Kevin. 2009. "Global Perspectives on the Demography of Aging." In Sokolovsky, *The Cultural Context of Aging,* 3rd ed., 13–29.

Lamb, Sarah. 2000. *White Saris and Sweet Mangos: Aging, Gender, and the Body in North India.* Berkeley: University of California Press.

Langsdorf, Susanne, Rudolf Traub-Merz, and Chun Ding. 2010. *Eldercare and Long-Term Care Insurance: China, Germany, and Japan: Models and Cases.* Shanghai, China: Shanghai Academy of Social Sciences.

Legge, James. 1933. *The Four Books*, transl. with notes. Shanghai, China: Chinese Book Company.

Long, Susan O., and C. Scott Littleton. 2003. "Demographic and Family Change: Problems and Solutions." In Traphagan and Knight, *Demographic Change*, 229–36.

Mehta, Kalyani, ed. 2005. *Untapped Resources: Women in Ageing Societies Across Asia*, 2nd ed. Singapore: Marshall Cavendish International.

Miller, Eric T. 2004. "Filial Daughters, Filial Sons: Comparisons from Rural North China." In Ikels, *Filial Piety*, 34–52.

National Statistics Republic of China (Taiwan) [Taiwan Department of Statistics]. 2018. "Life Expectancy and Death Rates." Retrieved 24 March 2020 from https://eng.stat.gov.tw/public/data/dgbas03/bs2/yearbook_eng/y006.pdf.

———. 2019. "Population and Housing." Retrieved 20 April 2019 from https://eng.stat.gov.tw/np.asp?CtNode=1525.

Palmore, Erdman. 1975. *The Honorable Elders: A Cross-Cultural Analysis of Aging in Japan.* Durham, NC: Duke University Press.

Palmore, Erdman, and Daisaku Maeda. 1985. *The Honorable Elders Revisited: A Revised Cross-Cultural Analysis of Aging in Japan.* Durham, NC: Duke University Press.

Powell, Jason L., and Ian G. Cook, eds. 2009. *Aging in Asia.* New York: Nova Science.

Raymo, James M., and Toshiko Kaneda. 2003. "Changes in the Living Arrangements of Japanese Elderly: The Role of Demographic Factors." In Traphagan and Knight, *Demographic Change*, 27–52.

Riley, Matilda White. 1974. "The Perspective of Age Stratification." *School Review* 83 (1): 85–91.

Santos, Goncalo, and Stevan Harrell, eds. 2017. *Transforming Patriarchy: Chinese Families in the Twenty-First Century.* Seattle and London: University of Washington Press.

Shea, Jeanne, and Yan Zhang, 2016. "Ethnography of Caregiving of Elders by Elders in Shanghai, China." *Ageing International* 41 (4): 366–93.

Shea, Jeanne, and Hong Zhang. 2017. "Introduction to Aging and Caregiving in Chinese Populations." *Ageing International* 42 (2): 137–41.

Shi, Lihong. 2009. " 'Little Quilted Vests to Warm Parents' Hearts': Redefining the Gendered Practice of Filial Piety in Rural North-Eastern China." *China Quarterly* 198 (June): 348–63.

Singer, Merrill, and Hans Baer. 1995. *Critical Medical Anthropology.* New York: Routledge.

Smith, James P., and Malay Majmundar, eds. 2012. *Aging in Asia: Findings from New and Emerging Data Initiatives.* Washington, DC: National Academies Press.

Sokolovsky, Jay. 2009. *The Cultural Context of Aging: Worldwide Perspectives*, 3rd ed. Westport, CT: Praeger.

———. 2020. *The Cultural Context of Aging: Worldwide Perspectives.* 4th ed. Westport, CT: Praeger.

Sorensen, Clark, and Sung-Chul Kim. 2004. "Filial Piety in Contemporary Urban Southeast Korea: Practices and Discourses." In Ikels, *Filial Piety*, 153–81.

Sun, Yuezhu. 2017. "Among a Hundred Good Virtues, Filial Piety is the First: Contemporary Moral Discourses on Filial Piety in Urban China." *Anthropology Quarterly* 90(3): 771–99.

Suzuki, Tori. 2014. *Low Fertility and Population Aging in Japan and Eastern Asia*. Medford, MA: Springer Science and Business Media.

Tham, Tat Yean, Thuy Linh Tran, Somjit Prueksaritanond, Josefina S. Isidro, Sajita Setia, and Vicknesh Welluppillai. 2018. "Integrated Health Care Systems in Asia: An Urgent Necessity." *Clinical Interventions in Aging* 13: 2527–38.

Traphagan, John W., and John Knight, eds. 2003. *Demographic Change and the Family in Japan's Aging Society*. Albany, NY: SUNY Press.

United Nations (UN). 2017. *World Population Prospects: The 2017 Revision*. United Nations Department of Economic and Social Affairs, Population Division. Custom data for original charts developed by author Jeanne Shea for this chapter acquired via website. Retrieved 1 June 2018 from https://population.un.org/wpp/DataQuery/.

———. 2019a. *Life Expectancy at Birth for Both Sexes Combined, 2018*. Retrieved 1 February 2019 from http://data.un.org/Data.aspx?q=Life+Expectancy&d=Pop Div&f=variableID%3a68.

———. 2019b. *World Population Prospects: The 2019 Revision*. Department of Economic and Social Affairs, Population Division. custom data for original charts developed by author for this chapter acquired via website. Retrieved 15 May 2019 from https://population.un.org/wpp/DataQuery/.

U.S. Census Bureau. 2017. "Taiwan TW: UCB Projection: Life Expectancy at Birth." Retrieved 15 May 2019 from https://www.ceicdata.com/en/taiwan/demographic-projection/tw-ucb-projection-life-expectancy-at-birth.

Walker, Alan, and Christian Aspalter. 2014. *Active Ageing in Asia*. New York: Routledge.

Wang, Danyu. 2004. "Ritualistic Coresidence and the Weakening of Filial Practice in Rural China." In Ikels, *Filial Piety*, 16–33.

Wolf, Margery. 1972. *Women and the Family in Rural Taiwan*. Stanford, CA: Stanford University Press.

World Bank. 2016. *Live Long and Prosper: Aging in East Asia and Pacific*. Washington, DC: World Bank. Retrieved 20 February 2019 from https://openknowledge.worldbank.org/handle/10986/23133.

———. 2017. "Population Ages 65 and Above." Retrieved 20 February 2019 from https://data.worldbank.org/indicator/SP.POP.65UP.TO.ZS?view=chart.

———. 2019. "Singapore Overview." Retrieved 20 February 2019 from https.worldbank.org/en/country/singapore/overview.

Yan, Yunxiang. 2016. "Intergenerational Initimacy and Descending Familism in Rural North China." *American Anthropologist* 118 (2): 244–257.

———. 2018. "Neo-Familism and the State in Contemporary China." *Urban Anthropology and Studies of Cultural Systems and World Economic Development* 47 (3,4): 1–44.

Yeh, Chung-Yang, Hyunwook Cheng, and Shih-Jiunn Shi. 2018. "Public–Private Pension Mixes in East Asia: Institutional Diversity and Policy Implications for Old-Age Security." *Ageing & Society* 40 (3): 1–22.

Zhang, Hong. 2009. "The New Realities of Aging in Contemporary China: Coping with the Decline in Family Care." In Sokolovsky, *The Cultural Context of Aging*, 3rd ed., 196–215.

———. 2017. "Recalibrating Filial Piety: Realigning the State, Family, and Market Interests in China." In *Transforming Patriarchy: Chinese Families in the Twenty-First Century*, ed. Goncalo Santos and Stevan Harrell, 234–55. Seattle: University of Washington Press.

———. 2020. "Globalizing Late Life in China and Realigning the State, Family and Market Interests for Eldercare." In Sokolovsky, *The Cultural Context of Aging*, 4th ed.

PART I
Aging and Caregiving in Chinese Contexts

1 OLD-AGE SUPPORT IN RURAL CHINA

Case Study of the Jiangxiang Model for Community-Based Filial Piety

Youcai Tang and Jeanne Shea

Introduction to the Problem

WITH CHINA'S RAPID AGING AND profound social transformation, rural old-age support issues have become an issue of substantial concern in both government and academic circles. China is one of the first developing countries in the world to have become an aging society, with over 7 percent of its population aged sixty or older, the benchmark that China and many other developing countries still recognize as the threshold to old age. In China, analysts characterize the situation as "having gotten old before getting rich," contrasting China's situation with the trajectories of countries like Australia, Canada, England, France, Germany, Japan, Korea, Singapore, and the United States, all of which were high-income countries before becoming aging societies. In Western countries, old-age security in the form of social insurance has largely been a product of industrial development. Although China's levels of industrialization and urbanization are continually increasing, rural dwellers still constitute a large portion of the population (42 percent) (World Bank 2018), among whom agriculture is still an important income source, although the rural economy has been diversifying over the reform era (1978–present).

In China, not only is the national proportion of the population that is elderly large and rising rapidly, but also rural areas there have both higher proportions of elderly folks and lower levels of economic development. According to China's 2015 National 1 Percent Population Sample Survey (China National Statistics Bureau [CNSB] 2015), by 2015 China's elderly population over sixty years old had reached a record 222 million people, accounting for 16.52 percent of the nation's population. Compared with the national census in 2010, the elderly portion of the population increased by 2.89 percentage points. By 2015, seniors accounted for 18.47 percent of the rural population, 4.27 points higher than for urban areas. At the same time, rural areas are still much poorer than urban areas. In 2016 per capita disposable income (after-tax income) of rural households was just 12,363 yuan (about US$1,825), almost three times less than that of urban households (CNSB 2016).[1] With China's decentralized system, this makes it difficult to establish a sufficient social security system for rural citizens, especially the elderly. Furthermore, the problem of rural old-age support is projected to deepen with the rising urban-to-rural migration of youth expected in the coming decades.

In this chapter we examine mixed-methods case study data on a famous reform-era innovation in rural old-age support based in Jiangxiang Cun, a village in Jiangsu Province. This "Jiangxiang Model" has been promoted by the national government and Chinese media as an exemplar of creative problem-solving by a village government to address the rural old-age support problem by cultivating local community resources. Our research questions include these: How was the Jiangxiang Model structured and accomplished in terms of types of supports for seniors, related revenue generation, negotiating resource distribution, and instilling filial piety (for definition, see Introduction) as a prioritized community value? How sustainable is it likely to be? What is the probable viability of scaling this model out to other rural locales?

In answering these questions, we show how the Jiangxiang Model involves reviving collective agriculture and enterprise in a new configuration in order to generate substantial public revenue to provide material support for seniors. In addition to such collective revenue generation, village leadership used central planning mechanisms to socially engineer intergenerational income distribution, and to provide free housing options for seniors not far from their children's homes, as well as incentives for intergenerational living. Driven by the charisma of the local Communist Party secretary, all of this was aimed at generating favorable conditions for continuing certain forms of filial piety like affective bonds, warm interactions, and family harmony. The moral authority of the aging village party secretary and the village reputation for being a model filial socialist village has been used to generate additional collective revenue through values-based tourism, further underscoring the continuing relevance of filiality. There are serious questions about the local sustainability of, as well as the broader scalability of, this model, given the heavy role that the charismatic authority and managerial acumen of one individual have played in its implementation.

In the pages that follow we begin with a review of typical issues of rural old-age support in China, followed by a theoretical framing. Then we examine how Jiangxiang's scheme was structured and accomplished, looking at the benefits provided to seniors and the mechanisms used for related resource production, negotiating elder-focused distribution, and building a village culture that prioritizes filial piety as a community value. Finally, we analyze how sustainable this mode of old-age support is likely to be in the village itself, and the probable viability of scaling this model out to other rural locations.

Theoretical Significance

This chapter connects with Ikels's (2004) remarks about the "role of state policy" in supporting, shaping, or even undercutting "the practice of filial piety" (12). Ikels wrote that earlier East Asian emphasis on the filial duty to obey parents and produce descendants has been "nearly completely overshadowed by the emphasis on supporting elderly parents" (12) as obedience to the state, gender equity, population control, and rapid modernization became priorities in China. Ikels noted the importance of "housing policy [in] family decisions about the relative merits of coresidence" with aged parents (14). In addition, she observed that "governmental decisions about whether, when, and how much they will encourage the development of programs and services that facilitate or complement family caregiving can be absolutely critical in determining how successfully families manage their filial responsibilities" (14). Likewise, in the case we will describe, village government is using local policy and programs to both support and transform filial practices of resident families through reform-era neo-collectivist resource production, civil engineering, redistribution, and redefinition of community values and their manifestations.

This chapter also connects with scholarly literature on post-socialism and the interplay, continuity, and discontinuity of market and collectivist ideologies and practices in post-socialist societies (Petrovici 2015). In China's case we have a society that characterizes itself as based on market socialism or "socialism with Chinese characteristics." Although China continues to describe itself as socialist, as early as the 1980s and 1990s many non-socialist states and territories including Hong Kong, Japan, Korea, Singapore, and Taiwan had far more redistributive systems of social welfare than China proper. While the overarching narrative of reform-era China has embraced the positives of market reform, there is also a storyline about the negative side effects, and losses with rising individualism and decline in collectivism. While stories abound of villages that avoided penury by secretly contracting land to individual households during Maoist times, this chapter relays a different, less common story about a village that bucked the de-collectivization trend and did a partial re-collectivization to good effect. It also relates to literature on the interplay between welfare states and the modern capitalist economies within which they are embedded (Polese, Morris, and Kovacs 2015) and on the promotion of the role of community in supporting social welfare efforts (Muehlbach 2012). It also engages the theme of regional inequality in old-age support in countries such as China with decentralized social welfare systems (Liu and Sun 2016). It echoes Sokolovsky's (2009) point that, rather than a choice of family or state, analysts should focus on how the family, community, and state interact with each other around eldercare. Likewise, it is not a case of either the market or collectivist efforts as superior, but of how the two coexisting forces may be used together to best support seniors under different circumstances.

Finally, the analysis connects with Weber's (1968) classic research on charisma and institution building and its relation to social transformation. According to Eisenstadt (1968: xxxii), Weber saw the path of social transformation as "greatly dependent not only on the objective forces of the market or of production but on a charismatic reformulation of the meaning of economic activities." Weber found charismatic leaders and the new answers to social problems that they offered to be pivotal at times of uncertainty when people were seeking new patterns of meaning and order (xxxii). This chapter also joins research on the role of Communist Party secretaries in navigating the transition from Mao to market, and the tensions between national policies and local conditions in reform-era China (Huang 1989).

Methods

This is a mixed-methods oral history case study carried out in Jiangxiang Village from 2008–17. Methods used include village records review, a questionnaire-based survey of villagers, key informant interviews with village leaders, years of participant observation in the village, and home visits and interviews with villagers and village seniors. The first author, Tang, is a sociologist and a native of China with reading proficiency in English. The second author, Shea, is an anthropologist and an American fluent in Chinese. The research progressed through years of follow-up research, involving archival, qualitative, and quantitative data. Shea is interested in rural "models" for senior support, and conducted participant observation and interviews in the village in summer 2014.

All study participants were informed of our intentions to conduct scholarly research and publish about their village. As an oral history case study, the name and location of the village were kept true to life. The real name of the party secretary was used as a public figure wishing to be credited, in accordance with the American Anthropological Association (AAA 2012) code of ethics. No real names are used for ordinary villagers or anyone not wishing to be named. For human subjects purposes, the research was approved by the IRB of the University of Vermont.

Validity was strengthened through building strong long-term rapport and data triangulation. Data was collected from multiple different villagers, including a variety of local leaders and ordinary residents, at many different points in time over a decade. Multiple data collection methods were used. This allowed us to compare what was recorded in village records, what people reported in surveys, what people said in casual conversations and interviews, and what people said and did in different participant observation situations.

Following data collection, the authors discussed the data in relation to this volume, and the first author wrote a draft in Chinese. The second author translated the draft and revised and added to the manuscript, orienting the argument toward our intended audience, and adding national context, historical background, additional theory, and references.

Old-Age Support in Rural China: Historical Background and Patterns of Social Change

Similar to the situation today, during the planned economy era of Maoist China (1949–76) prior to the market reforms, in rural areas self-reliance through work and familial assistance were the primary ways of getting by in old age. Similar to today, accessing governmental old-age support was much more difficult in rural as compared with urban areas, with far leaner provisions if that support was available at all. Urban areas had both non-means-based support for the aged via government employers and state-owned enterprises called "work units" and needs-based elder support via neighborhood-based street committees for those who had never been employed and who had no family and no capacity for self-support. In contrast, rural areas only had means-tested support for older adults (Wu et al. 2005). Each village was organized into an agricultural commune or collective composed of production teams, rather than work units. There were no retirement or pensions for rural dwellers who simply stopped working to then be supported by their families when they could work no more. Primary reliance on familial support and care was broadly feasible then due to "restricted geographic mobility, large families living in close proximity, relatively flexible work demands, and low consumption norms" (Shea 2019: 336). For those few childless infirm elders with no work ability, no family support, and no financial resources (known as the "three no's seniors"), the village collective was expected under the central-government's "five guarantees" policy to find a way to provide basic food, clothing, shelter, health care, and burial expenses (Lu et al. 2017; State Council of the People's Republic of China, Information Office [SCPRCIO] 2004; Urio 2010). Rudimentary health care was provided through cooperative medical services to which all villagers of any age or means had access.

During this period, the main mode of resource production to support rural seniors without adequate familial support was collective agriculture. All land was owned by the state and all goods and revenue produced through villagers' labor were owned by the village collective, with a portion set aside to support "three no's" seniors. While perverse incentives, policy missteps, and political turmoil contributed to low productivity and very lean times, a minimal level of subsistence was offered for a large portion of the Maoist period excepting famine times to extremely needy rural elders who passed the strict means testing.

The market reforms starting in 1978 two years after Mao's death brought both rapid economic development and increasing insecurity for rural seniors. Under the new nationwide household responsibility system, the rural collective system was dismantled in the 1980s as family households contracted with the state for land use rights and became able to keep the revenue generated through their labor, rather than relinquishing it to the collective. While this allowed some families to get rich, income inequality increased, and the formal subsistence guarantee previously promised by collectives to senior residents was lost in most of rural China in the 1980s and 1990s. Although the five guarantees policy continued, its application varied widely from place to place, and rural residents lost access to the basic "barefoot doctor" (chijiao yisheng) health care that the collectives had previously offered (Brandt et al. 2006).

Old-age support from the family under traditional Confucian ideals of filial piety has undergone considerable erosion in the reform era due to demographic, socioeconomic, and cultural reasons. Demographically, family size has declined under state-sponsored family planning, which began in the 1970s as a "late-spaced-few" (wan xi shao) policy (see glossary at end of chapter for definition), became a one- to two-child policy for rural areas from the 1980s on (two if first child was a girl or disabled), and then a two-child policy nationwide from 2015 on, becoming a three-child policy in 2021. Family planning policy, together with economic development, mechanization, and industrialization, and increases in maternal education and employment, led to a rapid decline in fertility levels. Whereas in 1960 the average number of children per woman of reproductive age in China was more than 5.8, in the 1970s it had fallen to 4, and by 2014 it was only 1.6 (World Bank 2016b). As a result, the number of younger family members per elderly parent has declined over time. In addition, as life expectancy has risen from only forty-three in 1960 to seventy-six by 2014 (World Bank 2016a), seniors have been living longer, requiring more resources, and incurring more health-care costs. In socioeconomic terms, the loosening up of former restrictions on geographic mobility has led to widespread migration of younger people from the countryside to urban areas in search of education and jobs, leaving older family members behind. Increases in the extent of women's formal employment in more-time-consuming, less-flexible jobs has also reduced unpaid familial sources of rural elder support. No longer sheltered by the collective, although earning far more, adult children today face much higher costs of living, rising inflation, increased financial risk, rising child education costs, and higher personal consumption expectations.

Finally, culturally in both Maoist and reform era times, there has been a widespread weakening of traditional cultural norms involving respect for elders and a sense of obligation to support elderly parents. Reduction in esteem for seniors began with the rapid modernization, steep increases in education, devaluation of tradition, and valorization of youths that emerged under Mao. It continued with the further weakening of traditional norms under the influence of Westernization and capitalism, leading to increasing individualization and emphasis on the young and the new, as well as the nuclear family unit and neolocal post-marital residence among the younger generations (Yan 2009). Together, this put the elderly into a precarious situation without stable support from either village government or younger family members. While most people in China, young and old alike, continue to express the belief that respect and support should be accorded to elders, follow-through can be challenging amidst the many competing demands and priorities complicating younger adults' lives today.

By the mid-2000s, China's social welfare system had become grossly inadequate, with widespread inequality in resource distribution, leading to discontent in disadvantaged populations such as seniors, especially in rural areas (Liu and Sun 2016). This led to the harmonious society policy (Guo and Guo 2008), with efforts to rebuild social welfare provisions (Liu and Sun 2016). Pronouncements followed concerning the importance of old-age support especially within the family, but also by the state and local communities. The most well-known is the Law for the Protection of the Rights and Interests of the Elderly of 2013 (Standing Committee of the National People's Congress of the People's Republic of China [SCNPCPRC] 2013), which despite spurring concrete improvements, is more moral policy admonition than law (Shea 2019).

TABLE 1.1. 2015 National 1 Percent Population Sample Survey.

Main Source of Support	National #	%	City	%	Town	%	Village	%
Income from employment	806,241	23.5	62,014	6.3	151,433	20.9	592,794	34.3
Pension from employment or local government	1,037,830	30.2	700,811	71.0	208,063	28.8	128,956	7.5
Minimum living subsidy for lowest income household	173,378	5.0	19,875	2.0	36,063	5.0	117,440	6.8
Income from property or rentals	18,156	0.5	5,788	0.6	4,914	0.6	7,454	0.5
Support from other family members	1,260,348	36.7	170,526	17.3	289,403	40.0	800,419	46.4
Other	139,911	4.1	27,366	2.8	34,530	4.7	78,015	4.5
Overall	3,435,864	100	986,380	100	724,406	100	1,725,078	100

Source: CNSB 2015.

In recent years, government provisions for the elderly have improved substantially (State Council of the People's Republic of China [SCPRC] 2016), yet large rural-urban inequalities remain, and benefits are typically low for most rural dwellers. While a combination of employer-, government-, and beneficiary-funded pension programs have achieved nearly 100 percent coverage of urban seniors, just 80 percent of rural older adults are covered. The social pension benefit level for rural self-employed agricultural workers is very low, averaging only 81 yuan (about US$13) a month, far below the urban level (Liu and Sun 2016). Also, even though nationwide health-care reforms launched in the mid to late 2000s had by 2016 reached a nearly universal level of basic insurance coverage nationwide (World Bank 2016c), benefit levels for rural residents under the New Rural Cooperative Medical Services are much lower than those for urbanites (Yu 2015). Wealthier areas also have set up community-based services for the aged such as senior meals, health promotion activities, and adult day programs (Chen and Han 2016), but these are still largely unavailable in poor and rural parts of the country. In general, reform-era government support for rural elderly has been rudimentary, sparse, and poorly funded.

Rural-urban disparity in old-age support in China also shows in the relative proportion of seniors covered by retirement income or social pensions, as seen in table 1.1. While 30.2 percent of the nation's elderly rely mainly on retirement income and/or social pensions, in rural areas only 7.5 percent of elders do so (CNSB 2015). In the relative absence of government- or employer-financed retirement support, up to 46.4 percent of rural elderly rely on family for material support, while another 34.3 percent support themselves through their own labor, gaining income by producing and selling vegetables, eggs, livestock, meat, or handicrafts and doing other manual labor. In contrast, only 6.3 percent of urban seniors rely on income from continuing employment and only 17 percent of urban elders rely on monetary support from family.

With the rapidly growing need for senior social security, much policy debate has focused on the responsibility of the family versus the government at national or provincial levels. Recently, community-based support for aging in place has become a popular theme in Chinese cities, but thus far it has rarely been applied to rural areas. As population aging deepens, finding ways to tap local communities for support beyond family and state will be an important part of efforts to establish comprehensive old-age support nationwide. Underused now, community-based supports may become even more important in rural areas where old-age support problems exist on a scale and level of urgency that exceeds the urban situation.

Old-Age Support Model of a Collectivist Village: The Case of Jiangxiang

Located in southeastern Jiangsu, Jiangxiang is a nationally recognized so-called "civilized" village (*wenming cun*) and model (*mofan*) for the development of "China's new countryside." Its location in a rapidly developing part of rural China surrounded by prosperous cities connected by convenient highways contributes to the village's relative good fortune. Perched propitiously near the southwestern shore of the Yangtze River, the large cities of Shanghai, Suzhou, and Nantong form a large triangle around the village, and the smaller cities of Changshu, Taicang, and Kunshan form a smaller triangle around the village (see figure 1.1).

A small village combining a modest base of agricultural land use with a variety of nonagricultural enterprises, Jiangxiang covers three square kilometers and has 1,700 acres of cultivated land. It has an official population of 835 citizens, consisting of 186 families, which are divided into twelve

FIGURE 1.1. Location of Jiangxiang Village in Jiangsu Province. Map by Jeanne Shea.

administrative groupings. Beyond this, the village also has some migrant settlers, with a total of 142 registered permanent residents who work in local factory and tourism jobs. For occupations, 524 residents are blue-collar workers and 12 are in management. Of the blue-collar workers, 43 are agricultural laborers, 326 are factory workers, and 143 are involved in sales, transportation, catering, and other services. This kind of employment structure, light on agricultural laborers, has become common in many Chinese villages during the reforms, with increasing mechanization of agriculture and economic diversification.

While nationally China de-collectivized the countryside in the early reform era, a small minority of villages such as Jiangxiang maintained, revived, and reinvented forms of socialist collectivist ideology and practice well into the reform period. While Jiangxiang is in a prosperous part of the temperate south along with Huaxi village of Jiangsu, another reform-era "collectivist" village (Zhou 2006), there is more lingering collectivism in rural areas in northern China (Van de Vliert et al. 2013), including Dazhai in Shanxi and Nanjie in Henan (Fu and Wang 2018). Not all collectivist villages emphasize old-age support to the extent that Jiangxiang does, although villages tend to include it in some fashion. Reform-era collectivist villages look back nostalgically to the subsistence guarantee theoretically offered to all in Maoist times. Yet, they also recognize that current economic development and living standards are stronger under market conditions. Therefore, the goal is to combine the best of collective social welfare and a capitalist market economy, rather than simply return to Maoist times. As such, they operate as government-sponsored corporations that employ capable villagers for a wage and channel profits back to all villagers through village infrastructure and other benefits.

Starting in the 1980s, Jiangxiang planned and worked toward the coordinated development of housing, agriculture, industry, and tourism under their long-time Communist Party secretary's lead. Villagers call their development plan "four parks on one base," consisting of four dedicated spatial areas: a housing development of new homes for villagers, a collective agricultural production park for organic produce, Changsheng Industrial Park, and the Jiangxiang Ecological Park for eco-tourism. The proceeds from these four parks form the collective funds through which community-sponsored old-age support is drawn.

With regard to housing, the village collective designed and built matching two-story freestanding houses called "villas" (*bieshu*) for all its 186 native-born families in a planned neighborhood (see figure 1.2). The villas were sold to villagers but at a subsidized price. Remaining profits went into the village collective fund, as did profits from the collective agricultural, tourism, and industrial ventures listed above and described below.

FIGURE 1.2. Two-Story Villa with Private Gated Yard for Adult Children, Jiangxiang. Photo by Jeanne Shea.

FIGURE 1.3. One-Story Row-House Apartments with Open Congregate Porch for Seniors across the Street from the Villas, Jiangxiang. Photo by Jeanne Shea.

The main priority for these collective funds has been to support a comprehensive social welfare guarantee for village elders who form a high and increasing proportion of the village population. At present, the village has 224 people age sixty and older, comprising 27 percent of the total native population (N = 835); of these, thirty-eight villagers or 4.6 percent are older than age eighty. With youths from newborn to fifteen years of age comprising 23 percent of the native village population, the remaining working-age adults between the ages of sixteen to fifty-nine make up half of the population. In demographic terms, this makes for a high population dependency ratio for the village. Although the village does not have the extremely high rates of blue-collar youth labor out-migration found in poorer rural areas, some of Jiangxiang's brightest and most ambitious young people are going to the city for college and remaining there for white-collar careers. This official population dependency ratio leaves out, however, the 142 migrant workers mentioned earlier, who are permanent residents of the village but not counted in the native village population of 835. Coming from other less-prosperous rural areas to work in Jiangxiang's enterprises, these migrant workers now make up about a third of working-age adults in the village, providing a substantial boost to economic output and the collective revenue base. While receiving some employee benefits, they are ineligible for collective social welfare benefits from the village collective.

Village collective revenues make it possible for Jiangxiang to provide native village seniors with a very high level of social welfare coverage. Old-age benefits there include free senior apartments, social pensions, returns on shares in collective village ventures, paid labor opportunities without any age cutoff, and medical benefits. In terms of housing, the village has built 150 fully equipped single-story row-style senior apartments (see figure 1.3) offered at no cost, all utilities included, to village seniors age fifty-five and up. The village made the decision to offer free stand-alone senior housing because they knew that in the reform era adult children preferred the freedom and convenience of neolocal post-marital residence, rather than the three- or four-generation households idealized in Confucian tradition. The senior apartments were positioned across the street from the adult children's villas in order to create convenient conditions for frequent intergenerational visits and close emotional bonds but also enough spatial distance to reduce conflict and promote family harmony across generations. At the same time, the village provided any adult children willing to take their elderly parents into their villa with a small bonus subsidy.

The income of the elderly in Jiangxiang is divided into three main sources and is remarkably high for a rural area in China. First, there is the social pension issued by the village to the elderly from collective revenues. The older a village elder is, the higher the amount of their pension, with amounts ranging from 500 yuan (US$74) for those in their late fifties to 1,500 yuan (US$222) for those in their nineties. Second, similar to all adult villagers, seniors receive 7,000 yuan (about US$1,000) per person a year through the village shareholding system for its various collective holdings. Third, based on individual abilities, seniors can earn income from employment in the villages' various collective ventures in agriculture, tourism, and manufacturing. Common jobs offered to village senior applicants include growing vegetables, breeding and caring for livestock, fisheries work, tending the eco-tourism biosphere areas, sweeping or raking common areas, cleaning guest bungalows and other buildings, greeting tourists, running errands, and gatekeeper duties. Average income from senior employment in the village is about 20,000 yuan per person per year (about US$3,000). Altogether, the income of Jiangxiang elderly is very high. Adding in social pensions, collective shareholder dividends, and labor remuneration, Jiangxiang senior incomes can reach as high as 30,000–40,000 yuan (about US$4,400–US$5,900) per senior per year. This is very high for a rural elder, given that the average per capita disposable income in rural China is only little more than 12,000 yuan (US$1,760) and even lower for rural elderly (Lu and Du 2015).

Finally, the village offers its seniors substantial subsidies to help protect their income from medical expenses in later life. Not only did the village pay into a New Rural Cooperative Medical Services fund for all of its villagers, but it also agreed to reimburse an additional 50 percent of seniors' remaining medical expenses over and above that fund's coverage. This level of health-care subsidy for the elderly is exceedingly rare in China today, even in other collectivist villages.

Mechanisms of Implementation

In order to understand how the Jiangxiang Model works, we need to probe its mechanisms of implementation. First, we examine where the collective resources for old-age support come from, how they are produced, and the historical process by which this became possible. Second, we analyze how distribution of those resources has been mobilized and managed over time. Third, we explore how sociocultural ideas and values have been used to publicly justify distribution to seniors within the broader village community.

Resource Production for Old-Age Support: Strong Collective Economy Essential

Economic development of the forces of production in Jiangxiang Village has gone through three main stages. As the villagers said, it had "agricultural development to begin with, followed by industrial development, and then tourism." The first stage ran from 1949 to 1983. During this period, the economic mainstay was agriculture. In 1978 the total industrial and agricultural output of the village was 568,200 yuan (about US$337,000 in that period's official exchange rate), of which total agricultural output value was 529,200 yuan (about US$313,880) and total industrial output value was 39,000 yuan (US$23,164).[2] By 1983 total industrial output value had risen to 127,200 yuan (US$66,000), still far lower than the agricultural sector of 499,700 yuan (US$258,510).

Called the phase of "walking on two legs" of agriculture and industry, the second stage started in 1984. China was well into the process of de-collectivization of agriculture. In that year, Jiangxiang began to implement the household responsibility system of contract-based agriculture, and to develop some manufacturing. Total industrial output of the village for this first year was 906,900 yuan (more than US$456,000), already higher than agricultural output of 667,800 yuan (US$335,915). Total industrial output steadily increased, reaching more than 5 million yuan (more than US$1 million) in 1990. Although industrial revenue steadily rose during this period, there were some problems, with many low-value-added products and trouble finding suitable markets. After the 1990s Jiangxiang began to produce steel building components and successfully established Changsheng Industrial Group, at which point the village began rapid economic development. Agriculture remained, but industrial revenue now far outstripped it. At this point, a large pool of collective funds began to accrue.

The third phase started in 2004 when Jiangxiang began to develop a "three-legged model" of agriculture, industry, and tourism. In 2004 Changsheng Industrial Group was restructured and parts were sold on a buyout basis, providing copious development funds for the village. Using part of these funds, Changsheng Tourism Development Company was established by the party secretary to develop agro-ecological tourism as a collective venture. Through this, the village accumulated 100 million yuan (more than US$12 million) in collective revenue for village planning and infrastructure improvements.

Thus, the resource base for community-based old-age support in Jiangxiang has been produced through a variegated set of collective enterprises across agricultural, tourism, and manufacturing sectors. For a rural area, Jiangxiang is an economic powerhouse, with a 2015 economic output exceeding 1.2 billion yuan (about US$193 million). Average per capita GDP of the village that year exceeded US$30,000, and villager per capita income was already nearly 30,000 yuan (more than US$4,833), excluding villa housing subsidies and collective welfare, with per capita community-shareholding dividends from collective enterprise valued at 7,000 yuan (more than US$1,100) per person a year.

Agriculture, manufacturing, and tourism have all done very well and produced much revenue for the village. In agriculture, money for the collective fund is produced through large-scale organic vegetable production, organic grain and cooking oil production, fisheries, and animal husbandry and breeding. Today forty-three villagers work in collective agriculture there, with much of the work mechanized. Yields are high and quality is excellent. Increasing appetite for clean sources of produce and meat in surrounding cities has meant a strong market for village agricultural products. Annual revenue from collective agricultural production in the village is now 30 million yuan (about US$4.4 million).

Industry now dominates the Jiangxiang economy in numbers of workers (326) and revenue. Changsheng Industrial Group is well-known in the province, and enjoys the reputation of an "advanced work unit." Consisting of four affiliated companies, the products manufactured by this group have a strong record of sales outside the village, and reach a national market. In 2015 alone sales value of its industrial output exceeded 1 billion yuan (about US$147 million), with steel building components still forming the bulk of sales. Today, industrial output accounts for 96 percent of total village output. As such, Jiangxiang has been called an "industrialized village," and is held up as a model for others.

With regard to tourism, the village has created an eco-park environment with demonstration areas that tourists can visit to learn how to farm organically and how to use sound land and water management practices to prevent pollution and clean soil and water of pollutants. There is also a village museum that presents the history and present situation of the village with many past and present photographs. Visitors rent rustic bungalows, tour the village, and dine on rustic organic fare in the village restaurant. Those who wish to do so may go walking, or fishing, or try out the ropes course. For many urbanites who visit, the fresh clean air is a major attraction, as is the slower pace of life and the neat and clean manner in which nature and agriculture are presented. With 155 villagers employed in service-related jobs, tourism has gradually become a steady source of collective revenue. Known as a filial village, a national civilized village, and a national agricultural demonstration site, Jiangxiang now draws more than 150,000 visitors per year for a combination of rest, relaxation, inspiration, and education. Most visitors are from China and include visiting Chinese cadres, political study groups, schoolchildren, and nostalgia-oriented travelers, but some visitors come from other parts of the world, such as African delegations interested in socialist development. Tourism and hotel revenues exceed 10 million yuan (US$1.4 million) annually.

Resource Allocation: Moral Authority of Village Party Secretary as Vital

In terms of villagers pouring energy into collective economic activity and buying into use of collective revenue for old-age support, the moral authority of Jiangxiang's Communist Party secretary has been pivotal. Seventy-five years old, as of this writing Chang Desheng has served as the village party secretary for fifty-four years. Over that time, he has built up a great store of trust and legitimacy. Villagers say that from the age of twenty-one Secretary Chang demonstrated selfless dedication and skilled management ability as he led the village from being a poor and backward rural area to a nationally renowned one with benefits for all. In the early years of the people's communes in the 1950s, Chang garnered villagers' respect by leading by example: He worked tirelessly at land reclamation, which both substantially increased arable acreage and wiped out the endemic schisto-somiasis. Then in the 1960s, when the central government tried to force villagers to plant two crops of rice a year, unlike the majority of cadres in other villages, Chang backed his farmers who by experience knew that double-cropping would not boost rice production in their area. Disobeying orders was a highly risky decision, but Chang's gamble paid off as villag-ers produced a bumper harvest. In the reform era, villagers admired how Chang found a way to combine collectivist social welfare with success in the market by "standing on three legs," successfully selling value-added agricultural products, high-value manufactured goods, and tourist expe-riences in eco-agricultural, socialist, and filial niches, bringing collective benefits to all native-born villagers.

Secretary Chang also earned respect by guiding the village through the difficult 1990s transition when state-owned and collective industry was under fire nationally due to concerns about unclear property rights, weak incentives for productivity, and unprofitable ventures propped up by iron-rice-bowl cadres stuck in the earlier Maoist-era ethos of valuing a secure meal ticket over productivity. Nationwide reforms required ownership to be separated from government, usually through internal buyouts by business operations managers, as in Jiangxiang's case. Unlike in other villages, Sec-retary Chang sold his own personal shares in Changsheng Industrial Group and combined that money with the other proceeds to develop collective village tourism. He also used his moral authority to cajole the new private owners of the bought-out industries to set aside some proceeds annually to support village welfare. Chang managed to persuade them, even though they did not have to and did not want to. Interviews showed that having been subordinate to Chang for years, the new owners could not bring them-selves to say no. Not only would that have dishonored Chang's years of sac-rifice, but also other villagers would lay on moral pressure not to be selfish.

Over the years Chang's personal character and actions worked together with the charisma of the office of party secretary to form a virtuous cycle feeding Chang's reputation as a cornerstone of both socialist morality and filial piety in the village. As Oi (1985) has shown, the institutional authority of the office of the village party secretary was most prominent during the era of collectivization when the party secretary's control of resource allocation by production teams and brigade cadres was the primary basis for both the power of the office and village social welfare. After the disintegration of the people's communes and decline of the collective economy, the authority of village party cadres weakened, but, in a minority of villages similar to Jiangxiang that retained or rebuilt a strong collective economy, the party secretary kept important powers. Such retained powers lay particularly in the arena of shaping the distribution of village welfare resources, as with Chang. For his achievements as party secretary in raising the torch of socialism through success in the market and forging a path for community-based support for aging in place, Chang has been recognized by provincial and national government and designated a "national model worker." In this way, he has garnered legitimacy from both above and below, for his person and his office, his past and present achievements, his socialist credentials and market clout.

Remembering Chang's acts back to early days, Jiangxiang elderly tend to attribute their good fortune to him personally, as well as to his continuance in office. A confidential village survey showed that although Jiangxiang elders felt that they enjoyed a very high standard of living and excellent social benefits, they nonetheless felt deeply insecure about their continuing material support. Participant observation and interviews with village elders showed that they credited Chang personally for bringing collective benefits to the village and its elderly. They credited his personal integrity, fine example, consistent generosity, and ability to persuade others to do the right thing for the good of all villagers. They did not feel confident in the inherent economic strength of the village or the systems and programs that government had put into place. While a normal age of retirement for a village party secretary is age sixty or so, each time Chang has tried to retire villagers have pressured him to stay on.

Many seniors expressed fear that if Secretary Chang were to retire, their collective welfare benefits may disappear. They worried that without the person of Chang in the office of party secretary the system of benefits would fall apart. They said that they wished that Chang could remain in good health and stay in power so that they could maintain a sense of security. They were concerned that a new younger party secretary would be selfish or corrupt or lack the authority to corral others to make village and senior welfare a top priority. Villagers were also aware that village industry's profit-sharing had no formal legal basis after the 2004 buyout, so once Secretary Chang steps down, they feared that no one else would be able to persuade the private owners to continue to donate to village social welfare.

Like hardware that does not work without software, this is a common story in collectivist villages today, with villagers fearing that once the current party secretary retires, the institutions and programs put into place will disintegrate without a moral leader to prop them up (Fu and Wang 2018). This harkens back not only to the Confucian notion of a benevolent leader to make up for institutional limits, but also to the importance of paramount leaders since Mao.

Rebuilding Filial Piety in the Village: Shaping Community Values

Kleinman (2007) has written about "local moral worlds" which form in communities over time and point the way to "what really matters." Classic Chinese anthropologist Fei Xiaotong (1983) wrote of the relationship between children and their parents in traditional China as one of the most important aspects of a Chinese person's life. That relationship, he argued, was one of a lifelong reciprocity involving heterogonous exchange figured over lifetimes, rather than in any given present moment, and at any rate, Confucian tradition held that the gift of life from parents was priceless. In later research in rural Hubei, Guo (2001) found that after China's market reforms, the traditional logic of long-term intergenerational exchange in families based in mutual love and reciprocal duty was being weakened in the younger generation by market-exchange logic focusing on short-term benefit to the individual. In his work in a village in northeastern China, Yan (2009) found that Western values involving individualization and focus on the young conjugal unit and the nuclear family were chipping away at intergenerational ties. While the vast majority still agree in principle that filial piety is important, many of its traditional expressions have become undesirable, inconvenient, challenging, or impracticable for many adult children, such as coresidence with, full economic support for, or hands-on caregiving for aging parents.

Sensing that filial piety was in jeopardy, Secretary Chang placed a high priority on shoring up the cultural value of filial piety and protecting the rights and welfare of village elders throughout the reforms. As such, the village has used a variety of governance mechanisms in order to shape residents' value orientations to prioritize distributing collective social welfare resources to seniors. In doing so, village leadership has had to reinterpret the pragmatics of what constitutes filial behavior in the context of rapid marketized development.

Village government has used a multipronged communications campaign to mobilize popular opinion in favor of prioritizing resource allocation to seniors. To generate ideological consensus, messages in favor of filial respect and support for seniors are relayed during village meetings, in village bulletins, in colorful signs planted in residential areas, in school, and in village museum displays. The village also holds regular "civilized family" appraisal activities to publicize and reward good deeds of children and grandchildren toward elders. This reinforces the importance of respect for seniors and encourages younger generations to try to think of elders first. (See also Thang and Mehta, chap. 6.)

A main form of messaging in village communications is that the elderly are *deserving* of respect and priority in collective resource allocation. These kinds of messages state that seniors have been a key force in village development for decades, making vital contributions and large sacrifices in agriculture, industry, and tourism, which form the basis for villagers' prosperity today. The example of Secretary Chang is invoked as an old man who has brought and is still bringing so many benefits to the village, further bolstering the idea of seniors as worthy contributors who deserve a return for their contributions. Tang's village survey showed that older villagers remain very grateful to Secretary Chang for the benefits he has brought; in participant observation one can often hear village seniors praising past and present deeds of the party secretary to each other, as well as to visitors. Older villagers also tell younger ones to be grateful for what their elders have done to create the benefits they enjoy today. The message of elder deservingness is joined with the idea that village seniors did not receive sufficient contemporaneous return for their labors, as earnings in the old days were so minor. In this way, village PR encourages thoughtfulness to seniors and a longer view of intergenerational reciprocity. At the same time, financial support for seniors is coming from collective village revenue, rather than from their children, as would have been the expectation under earlier renditions of filial piety. However, in the village PR this is not presented as making up for a failure of the younger generation; instead it is presented as an innovation to allow aging parents and their adult children to focus on a positive emotional bond.

Other PR messages spread mostly through informal channels appeal to the self-interest of younger generations. One such message is that collective economic support for village seniors is necessary to reduce the financial burden on younger people. This line also reminds younger villagers of how Jiangxiang seniors are very frugal and save their collective benefits to the point that not only do they not need financial support from their children, but also seniors generously provide financial assistance to descendants for large purchases, educational expenses, or weddings. Many elderly Jiangxiang residents we interviewed stated proudly that, due to their high collective earnings, they do not need to rely on their children for material support; rather, all they want is for their children to be emotionally concerned about them. With regard to the free housing for seniors, the argument is that it creates convenience for old and young and reduces tensions across the generations. Parents and adult children can live their own lifestyles without disturbing each other, but can still visit each other frequently. Seniors can conveniently talk and interact with other seniors, reducing the burden for adult children to keep their parents' company. For those with compatible lifestyles, the village still encourages children and the elderly to live together in three- or four-generation households if they would like. To this end, the village gives extra material rewards to families whose children live with folks more than sixty years old, including a yearly stipend of 2,000–3,000 yuan (about US$280-420. Very few take them up on that option, however, because most village seniors also like to have their own space and live by their own preferences. Not living together in a traditional multigenerational household is not presented as a failure on the part of younger generations to be filial. Rather, it is presented as a modern convenience and a way to maintain harmony in the family by maintaining a comfortable distance in space and the amount of time spent together.[3]

Finally, the external honors that the village has applied for and won, including "national civilized village" and "national moral model village," exert moral pressure on villagers to maintain the honor of their hometown by continuing to prioritize the elderly. Such honors have brought much political and economic capital to the village and many outside visitors and leaders seeking to learn from their experience. This makes residents proud to be Jiangxiang people, and the draw of their reputation promotes village tourism, which, in turn, brings in more money. As a result, filial ethics and behavior in Jiangxiang have become not just an internal family matter, but also a village problem. If a child is not filial, he may not face much moral pressure in other villages. However, in Jiangxiang unfilial behavior will be widely condemned since the village reputation for being a model filial socialist village is key social capital used to generate additional revenue.[4] Rather than seeing this as an incongruous mixing of Confucian and socialist collectivisms together with market commercialism, the syncretic virtuous cycle is presented as a useful social innovation.

Sustainability and Scalability of the Jiangxiang Model

With regard to sustainability, as we have already seen, there are serious concerns as to whether the Jiangxiang Model can be sustained, even in Jiangxiang itself. Elderly villagers, village leaders, and Secretary Chang have all expressed fears that the system will collapse as soon as the party secretary retires. They say things like, "We don't know how this is going to be maintained after Party Secretary Chang retires," and "We don't know of anyone in the village who can unify people around a collective goal like this. Everyone else is too individualized."

Reliance on the moral authority of one elderly man in the fading office of village party secretary has placed the model in a precarious position. With only moral pressure from Secretary Chang to compel the Changsheng Industrial Group ownership to donate a portion of the proceeds year after year since going private in 2004, the arrangement is running on borrowed time. Collective agriculture and tourism revenues pale by comparison and are unlikely to burgeon to a level that could compensate for loss of industry donations.

With regard to scalability of the Jiangxiang Model out to other rural villages, while it is a nationally recognized model, there is little hope of wholesale adoption elsewhere. The Jiangxiang Model is only a model in the sense that the village generated a creative solution that has, for the time being, worked for them. It is a model as in being exemplary, not a model in the sense of a precise recipe for others to follow, even though visitors come to study their example. Those visitors are generally looking for a feeling of creative inspiration, a story about a process of innovative problem solving, and perhaps a sense of whether there are some elements that might be adapted, and are not aiming to clone the model.

There are many reasons why the Jiangxiang Model would be hard to drop in ensemble into another village. Jiangxiang has a relatively small population to support and is much wealthier than most other Chinese villages. Jiangxiang had an extraordinary party secretary who combined integrity, technocratic skill, and charismatic persuasiveness, along with the ability to think systemically and to adapt deftly to changing circumstances. The village maintained a tradition of valuing collectivism throughout the reform era, even if the industry dimension was officially de-collectivized more than ten years ago. They were able to develop a multilegged approach including substantial agriculture, industry, and tourism. They benefited from innovating at the time when a village could own a profitable industry like steel production. The private buyers of the formerly collective village industry felt beholden to Secretary Chang who had been their boss. The village was one of the first on the scene, so there was little competition, which boosted demand for their products and tourism. They are positioned amidst many highly prosperous cities on convenient highways for travelers and shipping routes for goods. They have been attractive to working-age adults migrating from other poorer rural areas to work in Jiangxiang's local economy; these workers generate collective revenue, but do not draw on it due to outsider ineligibility for village collective benefits. The village was redesigned at a time when people's housing was still modest enough that a village-wide do-over was attractive. There are enough young people in the village to form an intergenerational neighborhood community, unlike in locales short of young and middle-aged folks. Their land and water were also clean enough to be able to credibly pull off organic agriculture, something impossible in China's "cancer villages" (Lora-Wainwright and Cheng 2016).[5]

Nonetheless, Jiangxiang's experience does provide some useful lessons. Capable and charismatic leadership is important, but so is stronger institutionalization of collective or community-based old-age support mechanisms. Institutional safeguards are needed for long-term viability. Strong revenue generation and clear contractual or local regulatory encumbrances dedicating a portion of funds to village social welfare are critical. How to get that is another story. The Jiangxiang case also shows how important it is to design for community-based old-age support in a holistic way, while accounting for the perspectives and interests of both aging parents and adult children. A sustained multimodal and multipronged intergenerational PR campaign appealing to both people's better nature and their self-interest is also highly important. Finding ways for village government to provide seniors with hard resources such as money and housing helps to raise their social status and the respect afforded them by younger family members. Many old folks themselves may not prefer some traditional manifestations of filial piety such as being financially supported by their children or living in the same household. Being old does not necessarily mean preferring everything old school. A village may undercut one or more traditional aspect of filial piety such as coresidence or child-sourced financial support in order to promote another aspect like positive emotional bonds, warm intergenerational relationships, or intergenerational family harmony.

If we take Jiangxiang to be not a recipe but an inspiration, then it is possible to consider other ways in which villages can use some kind of collective mechanisms to promote community-based support for the elderly in rural China. It is helpful to look for cases that do not require quite such a constellation of conditions as those found in Jiangxiang. One such example is the Feixiang Model of collective old-age support in Qiantun Village in Hebei Province in northern China where one author (Shea) visited in 2014. Qiantun has far fewer prospects for revenue generation through agriculture, industry, or tourism. It has generated its collective funds solely by applying for provincial and national grants to support innovative solutions to China's rural aging problem. In this case, local seniors who wish to do so apply to live two to a room in a dormitory constructed as free senior housing. Income level and need are taken into account, and the roommates pledge to keep each other company and look after each other. The dormitory is right in the village, so seniors can easily visit their children and/or their children can visit them. Being a dormitory, which is cleaned and maintained by the residents who also do their own cooking, the Feixiang Model has an economy of scale that it is much less costly than the Jiangxiang Model.

However, the Feixiang Model also has downsides. It has been beholden to winning competitive grant applications. As it moves from new innovative experimental demonstration project to a long-term scaled-out effort, those grants may become less forthcoming. As is the case in Jiangxiang, the Feixiang Model has also been reliant on a charismatic and capable village party secretary, who, together with his wife, conceived of the idea, applied for grants, first secured an abandoned schoolhouse, then built a new dormitory building, and manages the dorm's operations. There, too, everyone Shea ran into during her time in the village in 2014 said that the party secretary was pivotal to the whole operation. Currently being scaled out to other villages in Hebei, it will be important to track this model to see whether its funding becomes less contingent and its maintenance less dependent on charismatic authority. A final downside of both the Jiangxiang and Feixiang models, but even more so for the lightly financed Feixiang Model, is that in the case of serious illness, the family still needs to step in if hospitalization or complex long-term care is needed. However, both models do at least delay the need for heavy involvement by younger family members.

Discussion

Ikels (2004) pointed out the role of government in supporting, shaping, or undercutting filial piety in the family. Although it is hard to tell where government ends and community begins in a collectivist village like Jiangxiang, what we have seen in that case is that, by partially undercutting some traditional manifestations of filial piety that were in decline anyway, the village has been able to elevate some of its other dimensions. By providing collective economic support and free senior housing, the government obviated the need for adult children to provide material support or coreside with their aging parents. By doing so, however, the village has been able to elevate positive emotional bonds and interpersonal interactions between grown children and their parents, which became more feasible once money and coresidence were more or less removed from the equation. By giving seniors their own free housing and a large income from collective revenue, elders' social status rose in their own eyes and in the eyes of their children. With government relieving pressure financially and spatially, filial piety became an easier target for adult children to grasp.

Also apropos Ikels (2004), Jiangxiang was a case in which housing policy affected the merits of intergenerational coresidence, with folks pulled away from coresidence in favor of adequate distance to promote family harmony. This was similar to what Szawarska wrote (chap. 11) about geographic separation contributing inadvertently to family harmony among repatriated Sakhalin Korean elders and how removal of the need to support elders contributed to more positive affective bonds. However, both Korea's Happy Valley Home and the Jiangxiang Model lack community-based provisions for elders needing help with activities of daily living, something the Feixiang Model provides via mutual aid.

In relating to Moore's discussion of dependence versus interdependence (chap. 7), it is notable that Jiangxiang elders pride themselves on not being financially dependent on their children, while at the same time they boast of how their children still relied on them financially. It is also interesting how they did not see themselves as dependent on government or community handouts but rather as having earned those benefits by virtue of being a native of the village. Later in life, if their health falters, however, they expect that as a last resort they will need to rely on their children. The reciprocal return to aging parents is being compressed into higher age brackets as seniors are healthy until a later age.

Looping back to Weber, in the Jiangxiang case, charisma of both person and office together were important in negotiating collective old-age support throughout reform-era market transitions. However, for long-term sustainability and scaling out, reduced reliance on the charisma of person or office will be needed. Increased institutionalization in the form of binding regulations and contracts, especially for claims on revenue streams, will be vital.

Conclusion

China is facing a large issue of old-age support in its rural areas where a higher proportion of the population is older than age sixty than is the case in urban areas, at the same time as fewer family and state resources are available. Based on a mixed-methods case study of the collectivist village of Jiangxiang, this chapter examined their local implementation mechanisms for collectivist support for village elders and analyzed the local sustainability and broader viability of such a community-based collectivist approach to support of the aged in rural China. In previous pages we showed how the realization of the Jiangxiang Model has relied on three extant conditions. First, the collective economy of the village is highly developed, providing a strong material basis for community support for the aged. Second, the individual moral authority of the local party secretary and the priority he has placed on resource redistribution to the elderly has been pivotal. Third, through a variety of institutional innovations and mechanisms, the local leadership has strengthened community recognition of the continuing cultural importance of filial respect for the elderly and channeled public support in favor of such senior-directed allocation of collective enterprise revenue. However, given the breadth and depth of post-1978 de-collectivization during the reform era, in most rural areas the kind of collective resource base present in Jiangxiang is either very weak or nonexistent, and many local leaders lack the kind of moral authority or emphasis on filial values that are present in the leadership of Jiangxiang. Therein lies the predicament of old-age support in rural China today.

Moving forward, the Jiangxiang case suggests several important directions that could help to improve old-age support in rural China. The first would be to find ways to encourage Chinese villages to partially re-collectivize their local economies in a way that would produce a substantial pool of collective community resources. The precise manner and degree of partial collectivization could vary from village to village depending on local conditions. The second direction would be to identify systematic ways to strengthen the ethic of filial respect for the elderly among both ordinary villagers and local village leaders to encourage resource allocation in seniors' direction. The third would be to move from relying on individual moral authority of local leaders to institutionalize resource redistribution for old-age support. Each of these paths of action is challenging, but may be crucial for building a strong rural old-age support system. Further study and experimentation is needed since by the year 2050 as much as a third of China's population may be in the old-age bracket, with an even higher proportion in rural areas. Since rural old-age support and the associated interplay of family, community, and market forces are important in many societies today in East Asia and beyond, it is hoped that this case can help inspire new ideas for other sites.

Acknowledgments

We are grateful to the Jiangxiang and Qiantun communities for sharing their experiences and to Tsinghua University, East China University for Science and Technology, and the University of Vermont for their support.

Youcai Tang (唐有财) is associate professor of sociology at East China University for Science and Technology. He is secretary general of the Shanghai Center for Public Economy and Social Governance and the director of the Shanghai Lingyun Community Foundation. His research and teaching focus on family sociology, China's social transformation, Chinese migrant workers, community governance, nongovernmental organizations (NGOs), and public policy. His research on Chinese migrant workers and social governance has been published in *Social Sciences in China*, *Chinese Journal of Population Science*, and *Chinese Public Administration*. His research was awarded Outstanding Scientific Research Award of *Chinese Population Science* (2014).

Jeanne Shea (邵镜虹) is associate professor of anthropology and director of the Health and Society Program at the University of Vermont in Burlington, Vermont, USA. Recipient of two Fulbright Awards, she has published on menopause and midlife, marital relationships, the family, spousal caregiving, senior volunteering, evidence-based medicine, and community supports for aging in place in China. Most recently, she has published several research articles in *Ageing International* (2016, 2017, 2018) and a chapter on China's Senior Companions Program for *The Cultural Context of Aging: Worldwide Perspectives* (Sokolovsky 2020).

Glossary

bieshu		Villa—a nice single-family home in the countryside, generally of two stories.
chijiao yisheng	赤脚医生	Barefoot doctor—a medic with a very low level of training who was deployed to rural areas during Maoist times.
mofan	模范	Model or exemplar.
Jiangxiang cun	蒋巷村	Jiangxiang village.
wan xi shao	晚稀少	Late-spaced-few policy, 1970s family planning policy that encouraged later age of first birth, spacing of pregnancies, and fewer children.
wenming cun	文明村	Civilized village.

Notes

1. Recent exchange rates use https://www.oanda.com/us-en/ for 1 January of the relevant year.
2. Historical exchange rates use http://fxtop.com/en/historical-exchange-rates.php for 1 January of the relevant year. Early exchange rates were artificially inflated in favor of Chinese currency. With deepening of market reforms, China's currency became more subject to world market rates, resulting in the yuan exchanging at a lower rate relative to the U.S. dollar than in pre-reform and early reform years.
3. This relates to what Ikels (2004) observed: "Both Miller in Lijia and Zhang in Zhongshan found parents who chose to live independently in order to avoid having to do such chores [for their descendants] and to have more freedom" (6).
4. This connects with Ikels's (2004) observation, "As Janelli and Yim point out [for Korea], filial demonstrations testify to a person's moral worth and provide him or her with a form of symbolic capital that accrues not only to the self but also to the lineage and the village. Justice Doolittle . . . makes it clear that just as filial behavior could bring honor to a community [in China], unfilial behavior could bring dishonor and shared punishment" (5).
5. "Cancer villages" are communities near polluting factories where cancer rates are far above the national average.

References

American Anthropological Association (AAA). 2012. "Principles of Professional Responsibility." Retrieved 1 August 2018 from http://ethics.americananthro.org/category/statement/.

Brandt, S., M. Garris, E. Okeke, and J. Rosenfeld. 2006. "Access to Care in Rural China: A Policy Discussion." Paper for Gerald Ford School of Public Policy, University of Michigan, Ann Arbor. Retrieved 1 August 2018 from http://www.umich.edu/~ipolicy/IEDP/2006china/1)%20Access%20to%20Health%20Care%20in%20Rural%20China,%20A%20Policy%20Discussion.pdf.

Chen, Lin, and Wen-Jui Han. 2016. "Shanghai: Front-Runner of Community-Based Eldercare in China." *Journal of Aging and Social Policy* 28 (4): 292–307.

China National Statistics Bureau (CNSB). 2015. *2015 China 1% National Population Sample Survey.* Beijing: Zhongguo Tongji Chubanshe.

———. 2016. "2016: A Good Start for China's Economy During the 13th Five-Year Plan Period." *China National Statistics Bureau Press Release.* Retrieved 1 August 2018 from http.stats.gov.cn/english/pressrelease/201701/t20170120_1455922.html.

Eisenstadt, S. N., ed. 1968. *Max Weber on Charisma and Institution Building: Selected Papers.* Chicago: University of Chicago Press.

Fei Xiaotong. 1983. "The Old-Age Support Problem in the Context of Change in Family Structure." *Beijing University Newsletter: Philosophy and Sociology Edition* 3: 6–10.

Fu, Danni, and Yiwei Wang. 2018. "China's Collective Villages Struggle to Keep it Together." *Sixth Tone.* Retrieved 1 August 2018 from https.sixthtone.com/news/1003362/chinas-collective-villages-struggle-to-keep-it-together.

Guo, B., and S. Guo. 2008. "Introduction: China in Search of a Harmonious Society." In *China in Search of a Harmonious Society,* ed. Sujian Guo and Baogang Guo, 1–12. New York: Lexington Books.

Guo, Yuhua. 2001. "Fairness Logic in Intergenerational Relations and its Transformation: Analysis of Old-Age Support in Hebei." *Chinese Studies (Zhongguo Xueshu)* 4: 221–54.

Huang, Shumin. 1989. *The Spiral Road: Change in a Chinese Village through the Eyes of a Community Party Leader.* San Francisco: Westview Press.

Ikels, Charlotte, ed. 2004. "Introduction." In *Filial Piety: Practice and Discourse in Contemporary East Asia,* ed. Charlotte Ikels, 1–15. Stanford, CA: Stanford University Press.

Kleinman, Arthur. 2007. *What Really Matters: Living a Moral Life Amidst Uncertainty and Danger.* Oxford: Oxford University Press.

Liu T., and L. Sun. 2016. "Pension Reform in China." *Journal of Aging and Social Policy* 28 (1): 15–28.

Lora-Wainwright, Anna, and Ajiang Cheng. 2016. "China's Cancer Villages Contested Evidence and the Politics of Pollution." In *A Companion to the Anthropology of Environmental Health,* ed. Merrill Singer, 396–416. Hoboken, NJ: John Wiley.

Lu, Bei, Xiaoting Liu, and Mingxu Yang. 2017. "A Budget Proposal for China's Public Long-Term Care Policy." *Journal of Aging & Social Policy* 29(1): 84–103. https://doi.org/10.1080/08959420.2016.1187058.

Lu, Jiehua, and Peng Du. 2015. "Income Security Schemes of Chinese Elderly: Situations, Gaps, and Policy-Reorientations." Paper presented at Sharing Knowledge and Experiences towards Sustainable Ageing Societies in North-East Asia, Tokyo, 6–7 November.

Muehlbach, Andrea. 2012. *The Moral Neoliberal: Welfare and Citizenship in Italy.* Chicago: University of Chicago Press.

Oi, Jean C. 1985. "Communism and Clientelism: Rural Politics in China." *World Politics* 37 (2): 238–66.

Petrovici, Norbert. 2015. "Framing Criticism and Knowledge Production in Semi-Peripheries Post-Socialism Unpacked." *Intersections* 1 (2): 80–102.

Polese, Abel, Jeremy Morris, and Borbala Kovacs. 2015. "Introduction: The Failure and Future of the Welfare State in Post-Socialism." *Journal of Eurasian Studies* 6 (1): 1–5.

Shea, Jeanne L. 2019. "Dominant Chinese National Policies on Aging and their Degree of Attention to Eldercare by Seniors." *Ageing International 44: 331-51.* Retrieved 1 November 2019 from doi: 10.1007/s12126-017-9318-2.

Sokolovsky, Jay. 2009. *The Cultural Context of Aging: Worldwide Perspectives.* 3rd ed. Westport, CT: Praeger.

Standing Committee of the National People's Congress of the People's Republic of China (SCNPCPRC). 2013. Law of the People's Republic of China on the Protection of the Rights and Interests of the Elderly. Promulgated 28 December 2012, in effect as of 1 July 2013. Retrieved 1 March 2013 from http.jzga.gov.cn/jzjws/wxjws/xiazhuang/fazhi/201307/2086.html; available as of 11 March 2020 at http://en.pkulaw.cn/display.aspx?cgid=252608&lib=law.

State Council of the People's Republic of China, Information Office (SCPRCIO). 2004. *Social Security in Rural Areas.* Retrieved 1 August 2018 from http.china.org.cn/e-white/20040907/10.htm; available as of 11 March 2020 at http://www.chinadaily.com.cn/english/doc/2004-09/07/content_372369.htm.

State Council of the People's Republic of China (SCPRC). 2016. *Development of China's Undertakings for the Aged for the 13th Five-Year Plan.* Retrieved 1 August 2018 from http://m.guolitv.com/html/hcgpnc qcijepbkcdlechdlbk.html, 2016. 14 March.

Urio, P. 2010. *Reconciling State, Market, and Civil Society in China: The Long March toward Prosperity*. New York: Routledge.

Van de Vliert, E., H. Yang, Y. Wang, and X. Ren. 2013. "Climato-Economic Imprints on Chinese Collectivism." *Journal of Cross-Cultural Psychology* 44 (4): 589–605.

Weber, Max, 1968. *Max Weber on Charisma and Institution Building: Selected Papers*, ed. and introduced by S. N. Eisenstadt. Chicago: University of Chicago Press.

World Bank. 2016a. "Life Expectancy at Birth." Retrieved 1 August 2018 from http://data.worldbank.org/indicator/SP.DYN.LE00.IN.

———. 2016b. "Fertility Rate, Total (Births per Woman)." Retrieved 1 August 2018 from http://data.worldbank.org/indicator/SP.DYN.TFRT.IN.

———. 2016c. "Report Recommends Deeper Healthcare Reforms in China." Retrieved 1 August 2018 from http.worldbank.org/en/news/press-release/2016/07/22/report-recommends-deeper-healthcare-reforms-in-china.

———. 2018. "Rural Population (% of Total Population)." Retrieved 14 January 2019 from https://data.worldbank.org/indicator/SP.RUR.TOTL.ZS.

Wu, B., M. W. Carter, T. R. Goins, and C. R. Cheng. 2005. "Emerging Services for Community-Based Long-Term Care (CBLTC) in Urban China: A Systematic Analysis of Shanghai's Community-based Agencies." *Journal of Aging and Social Policy* 17 (4): 37–60.

Yan, Yunxiang. 2009. *Transformation in Private Life: Love, Family, and Intimacy in a Chinese Village*. Shanghai, China: Shanghai Shudian Chubanshe.

Yu, H. 2015. "Universal Health Insurance Coverage for 1.3 Billion People: What Accounts for China's Success?" *Health Policy* 119 (9): 1145–52.

Zhou, Yi. 2006. *Huaxi Village: Post-Collectivism in a Transitional Economy*. Oxford: Oxford University Press.

2 MEANINGS OF SPOUSAL ELDERCARE IN LIFE AND DEATH IN CHINA

Jeanne Shea

Introduction

GIVEN TRADITIONAL CULTURAL EMPHASIS ON filial piety (*xiao*) (for definition, see Introduction) in China, public discourse and research on eldercare
in Chinese populations have tended to focus on intergenerational issues of
respect, support, assistance, and care from adult children for their aging parents (Shea and Zhang 2017). However, studies in many nations have found
spouses to be the most common primary caregiver for seniors and that, overall, the years and amount of eldercare performed by spouses outstrip that of
adult children (Shea and Zhang 2016). Yet until recently spousal eldercare
in China has been glossed as a sign of modern decline in filial values, rather
than as a phenomenon unto itself. China's populace has aged rapidly in tandem with modern family planning and rising longevity, reaching a rate of
12 percent age sixty and older by 2009 and 16.1 percent by 2016 (chap.
1), with age sixty as the threshold for old age still commonly used in China.
Thus, many studies have noted the burden of eldercare on adult children
and the risks of a high old-age dependency ratio for national well-being.

Some recent research has revealed quantitative evidence on the importance of spousal caregivers in providing direct care to sick and disabled seniors in China. A national sample of 32,494 households from rural and
urban areas of thirty-one provinces found that a large proportion of older
adults relies on spouses for support and care (National Health and Family
Planning Commission [NHFPC] 2015; Wang 2015). The survey also found
that half of all elderly people in China now live in empty-nest households,
including about 40 percent with just their spouse, and 10 percent living
alone. Smaller regional studies have reported similar findings for Zhejiang,
Tianjin, and Shanghai (Shea and Zhang 2016).

Given this, it is important to learn more about the experiences of spousal
caregivers in China, especially since its population is projected to reach over

30 percent elderly by 2050 (chap. 1). When considering an area to study I chose Shanghai as the city in China with the oldest population; by now, more than 30 percent of its residents are over the age of sixty (Xinhua 2016). As spouses in my study began to pass away, I extended my research from 2013 to 2018 to include spousal death. As an anthropologist, I am interested in the kinds of meaning that people find in their life experiences. In this chapter, I explore these questions: What are the expressed meanings of spousal caregiving among Chinese seniors doing dementia caregiving at home? Do ideas of spousal caregiving get extended into dying and death, and if so, how? Using qualitative methods and an interpretive approach, I analyze what spousal caregiving and death mean to Chinese wives and husbands.

I argue that ideals and concerns beyond presence or absence of filial piety were deeply important for these caregivers. Meanings of spousal caregiving included not wanting to burden their children; having no other viable or acceptable options; caregiving as difficult but generally not a burden; self-reliance and capability; spousal reciprocity; marital responsibility; feelings of affection or love; notions of fate; and issues of regret. In interviews, often the same caregiver expressed many different meanings of spousal caregiving. As expected, those with happy marriages tended to give the most sanguine spin, although seemingly very negative and very positive caregiving experiences often coexisted in the same person. Some widowed caregivers talked about how they continued to take care of their husband or wife in death and how the deceased extended care toward the family during dying or from beyond the grave. Even so, not just the unhappily married caregivers found liberation in the death of their spouse.

Review of the Scholarly Literature

This chapter connects with social science research on eldercare in Chinese populations, and adds to anthropological and sociological studies of the family in China. It also brings qualitative insights to work on spousal caregiving and widowhood in social gerontology and social work.

The Theme of Change in Filial Piety, Eldercare, and the Family in China

Social research on eldercare in China has focused on themes of a decline in filial piety and a decrease in traditional forms of support and assistance for elders by adult sons and daughters-in-law. It has traced how the traditional way of raising sons for support in old age (*yang'er fang lao*) has ceased working as it once ideally had. Chapters on China in Ikels's (2004) volume examined related themes. Later eldercare research in China has also been focused on decline or change in respect, support, assistance, and care from adult children to aging parents (Sun 2017).

A major theme in anthropology and sociology of the family in modern China, of which Ikels's volume (2004) is part, has been the decline in traditional parental authority and Confucian familism (Yan 1997), increased autonomy of youths, and a greater emphasis on young people's marital relationships and nuclear families (Yan 1997, 2009, 2016). With the 1949 Revolution, the Communist Party strived to decrease the influence of the traditional patriarchal family in an effort to promote gender equality and to increase the authority of party and government (Ikels 2004: 12–13). Elders following traditional customs and arranged marriages were criticized as "feudal" (*fengjian*). The modernity of youths and love marriages of comrades (13) were lauded as ideal. With the market reforms from 1978 on and the Single Child Family Policy from the 1980s to 2015, a steep rise in individualism occurred (Yan 2009). Value placed on youths and their conjugal relationships, nuclear families, and neolocal residence rose, further weakening intergenerational ties and reducing obedience to and respect, support, and assistance for elders. This chapter extends this work by exploring senior conjugality there today.[1]

The Issue of Burden versus Positive Aspects of Caregiving

In gerontological and social work research on dementia caregiving, much attention has been paid to the burden experienced by caregivers and its implications for mental and physical health. Much of such research uses the Zarit Burden Interview (Zarit and Zarit 1987) to measure dementia care burden in different populations, including Chinese ones (Yu, Yap, and Liew 2018). Not spouse-specific, the Zarit Burden Interview asks caregivers to rate self-perceived caregiving burden, including feeling role strain, stress, or burden, facing excessive demands or insufficient time for self, and perceiving related financial strain or bad health effects. Scores are summed, with high scores signifying high burden.[2] The hope is to identify caregivers who may benefit from assistance. Such research, however, misses potential positive aspects of caregiving.

Developing a Positive Aspects of Caregiving scale, Lou, Lau, and Cheung (2015) tested a Chinese version on 374 Hong Kong Chinese informal dementia caregivers, more than half of them spousal. Numerous caregivers endorsed many positive aspects of caregiving, and the Positive Aspects of Caregiving scale's eleven items broke down into two principal components of enriching life (feeling useful, good about self, needed, appreciated, important, strong, and confident) and affirming self (learning new skills, gaining more positive attitude and more meaning and appreciation for life, and strengthening relationships). Lou, Lau, and Cheung (2015) found Positive Aspects of Caregiving instrument to be valid and uncorrelated with the Zarit Burden Interview, and found that "caregivers may experience high levels of positive appraisal despite feelings of burden" apropos their caregiving role (5), showing how considerable perceived burden can coexist with feeling highly rewarded.

Research on Spousal Eldercare in Chinese Populations

Most research focused on spousal eldercare in Chinese populations has occurred in places other than in mainland China, such as Hong Kong (Holroyd 2005; Lou, Kwan, et al. 2015; Wong et al. 2018) or Taiwan (Wang et al. 2015). There are a few recent instances of related research on the mainland by this author and others (Shea and Zhang 2016; Zhao 2013). Here I focus on findings from Holroyd for Hong Kong and Zhao for Shanghai.

In analyzing interviews with twenty elderly Chinese women caring for husbands with various health conditions in 1990s Hong Kong, Holroyd (2005) found several distinct schemas. One was a Confucian duty to be a self-sacrificing wife. Second was equity concerns regarding reciprocity over time with one's husband and children. Third was social pressure to uphold the reputation of self and family apropos traditional expectations and government messages. Fourth was emotional bonds with one's spouse from a shared history of experiences, mutual support, and interactions. Many women used more than one schema, often revealing tensions among them. Overall, some felt resentment at being trapped by tradition and the need to save face in a chore with high expectations and little gratitude. Others felt pride in making good on duty, reciprocity, affection, and/or reputation.

Zhao's (2013) research is based on qualitative interviews with twenty-six elderly spouses taking care of a husband or wife with Alzheimer's disease in Shanghai from 2008 to 2010. Analyzed through the framework of adaptation and coping, Zhao reported a rich array of positive, negative, neutral, and ambivalent meanings connected with spousal dementia caregiving. Zhao grouped themes from the interviews into categories of adjustment, including adjustment to diagnosis, inner adjustment, and adjustments in spousal interaction, family system, social network, and life management. Zhao uncovered a long list of themes in relation to each of these categories, much too long to list here. I will return to relevant themes in the discussion. Another important point from Zhao is that many of the meanings expressed by the caregivers studied varied depending on the quality of their spousal relationship. Also, as in Lou, Lau, and Cheung (2015) and Holroyd (2005), often the same caregiver reported many different meanings.

Tendency to Separate Caregiving from Bereavement

Literature in social gerontology has tended to treat caregiving for an ailing spouse in separation from bereavement (Long and Campbell, chap. 9). As Kellehear notes (2009), scholarship has likewise tended to separate research on suffering and illness from studies of dying and death. For Chinese populations, a number of sources address coping in elderly widowhood and bereavement, largely in isolation from caregiving, most emerging from Hong Kong (Ng et al. 2016). Among sources written about mainland China, many are on demographics of widowhood (Jiang, Li, and Sánchez-Barricarte 2015) or on coping, depression, or quality of life in widowhood (Zhou and Hearst 2016). Here I aim to bring caregiving in life and death together.

Methods and Sample of Spousal Caregivers

This research was conducted among Chinese men and women between sixty and ninety years of age or older in 2012 (born between 1920 and 1952) serving as primary caregivers for spouses in their own homes (Shea and Zhang 2016). Research occurred in two naturally occurring lower-middle-income retirement communities in Shanghai from 2012 to 2018. Methods involved in-depth interviews and home visits with spousal caregivers, and community participant observation with senior neighborhood volunteers who knew them. Interviews were done with thirty caregivers taking care of a husband or wife with either dementia or another noncognitive ailment. Eligible caregivers were identified through the knowledge of local neighborhood residents' committees, nonprofits engaged in community work with seniors, and senior neighborhood volunteers.

Each caregiver was interviewed between one and three times in 2012, and the majority participated in one or more follow-up interviews from 2013 to 2018. In-person interviews after 2012 were not possible for all cases because neighborhoods were being dismantled for urban renewal, with residents relocated to scattered suburbs. Also, some care recipients and caregivers had passed away. For all cases, however, follow-up news was relayed through senior neighborhood volunteers. Over the six years of the study, interviews and home visits were conducted by the author and four Chinese graduate students supervised by the author. All interviews were audio-recorded and transcribed verbatim into Chinese characters. The author entered the data into NVivo and coded it for qualitative analysis regarding meanings of spousal caregiving.[3]

This chapter focuses on themes drawn from the thirteen cases of dementia caregiving. These included vascular dementia or Alzheimer's disease as reported to us by the caregivers. The degree of dementia was mostly moderate, but in one case it was severe. All care recipients also had other health issues such as high blood pressure, heart disease, stroke history, physical weakness, diabetes, chronic bronchitis, arthritis, and so on. All ailing spouses required help with two or more activities of daily living, such as eating, dressing, bathing, toileting, or transferring.

The sample included five male and eight female dementia caregivers. All had at least one child, and some as many as four. All lived in their own home, and the majority lived alone, but one couple had their son's family living with them. Each caregiver had been caring for a spouse from three to more than fifteen years. All caregivers had their own health problems, such as high blood pressure, heart disease, or arthritis, and attributed those problems to aging and/or caregiving. Given their ages, some had had an arranged marriage which was common in earlier decades, but self-perceived relationship quality was not reliably predicted by this. Eleven caregivers reported a good, and two a bad, relationship. Caregivers' education ranged from elementary to high school, which is common for these generations. Most had had blue-collar or service jobs. All were retired with middling monthly pensions of 3,500–6,000 yuan in 2012 (US$549–US$941) and health insurance from past employers.

All caregivers are called by pseudonymous surnames preceded by Grandma or Grandpa, as is common in China. Pseudonyms and age in 2012 are in table 2.1. Since Chinese spouses have different surnames, I refer to care recipients as the caregiver's husband or wife. This chapter features stories and quotes from six of the spousal dementia caregivers, indicated in table 2.1 with one or two asterisks; these caregivers were chosen to achieve a full range and saturation of themes for the sample. Featured interviewees were all living alone as of 2012. Those two caregivers with a double asterisk reported a poor relationship.

Having No Other Viable or Acceptable Options

Whether perceiving their relationship as good or bad, all caregivers at some point said "*mei you banfa*" in relation to spousal caregiving. In a literal sense, *mei you ban fa* means "no way to do it." It also means that there is no way around it, no choice, or no alternative. For all caregivers, it meant that it was an immutable reality that their spouse was sick and someone had to care for them. It also meant not wanting to or not being able to burden their children, and that there were no other viable options.

There were distinctions in how *mei you banfa* was used, depending on relationship quality. In good relationships, it did not necessarily mean no choice at all. Rather, it meant no choice but to make the morally right choice and to take care of their spouse. In poor relationships, it meant no choice but to be the one stuck with caregiving. Overall, whereas caregivers in unhappy unions emphasized external constraints, the happily married described themselves as both constrained and agentive in caregiving.

The Notion of Burden in Relation to Spousal Caregiving

All caregivers found aspects of caregiving difficult, but there was a difference by relationship quality in orientation to caregiving as a burden (*fudan*). Happily married caregivers said that although taking care of their spouse was difficult, it was not a burden, or that although it was a burden, it was a positive labor they chose as the right thing to do. They believed that a decent husband or wife should willingly take on this task and not *feel* it as a burden. For instance, Grandma Mi, who had a good marital relationship, never used the word "burden" when talking about caring for her hus-

TABLE 2.1. Research Participants, Spousal Eldercare in China.

Caregiver Pseudonym	Caregiver Age	Care Recipient Pseudonym	Care Recipient Age
Grandpa Zhao	81	Zhao's wife	80
Grandpa Weng*	72	Weng's wife	76
Grandma Han*	79	Han's husband	84
Grandma She	79	She's husband	86
Grandma Lei	81	Lei's husband	89
Grandpa Yin	79	Yin's wife	84
Grandma Zhuo	66	Zhuo's husband	72
Grandpa Ling	95	Ling's wife	98
Grandma Zuo*	80	Zuo's husband	85
Grandma Shang	86	Shang's husband	90
Grandma Mi*	75	Mi's husband	80
Grandma Rong**	61	Rong's husband	66
Grandpa Wei**	80	Wei's wife	83

Note: * = Spousal dementia caregivers featured in this chapter; single asterisk indicates self-identified positive spousal relationship; ** = Spousal dementia caregivers featured in this chapter; double asterisk indicates self-identification of a bad spousal relationship.

Source: Author data.

band although she did use it regarding her unfilial son "gnawing on the old folks" (*kenlao*)—that is, taking advantage of aging parents. Grandma Zuo, who considered her husband a soulmate predecline, did sometimes refer to taking care of him as a burden, but also as a meaningful responsibility that she willingly shouldered. Although her husband only slept a few hours a night and often acted out at home and in the neighborhood, she felt that, after sixty years of marriage, taking care of him was her burden to bear.

In contrast to the happily married, those caregivers with poor spousal relationships said that taking care of their spouse was an unmitigated burden that they were forced to take on. Both Grandma Rong and Grandpa Wei felt that way, as shown in the section on "Spousal Responsibility or Duty" below.

Not Burdening the Children and a Modest Bar for Filial Piety

Whatever their relationship, all caregivers expressed the intent to not burden their children. Not burdening or bothering one's children and not asking them for things was often spoken of as an ideal to which old people today should aspire. Caregivers said things like, "I do not want to increase our children's burden," or "I do not want to bother our children," or "I do not want our children's help." At other times, rather than an ideal, such talk was more of an acknowledgment of the reality that their children were not able to do more to support or assist them. When caregivers spoke of children they considered filial, they cast them as not able to help (more) due to having their own burdens, including their own families, households, work, retirement, finances, children, and/or grandchildren to tend.

In some cases, the caregiver's children were still working and had a teenage child of their own still at home, but in others the caregiver's children were retired, and their grandchildren had already graduated and were working and sometimes even had a child of their own. However, since Chinese parents generally continue to help their children with getting married, getting an apartment, and raising and cultivating grandchildren, the heavy burden of nurturing children does not end when one's child hits age eighteen or graduates from college. This was described as being due to China's tradition of helping descendants long into adulthood, the competitive environment of today, and how "children's ability to do things themselves today is weaker than in the past."

Another dimension of not wanting to burden children was not wanting to *ask* them for help or money. Caregivers considered it a good thing if children came up with the idea to help or give money, but they felt that the act of asking them could put their children into a tight spot that might force them either to overtax themselves or to have to decline the request, thus losing face for both parties. Caregivers did not want to ask their children for help except as a last resort.

For the most part, caregivers attributed the fact that children help little to the times and social change, rather than to shortcomings of their children. They said that the current societal situation made it no longer viable to rely on your children in old age, so it was best to rely on spousal care.

Reluctance to burden children was also a reflection of how elders were balancing the ideal of filial piety toward aging parents against the traditional ideal of nurturing descendants. Caregivers were very invested in the success of their children and grandchildren and did not want to jeopardize that investment by taking time, energy, or money from descendants. For example, Grandpa Weng said, "We don't want to be any more of a drag on our children than we have to." Similarly, Grandma Zuo said, "We don't want their money. Because us two, we are of no use any more [to society]. We can just use our pension money and get by fine." Both considered their children to be filial. Such sentiments show how caregivers tended to see themselves and their time as less valuable than their descendants' time was. Caregivers often referred to how their own needs were very modest since they were used to getting by with little due to their materially Spartan lives when younger. Their children and grandchildren, however, were not used to such a simple life, and caregivers did not want descendants to have to sacrifice lifestyles or aspirations.

One caregiver with a poor marital relationship said that she did not want her daughter helping with her husband's care due to how, since coming down with dementia, he had hit not only her, but also their daughter and granddaughter. Luckily, he was too weak and in pain with arthritis to hit hard, but she still did not want to expose the younger generation to that. Grandma Rong wanted to do the caregiving herself to save their descendants from her husband's temper.

Grandma Mi, who identified as having an unfilial son, worried that asking her children for help could threaten their nuclear family harmony. She had seen how her daughter-in-law complained whenever her son did anything for or gave anything to her. This made her worry that if either her son or daughter gave her much help, it could cause conflict in their marriages.

All but one of the caregivers said that all of their children were filial. Even Grandma Mi, the one caregiver who complained of an unfilial child, had another child who she considered filial. Given the times and desire to not hold descendants back from success, all caregivers set a modest bar for calling their children filial. Rather than expecting their children to live with them, use a substantial portion of their income to support them, or help them daily with housework and direct care tasks, the caregivers expected relatively little. Caregivers praised their children as filial for relatively small gestures in comparison with the traditional ideal. Many including Grandma Mi and Grandma Zuo said things like, "The children sometimes bring us things we like to eat. That is enough." Such small gestures engendering praise included things like calling their parents for a few minutes most days to check in, visiting them at home once every week or two and on holidays, and/or bringing them groceries and food they liked to eat when they visited. They also included doing some household chores when they visited, helping with heavy-duty parts of the laundry, giving them some money during spring festival and other holidays, visiting them at the hospital if they were admitted for a serious illness, and/or helping them to transition home from the hospital.

Grandpa Weng, age seventy-two with high blood pressure, felt that both his daughters were very filial, but that they could only do so much to help since they were busy with work. One daughter worked in banking, and the other worked as a cashier. Grandpa Weng said that unlike the iron-rice-bowl period (1949–78) in which productivity was often not carefully monitored, today work consumed a lot of time and energy and getting time off was hard. He said that his daughters were "very good children." Beyond work, one also had a teenage daughter of her own still at home. Grandpa Weng said that both daughters took time off work and away from "their own families" to help with caregiving each time their mother was hospitalized and then later when she transitioned back home. But after those short-term crises were over, they had to go back to work or risk their employment. Due to work, they were unable to offer much instrumental assistance on a regular basis beyond bringing some food and doing some chores on weekends and vacations. Regarding his granddaughter, Grandpa Weng noted how children nowadays need more help from their parents.

Grandma Zuo, age eighty with heart disease, was very satisfied with her four retired children's filiality even though she herself had had to do all of the direct care for her husband and nearly all of the housecleaning and cooking. Two children lived in the same neighborhood and two within an hour by public transport. Each child called Grandma Zuo on the phone regularly, who especially appreciated talking with her daughters who "knew how to talk about matters of the heart." Since Grandma Zuo's apartment lacked indoor plumbing, one daughter took the laundry home each week to wash it in her machine, and her son came once a week to help his unruly father to shower at the public bath facilities. There were two reasons they did not help more. First, Grandma Zuo did not want to divert them from their responsibilities of taking care of "their own families," that is, their children and/or grandchildren. Second, her husband was paranoid that his children were trying to take his money and poison him. He would shout them away if they tried to enter the apartment and refuse food from them, fearing that it was tainted.

There are several reasons behind the low contemporary bar for filial piety. First, such a low bar is possible due to the pensions, health insurance, and low-cost Mao-era work-unit-issued housing that allowed these caregivers to be fairly independent and healthy. Another reason is that most aging parents in China today consider their children's and grandchildren's success one of the most important parts of being "good children" (Yan 2016: 249). Caregivers often spoke with pride about descendants' education and/or careers and about how descendants were much better off than they were. The ideal for parents to nurture their children and make their descendants as successful as possible has become much stronger than traditional filiality in which children coreside with and respect, obey, support, assist, and care for aging parents. A further reason may also be that it is difficult to admit to oneself or others that your own child is not filial. According to a community leader in a local Old People's Association that mediates family disputes, admitting or complaining that your child is unfilial can result in a public loss of face as people wonder "what you as a parent did wrong to raise a kid who would not treat his/her parents well."

Self-Reliance and Capability

Whatever their relationships, all caregivers spoke with pride of their self-reliance and capability to support and take care of themselves and their spouse. Grandpa Weng said, "Now it is primarily a matter of old husbands and wives taking care of each other, rather than relying on their children." This theme closely intertwined with sentiments of not wanting to burden one's children. In this respect, the caregivers talked not only about not wanting, but also about *not needing*, their children's help. Instead, they said, they were able to live independently (*zi li*) from their children thanks to their own pensions, health insurance, and resourcefulness. Regarding money, Grandma Zuo insisted, "We do not want money from them. We have our own, we two. We have enough for our needs. We do not need their money." Combining sense of personal efficacy and self-sufficiency, Grandma Mi stated, "Our pensions are enough to cover our expenses. For all of our expenses, we use our own pensions. I am very thrifty. If we need an expensive medicine that our health insurance can't cover, I just buy less-expensive things when I go grocery shopping. We do not want their [our children's or grandchildren's] money." With regard to the ability to carry out household and caregiving tasks, caregivers emphasized with pride their abilities and will to exercise them as long as possible. As Grandma Han said, "I am still capable. I don't need anyone to help me. I can do it myself. I can meet this difficulty on my own. I don't need help." Grandpa Weng stated, "For now I still have the ability to take care of her. As long as I have the ability, I will do my best to take care of her." Self-reliance also meant "exercising" yourself to avoid losing abilities and not wasting money on things you could do yourself.

Self-reliance and being capable were spoken of in relation to not only self-satisfaction and practical utility, but also as moral ideals, which the caregivers tried their best to manifest in daily life. These moral ideals were often in direct competition with the idea of easing old people's burdens with more assistance from children or from services including domestic helpers or nursing homes. Grandpa Weng, for instance, declared, "It is best to do it yourself. It is important to mainly rely on yourself. You should not depend on others. Unlike our children's generation, people our age feel that we should be self-sufficient. From the communist revolution [in 1949] until now, we feel that everything should be done self-sufficiently. You should not lean on other people."

Caregivers talked about their pride in their accomplishments as caregivers. Some marveled at their own resilience and ability to cope. Grandpa Wei boasted, "Look at me. I am over eighty, but I only get two or three hours of sleep at night, yet my spirits are not too bad given that!" Some shared good outcomes of their caregiving labors or ingenious low-cost solutions for caregiving, such as using mirrors to allow an immobile spouse to watch television when lying on his back.

> Grandpa Weng: I should do my best to take care of her as well as possible so that she won't have another stroke and do my best to give her a bit of longevity. For someone like her with this kind of sickness to be this well off, I think that I've done really well. All the people who were in the hospital ICU with her have already died, but she's improved. . . . I feel peace of mind that over these seventeen years I have been able to maintain her this well.

Happily married caregivers often spoke of spousal caregiving not only as the only viable option, but also as the best option or the ideal in quality care. In expressing this, the caregivers said that spousal care was better than caregiving by children, domestic helpers, or nursing homes. A large reason was that they knew their partners the best, saw them as whole people, and attended not just to tasks and physical needs of the body but also to their emotional needs of the spirit.

In comparing spousal care to caregiving by adult children, such caregivers said that their children mostly helped with chores around the house and were only there for short periods of time. They also said that their children had grown apart since moving out and starting their own families and were not familiar with their parents' current needs and preferences, or with how to talk to and interact with them in a way that satisfied their emotional needs. Even though they were grown, children also still tended to treat their mother or father as a parent and not as a full person.

> Grandma Han: Spousal care is better because children are not as close and familiar with you. Our children don't know what my old man likes to eat and what he likes to use, because they don't live with him. They have lived apart for twenty years. After they married, they didn't live with us. . . . [Now] they have their business, and we have our business, separate lives. . . . He doesn't want our children or any other family members than me to take care of him.

> Grandpa Weng: It's always best if a spouse does most of the caregiving themselves. Like when my daughters help, they mostly help with doing tasks. As for caring for her spirits, they don't necessarily know how to do that, they aren't necessarily clear what she wants. . . . When elderly spouses care for each other, they do so in a way that is most heartfelt (*zui tiexin*). When children take care of their parents, there is a generation gap, and they have different ideas about things. So when you get old, if you need to be taken care of, the best strategy is for spouses to take care of each other.

For happy unions, intimacy of aged spouses was seen as greater than intergenerational intimacy. Although many eventually had to avail themselves of such assistance as the years passed and health problems mounted, happily married caregivers viewed care by domestic helpers or nursing homes as inferior to spousal care. They felt that domestic helpers took care of physical tasks, but not personal emotional needs. Such helpers were even less familiar with the ailing person than adult children were. Caregivers wondered why some people encouraged them to hire help when they could do it themselves and save money in the process. Caregivers also expressed concerns that hired helpers, who were from a lower class bracket and often were rural migrants, may have lower hygiene standards, which might negatively impact a spouse's health. Concerns about nursing homes included worries about lack of emotionally satisfying care. There were also concerns that too much standardization and lack of adequate staffing might lower quality of care.

Spousal Reciprocity

Many caregivers spoke of spousal reciprocity as an ideal underlying their caregiving, but the form varied, and spouses with a poor relationship did not endorse this meaning. Variants on the theme of reciprocity among happily married couples included consonance with long-term marital companionship, the spouse deserving good treatment based on past interactions, continuing give-and-take in the current relationship, and the spouse's hypothetical response had roles been switched.

Consonance with long-term marital companionship was often expressed using the phrase "*baitou xielao*," an idiomatic ideal for spouses growing old together. It means an old married couple accompanying and caring for each other on the journey throughout old age, through thick and thin, whatever occurs, somewhat like "until death do us part." It also means later-life happiness through having a close companion for company and to look out for you. A related expression also used by the interviewees is, "elderly spouses caring for each other" (*lao fuqi huxiang zhaogu*).

Another variant of spousal reciprocity was the idea that the ailing spouse deserved good treatment based on actual past interactions earlier in the marriage. This included the current care recipient having taken care of their husband or wife during sickness before dementia struck. Sometimes it connoted that the care recipient had once done a fair portion of the housework.

Some caregivers also mentioned continuing reciprocity in the current relationship. In this case, the bar for contribution was significantly lowered. Pitching in in small ways such as washing a couple of dishes when feeling well enough was enough for a caregiver to insist that "we take care of each other." Just cooperating well with their care, being a good eater, or holding their urine were considered current reciprocal contributions. Expressing gratitude was another way that spouses with dementia could reciprocate caring in the present.

Finally, imagining the spouse's favorable hypothetical response had the tables been switched was a last form of spousal reciprocity. It involved the conviction that, had the caregiver been the one to get sick, then their spouse would have likewise taken care of them.

One happily married caregiver, though, said that her caregiving had nothing to do with reciprocity. Grandma Han said that her husband was a traditional man who just worked when they were younger and never helped with childcare or eldercare or any more housework than dishes. Nonetheless, hardworking and good tempered, he was a good man for their generation.

Spousal Responsibility or Duty

Whether their marital relationship was good or bad, caregivers spoke of their caregiving as a spousal responsibility (*zeren*) or duty (*yiwu*). As Grandpa Weng said, "For husbands and wives to take care of one another, this is a duty. You should do your best to fulfill this duty. Basically, I have a feeling of responsibility toward the family. The smallest unit of family is the old couple. It's a kind of feeling of responsibility."

Although caregivers often spoke of "Chinese tradition" in referring to children's obligations to parents, unlike in Holroyd's (2005) study they rarely mentioned tradition when speaking of spousal obligations. This was probably in large part because Communist Party teaching has portrayed Confucian gender roles and traditional forms of marriage as "feudal" and stinking of gender inequality. This may be why, instead of tracing this idea to traditional family values, Grandpa Weng considered spousal responsibility to be grounded in "materialist thinking" stemming from Marxism, probably because in his mind spousal responsibility was not gender-differentiated.

Spousal responsibility was variously discussed as going beyond reciprocity, as more solid than love, as a necessary addition to love, or as a burdensome role to be endured. Among the happily married, spousal responsibility was an ideal to which they aspired. For the others, it was an external expectation they had to meet or risk their reputation or relationships with children.

Spousal Responsibility as More Solid than Love

Even among the happily married, caregivers tended to see spousal responsibility as far more solid, real, lasting, and dependable than reciprocity or love. For Grandma Han, taking care of her husband was her responsibility as his wife, going beyond both reciprocity and love. She explained, "Because he is sick, as his wife I should take up this responsibility. . . . If I don't shoulder this responsibility, who will? . . . Caring for your spouse is your family responsibility. You can't pass it off onto someone else. If I have the ability, then I need to shoulder this." In answering whether love (*aiqing*) or affection (*ganqing*) played a role, Grandma Han insisted that neither did. Instead, it was about her spousal responsibility to support her husband's health. "What love?" she said. "We don't see it as love. We are already old. It is just that we have been together for decades. What affection? It's not about affection. It is just something that I should do." Airing frustration over her husband sneaking cigarettes, she expressed exasperation, underlining that responsibility, not affection, kept her going: "I really do not love him. *Mei you banfa*. I really have no other choice. Over sixty years, the two of us have been this way."

Grandma Zuo, who saw her husband as a soulmate before dementia, said that the love was no longer there, because he was no longer the same person, and he did not even know any more that she was his wife. Instead, it was her sense of responsibility as his wife that kept her serving him sometimes as many as six hot meals a day to keep him from having tantrums.

"It is not love," Grandma Zuo explained. "He doesn't understand any more what love means. He doesn't even know that I'm his wife. After all we've been through, now at the very least, each day I give him three meals to eat, often many more [because he forgets he has already eaten]. Every day feeding him, that is my responsibility. I feel like if I do my best to carry out my responsibility, then that's good enough. I have no way to do anything more."

Other caregivers said feelings for their spouse came into play, but that those feelings were not love (*aiqing*) and that feelings were insufficient. Grandpa Weng felt that his caregiving was partly based in feelings of familial intimacy (*qinqing*) built up through so many years together. However, he said that such feelings of affection (*ganqing*), as well as marriage vows, were worthless unless regularly put into mundane practical action. For him as with many older Chinese caregivers, actions speak louder than feelings, words, or promises.

Spousal Duty as Burdensome and Driven by External Constraints

The two caregivers with poor relationships, Grandma Rong and Grandpa Wei, spoke of spousal duty as burdensome and externally compelled. Their reasons for dissatisfaction with their spouse and seeing caregiving as burdensome were rooted in the long-term dynamics of their marriages.

Grandma Rong had married for convenience during the Cultural Revolution era (1966–76). Soon after marriage she found that her husband was a "selfish, unreasonable person" who wanted her to "wait on him" and was "only interested in his reputation." Throughout their marriage they argued bitterly. After developing dementia, her husband increased his habit of shouting and cursing at her and began to hit her and forbid her from speaking. Since he was too weak and in pain from arthritis to hit hard and since he had been telling his siblings that Grandma Rong was neglectful, she had decided to bear the burden of taking care of him alone at home. "I know that I should take care of him," she said with a sigh, "because I am his spouse."

Grandma Rong saw bearing her duty stoically as a way to protect her reputation. Recently when her husband yelled at her loudly and hit her and threw things in the apartment, she took a piece of paper and wrote a large Chinese character for "forbearance" (*ren*), meaning to endure suffering. She taped it to the outside of their door for neighbors to see. Although her husband soon tore it down, some neighbors saw it. With regard to reputation, Grandma Rong said that she would take care of her husband as long as necessary to save face. She said, "I haven't reported him to the police, because he is too weak to do more than bruise, and I don't want to lose face."

She said that her husband frequently told his brother and sister and other relatives on his side of the family that she was not taking good care of him. They complained to her about alleged negligence, making her worry that they might report her to the residents' committee. As a result, she wanted to prove them wrong by taking decent care of her husband until he was sick enough to no longer protest going into a nursing home.

Grandpa Wei also felt that taking care of his wife was a negative burden that caused him a "great deal of suffering" due to her sleeplessness and incontinence. He and his wife had an arranged marriage, and their relationship had never been close. He considered her "pretty stupid" and below his level. After they married, he learned that her parents were cousins. Despite his lack of closeness with his wife, he felt that he had no choice but to take care of her at home with some help from an adult day-care center. It was his duty as her spouse, and, more importantly, he could not afford a nursing home on his own, and his children would not agree to pitch in funds because they feared that seniors who entered nursing homes often died shortly thereafter.

Feelings of Affection or Love

As we saw above, many of the caregivers with good relationships, let alone poor ones, did not see their caregiving as animated by feelings of love (*ai-qing*). Love, as Jankowiak (2008) and others have noted, is considered by many older generations in China to be a modern frivolity from the West. A form of steady companionate affection (*ganqing*) through years of living together was what more of the caregivers felt was at play, although, as we saw above, one happily married caregiver said that even affection was not a factor in her caregiving experience, and another said that you need both love and responsibility together or else love was useless in caregiving.

There was one caregiver, though—Grandma Mi—who did emphasize the role of love. She felt that responsible action was important, but that such action was made potent by a strong infusion of loving kindness. She combined a sense of spousal love with feelings of compassion and a kind of motherly love for her husband. Although they had had an arranged marriage, they always had a very close and affectionate relationship. By 2012 her husband had reached late-stage vascular dementia and had been unable to sit up or turn over for three years.

Instead of focusing on the bitterness of her own suffering, Grandma Mi focused on alleviating the suffering her husband was enduring. When asked about the meaning of caregiving for her, she said that when he was young her husband had been like an orphan who never knew a mother's love. Not long after he was born, his mother, who was only nineteen, died of a seizure. His young father thought that she had died because he had given her cold water to drink during the postpartum, and he was not able to handle the trauma and had no idea how to care for a baby. So, Grandma Mi's husband was raised by his step-grandmother and grandfather. Grandma Mi felt that now that her husband was old and sick and needed to be taken care of, it was a chance to shower him with all the loving care that he never got from his mother as a child.

> Grandma Mi: He has had so much bitterness in his life. From the time he was little, he had no mother. I said to myself, his mother died just fifteen days after she gave birth to him. To not have a mother is the bitterest thing that a person can experience. He didn't even get to drink mother's milk. So I said to my old man, "Don't worry, I am going to help you, okay? Before your mother wasn't able to give you diaper changes, so now I will do that for you. Your mother wasn't able to wipe the poop off your body, so now I will wipe it for you." I said to him, "Let me do this for you, okay?" And he said, "Okay."

Notions of Fate

Whatever one's relationship quality, notions of fate (*ming*) were common. For example, unhappily married Grandma Rong said, "My fate is bitter." Despite good relationships, Grandpa Weng also said, "My fate in this life is bitter," and Grandma Zuo said, "My fate is not good."

Meanings surrounding that fate, however, varied by relational caliber. Only happily married caregivers linked fate with the universality and inevitability of suffering. Likewise, Grandma Mi said, "No one has a perfect life. There is always some hardship." The happily married also used fatalism to console themselves that they could not have prevented their predicament, saying things like, "It can be no other way." Instead of finding these thoughts depressing, caregivers with positive relationships found them bolstering. Everyone suffers. This is unavoidable. There is no point in feeling sorry for yourself. Grandma Zuo said, "You can't go on complaining. It's your own fate that's no good. I console myself by telling myself this." Likewise, Grandma Mi said, "It is your own fate, so you have no choice. This is my fate. You should not envy others. You should do what you can with what you've got."

It was also only the happily married who referred to a predestined relationship (*yuanfen*) and the need to repay a karmic debt. Caregivers used these ideas to comfort themselves and to make sense of why their spouse got sick and why they had to watch them suffer and toil in their care. Grandma Han said, "It is fated for us to be together. *Mei you banfa.*" Grandpa Weng said, "Taking care of her is a kind of predestined fate." They reasoned that in a past life, they must have done something horrible to the person embodying their spouse's spirit. As a result, in their present reincarnation the caregiver owed a debt of service to them (*qian shi qian ta*). Along these lines, Grandma Han said, "It is your own fate, and you need to acknowledge your debt. It is what I should do. It is that I owe him from a past life." Grandma Zuo said, "In a previous life, I incurred a debt to him. This life I am paying him back. I must have wronged him in a past life, so it is my burden to bear." In this sense, it was important to do as much as possible of the caregiving by yourself as well as possible, because it was "your own debt," and not something unfairly imposed. If others were to take on too much of your burden, you could fail to pay your debt in full, such that in your remaining life or your next reincarnation you would suffer even more. In this way, bearing the burden yourself to the full extent possible, though difficult, was a positive thing.

Meanings of Spousal Caregiving in Relation to Dying and Death

There were four main themes related to spousal caregiving apropos dying and death. These include absence or presence of regrets, continuing care for ailing spouse in dying and after death, finding liberation in spousal death, and dying or deceased spouse showing care for the family.

Absence or Presence of Regrets

The issue of regret (*yihan*) after spousal death varied by quality of spousal relationship. Caregivers in happy marriages talked about striving for an absence of regrets. For them, caring well for their spouse each day bolstered their conviction that they would emerge from the experience regret-free. Grandma Han said, "Now I just do my best to give him whatever he wants to eat. Then when the time comes I won't have any regrets. I have the feeling that I haven't done all of this for nothing. We saved his life, and his health is better now. That makes me happy. I feel that I have done right by him." Grandpa Weng had stated that taking care of his wife was not a burden, because he was doing it not just for her, but also for himself. He wanted to keep her as healthy as possible to avoid a lonely widowerhood regretting he had not done more.

Caregivers with poor relationships spoke of regret over having married their spouse. For them, tending to their spouse day after day heightened feelings of regret. Grandma Rong said, "Now more than ever, I ask myself, why did I ever marry this man?" Grandpa Wei grumbled, "Taking care of her is annoying to death. I wish we hadn't listened to our parents [on marriage]."

Caregiver Providing Continuing Care for Spouse in Dying and After Death

Relationship quality affected orientation to spousal death. I only had a chance to speak with happily married caregivers after they became widowed, but those in unhappy relationships spoke with anticipation of their hope to eventually put their spouse into a nursing home where others could deal with them until they died. By contrast, those in happy marraiges talked about their continuing efforts to give tender care to their spouse as they were dying and to do everything properly for them after their death.

Just six months after his wife's death, caregiver Grandpa Weng died. A neighborhood volunteer who visited him said that he became very depressed after his wife's passing, and he had died of a second stroke after suffering a mild one a year or so before his wife's passing. Although we do not know how Grandpa Weng felt about his death, we know that he had expressed fear of being a lonely widower. The volunteer said that enjoying life "was not his fate. Instead, his fate was to continue to take care of his wife by accompanying her into death."

Grandma Han talked about keeping her husband company after his death, but for her it did not require dying. After her husband died, their son asked her to come live with him and his wife. Grandma Han thanked him but refused: "My son asked me to come live with him, but I said I wouldn't because I am used to it here, and I am keeping my old man company here."

When I visited Grandma Zuo after her husband died, she was getting ready to have lunch in her home with her daughters. Her son was occupied, otherwise he would have been there, too. Grandma Zuo talked about how she had continued to take care of her husband at home until the end of his life. He had tripped and hit his head one day when he had once again insisted on going out walking in the neighborhood as he had done for years. When he got home, Grandma Zuo noticed the side of his pant leg was dirty and when she asked about it, he touched the hair on the side of his head indicating he had bumped it, but otherwise seemed fine. The next day he went out walking again, and this time he fell and slammed his head hard into the curb. The whole side of his head and face turned purple. The family tried to get him to go to the hospital, but he refused, and yelled at and hit them. Grandma Zuo talked with her children, and they decided that since he did not want to go and his dementia would only worsen, they would respect his wishes and let him stay home. They took turns watching him, giving him warm water when he was thirsty and trying to feed him bits of porridge when he might be hungry. But mostly he just slept and got up with their help to relieve himself in the chamber pot (makeshift commode) by the bed, which was there to avoid nighttime trips to the public toilet. On the third day he was unresponsive and died in his sleep in his bed. Grandma Zuo was happy that she had taken care of him until the end in the way he had wished.

When I visited Grandma Mi after her husband's passing, he had been gone a week. She greeted me in tears, saying, "Last time you came my old husband was still alive, but this time he is gone." At that and subsequent visits, she recounted how she had done everything possible first to save her husband and then to ease his suffering and care for him after his death. Homebound for seventeen years and unable to sit up for three, her husband came down with pneumonia and a high fever. Grandma Mi and her visiting daughter and son-in-law called the ambulance and rode with him to the hospital. From there, Grandma Mi called her unfilial son and daughter-in-law telling them to come quickly. Grandma Mi gave the hospital a deposit of 50,000 yuan (US$7,500) to ensure good care. Her husband was given IV fluids and medicine and even a blood transfusion. Her son and daughter-in-law visited the hospital daily, but not to the extent that her daughter and son-in-law did, the latter rotating to keep watch night and day between breaks to rest at home. Grandma Mi's husband just kept getting worse. The doctor suggested a feeding tube and surgery, but the family realized that he would only suffer. So, after two days, they allowed him to die.

Continuing Care and Finding Liberation in Spousal Death

Grandma Mi felt that her husband had had a good death and that she had taken good care of him until the end. She recounted using gauze to mop up phlegm to ease his breathing and putting a drop of porridge to his lips for his last taste of food. Then she encouraged him to let go: "I said to him, "Don't you worry! You go now. I have taken care of everything for you. You didn't have a good road to walk. I have laid everything out for you. Everything is all set. Old man, you can go to heaven now and enjoy things there! The debt is paid in full. The sickness debt is paid in full. Be brave and go!'" Grandma Mi said that half an hour later, her husband died peacefully, and she helped him to close his eyes and mouth. In life, she had referred to her fate as being to care for her husband, but near death she had switched registers, reassuring her husband that he had paid off any karmic debt of his own through enduring illness all those years and could now die in peace. She vowed not to cry when he died, since she had no regrets. "All along I said that "while he is alive, I will be really good to him and after he's dead I will not weep.' There is no need for weeping. I was very good to him while he was alive." Relieved to see her husband finally free from suffering, she cried little. "I only had a few little tears," she said. "I didn't cry terribly. I thought, 'now he is liberated [*jiefang le*]. All his pain is gone.'"

Grandma Mi detailed how she took care of her husband after his death, saying, "You should always do your best for your old companion." To make sure to "do things properly," she hired One Dragon, a death ritual assistance company.[4] In the hospital they showed her and her children how to wash and dress her husband's body. At the crematorium, Grandma Mi paid hundreds of yuan extra for a solo cremation so the ashes would be "all him." She asked crematorium staff's advice and learned how to place some of her son's hair wrapped in red cloth onto her husband's body as a lamp to light his way to the underworld. At home, with One Dragon's help, she set up an ancestor table with her husband's ancestor portrait, foods he liked, and an audio player chanting Buddhist sutras. Per their instructions, she wore a white fabric flower blossom in her hair and a black swatch on her sleeve, which she was to burn after thirty-five days. Her daughter, son-in-law, and son stayed with her at her apartment the first seven nights postmortem to help guard her husband's spirit and light incense at set times. In this, Grandma Mi said that both her "son and daughter were very filial." She was to play the sutras for seven sets of seven days, cooking an increasing number of her husband's favorite dishes each week. After forty-nine days mourning would be complete. She also bought a grave in her husband's rural hometown to bury his ashes to maintain ties with relatives during Qingming grave-sweeping festival. In later years, Grandma Mi described plans for a Buddhist third anniversary ceremony of her husband's death, which she would do with her daughter and son-in-law, but not her son and daughter-in-law who had reconfirmed their lack of filiality by taking some of her assets without permission.

It was also not just unhappily married caregivers who found what they called "liberation" in spousal death. Those with poor relationships spoke of their spouses' eventual death as freedom from the burden of having tend to them. Yet happily married Grandma Zuo also spoke of her husband's death as her *own* liberation. She said that when her husband died she was liberated from her karmic debt, having cared for him as he had wished to the end. I visited her and her daughters six months after the death. Grandma Zuo's husband was smiling down on us from his ancestor portrait on the wall beside the table. She and her daughters were smiling as well, bittersweet. Grandma Zuo sighed. "I took care of him well until the end. I have freed myself from my karmic debt [*jietuo le*]." Her daughters affirmed, "Yes, she has freed herself from her debt."

Deceased Spouse Extending Care toward the Family in Dying and After Death

Some of the happily married caregivers also talked about how the deceased spouse himself extended care toward the family as they were dying or dead. Grandma Zuo relayed how her husband had taken care of her and her children in his dying days by resting quietly and not relieving himself in the bed until the very last day: "In the end, he took good care of us. He slept and slept and even got up to use the chamber pot. It was only the last day that he couldn't get up any more to go. He took good care of us."

Grandma Mi praised her husband for taking care of them in the way he died. She said that he "timed his death" in a way that showed consideration for the whole family: "He took care of us in his final days." She said that by spending his last days in the hospital, he gave her a chance to have someone come replace their broken stove. With his death near Dragon Boat Festival, family did not need to take time off work to come to the memorial. He even died early in the morning, such that her son-in-law could go clean up the apartment before Grandma Mi got back home. It also meant that they could take the body from the morgue to the crematorium that same afternoon. Unlike some, they did not believe three days were needed for the soul to exit, and with the pneumonia it made sense to hasten cremation. Grandma Mi said the timing was so perfect that on the way, "there was not a single red light" and "when we got there, they got him right in."

Grandma Han said she experienced her husband's caring from beyond the grave in two ways. First, he became a spirit to whom she could pray. Second, he had left instructions with their children to take good care of her after he was gone. In the first sense, after her husband's death Grandma Han began to worry about lingering and suffering herself in old age as happened to her husband. So she sought comfort by praying to him to take care of her either by "casting blessings upon her health," or "taking her with him sooner into death." The second sense came up when, some time after her husband died, Grandma Han had dizzy spells and a rapid heartbeat. She was diagnosed with stroke risk and had to stay in the hospital several nights. When she told her children to go home to sleep instead of rotating nights in the hospital with her, her children refused, saying that their father had made them promise to take good care of her.

Discussion and Conclusion

We have seen how these elderly Chinese dementia caregivers expressed many meanings of spousal caregiving in life and death, going beyond the presence or absence of filial piety. Issues of filial piety were, of course, still there, but they did not dominate. The dementia caregivers set a modest bar for filial piety and talked about how they did not want to burden their children. They described why they felt that spousal caregiving was the only viable option at that point in their lives. Most of them spoke of caregiving as difficult but not a burden, or as a positive burden they chose to bear, with the exception of those with a poor spousal relationship.

Regarding meanings of spousal caregiving in life, marital responsibility or duty was important for all caregivers, as were the values of self-reliance and/or personal capability. Spousal reciprocity was a theme for some of the happily married caregivers, but not for those in unhappy unions. Among those with happy marriages, feelings of affection were more likely to be endorsed than feelings of love, because the latter was interpreted by most as a frivolity of modern youth, and love or affection without responsibility were considered empty. Only one caregiver emphasized love, and in doing so she mixed spousal and motherly love. As to regrets, the unhappily married regretted ever having married and found caregiving amplified regret. Happily married caregivers talked about their labors to try to prevent regrets. Notions of fate were present for all caregivers. In poor relationships, notions of fate were limited to a sense of bad luck. In strong relationships, talk of fate included musings on the universality of suffering and on ideas of predestined relationships and the need to pay off karmic debts to their spouse.

The same caregiver espoused many different meanings of spousal caregiving in life and often mixed positive and negative sentiments about their caregiving experiences. As expected, those spouses with good relationships tended to express the most sanguine spin on spousal caregiving, although they too felt that it was a difficult trial, though worth it.

With respect to spousal caregiving in dying and death, some happily married widowed caregivers talked about how they continued to take care of the spouse and even how the deceased spouse took care of them and their families in dying or after death. Given beliefs in karmic debt, not just those with poor relationships found what they called "liberation" in their spouse's death. One happily married caregiver felt that she herself was liberated from debt to her husband when he died. Another not only saw herself as having been paying off karmic debt as a caregiver, but also saw her husband as liberated from whatever karmic debt he had of his own when he passed.

These findings resonate with the scholarly literature, while also showing small areas of contrast. For example, the findings reinforce recent work by Yan (2016, 2018) on descending familism in which grandparents and parents prioritize the nurturance of descendants over ascending attention to seniors or ancestors. These results also contrast with Yan's work on increasing emotional intimacy across generations in showing how these caregivers tended to feel that intimacy with their spouses was greater than their intergenerational intimacy. Below I focus on connections with Holroyd (2005) and Zhao (2013) and some chapters in this volume.

All the general themes that Holroyd (2005) found for female spousal caregivers in Hong Kong, including duty, reciprocity, reputation, and affection, were present in my study. A major difference is that my study also included men, men talked about those same themes, and the women I interviewed did not express nearly as many concerns about gender as Holroyd's did. Confucian moral duty to be a self-sacrificing wife was not mentioned by my informants, probably because such virtues were so vilified under Mao in their younger days. Caregivers in my study talked not just about actual past reciprocity but also about present and hypothetical reciprocity. I did not find resentment or complaints about ingratitude to be the overall sentiment; rather resentment, such as caregiving to save face, was only dominant in those with unhappy marriages. Different samples, settings, and histories, as well as the time gap, may play a role in the study differences.

Although my analysis was framed differently than Zhao's (2013), with Zhao's focusing on coping and adaptation and mine on meanings in cultural and life-course context, our findings have many parallels. One similarity was how relationship quality shaped caregiving experiences. This did *not* mean, however, that love drove the happily married, while duty drove those in unhappy marriages. Rather, duty was important to caregivers in both good and bad relationships, and, for most in good marriages, responsibility trumped love. Another commonality, also in Holroyd (2005), was that the same caregiver often reported many different meanings and ambivalence. By grouping Zhao's (2013) data into the themes of my chapter, we see many parallels. These include wanting to reduce burden on children (176, 281), low expectations for filial piety (201–2, 206–7, 216–17, 237, 297), having no other good options (181, 298), the idea that spouses should not *feel* burdened (159–60), and self-reliance and capability (161–62, 243). They also include: reciprocity (120, 176, 287), responsibility or duty (121, 123, 158–60, 163, 176, 181), reputation maintenance (295), feelings of affection, compassion, or love (120, 125, 136, 158), notions of fate, karma, and inevitability of suffering (143–48, 157, 162), and the issue of regrets (165–66, 173, 268, 282). A difference was that some in Zhao's sample brought Christian interpretations to their experiences.

These findings also connect to other chapters in this volume, most notably Long and Campbell's on eldercare (chap. 9), but also Moore's on self-reliance (chap. 7) and Han and Shea's on end of life (chap. 12). Focusing on chapter 9, my findings resonate in many ways. Both chapters follow family caregivers for the aged longitudinally, including some time after death. Both explore how traditional ideals for eldercare are being challenged, unpack recent meanings of eldercare, question simplistic measures of burden, and examine continuities in care before and after death. Both address the import of preexisting relationships, issues of pride versus regret, and feelings about aging in place versus in nursing homes. The theme of destiny was another commonality. Our chapters differ as well. The lower end of the Japanese age range was younger. Whereas the China study had all spouses, the Japan one had a mix of children, daughters-in-law, and spouses. The China one focused on meanings of caregiving, whereas the Japan one also examined how patterns, styles, and experiences of eldercare vary by illness stage and family relationships and how caregivers build a post-caregiving life.

As with any study, this one has its limitations. The small qualitative sample in the oldest urban population in China cannot represent all dementia spousal caregivers across the urban and rural expanse of China. Subjects were specifically chosen to be primary caregivers for their spouses. In other situations, there can be a more even distribution of caregiving labor between spouses and adult children. Also, not all Chinese families avoid nursing homes.

These findings have important implications for future research on, and for practitioners working with, spousal caregivers. They help to illustrate the complexity of what spousal caregiving "burden" can mean. The idea of karmic debt, for instance, means that, for some caregivers, relieving them of their burdens may condemn them to worry about a more difficult life to come. This amplifies the point made by Lou, Lau, and Cheung (2015) that very negative and very positive meanings of care may coexist for the same caregiver. For most, the nature of their experience and its implications for their health and the kinds of assistance they may want or need cannot be easily captured on a ratings scale, because experience is a symphony or cacophony of many different parts, which often do not align with each other on a positive versus negative scale. It is also often difficult to discern what is positive and what is negative. Even ambivalence does not quite capture the nuance, because sometimes it is more of a narrative arc in which what was negative becomes positive. As a result, it is imperative that ratings scales be accompanied by contextualized qualitative data. On a practical level, geriatricians, gerontologists, and social workers should read burden rating-scale scores with caution and not assume caregiver needs. Not only is there more than meets the eye beneath those ratings, but also what lies beneath really matters.

Acknowledgments

I wish to thank the Fulbright Foundation and the University of Vermont for their financial support for this research; Tianshu Pan for his support as my host at Fudan University; and Jinjin Feng, Ran Feng, Yan Shen, and Yan Zhang for research assistance. I extend my deepest appreciation to the spousal caregivers, neighborhood volunteers, community leaders, and nonprofit staff who shared their experiences.

Jeanne Shea (邵镜虹) is associate professor of anthropology and director of the Health and Society Program at the University of Vermont in Burlington, Vermont, USA. Recipient of two Fulbright Awards, she has published on menopause and midlife, marital relationships, the family, spousal caregiving, senior volunteering, evidence-based medicine, and community supports for aging in place in China. Most recently, she has published several research articles in *Ageing International* (2016, 2017, 2018) and a chapter on China's Senior Companions Program for *The Cultural Context of Aging: Worldwide Perspectives* (Sokolovsky 2020).

Glossary

aiqing	爱情	Romantic love.
baitou xielao	白头偕老	Accompanying each other in growing old together.
fengjian	封建	Feudal, as in unfair traditions from before the communist revolution.
fudan	负担	Burden.
Lao fuqi huxiang zhaogu	老夫妻互相照顾	Old husbands and wives taking care of each other.
ganqing	感情	Feelings of affection.
jiefang le	解放了	To be liberated.
jietuo le	解脱了	To be freed from karmic debt.
kenlao	啃老	To take advantage of or take from the elderly.
mei you banfa	没有办法	Having no other choice or option or having no way around it.

ming	命	Fate.
qian shi qian ta	前世欠他 / 她	To owe a karmic debt to him or her from a previous life.
qinqing	亲情	Feelings of familial intimacy.
ren	忍	To tolerate, to withstand, forbearance.
xiao	孝	Filial piety.
yang'er fang lao	养儿防老	Raising sons (or children) for support in old age.
yihan	遗憾	Regret.
yiwu	义务	Duty.
yuanfen	缘分	Predestined.
zeren	责任	Duty or responsibility.
zi li	自理	Able to live independently or take care of oneself.
zui tiexin	最贴心	Most heartfelt, closest to one's heart.

Notes

1. Shea (2011) has documented a public health campaign in China that has encouraged old people to get married or remarried, in part so they could take care of each other.
2. Many versions of the Zarit Burden Interview exist, from the original twenty-two-item scale to short versions.
3. The study was approved by the University of Vermont Institutional Review Board and Fudan University. All participated voluntarily with informed consent.
4. Simplification of funeral practices under Mao (Ikels 2004: 13) gave way to re-elaboration under the reforms. Now some do less, and others more, than Grandma Mi. Not all follow Buddhist practices. Rural, but not urban, burial is tolerated.

References

Holroyd, Eleanor. 2005. "Developing a Cultural Model of Caregiving Obligations for Elderly Chinese Wives." *Western Journal of Nursing Research* 27 (4): 437–55.

Ikels, Charlotte, ed. 2004b. "Introduction." In *Filial Piety: Practice and Discourse in Contemporary East Asia*, ed. Charlotte Ikels, 1–15. Stanford, CA: Stanford University Press.

Jankowiak, William R., ed. 2008. *Intimacies: Love and Sex across Cultures*. New York: Columbia University Press.

Jiang, Quanbao, Xiaomin Li, and Jesus J. Sánchez-Barricarte. 2015. "Elderly Widowhood in China." *Asian Population Studies* 11 (1): 7–16.

Kellehear, Allan. 2009. "On Dying and Human Suffering." *Palliative Medicine* 23 (5): 388–97.

Lou, Vivian W. Q., Chi Wai Kwan, Ming Lin Alice Chong, and Iris Chi. 2015. "Associations between Secondary Caregivers' Supportive Behavior and Psychological Distress of Primary Spousal Caregivers of Cognitively Intact and Impaired Elders." *Gerontologist* 55 (4): 584–94.

Lou, Vivian W. Q., Bobo Hi-Po Lau, and Karen Siu-Lan Cheung. 2015. "Positive Aspects of Caregiving (PAC): Scale Validation among Chinese Dementia Caregivers (CG)." *Archives of Gerontology and Geriatrics* 60 (2): 299–306.

National Health and Family Planning Commission (NHFPC). 2015. "Press Release of the National Health and Family Planning Commission of the People's Republic of China's 'Development of the Family in China, 2015 Report.'" *NHFPC Website*. Retrieved 5 January 2016 from http.china.com.cn/zhibo/2015-05/13/content_35539813.htm?show=t.

Ng, Petrus, Wing-Chung Ho, Angela Tsun, and Daniel K. W. Young. 2016. "Coping with Bereavement of Widows in the Chinese Cultural Context of Hong Kong." *International Social Work* 59 (1): 115–28.

Shea, Jeanne. 2011. "Older Women, Marital Relationships, and Sexuality in China." *Ageing International* 36, 361–77.

Shea, Jeanne, and Hong Zhang, eds. 2017. "Introduction to Aging and Caregiving in Chinese Populations." *Ageing International* 42 (2): 137–41.

Shea, Jeanne, and Yan Zhang. 2016. "Ethnography of Caregiving of Elders by Elders in Shanghai, China." *Ageing International* 41 (4): 366–93.

Sun, Yuezhu. 2017. "Among 100 Good Virtues, Filial Piety Is the First: Contemporary Moral Discourses on Filial Piety in Urban China." *Anthropological Quarterly* 90 (3): 771–99.

Wang, Ching-Lin, Yea-Ing Lotus Shyu, Jing-Yun Wang, and Cheng-Hsien Lu. 2015. "Progressive Compensatory Symbiosis: Spouse Caregiver Experiences of Caring for Persons with Dementia in Taiwan." *Aging and Mental Health* 21 (3): 241–52.

Wang, Qi, ed. 2015. "Development of the Family in China Report 2015: Half of the Elderly Are Living in an Empty Nest." *Changsha Evening News* (*Changsha Wanbao*). Retrieved 5 January 2016 from http://news.xinhuanet.com/edu/2015-05/14/c_127800298.htm.

Wong, Daniel Fu Keung, Ting Kin Ng, and Xiao Yu Zhuang. 2018. "Caregiving Burden and Psychological Distress in Chinese Spousal Caregivers: Gender Difference in the Moderating Role of Positive Aspects of Caregiving." *Aging & Mental Health*. Advance online publication. Retrieved 8 January 2019 from https://doi.org/10.1080/13607863.2018.1474447.

Xinhua. 2016. "Shanghai Sees Increasing Aging Population in 2015." *China Daily*. Retrieved 5 January 2016 from http.chinadaily.com.cn/china/2016-03/31/content_24197357.htm.

Yan, Yunxiang. 1997. "The Triumph of Conjugality: Structural Transformation of Family Relations in a Chinese Village." *Ethnology* 36 (3): 191–212.

―――. 2009. *The Individualization of Chinese Society.* Oxford: Berg.

―――. 2016. "Intergenerational Intimacy and Descending Familism in Rural North China." *American Anthropologist* 118 (2): 244–57.

―――. 2018. "Neo-Familism and the State in Contemporary China." *Urban Anthropology and Studies of Cultural Systems and World Economic Development* 47 (3,4): 1–44.

Yu, Junhong, Philip Yap, and Tau Ming Liew. 2018. "The Optimal Short Version of the Zarit Burden Interview for Dementia Caregivers: Diagnostic Utility and Externally Validated Cutoffs." *Aging & Mental Health.* Retrieved 8 January 2019 from doi: 10.1080/13607863.2018.1450841.

Zarit, Steven H., and Judy M. Zarit. 1987. *Instructions for the Burden Interview.* University Park: Pennsylvania State University.

Zhao, Huan. 2013. *Living and Loving: Adaptive Experiences of Caregiving to a Spouse with Alzheimer's disease in Shanghai, China.* Saarbrucken, Germany: Lambert Academic.

Zhou, Jianfang, and Norman Hearst. 2016. "Health-Related Quality of Life of Among Elders in Rural China: The Effect of Widowhood." *Quality of Life Research* 25 (12): 3087–95.

3 "TOO BUSY TO DO ANYTHING ELSE"
How Caregiving and Urban Sojourning Impact the Aging Experience of China's Migrant Grandparents

Min Zhang

Introduction

CHENCHEN'S GRANNY IS A RETIRED middle-school teacher in her early sixties. She has recently moved to the city of Shenzhen where she is living with her son's family. Like many elderly residents in this middle-class neighborhood, she and her husband relocated to take care of their newborn grandson. With all the joy of becoming a grandmother and helping out her son's family, she also found herself a bit overwhelmed with taking care of Chenchen in her new surroundings. "Life was more relaxing back home," she remarked.

During their sojourn away from her hometown, she and her husband hardly have time to step beyond the gated community in which their son and daughter-in-law's home is located. "It is just too busy to do anything else." She feels that it is nice to stay in a cosmopolitan city like Shenzhen, but she rarely considers herself a local, nor does she attempt to become one. The location is not the point after all. What really matters is that she can stay with her son and provide care on a daily basis for his family and especially for her grandson Chenchen.

She has been thinking about returning to her hometown, a small city in northern China for a break, since her husband even more frequently than her feels out of place in Shenzhen. Occasionally, she too gets frustrated, sometimes with what she thinks of as her son's ungratefulness. However, she hesitated when her son asked her to stay until their in-laws come to take a stint at childcare. The original arrangement was for both sides to switch every six months. But the other in-laws' visit had to be postponed because that grandpa was recovering from a hip fracture at their Xian home. On International Children's Day she shared with me a short poem widely circulating among her friends on WeChat Moment, a popular smartphone app in China.[1]

> What tires grandma most?
> Caring for a baby.
> What challenges grandpa most? Caring for a baby.
> What is a grandparent's greatest joy?
> Caring for baby's baby.
> On the eve of International Children's Day,
> I salute you, fellow grandmas and grandpas!
> Stay strong!
> The strollers are rolling.
> We must keep moving.

Chenchen's granny is one of hundreds of thousands of elderly Chinese who travel long distances to and temporarily sojourn in major cities in order to provide care for their adult children and grandchildren. Widely referred to as migrant grandparents (*houniao laoren*) or floating elderly (*lao piao*), the size of this demographic segment has risen sharply over the past several years amidst China's rapidly aging process and socioeconomic-cultural transformation (Zhang 2018a, 2018b).[2] By 2016 the number of grandparents migrating within China to take care of their grandchildren already accounted for more than 43 percent of China's 18 million elderly migrant population, and its size is expected to expand significantly in the next decade.[3]

Although providing care for their adult children's families has long been a common experience for Chinese elders (Chen and Liu 2011; Chen, Liu, and Mair 2011; Goh 2011; Ikels 1993; Ko and Hank 2013), the increasing prominence of migrant grandparents is a very recent phenomenon.[4] Thus far, empirical and policy studies have shown strong evidence that migrant grandparents' engagement in domestic care has significantly facilitated the young generation's workforce participation, and at the same time has complicated China's intergenerational family relations (Huang 2017; Qi 2018; Zhang 2018a, 2018b). What is yet to be determined is the impact of that care on migrant grandparents' experiences of aging. What does the extensive involvement in caregiving mean to China's elderly caregivers over the course of urban sojourning? How do domestic migration and urban sojourning in old age to care for grandchildren affect elderly people's caregiving practices? Ultimately, how do trans-local mobility and caregiving for descendants affect Chinese elders' attitudes and practices toward aging?

As reflected in the vignette of Chenchen's granny, migrant grandparents' understanding of themselves and the prospect of aging are closely associated with their caregiving practices as they move *to* urban areas where their children are living and *into* adult children's residence units. Over the course of urban sojourning, migrant grandparents dedicate their lives to providing care and economic support for their grown-up children's families, a task that they consider to be crucial for having a happy, fulfilling life in their old age. Even though the migrant grandparents I observed in Shenzhen understood themselves to be socially valuable persons based on their commitment to their children and grandchildren, their sense of self was also undermined in some ways by that experience. This was especially the case because they confined their experiences to the domestic sphere, adrift in an unfamiliar setting with their caregiving activities increasingly taken for granted. I contend that caregiving practices both enrich and constrain the floating elderly's experiences of getting old as they search for a meaningful way to accomplish good aging. In the long term, the floating elderly encounter grave challenges as they transition from healthy young-old to old-old seniors.

In what follows, I first review the phenomenon of the floating elderly in the context of China's extraordinary social transformation, and then give a brief sketch of the research setting and methods. Subsequently, I ethnographically examine the busy-ness of migrant grandparents' everyday life, at a given point and over the prolonged period of their urban sojourning. In doing so, I analyze the positive and negative impact of caregiving on migrant grandparents' aging experience. Finally, I address the theoretical and empirical significance of this study in the conclusion.

Moving for the Sake of Caring for Descendants: The Rise of the Floating Elderly

The sharp rise of the floating elderly can only be understood when framed in China's social-economic-cultural transformation, especially the intensified parenting, the insufficient public service provision, and the rise of new immigrants in contemporary Chinese society.

Intensified Parenting/Grandparenting

The fact that nearly 50 percent of China's elderly migrants relocate to urban areas to tend to the needs of adult children and grandchildren reflects the nationwide trend of grandparents today being extensively involved in childcare. Over the past three decades of the one-child policy, parents and grandparents have come to increasingly cooperate in raising the precious third generation. A high investment in childrearing is needed in China today due to fierce competition in education and the market economy. This changing landscape has reshaped Chinese people's values and practices into intensified childrearing (Fong 2004; Kuan 2011, 2015; Woronov 2007) and meticulous attention to the needs of children of different ages (Naftali 2009, 2014). Parents alone cannot do all that needs to be done, given their work commitments, so intensive grandparenting has become essential.

Rearing precious singletons has come to require a multigenerational task force (Goh 2011; Gong and Jackson 2012), backed by copious investment of funds and time. Young parents, especially the middle class in urban areas, are willing to invest extensively in childrearing for the sake of developing a child's capabilities (Crabb 2010; Fong 2004; Kipnis 2011; Zou, Anderson, and Tsey 2013). A 2011 survey by the Shanghai Academy of Social Sciences found that raising a child costs on average appropriately RMB 32,000 a year (about US$4,855 at that time), whereas average disposable income was only RMB 31,838 (US$4,683) in the preceding year (Swanson 2015). Nationwide, expenditures for childrearing accounted for approximately 50 percent of annual household income in 2017 (H. Li 2017).

Socioeconomic Factors

The growing prevalence of migrant grandparents is also induced by economic concerns because China's welfare system has increasingly adopted a neoliberal logic (He and Wu 2009; Li 1999). Despite the expansion of formal childcare services, accessible and affordable public childcare facilities still cannot meet the increasing demands. Private service is burgeoning, but it has yet to grow in popularity due to financial concerns and/or distrust of strangers. In 2015 only 4 percent of children between newborn and three years old attended nursery schools or other related childcare facilities, far below the 50 percent in developed countries (H. Li 2017).

China's middle-class parents, particularly young mothers, face tremendous pressure to balance career and family, leaving young couples with little time to personally raise their children (Du and Dong 2013; Y. Li 2017). Consequently, despite the conflicts between the new and traditional ways of rearing their children (Binah-Pollak 2014; Zhu 2010), it has become increasingly common for young couples to turn to their aged parents, many of whom are recent retirees and more than willing to invest time, money, and love in their grandchildren. They are known as nannies who bring their own money (*daixin baomu*).

Within such a landscape, not only do grandparents participate in their grandchildren's upbringing, but at the same time the burden of childcare shifts toward elderly grandparents. Since multigenerational childcare has become normative, Chinese grandparents are now expected to provide live-in help. In Shanghai, for instance, approximately 90 percent of children under the age of three are cared for and reared by at least one grandparent (Scull 2017). China's grandparents now essentially assume most of the childrearing responsibilities, particularly during the early stages of childcare.[5]

The Emergence of New Immigrants

The ongoing process of differentiation among migrants in China is the third crucial factor, which is related especially to the emergence of new immigrants amidst the accelerating stratification of Chinese society. Starting in the early 1980s, economic reform and unbalanced development have spurred massive internal migration in China, largely from the countryside to cities and from interior provinces to coastal regions for higher income and better jobs. In less than forty years, the size of the migrant population grew from less than 16 million in the 1980s to approximately 261 million today (National Bureau of Statistics of China 2011).

Until recently, despite their crucial role in China's economic development, rural-to-urban migrants have been relegated to second-class status (Solinger 1999). Migrant workers, known as the floating population, have been denied permanent urban residency and do not have access to basic public services such as education and health care that are associated with urban household (*hukou*) residency status (Chan and Zhang 1999; Zhang 2001). Without a permanent home in cities, it is common for migrant workers to leave their children in the custody of elderly grandparents that reside in the countryside (Silverstein 2009; Xiang 2007).[6]

Over the past decade, a new segment of the population has started to differentiate itself from the once homogeneous migrant population along the lines of occupation, household registration status, and education (Lian 2013; Mason 2016). These urban residents are mostly young professionals with college degrees. Similar to the migrants who made up the floating population, these young professionals originally came from the countryside or small towns, yet they are able to secure well-paid, white-collar jobs that suit their training and education (Zhang and Lei 2017). They are also more likely to obtain legal residence status for permanent settlement in major cities.[7] These new urban residents, now subjectively identifying themselves as "new immigrants" (*xin yimin*), are well educated and more willing to culturally assimilate into urban life.[8] These young residents are also financially capable of hosting their parents to bring them to the city to help them with childrearing.

Consequently, instead of being left behind in the community of origin, a growing number of aged parents, especially those in relatively affluent middle-class families, have relocated to major cities to tend to their children and grandchildren. In the meantime, different from their local counterparts, migrant grandparents are strangers in these cities and their stays in urban areas are periodical, representing a form of urban sojourning (*chengshi douliu*).

Research Setting and Methods

The data for this study are drawn from a larger project that examines migrant grandparents' experiences and practices toward aging in China's cosmopolitan areas. Shenzhen, marked by its rapid economic ascent and enormous migrant population, provides a particularly suitable setting to study migrant grandparents. Designated as China's first special economic zone, the city has transformed from a small fishing village to a high-tech hub of more than 12 million urban people within just four decades (Shenzhen Municipal Bureau of Statistics 2018). As of 2017 Shenzhen's GDP was reportedly ranked third among all cities nationwide (Wu 2018).

As in China's other first-tier cities, Shenzhen's fast development has attracted a large influx of internal migrants from the countryside. Notably, with 60–80 percent of its population made up of immigrants, Shenzhen is the only Chinese city where the migrant population outnumbers local residents, yielding its reputation as a city of immigrants (Liang and Yiu 2004). To date, Shenzhen's migrant population has further diversified into more distinct categories, including a population of highly educated professionals with legal residential status in contrast to migrant workers without *hukou* (Mason 2016).

Located in the inner city, the neighborhood (referred here by the pseudonym Rose Garden) where I carried out fieldwork is made up of about 5,000 residents, of whom only 20 percent are considered local. The vast majority of the neighborhood's residents are young, white-collar professionals who grew up in other parts of China. Of the 1,500 households living in this community, 87 percent have children. Over 90 percent of these households have at least one grandparent coresiding with married children and grandchildren. Hence, this community has formed in a typical process of "congregation" (McCarthy 1983), a term used to describe the process of both aging and young residents moving into the community. Grandparents usually move in weeks before the birth of their grandchildren and stay until they start primary school. In some cases, maternal and paternal grandparents take turns sojourning to provide care for their grandchildren.

In this study I focus on one of the most basic elements of migrant grandparents' daily experiences: their everyday routine. Methodologically, I conducted semi-structural interviews on a day in the life (del Rio Carral 2014). Respondents were encouraged to tell their story about what an average day of their life was like, and what challenges they have run into over a longer period. I also observed their daily activities and practices as they moved within and beyond the neighborhood's geography. The remainder of this chapter examines how the busy-ness (*manglu*) manifested in their everyday life helps to both enrich and constrain migrant grandparents' aging experiences during their urban sojourns.

Understanding Migrant Grandparents' Busy Life

As aforementioned, older adults in China are now extensively involved in their grandchildren's upbringing and education. In the case of migrant grandparents, taking on the responsibility of care is accompanied by a physical movement to major cities and into grown-up children's small residential units. During their urban sojourns, migrant grandparents' daily activities are organized around adult children's and grandchildren's needs in the domestic sphere. As they bury themselves in integrating and absorbing new childrearing notions and skills, their lives slowly sink into the tedious trivialities from which they are shielding their children, and they are largely excluded from other aspects of social life in an unfamiliar environment.

"Busy but Fulfilling"

Migrant grandparents' experience of urban sojourning is imbued with a sense of busy-ness. Once relocated to Shenzhen, aged parents must quickly adapt to the fast-paced caregiving practices and synchronize their daily activities to the needs of grandchildren and grown-up children. Because most young couples are full-time professionals, it is common for grandparents to take up full responsibility of childcare and household chores. Breakfasts and dinners have to be ready before the young couple leave for and return from work. Schedules are carefully set to ensure that grandchildren have sufficient time for sleeping and outdoor activities. Adding to the challenge is the difficulty of becoming familiar with their new surroundings, a demanding task since the majority of migrant grandparents come from the countryside or underdeveloped regions.[9]

Returning now to the case of Chenchen's granny, her son and daughter-in-law, an IT engineer and an online customer service representative, respectively, usually leave home before 8:00 a.m. and rarely get home from work until 9:00 p.m. Immediately after her daughter-in-law leaves for work,

Granny gives Chenchen a glass of warm water. Twice a day, she also feeds the baby bottled milk, using infant formula purchased from Hong Kong. Like their counterparts across the nation (e.g., Gong and Jackson 2012), the young couple now rely heavily on imported formula. In addition to preparing two meals for adults, the grandmother makes three separate meals for her grandson. Her husband helps her look after Chenchen while she cooks. Her daughter-in-law regularly rearranges meal content to ensure the baby's nutrient balance.

Although migrant grandparents try not to put too much pressure on children about marriage and fertility, they never hesitate to point out how important it is to have a grandchild so that they can become a grandparent (Davis 1991) and get busy playing that crucial role "at this stage of life." Immediately after moving to this community, Ms. Wang converted her WeChat nickname from Teacher Wang to Chenchen's Granny, a common practice among her friends. Indeed, elderly residents in this neighborhood usually addressed each other as somebody's grandmother or grandfather. In her study of name and naming practices in Hong Kong in the late 1960, Rubie Watson (1996) argued that the number of names signifies a person's social position in traditional Chinese society. In the case of migrant grandparents, changes to an online nickname and to the way of addressing each other can be viewed as a quick signifier of the change of their status from "somebody" in their own right into "somebody's grandparents."

Here, it must be noted that simply having a grandchild is not equivalent to taking on the role of grandparent in Chinese culture. Rather, it is through intimate, embodied care practices that migrant grandparents embrace this new role as somebody's grandparents. As illustrated in the busy routine of Chenchen's granny, she and her husband commit to looking after Chenchen, their now eighteen-month-old grandson, virtually full time. Day in and day out, migrant grandparents busy themselves with attending to their grandchildren' most trivial, practical needs: dressing, cooking, feeding, bathing, toileting, playing, and periodically taking them to the hospital for vaccines. Ms. Lin, a retired nurse who recently moved to Shenzhen to care for her daughter's family, mentioned that several friends, who have not yet relocated to their children's city to look after their grandchildren, have nothing to do but wander around supermarkets. She felt that leading such a life might be cool (*xiaosa*), but it is also empty (*kongxu*). By comparison, Ms. Lin is happy to "have a granddaughter to keep me well-occupied." In China today a well-managed daily life with a tightly scheduled routine of grandchild caregiving activities has become a crucial symbol of good and positive aging. Grandparents' lives may be full of trivial details, but they are important details, rather than the alternative, of living a cool but selfish and empty existence.

Caring activities, in the meantime, help aged parents connect to their adult children, who are otherwise available only via phone or WeChat. It is a way to reestablish intimacy between aging parents and adult children. As is common in many Chinese families, adult children usually visit their parents during Spring Festival after they land their first job. Over time, young professionals get married and become too busy to visit home. Aged parents' periodic visits then replace adult children's home visits, usually until around the time young couples consider starting a family. At that time, aged parents' annual visits become a long-term sojourn. Like other migrant grandparents elsewhere in China (Qi 2018), most migrant grandparents are recent retirees. At Rose Garden some aged parents opted to retire early to better coordinate with their offspring's plan to start their own family. One grandmother persuaded her husband to retire a year early after their daughter-in-law got pregnant. The retired clerk believed this was a necessary sacrifice (*xisheng*) to help with her son's career. She is happy to be able to "lend a hand [and] reduce a young couple's burden" by providing care to her adult children's family. Caregiving practice hence grants her a sense of usefulness as she transitions to a later stage of life.

The value of the care and support they provide is a common theme among migrant grandparents. These grandparents remark on the economic contribution of their caregiving practices, eagerly pointing out how much a professional babysitter costs in a city like Shenzhen, as well as how much they spend on adult children's families every month. They constantly point out that adult children could not advance their careers without their aged parents' commitment to the younger generations' care and support. Migrant grandparents recognize their sacrifice in having to give up a casual life, spacious living, and their old social network back home, but they see such sacrifice, crystalized in the busy-ness of their daily life, as worthy and fulfilling. Ultimately, what really matters to migrant grandparents is building intimate connections with their children and grandchildren and gaining their respect and appreciation in order to remain a socially and morally valuable person into old age. To these seniors, such considerations are no less important than future monetary or instrumental support (Newendorp 2017).

Too Busy to Do Anything Else

The extensive care practices also constrain elderly caregivers' sense of good aging in old age. As migrant grandparents' role as caregivers becomes paramount in their identities, their daily life is submerged in trivial, repetitive activities. Oftentimes, their lives become contained within the domestic sphere, with little interaction with other domains of life.

Providing care for the precious singletons is a continuous process of learning and synchronizing the modern skill-based parenting styles that China's middle-class parents pursue (Kuan 2011, 2015; Woronov 2007). In the high-stakes childrearing environment of today, banal activities, as trivial as what children eat, how to feed them, napping practices, or how to handle injuries, can easily become a battlefield between generations with distinct beliefs and practices (Binah-Pollak 2014; Goh 2011; Zhu 2010). During their sojourns, aged parents must constantly deal with detailed modern childrearing requests from their adult children. Many grandparents complained that adult children now trust the "Internet mom" more than elders' wisdom.

Incorporating modern parenting methods into caring practice can be a mentally and physically demanding task for migrant grandparents. The situation is especially challenging for grandparents who travel alone. A grandmother who moved from the countryside to Shenzhen alone because her husband had to stay behind to care for his own ailing parents, reported, "I take care of both the young and the old: preparing breakfast for the whole family, feeding my granddaughter, cleaning the house, making lunch, doing grocery shopping, and making dinners. I'm exhausted, but there is nobody I can complain to. I tell my relatives I am doing fine in Shenzhen, because you are supposed to sweep bad news under the carpet [*bao xi bu bao you*]." Such grandparents say that they "have no time" (*mei shijian*) for themselves.

As reflected in the comment above, as the role of caregiver becomes the primary piece of their identity, migrant grandparents often find themselves stuck in the domestic domain, but unable to vent that sense of stuckness. This is because the dominant social narrative is that grandparenting in the big city should be extremely fulfilling, so a grandparent who complains would risk losing face (*diu lian*).

Migrant grandparents' isolation is clearly reflected in the limited radius of their activities. Except on special occasions such as grandchildren's birthday or national holidays, migrant grandparents spend a great deal of their time on domestic chores. Mr. Zhang, a retired factory manager who had relocated to Rose Garden to look after his grandson, once described to me his daily living trajectory. Twice a day he takes his grandson to a playground located at the center of the neighborhood. At night, when his wife attends square dancing at the park across the street from the gated community, he usually chats with other grandfathers and then visits neighborhood grocery stores. On weekends, when the young couple takes over the childcaring responsibilities, he and his wife take the bus to Ren Ren Le, the closest large supermarket in the area. If we put his routine activities on the map (see figure 3.1), a materialized representation of time-geography

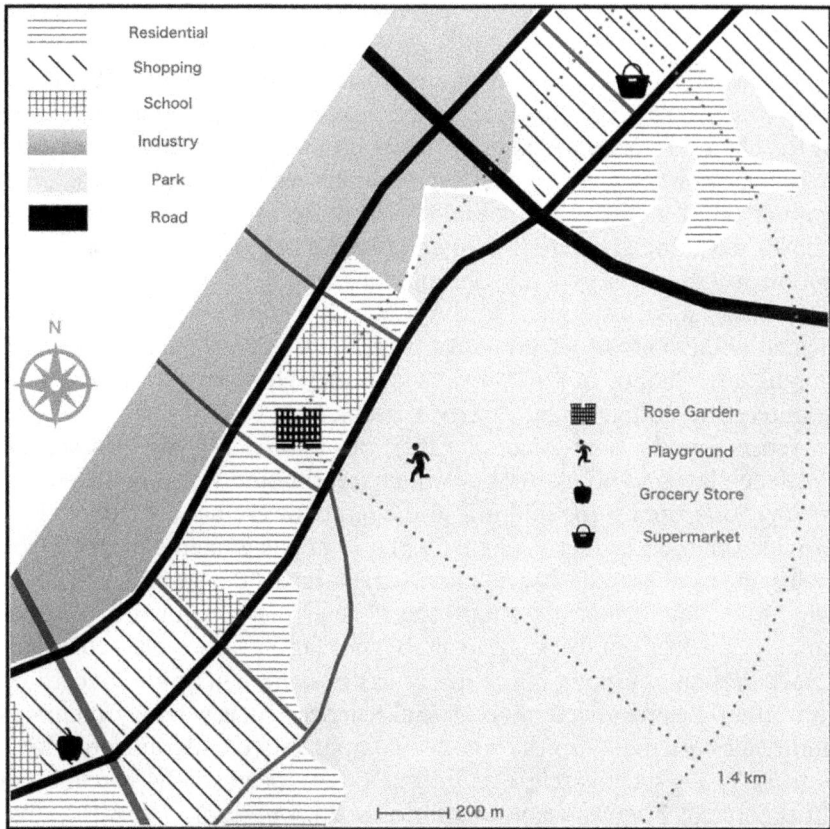

FIGURE 3.1. Geographic Radius of a Migrant Grandfather. Map by Min Zhang.

(Giddens 1984: 111–19), it becomes clear that Mr. Zhang's activities are largely limited within the boundary of the neighborhood, except for the three supermarkets frequented by him and other fellow grandparents. Busy with adult children and grandchildren's practical needs, elderly parents' geographical terrain is limited.

The map in figure 3.1 illustrates the surrounding areas of Rose Garden and the major sites a migrant grandfather frequents during his sojourning. His daily activities mostly consist of looking after his grandson inside, taking his grandson to the playground, or visiting the nearby grocery stores. His life is located within a geographic radius of approximately 1.4 kilometer from his son's apartment, as marked by the dotted circle in the map.

While they did interact with some other fellow grandparents in the course of caregiving activities and errands that took place in the neighborhood, the extent of childcare and household chores that took place in their adult children's apartments kept migrant grandparents from developing deep relationships or strong informal support networks. When visiting Rose Garden, I often saw grandparents cordially greeting each other at the children's playground or at neighborhood grocery stores and sharing happy news regarding milestones in their grandchildren's lives. Information about a special promotion of vegetables at a nearby store passed quickly from one grandmother to another. An absence of a fellow grandparent would be noticed, and speculations would be shared. Sometimes, newcomers were introduced to the circle. Grandfathers often engaged in heated discussions about the latest political news, with some presenting this as an evidence of their male superiority compared to their female counterparts' "nitpickings over trivial issues."

Yet, no matter how frequently they ran into each other at a certain time each day and no matter how much information was exchanged, the connections among the migrant grandparents were not deep enough to provide them with moral support when family arguments arose. A sixty-five-year-old grandfather poignantly remarked, "People only talk about where we came from and what kind of food is well-known in that region. It just does not feel right to share your family issues." His comment clearly resonates among his counterparts elsewhere in China. According to a 2017 Beijing Academy of Social Sciences survey, family members and neighbors made up the top two components of migrant grandparents' everyday social circle, accounting for a respective 30.4 percent and 24.6 percent. Friends accounted for only 23.5 percent (Yin 2017). Because migrant grandparents usually take turns sojourning, their isolation was compounded. Some migrant grandparents leave the city abruptly due to family controversies, and many return to their community of origins once grandchildren attend primary school. The migrant community is hence superficial and unstable, providing temporary social convenience but no moral buttress.

When Being Busy Is Taken for Granted

According to classic Confucian texts, adulthood is a continuous process of self-cultivation and self-transformation. Coming to old age, which itself is one of the most crucial components of adulthood, is not just reaching a physical stage of life, but also means arriving at culmination of a holistic process of reaching one's full humanity (Tu 1979). In this sense, providing care and support to adult children's families plays a crucial role in helping older adults build social connections and establish a sense of realizing their moral selves.

Yet as they become submerged in trivial, repetitive caregiving activities on a daily basis, migrant grandparents are vulnerable to disregard and contempt, with their moral status relegated to the perspective of their children's generation. For many elders, the time pressure in their busy lives is as much a social duty toward their adult children as a voluntary personal sacrifice, because "everyone else [at our age] is doing this." Yet even when migrant grandparents believe their children to be under tremendous pressure at work, aged parents often find it frustrating to see them "do nothing but play on their cellphones" after getting off work.

What makes the situation even more unacceptable is the young generation's attitude: "They just take it for granted that the elders sacrifice our time to help them." Both generations take it for granted that elders should attend to the needs of adult children and their grandchildren, with a seemingly different interpretation of this taken-for-grantedness. A grandfather in his late sixties who felt strained by the heavy burden of care remarked that the young generation seems not to realize that "it is not easy to travel this far away and live in such a crowded apartment." As providing care becomes a social norm, migrant grandparents' sense of usefulness has become trivialized into a utilitarian role, losing the moral dimension that they wish to emphasize on a relational and personal development level.

The situation becomes even more complicated in the long run. The floating elderly's daily routines are subject to change in accordance with grandchildren's age-based needs. Once their grandchildren enroll in primary school, elderly grandparents generally either choose to or are asked to move out. Unfortunately, it is also near this time that this demographic group begins to transition from healthy young-old to old-old senior. Whereas urban retirees usually do not need to worry financially and tend to have children who live close by, those from rural areas often have grave concerns about their economic futures and who will care for them if they get sick.

Socially, even if they have long forsaken an expectation of elder support from their adult children, the floating elderly express a bitter sense of betrayal. Many of them speak of the post-caregiver stage with a great sense of uncertainty. More than one migrant grandparent told me that young people simply "dumped" their aged parents when the latter are no longer of use. A story widely circulating among the migrant grandparents was about an old couple sent to a new commercial apartment development located three hours' drive from their adult children's home. In other cases, aged parents encountered challenges when returning to their community of origin. A grandparent actively caught up with her relatives and friends once she returned; however, after the initial excitement, she was hit by waves of melancholy over her life in Shenzhen. Home was just not feeling as warm as before.

The younger generation, on the other hand, find themselves mired in a dilemma regarding when and how to end aged parents' role as caregiver with dignity and decency. Many of them insisted that it is good for aged parents to step back and enjoy a carefree life once the grandchildren enroll in primary school. Some admitted that aged parents were getting old and were no longer as helpful as they once were. Still, some of them felt obliged to ask their aged parents to continue staying with them. "It is really difficult to decide [whether to ask them to stay]," a young engineer explained. "They feel exploited if continuously taking care of [my child], but they feel abandoned if asked to leave." Both adult children and sojourning grandparents find themselves between a rock and a hard place if the topic of early exit is broached.

Conclusion

Against the backdrop of a rapidly aging population and a growing gap between caregiving demand and supply (Glenn 2010), over the past two decades a rising number of older adults have taken on the responsibility for caring for others. This includes caring for grandchildren, frail spouses (see chap. 2), and/or other aging family members (Gibson 2002a, 2002b; Gray 2005; Haglund 2000; Hank and Buber 2009; Hong and Kim 2008; Shea 2018; Solomon and Marx 1995; Williams 2011). Thus far, the phenomenon of grandparents taking care of grandchildren has been more prominent in many contemporary East Asian contexts (Goh 2011; Ko and Hank 2013; Mehta and Thang 2011) compared with grandchildren taking care of grandparents (for the latter, see chap. 5). Worldwide grandparenting practices profoundly affect elderly caregivers' economic, physical, and emotional well-being (Baker and Silverstein 2008; Conger et al. 2002; Conway, Jones, and Speakes-Lewis 2011; Hughes et al. 2007). What makes China's migrant grandparents' situation even more complicated is that their involvement in care is accompanied by geographical movement, both domestically and sometimes internationally (Newendorp 2017; Zhang 2018a, 2018b). In this study, I have ethnographically shown how urban sojourning to care for younger generations complicates elderly caregivers' own aging experiences.

My ethnographic accounts have shown how migrant grandparents' daily life is predominantly organized around caregiving activities and how the busy-ness of their daily lives both enriches and detracts from migrant grandparents' experience of getting old. I contend that, for China's floating elderly, providing care and economic support for adult children and grandchildren serves as a meaningful way to enact good aging for themselves. However, as migrant grandparent sojourning labors for the younger generations have become taken for granted, their family contributions have become devalued and their experience of aging well is threatened by the devaluation of domestic labor and by the liminal nature of urban sojourning. Today's migrant grandparent's aging well may be tomorrow's old person returning to their hometown far away from their children or grandchildren. The impact is exacerbated when the floating elderly transition from healthy young-old to old-old senior with health problems. Can such temporary grandparenting sojourns serve as a source of long-lasting meaning like a rite of passage in which the experience is liminal but with extended positive after-effects? Or will these experiences more often lead to a sense of disjointedness and imbalance, of investing heavily in descendant care without hope of lasting sense of moral elevation or adequate future return in filial care (for definition, see Introduction)?

As this demographic segment advances to a new stage in their life cycle and as China rapidly evolves as an aging society, this study reveals numerous challenges to policymakers regarding the issue of elder support. Various policies and programs must be formulated to allow better integration of the migrant grandparents into urban life. Whether the host city is capable of providing sufficient medical support becomes an urgent issue under the weight of already-heavy medical demands of older official residents. Because many migrant grandparents return to their community of origin due to the high cost of living in cities, the issue of who should be responsible for and who would be able to care for the elders remains a big question. Aging is growing into a pressing issue worldwide and the elderly population is increasingly involved in informal caregiving activities later in life, so this research also sheds light on the challenges faced by elderly caregivers on a global scale.

Min Zhang (张敏) is a faculty member in the School of Ethnology and Sociology at Minzu University of China in Beijing. Prior to teaching at Minzu University, she was a research fellow at the Harry S. Truman Research Institute at Hebrew University of Jerusalem, Israel, and a visiting research fellow at East Asian Institute at National University of Singapore. Her current project examines the dynamics among grandchild care, urban relocation, and elderhood in cosmopolitan China. Her work has appeared in *Social Anthropology/Anthropologie Sociale, Ethnography and Education, Ethnography,* and other journals.

Glossary

bao xi bu bao you	报喜不报忧	Sweep bad news under the carpet; to report the good things but not the bad.
chengshi douliu	城市逗留	Urban sojourning.
daixin baomu	带薪保姆	Nanny who brings her own salary in her pocket, meaning a nanny who not only provides free service, but also brings her own money to the family.
diu lian	丢脸	Losing face.
houniao laoren	候鸟老人	Migratory bird old folks, used to describe sojourning migrant grandparents.
kongxu	空虚	Empty; not meaningful.
lao piao	老漂	Floating elderly or migrant elders.
manglu	忙碌	Being busy; busy-ness.
mei shijian	没时间	Does not have time.
Ren Ren Le	人人乐	Everybody's Happy, the name of a grocery store chain.
xiaosa	潇洒	Cool or chic.
xin yimin	新移民	New immigrants.
xisheng	牺牲	Sacrifice.

Notes

1. The poem reads as follows in Chinese: 什么最累, 看孩子; 什么最难, 看孩子; 什么最幸福, 看自己的孩子的孩子. 在此六一儿童节到来之际, 送给各位爷爷奶奶姥姥姥爷们. 再接再厉, 小车不倒, 只管推. I thank Dr. Nick Walmsley for helping me edit the English translation.
2. Other terms for these grandparents also circulate in public media, such "floating vagabonds" or "floating grandparents." In this chapter, I use the terms "floating elderly" and "migrant grandparents" interchangeably. According to the fifth population census, people sixty-five years of age and older represented 6.96 percent of China's 1.295 billion total population, indicating China had already become an aging society in 2000 (National Bureau of Statistics 2001).
3. The rate of migrating grandparents is even higher in China's most-developed cities. According to Beijing Academy of Social Sciences survey, more than 54 percent of China's elderly migrants moved to Beijing in 2017 in order to provide care for children or grandchildren there (Yin 2017). According to the 2016 National

Health and Family Planning Commission (NHFPC) survey, the population of elderly migrants (aged sixty and older) reached 18 million in 2015, accounting for 7.2 percent of China's 247 million migrant population. Caring for the younger generation (both adult children and grandchildren), reuniting with adult children due to the elder's advanced age, and finding jobs are the top three reasons for elder migration, accounting for 43 percent, 25 percent, and 23 percent, respectively. This figure is likely an underestimation of the actual size of the floating elderly population as it only counts individuals officially registered as temporary residents in host cities. In reality, many are not officially registered and are not counted in the cited study.

4. See, for instance, "The Changing Face of China's Migrant Population" (2016) and "Grandparents Without Borders" (2013) report on this phenomenon.

5. Eighty percent of participants of parenting schools in Guangzhou and Shanghai were grandparents (Yang 2013). As Ikels (2004) noted, the trend of the old increasingly serving younger generations had already begun earlier in the reform era (6), but it has ramped up since then as expectations for cultivation of children and grandchildren have intensified.

6. The estimation varies from 9 million to 61 million in different surveys, depending on the definition. For instance, a Ministry of Civil Affairs survey found that of more than 9 million left-behind children in 2016, 89.3 percent lived with grandparents (Cai and Wang 2016).

7. Overall, China's household registration system has become less restrictive in recent years, but the criteria for obtaining urban *hukou* have become more stringent in large cities. Such criteria usually favor migrants with higher education or financial means.

8. Migrants with higher education tend to permanently settle in major cities and assimilate into the urban environment. The 2017 NHFPC survey suggested an inverse link between education level and chances of returning to original place of residence (NHFPC 2017: 45).

9. According to a 2017 Beijing Academy of Social Sciences survey, the ratios of migrant grandparents moving from countryside, towns, small cities, and major cities were 36 percent, 18 percent, 32 percent, and 14 percent, respectively (Yin 2017).

References

Baker, Lindsey A., and Merrill Silverstein. 2008. "Depressive Symptoms among Grandparents Raising Grandchildren: The Impact of Participation in Multiple Roles." *Journal of Intergenerational Relationships* 6 (3): 285–304.

Binah-Pollak, Avital. 2014. "Discourses and Practices of Child-Rearing in China: The Bio-Power of Parenting in Beijing." *China Information* 28 (1): 27–45.

Cai, Yiwen, and Lianzhang Wang. 2016. "How Accurate Is China's 2016 Figure for Left-Behind Children?" *Sixth Tone*. Retrieved 19 December 2018 from http://www.sixthtone.com/news/1540/how-accurate-is-chinas-2016-figure-for-left-behind-children%3F.

Chan, Kam Wing, and Li Zhang. 1999. "The Hukou System and Rural-Urban Migration in China: Processes and Changes." *China Quarterly* 160 (Dec.): 818–55.

Chen, Feinian, and Guangya Liu. 2011. "The Health Implications of Grandparents Caring for Grandchildren in China." *Journals of Gerontology Series B: Psychological Sciences and Social Sciences* 67 (1): 99–112.

Chen, Feinian, Guangya Liu, and Christine A. Mair. 2011. "Intergenerational Ties in Context: Grandparents Caring for Grandchildren in China." *Social Forces* 90 (2): 571–94.

Conger, Rand D., Lora Ebert Wallace, Yumei Sun, Ronald L. Simons, Vonnie C. McLoyd, and Gene H. Brody. 2002. "Economic Pressure in African American Families: A Replication and Extension of the Family Stress Model." *Developmental Psychology* 38 (2): 179–93.

Conway, Francine, Samuel Jones, and Amandia Speakes-Lewis. 2011. "Emotional Strain in Caregiving among African American Grandmothers Raising Their Grandchildren." *Journal of Women and Aging* 23 (2): 113–28.

Crabb, Mary W. 2010. "Governing the Middle-Class Family in Urban China: Educational Reform and Questions of Choice." *Economy and Society* 39 (3): 385–402.

Davis, Deborah. 1991. *Long Lives: Chinese Elderly and the Communist Revolution.* Stanford, CA: Stanford University Press.

del Rio Carral, Maria. 2014. "Focusing on 'A Day in the Life': An Activity-Based Method for the Qualitative Analysis of Psychological Phenomena." *Qualitative Research in Psychology* 11 (3): 298–315.

Du, Fenglian, and Xiao-yuan Dong. 2013. "Women's Employment and Child Care Choices in Urban China during the Economic Transition." *Economic Development and Cultural Change* 62 (1): 131–55.

Fong, Vanessa. 2004. *Only Hope: Coming of Age under China's One-Child Policy.* Stanford, CA: Stanford University Press.

Gibson, Priscilla. 2002a. "African American Grandmothers as Caregivers: Answering the Call to Help Their Grandchildren." *Families in Society: The Journal of Contemporary Social Services* 83 (1): 35–43.

———. 2002b. "Caregiving Role Affects Family Relationships of African American Grandmothers as New Mothers Again: A Phenomenological Perspective." *Journal of Marital and Family Therapy* 28 (3): 341–53.

Giddens, Anthony. 1984. *Constitution of Society: Outline of the Theory of Structuration.* Berkeley: University of California Press.

Glenn, Evelyn N. 2010. *Forced to Care: Coercion and Caregiving in America.* Cambridge, MA: Harvard University Press.

Goh, Esther C L. 2011. *China's One-Child Policy and Multiple Caregiving: Raising Little Suns in Xiamen.* New York: Routledge.

Gong, Qian, and Peter Jackson. 2012. "Consuming Anxiety? Parenting Practices in China after the Infant Formula Scandal." *Food, Culture & Society* 15 (4): 557–78.

"Grandparents Without Borders." 2013. *China Daily,* 27 January. Retrieved 23 September 2018 from https://www.chinadaily.com.cn/china/2013-01/27/content_16177853.htm

Gray, Anne. 2005. "The Changing Availability of Grandparents as Carers and Its Implications for Childcare Policy in the UK." *Journal of Social Policy* 34 (4): 557–77.

Haglund, Kristin. 2000. "Parenting a Second Time Around: An Ethnography of African American Grandmothers Parenting Grandchildren Due to Parental Cocaine Abuse." *Journal of Family Nursing* 6 (2): 120–35.

Hank, Karsten, and Isabella Buber. 2009. "Grandparents Caring for Their Grandchildren: Findings from the 2004 Survey of Health, Ageing, and Retirement in Europe." *Journal of Family* 30 (1): 53–73.

He, Shenjing, and Fulong Wu. 2009. "China's Emerging Neoliberal Urbanism: Perspectives from Urban Redevelopment." *Antipode* 41 (2): 282–304.

Hong, Gwi-Ryung Son, and Hyojeong Kim. 2008. "Family Caregiver Burden by Relationship to Care Recipient with Dementia in Korea." *Geriatric Nursing* 29 (4): 267–74.

Huang, Yu. 2017. "Stay or Back: Chinese Migrating Parents Experience of Social Inclusion under Intergenerational Support." Master's thesis, Nord Universitet, Bodø, Norway.

Hughes, Mary Elizabeth, Linda J. Waite, Tracey A. LaPierre, and Ye Luo. 2007. "All in the Family: The Impact of Caring for Grandchildren on Grandparents' Health." *Journals of Gerontology Series B: Psychological Sciences and Social Sciences* 62 (2): S108–S119.

Ikels, Charlotte. 1993. "Settling Accounts: The Intergenerational Contract in an Age of Reform." In *Chinese Families in the Post-Mao Era*, ed. D. Davis and S. Harrell, 307–33. Berkeley: University of California Press.

———, ed. 2004. *Filial Piety: Practice and Discourse in Contemporary East Asia*. Stanford, CA: Stanford University Press.

Kipnis, Andrew. 2011. *Governing Educational Desire: Culture, Politics, and Schooling in China*. Chicago: University of Chicago Press.

Ko, Pei-Chun, and Karsten Hank. 2013. "Grandparents Caring for Grandchildren in China and Korea: Findings from CHARLS and KLoSA." *Journals of Gerontology Series B: Psychological Sciences and Social Sciences* 69 (4): 646–51.

Kuan, Teresa. 2011. "The Heart Says One Thing but the Hand Does Another: A Story about Emotion-Work, Ambivalence and Popular Advice for Parents." *China Quarterly* 65: 77–100.

———. 2015. *Love's Uncertainty: The Politics and Ethics of Child Rearing in Contemporary China*. Berkeley: University of California Press.

Li, Hongmei. 2017. "Yangwa Chengben Taigao, Qicheng Buyuan Zaiyao" [70 percent of Chinese do not plan to have the second child due to rising cost of raising a child]. *People's Daily*, 23 January. Retrieved 6 March 2020 from http://news.sohu.com/20170123/n479381265.shtml

Li, Xing. 1999. "The Transformation of Ideology from Mao to Deng: Impact on China's Social Welfare Outcome." *International Journal of Social Welfare* 8 (2): 86–96.

Li, Yunrong. 2017. "The Effects of Formal and Informal Child Care on the Mother's Labor Supply—Evidence from Urban China." *China Economic Review* 44: 227–40.

Lian, Si, ed. 2013. *2013 Zhongguo Qingnian Fazhan Baogao 2013: Chengshi Xin Yimin de Jueqi* [2013 report on youth development: The rise of new immigrants in urban China). Beijing: Social Sciences Academic Press.

Liang, Zai, and Por Chen Yiu. 2004. "Migration and Gender in China: An Origin-Destination Linked Approach." *Economic Development and Cultural Change* 52 (2): 423–43.

Mason, Katherine. 2016. *Infectious Change: Reinventing Chinese Public Health after an Epidemic*. Stanford: Stanford University Press.

McCarthy, Kevin F. 1983. "The Elderly Populations Changing Spatial Distribution: Patterns of Change since 1960." Rand Report No. R-2916-NIA. Rand Corporation, Santa Monica, CA.

Mehta, Kalyani K., and Leng Leng Thang, eds. 2011. *Experiencing Grandparenthood: An Asian Perspective*, vol. 47. Dordrecht/Heidelberg/London/New York: Springer Science & Business Media.

Naftali, Orna. 2009. "Empowering the Child: Children's Rights, Citizenship and the State in Contemporary China." *China Journal* 61: 79–103.

———. 2014. *Children, Rights and Modernity in China: Raising Self-governing Citizens.* New York: Springer.

National Bureau of Statistics of China. 2001. "Diwuci Quanguo Renkou Pucha Gongbao, Diyihao" [Communiqué of the National Bureau of Statistics of People's Republic of China on major figures of the 2000 population census, no. 1]. Retrieved 6 March 2020 from http://www.stats.gov.cn/tjsj/tjgb/rkpcgb/qgrkpcgb/200203/t20020331_30314.htm.

———. 2011. "Diliuci Quanguo Renkou Pucha Zhuyao Shuju Gongbao, Diyihao" [Communiqué of the National Bureau of Statistics of People's Republic of China on major figures of the 2010 population census, no. 1]. Retrieved 8 May 2020 from http://www.stats.gov.cn/tjsj/tjgb/rkpcgb/qgrkpcgb/201104/t20110428_30327.html.

National Health and Family Planning Commission (NHFPC). 2017. *2016 Zhongguo Liudongrenkou Fazhan Baogao* [2016 report of China's migrant population development]. Beijing: China Population.

Newendorp, Nicole. 2017. "Negotiating Family 'Value': Caregiving and Conflict among Chinese-Born Senior Migrants and Their Families in the US." *Ageing International* 42 (2): 187–204.

Qi, Xiaoying. 2018. "Floating Grandparents: Rethinking Family Obligation and Intergenerational Support." *International Sociology* 33(6): 761-777.

Scull, J. C. 2017. "China's Grandparent Trap: How China's Children Are Being Cared by Their Grandparents." *ExtraNewsfeed.* 17 June. Retrieved 6 March 2020 from https://soapboxie.com/social-issues/How-Chinese-Children-are-Raised-by-Grandparents.

Shea, Jeanne L. 2018. "Dominant Chinese National Policies on Aging and Their Degree of Attention to Eldercare by Seniors." *Ageing International, 44(4), 331-351.*

Shenzhen Municipal Bureau of Statistics. 2018. "2017 Nian Shenzhen Jingjin Youzhiliang Wending Fazhan" [Shenzhen economy had stable quality and development in 2017]. 1 February. Retrieved 13 January 2019 from http://wemedia.ifeng.com/47549008/wemedia.shtml.

Silverstein, Merrill. 2009. "Intergenerational Reciprocity and the Well-being of Older Adults in Rural China." In *Family Support Networks and Population Ageing*, ed. Alberto Palloni, Guido Pinto, and Rebeca Wong, 25–28. Retrieved 4 March 2020 from https://www.difi.org.qa/wp-content/uploads/2017/11/MerrillSilverstein.pdf.

Solinger, Dorothy J. 1999. *Contesting Citizenship in Urban China: Peasant Migrants, the State, and the Logic of the Market.* Berkeley: University of California Press.

Solomon, Jennifer Crew, and Jonathan Marx. 1995. "'To Grandmother's House We Go': Health and School Adjustment of Children Raised Solely by Grandparents." *Gerontologist* 35 (3): 386–94.

Swanson, Ana. 2015. "Why Many Families in China Won't Want More Than One Kid Even If They Can Have Them?" *Washington Post*, 30 October. Retrieved 6 March 2020 from https://www.washingtonpost.com/news/wonk/wp/2015/10/30/why-many-families-in-china-wont-want-more-than-one-kid-even-if-they-can-have-them/.

"The Changing Face of China's Migrant Population—Reuniting the Three-Generation Family." 2016. *The Economist*, 3 December. Retrieved 4 March 2020 from https://www.washingtonpost.com/news/wonk/wp/2015/10/30/why-many-families-in-china-wont-want-more-than-one-kid-even-if-they-can-have-them/.

Tu, Wei-ming. 1979. *Humanity and Self-Cultivation: Essays in Confucian Thought*. Berkeley: Asian Humanities Press.

Watson, Rubie S. 1996. "The Named and the Nameless: Gender and Person in Chinese Society." *American Ethnologist* 13 (4): 619–631.

Williams, Molly N. 2011. "The Changing Roles of Grandparents Raising Grandchildren." *Journal of Human Behavior in the Social Environment* 21 (8): 948–62.

Woronov, Terry. E. 2007. "Chinese Children, American Education: Globalizing Child Rearing in Contemporary China." In *Generations and Globalization: Youth, Age, and Family in the New World Economy*, ed. Jennifer Cole and Deborah Durham, 29–51. Bloomington: Indiana University Press.

Wu, Xiaobo. 2018. "Shenzhen's 2017 GDP to Top $340b." *China Daily*, 18 January. Retrieved 19 September 2018 from http://usa.chinadaily.com.cn/a/201801/18/WS5a602cbda310e4ebf433eb4f.html.

Xiang, Biao. 2007. "How Far Are the Left Behind Left Behind? A Preliminary Study in Rural China." *Population, Space and Place* 13 (3): 179–91.

Yang, Kelly. 2013. "In China, It's the Grandparents Who 'Lean In.'" *The Atlantic*. 30 September. Retrieved 4 March 2020 from https://www.theatlantic.com/china/archive/2013/09/in-china-its-the-grandparents-who-lean-in/280097/

Yin, Xincheng, ed. 2017. *Beijing Lanpishu: Beijing Shehui Zhili Fazhan Baogao (2016–2017)* [Blue book of Beijing: Annual report on social governance development of Beijing (2016–2017)]. Beijing: Social Sciences Academic Press.

Zhang, Li. 2001. *Strangers in the City: Reconfigurations of Space, Power, and Social Networks within China's Floating Population*. Stanford, CA: Stanford University Press.

Zhang, Min. 2018a. "The Rise of the 'Floating Elderly' (I): A Signal Trend of China's Ageing Population." *Background Brief*, # 1348, East Asian Institute, National University of Singapore, Singapore.

———. 2018b. "The Rise of the 'Floating Elderly' (II): Challenges and Long-Term Implications." *Background Brief*, # 1349, East Asian Institute, National University of Singapore, Singapore.

Zhang, Wenhong, and Kaichun Lei. 2017. *Chengshi Bailing Xin Yimin Yanjiu* [A study on the new immigrants of white collar in urban China]. Beijing: Social Sciences Academic Press.

Zhu, Jianfeng. 2010. "Mothering Expectant Mothers: Consumption, Production, and Two Motherhoods in Contemporary China." *Ethos* 38 (4): 406–12.

Zou, Wuying, Neil Anderson, and Komia Tsey. 2013. "Middle-Class Chinese Parental Expectations for Their Children's Education." *Procedia: Social and Behavioral Sciences* 106: 1840–9.

4 POPULATION AGING AND CARE OF THE ELDERLY IN HONG KONG

Michelle Shum and Terry Lum

Introduction

AS A CONFUCIAN HERITAGE SOCIETY, Hong Kong is now confronting the weakening of its cornerstone, the family, for provision of care for the elderly. Over recent decades Hong Kong has been transformed from a small fishing village and trading port in south China to an international financial center at a pace and scale that are legendary. The successful economic development and modernization have inevitably led Hong Kong to immense sociodemographic change. This change has altered the traditional Chinese family system and weakened adult children's ability to take care of their elderly parents in accordance with the traditional virtue of filial piety (for definition, see Introduction).

Despite these changes, a recent survey reveals that children's affective altruistic concern for their parents indeed persists in Chinese adults in Hong Kong; whether this leads to provision of care for their elderly parents, however, depends on the children's abilities and resources. Yet the conventional policy for care of the elderly in Hong Kong provides only residual support to family caregivers. The policy's deficit approach to the provision of services for the care of the elderly primarily targets the development of residential care services (RCS) for the dependent elderly people whose family members are no longer able to provide support. Without the availability of family support services tailor-made for individual needs, a family caregiver with only limited resources or capacity has no alternative but to resort to RCS. The lack of family support engenders a high institutionalization rate among the elderly of around 7 percent in Hong Kong (Chui et al. 2009: 10). This figure keeps rising, and there is a long waiting list for RCS. Only in recent years has the government of the Hong Kong Special Administrative Region (HKSAR) considered a revamp of the compensatory services for the care of the elderly.

Given the worldwide trend in population aging, we argue that a new policy paradigm of a shared-care model—that empowers the family and the community to promote "aging in place" and care in the community by the community—is needed to support the rapidly increasing elderly population while maintaining decent economic growth. In this chapter, we first provide information on population aging in Hong Kong. With this as the context, we discuss family caregiving for frail elderly people in Hong Kong against the backdrop of the societal changes. We then critically review the deficit-focused compensatory policy of care for the elderly, which has fostered a prolonged neglect of the needs of family caregivers. Finally, we discuss recent changes in the policy for care of the elderly in Hong Kong toward this new empowerment-based paradigm.

Population Aging in Hong Kong

Hong Kong is aging very quickly. In 2011 only 13 percent of the population were sixty-five years or older, but by 2041 the figure will have increased to 30 percent. The median age will have increased from forty-two years in 2011 (Census and Statistics Department of Hong Kong [C&SD] 2012a: 9) to fifty years in 2041. The elderly dependency ratio (defined as the number of persons aged sixty-five years and older per 1,000 persons aged between fifteen and sixty-four) will have increased from 177 in 2011 to 497 in 2041. The oldest elderly (those eighty-five years of age and older) will have increased from 125,000 people in 2011 to 490,000 people in 2041 (C&SD 2013c: 8, 23). The ratio of working-age people to elderly people will have fallen from 5.3 to 1 in 2011 to 1.8 to 1 in 2041 (Government of the HKSAR 2013).

The rapid population aging is caused by several factors. First, the population of Hong Kong has grown rapidly since World War II. Immediately after the war, Hong Kong had only 600,000 residents. Between 1945 and the 1970s the growth was mainly fueled by immigration. By 1947 the population had increased to 1.8 million people, by 1960 it had reached 3 million people, and by 1974 it had increased to 4.3 million (C&SD 1975). Most of these new residents were young adults who came to Hong Kong as refugees because of political unrest in mainland China. Between the 1970s and now, the population has grown naturally, with the children and grandchildren of these young immigrants being born. By 2011 the population of Hong Kong had reached 7.1 million people and about 13.3 percent were sixty-five years or older (C&SD 2012a: 9). The cohorts of successive waves of young immigrants have aged together, and they have created a very large cohort of elderly people in Hong Kong.

Second, the fertility rate in Hong Kong has been persistently low since the early 1980s, when Hong Kong faced political uncertainty due to its imminent return to China (it was returned in 1997). The total fertility rate (the average number of children that 1,000 women give birth to during their lifetime) decreased from 1,933 in 1981 to 901 in 2003, although it rebounded to 1,285 in 2012 (C&SD 2018: 7). For comparison, in 2010 the total fertility rates in Japan and Singapore were 1,390 and 1,150, respectively (C&SD 2012a: 31). As the population of a society ages, it has proportionately fewer and fewer young people.

Third, Hong Kong people have a very long life expectancy. For males the life expectancy at birth increased from 67.8 years in 1971 to 81.2 years in 2014, and for females it increased from 75.3 years to 86.9 years over the same period (Department of Health of Hong Kong 2016). In fact, according to a report published by the United Nations (UN) in 2015, Hong Kong has the world's highest life expectancy at birth, for both genders (UN 2015: 44).

Overall, Hong Kong is a small city that houses elderly people living some of the longest lives in the world with a rapidly increasing dependency ratio (that term refers to the above calculation of the dependency ratio). At present Hong Kong is, and in the decades to come will be, projected to remain one of the ten places in the world with the oldest median age (UN 2015: 32). The unprecedented pace of population aging in Hong Kong means that the previous experiences of advanced Western economies will provide limited guidance to the city. The city's successful adaptation to the rapidly changing population structure will be vital to its sustainable economic and social development. The city needs to find a way to provide adequate support and care for the elderly without jeopardizing its economic growth.

The Societal Context of the Rise of Contemporary Family Caregiving in Hong Kong

This section introduces the immense sociodemographic changes in Hong Kong during the process of modernization; these changes have inevitably altered the traditional Chinese family system and weakened adult children's ability to take care of their elderly parents. These changes are unfavorable for Hong Kong to adapt to the rapidly aging population.

The Traditional System of Care for the Elderly in Hong Kong

In Hong Kong the traditional Chinese family structures together with the Confucian virtue of filial piety form the foundation for the provision of care for the elderly. Traditionally, the Chinese family displayed characteristics of the gemeinschaft community, which encompasses a network consisting of social relationships with communal attachments, small-scale interactions, meaningful personal relationships, and intimate ties (Tönnies 1957; Weber 1921). The Chinese family has a broader informal caring network than the family in the West. The network of kin, friends, and neighbors extends to include not just the lineage but also the extended clan in terms of kin, and to often encompass non-kin from the neighborhood (*kaifong*) (Ngan 1990).

The size of a Chinese family system is indefinite, similar to highly elastic social circles. It can be expanded or contracted based on the present configuration of power at its center. Merely through the social relationship of kinship it can be extended to embrace countless numbers of people in the past, present, and future by marriage and reproduction. Furthermore, the Chinese may also include whomever they want to add to their own circle as family members and call them "my own people" (*zijia ren*) to indicate a level of intimacy with them (Fei 1992).

With such broad informal networks setting the foundation for care of the elderly, the value placed on the family taking on the ultimate responsibility for caring for its older adults is bolstered by the Confucian virtue of filial piety. Filial piety involves an intricate value system that shapes the intergenerational relationships between parents and children through defining their respective duties and obligations (Ikels 2004; Lum et al. 2015). It emphasizes the responsibility of the younger generation to take care of their elderly parents and grandparents.

Societal Changes Leading to Decline of the Traditional System of Care for the Elderly

The Rise of the Nuclear Family

As mentioned above, in the past Hong Kong was a gemeinschaft-type community, when it was a fishing village before it was ceded to Britain in 1842. Even in the 1960s and early 1970s community sentiment still prevailed in the urban areas. Particularly where people of lower socioeconomic status were concentrated (such as public housing estates, squatter areas, cottage areas, and temporary housing areas), neighborliness—with its mutual trust, care, concern, and support—prevailed (Chui 2003: 152).

However, urban renewal and massive public housing programs implemented in the urbanization process that occurred after 1973 dismantled the gemeinschaft-type community and thus broke down the traditional Chinese family system in Hong Kong. This dismantling weakened the bonds of kinship, neighborliness, and friendship that had facilitated the care of the older adults in the community (Chui 2003).

Furthermore, because urban space in Hong Kong is limited the housing units are normally quite small; this has given rise to a sharp increase in the number of small nuclear families (Chui 2007). There has been a prodigious increase in the number of domestic households in Hong Kong—from 0.69 million in 1961 to 2.37 million in 2011.[1] During this fifty-year period the highest average annual growth rate was seen in 1981, at 4.3 percent. The average household size dropped from 4.5 in 1971 to 2.9 in 2011 (C&SD 2012b: FA8).

Decrease in the Incidence of Coresidence with Older Parents

At the same time, industrialization has also led to social and cultural changes that alter adult children's attitudes to, and ability to abide by, the traditional virtue of filial piety in providing direct personal care for their elderly parents. The rise in the number of nuclear families, smaller apartment sizes, and Western individualistic values engenders a decrease in the incidence of coresidence with older parents as well as an evolution of the modern ethics of filial piety with new interpretations put to an old moral value, as Janelli and Yim (2004) suggested for Korea in Ikels's (2004) edited volume. Surprisingly, the pursuit of independence based on the Western concept of individualism appears not only in the younger generation but also in the older parents. Modern Chinese older persons in Hong Kong are increasingly prepared to live separately from their children (Chi and Chow 1997; Chow 1999; Chow and Lum 2008; Chui 2007).

The number of domestic households exclusively comprising a couple increased from 271,000 in 2001 to 354,000 in 2011, increasing from 13 percent of all households in 2001 to 15 percent in 2011. Among the domestic households comprising a couple only, significant increases from 2001 to 2011 were noted in the number of elderly couples (i.e., both individuals aged sixty-five or older) and in the number of couples comprising individuals aged forty-five to sixty-four (C&SD 2012b: FA10). The proportion of older persons living alone increased from 11.3 percent in 2001 to 12.7 percent in 2011 (C&SD 2013a: FA3).

This trend also reflects the fact that the positive policies adopted by the Hong Kong government provide insufficient inducements to encourage adult children to take care of their older parents. The positive policies include tax relief for married children who live with their parents. In addition, since 1982 priority has been given to families with an older person who are on the waiting list for public housing, under the Families with Elderly Persons Priority Scheme. Moreover, since 2008 this scheme has been combined with the Special Scheme for Families with Elderly Persons under the Harmonious Families Priority Scheme (Hong Kong Housing Authority 2018).[2] Despite these incentives, there is still a decline in the incidence of intergenerational coresidence of adult children and their aging parents.

The Rise of the Dual-Earner Family Due to Economic Needs

Modernization, economic development, and the higher educational attainment of women create more employment opportunities for women in the manufacturing, commercial, and service sectors and increase the labor participation of women (Chui 2007). At the same time, in pursuit of a better standard of living and homeownership encouraged by the Hong Kong government's property-led economy, Hong Kong couples usually use the dual-earner strategy to increase household income to pay for home mortgages, insurance plans, and a better education for their children, and to cover related household expenses (Chui 2007). All these have imperiled the conventional strategy for caring for the elderly, one based on community care or family care.

Contemporary Family Caregiving in Hong Kong

Although filial piety is a cornerstone of Chinese societies, modernization and social changes have diminished the capacity of the family to provide care for the elderly (Chow and Lum 2008; Lum et al. 2015). Such changes include longer life expectancy, the higher educational attainment of women, a greater devotion to work, greater geographic mobility, smaller families, and the decrease in the incidence of intergenerational coresidence.

The decline of the gemeinschaft-type community and the rise of the nuclear family have seriously shrunk the available sources for the provision of care for the elderly. The families of elderly people remain the main source for the provision of care for the elderly. Neighbors and social service networks merely play a supplementary role: they provide care for those who have no family of their own but are fortunate enough to be able to obtain help from their neighbors or social welfare agencies (Chow 2007). This theme of help from neighbors is similar to what Moore (chap. 7) describes for Japan.

Even though close relatives remain important for the provision of care for older people, such relatives are now often confined to one or two immediate family members (Mulvey 2005; Ngan 1990). When sick or injured, fewer than two people were ready to provide help to elderly respondents, as found by a study of elders' health situation since the late 1980s (Lee and Chi 1999).

Some researchers found that, in the early 1990s, elderly people in Hong Kong had very limited social networks and received the least social support from others, compared with elderly Chinese people residing in mainland China and Los Angeles (Lubben and Chi 1993). This problem of the diminishing availability of help from informal networks has persisted in recent years. In a comparative study of care and support for elderly people in three Chinese societies (Guangzhou, Taiwan, and Hong Kong) in the early 2000s, only about 75 percent of the elderly Chinese participants in Hong Kong answered "yes" when asked whether they had someone to help them if they were sick or disabled. In contrast, almost all of the elderly Chinese in Guangzhou and Taipei gave a positive answer (Lai 2013). With regard to social support, the study also found that the elderly Chinese respondents in Hong Kong tended to report the lowest level, compared with those in Guangzhou and Taipei. Over a third of the elderly Chinese participants in Hong Kong reported not having someone they could trust and confide in, whereas only 23.4 percent in Guangzhou and 14.5 percent in Taipei reported this. Compared with Guangzhou and Taiwan, a much smaller percentage of the elderly Chinese participants in Hong Kong reported talking to friends, relatives, or others on the telephone once a day, or spending time with someone with whom they did not live (Lai 2013).

The decrease in the incidence of coresidence with elderly parents poses a threat to the practice of filial piety with regard to the provision of care for elderly parents by their adult children. Data from the latest census shows that 51 percent of the elderly people in Hong Kong were living with their adult children in 2011, down from 56.8 percent in 2001 (C&SD 2013b). However, regarding elderly people who needed assistance from others in their daily living, only 47.6 percent had caregivers; of these, 37.3 percent had their children, 26.3 percent had their spouses, and 25.6 percent had domestic helpers or nurses as their major caregivers (C&SD 2009).

For elderly parents living with their adult children, family caregiving also confronts a rising threat to family harmony and caregiver well-being. The rise in the number of small households consisting of merely two to three persons, most of whom are dual-wage earners, makes family caregiving difficult. Because of the busy modern lifestyles and the dual roles of both wage earner and homemaker, the strain on family caregivers that comes from caring for frail elderly persons is of deep concern.

For families with the financial resources, there is a recent trend of employing foreign domestic helpers to take up or share the household chores of childcare and care for the elderly. The number of foreign domestic helpers increased from 227,000 in 2001 to 292,000 in 2011 (C&SD 2012b). Most of them come from economically less-developed countries, such as Indonesia, the Philippines, and Thailand. Care of the elderly is a significant part of their work. A survey indicated that 22.3 percent of the surveyed foreign domestic helpers in Hong Kong were working in families with an elderly person aged sixty-five or above (Chiu 2005; see Wang 2016 for foreign domestic eldercare situation in Taiwan). However, cultural differences and language barriers, as well as high market demand for such workers, often lead to issues of turnover and coverage gaps.

To conclude, the changing structure and functions of the family in the context of industrialization and modernization are shaking the cornerstone of the traditional system of care for the elderly. There is doubt whether the policy for care of the elderly can continue to pivot on the significant role of the family. This situation is exacerbated by the lack of adequate community care services (CCS) to support family caregiving.

Without government provision of a wide range of family support services tailored to individual needs, overburdened families have no alternative but to make compromises in their traditional filial responsibility of taking care of their parents and thus have to resort to institutional care (i.e., the RCS). In a study of adults who provided care for their elderly parents and who, having applied for government-subsidized long-term care (LTC) services, were on the government's centralized waiting list in 2008, it was found that about 35 percent of these caregivers showed signs of psychological distress, such as anger and depression (Lou et al. 2011). There is a clear need for more community-based support for familial care in the home.

Hong Kong currently has a higher institutionalization rate than many other countries in the East and West at nearly 7 percent of the elderly people aged sixty-five or above in 2009. Notwithstanding the high institutionalization rate, there have still been long waiting lists for the subsidized RCS services. It takes an average of twenty-three months for a normal case to be admitted successfully to the services (Social Welfare Department of Hong Kong 2018). On the surface, the substantial demand for RCS seems to show a general preference of elderly people or their family members for RCS rather than CCS, but it actually indicates the underdevelopment of CCS. In turn, this demand for RCS also helps to foster the imbalance in the development of RCS and CCS in Hong Kong. It is a vicious cycle: Inadequate CCS leads to familial resort to institutionalization, which further diverts resources away from CCS. Hence, a new policy paradigm of a shared-care model that supports aging in place and care in the community by the community is required.

Review of Hong Kong's Policy for Care of the Elderly

Before introducing the new policy direction, it is necessary to discuss the emergence of an imbalance in the development of RCS versus CCS in Hong Kong. The aforementioned vicious cycle is basically due to the residual-deficit approach to the elderly care policy that has existed since the colonial era. The limited amount of community care services provided by the government has been a large part of the failure to sufficiently support familial efforts to take care of elderly parents amidst rapid population aging in Hong Kong. This section first introduces the imbalanced development of the LTC services in Hong Kong, then discusses the contributions to such imbalances.

Imbalances in the Long-Term Care System in Hong Kong

There are several imbalances in the LTC system in Hong Kong. First, most of the LTC money goes to RCS rather than to CCS, despite the fact that the government has made aging in place a policy objective since the 1970s. According to the budget of the Social Welfare Department of Hong Kong, during 2014–15 the government funded a total of 26,638 RCS places, but only 7,600 home care places and 2,981 adult day-care places. The total spending on RCS was HK$3,901 million (US$ 501.93) versus only HK$851 million (US$109.49) on home care and adult day-care services combined (Government of the HKSAR 2014).

Second, although there are many private RCS providers, most are perceived as providing low-quality services. In fact, this perception has created an imbalance in the demand for publicly funded RCS places. On average, elderly people need to wait for about three years for a government-funded RCS place, while there are vacant beds in private RCS homes. Many middle-class elderly people are also applying for publicly funded RCS places because of the better quality, competing with low-income and disadvantaged elderly people for limited government resources.

The Welfare Ideology of Hong Kong's Policy for Care of the Elderly

Conventional policy for care of the elderly in Hong Kong is a result of two social forces converging in Hong Kong, a colonial city that was populated by refugees and their children after World War II. On the one hand, the colonial government began a social policy to strengthen the legitimacy of colonial rule, being greatly concerned about political and social stability (Wilding 1997) and maintaining economic growth to benefit British companies. On the other hand, the rapidly increasing refugee population had a strong ethic of self-reliance. These refugees came to Hong Kong to escape suffering and persecution from their own government in mainland China and mainly wanted to be left alone, without much government interference in their daily lives.

The desire to have a social policy for tripartite goals of social and political stability, strong economic growth, and minimal engagement between the political elites and the rest of society has led to the adoption of a residual-productivist model of social policy in Hong Kong. The colonial government placed a high priority on economic growth as the main mechanism for improving the welfare of the citizens (Fung 2014). Social policy is subordinated to economic policy, serving a pro-production role (Gough 2004; Holliday 2000, 2005). Apart from assisting in social investment to promote economic development, such as investment in education and health care (Wong 2008), Hong Kong welfare policy is generally based on "familistic residualism." This means that family shoulders the duty of meeting an individual's unmet needs, under the concept of "obligation" in traditional Chinese familism, and state assistance is only the last resort (Chiu and Wong 2005).

Since 1973 the policy for care of the elderly has developed within the same framework. Since the mid-1970s, the Hong Kong government has adopted a community approach as the guiding principle. The term "community" can be broadly interpreted as either "the environment that the elderly know" or "the local sources from which the elderly could possibly obtain care and attention" (Working Party on the Future Needs of the Elderly 1973: 15). This policy orientation was stipulated clearly in the 1991 White Paper on social welfare and has been consistently upheld in the policy addresses of various years since then. In order to achieve its objective, the Hong Kong government has encouraged an approach that enlists the support of the community through "the establishment of networks of informal care and support provided by families, friends and neighbors" (Hong Kong Government 1991: 18). In recent years, the government of the HKSAR has adopted the principle of "aging in place as the core, institutional care as the backup" for developing care services for elderly people (Legislative Council of the HKSAR 2013: 1).

Care Services for the Elderly in Hong Kong

Despite the grand ideal declared in governmental policy papers, the policies and services formulated under the residual model causes the imbalance of development between RCS and CCS, which ultimately leads to the high institutionalization rate in Hong Kong, leaving the principle of "aging in place" as empty rhetoric. The residual model adopted in social policy focuses on deficit instead of strength. It puts the ideology of traditional Chinese familism at its core, engendering a design of welfare programs that would never substitute for or erode the traditional functions of the family (Hong Kong Government 1965). It places emphasis on self-reliance and on not creating a dependency culture (Hong Kong Government 1991: 14). This principle has long weakened the partnership between the government and the family for providing care for the elderly in Hong Kong.

Currently, the provision of both RCS and CCS in Hong Kong is dominated by the government under a publicly funded model that depends heavily on public revenue, mainly from taxes. Conforming to the conventional way services are delivered in Hong Kong, instead of the government delivering the services directly, instead it partners with numerous service operators/ providers, which are usually nongovernmental organizations (NGOs). The government then provides funding for those external service providers to deliver the services, and the Social Welfare Department of Hong Kong manages quality assurance (Chui et al. 2009).[3]

There are three tiers of care services for the elderly that are provided by this government-NGO partnership. The first tier is community support services providing care that is not LTC service. The government funds NGOs to run neighborhood- and district-level care centers for the elderly. These centers promote positive aging in the community through social and educational services. They also provide limited community support, such as meal services and support for caregivers, to promote aging in place in the elderly people's own communities. All members of the centers can enjoy these services and no assessment is needed. During the financial year 2014–15, the government funded forty-one district-level community centers for the elderly; these provided services to frail elderly people to support their living in the community. The government also funded 170 neighborhood-level centers for the elderly; these enable elderly persons to remain in the community, to lead healthy and dignified lives, and to enhance their positive and contributing role in society (Government of the HKSAR 2014). In recent years, the government has also upgraded some of these centers, with the goal of enabling them to provide social care for frail elderly people, including those with dementia. As well as funding the center services, the government has also funded NGOs to provide limited home support services to the elderly through their integrated home care services.

The second tier is community support services for the LTC of frail elderly people. These include the enhanced home and CCS, and adult day-care centers. The enhanced home and CCS provide nursing and social care services in the homes of frail elderly people to promote aging in place. To a lesser extent, they also provide support services to caregivers. To be eligible, an elderly person must be sixty-five years or older and be assessed by the government of the HKSAR (using a standardized instrument) as having either a moderate or severe level of impairment. The services include visiting nurse and rehabilitation services, meal delivery, escort services for medical appointments, helping with chores, and so on. During the financial year 2014–15, there were 7,600 places for enhanced home and CCS.

The third tier is the RCS. In September 2015 Hong Kong had 73,685 residential-care beds for frail elderly people. Of these, the government funded 26,604 beds (36 percent). The rest (64 percent) were in private nursing homes (Social Welfare Department of Hong Kong 2015). However, a majority of these beds in private nursing-home beds are also funded by the government through the welfare system: low-income elderly people can move into these private nursing homes and apply for the welfare program to pay for their stay. The welfare program pays for their housing and living expenses, and the universal health-care system pays for medical care. Thus, the government also pays for their medical care.

New Policy Direction for Care of the Elderly

The polarized development of RCS under the residual-deficit approach of the policy for care of the elderly implies the irreconcilability of government policies in enshrining community care and aging in place. It is a concern whether the current policy framework of forming partnerships with the family and the community for the provision of care for the elderly is in vain and whether it will be able to meet the challenges posed by rapid aging in the coming century. It is conceivable that a system of care for the elderly that relies on government provision of professional-led formal health-care services is unviable and unsustainable. However, as previously mentioned, the compensatory policy model has left the CCS in Hong Kong underdeveloped. Hence, Hong Kong is now overreliant on professional and institutional care.

Efficacious care for the elderly amid the trend of rapid population aging requires strengthening the family and community to form a sustainable system for providing such care. Although there is an inevitable trend toward the weakening of filial piety and familial support, more elderly people in Hong Kong benefit from the help of their families relative to Western countries (Bartlett 2009), and Hong Kong also still has relatively high levels of coresidence of adult children and their older parents. Fifty-one percent of elderly people in Hong Kong were living with their adult child or children in 2011 (C&SD 2013a); in Australia the figure was 9 percent, in Canada 12.7 percent, in the United Kingdom 16 percent, and in the United States 25 percent in the early 2000s (Chui 2007).

A contemporary filial-piety scale, recently developed by Lum et al. (2015) to capture the changing experience and practice of filial piety, has shown that children's affective altruistic concern for their parents—one stemming from the notion of benevolence (*ren*), the very root of filial piety in traditional Confucian thought—still figures prominently in Hong Kong society. Yet, pragmatic accomplishment of filial piety in terms of the children's caregiving practices depends not just on their feelings, but also on their abilities and resources. According to the ten-item two-factor structural model for assessing contemporary filial piety, children still "always care about their parents' well-being" (Lum et al. 2015: 7). This shows that the genuine affection and empathetic bonding between parents and children still exist. Yet, these filial feelings are often translated into actions that do not involve direct in-person intimate care. Hence, children provide financial assistance to their parents when the elders are no longer able to support themselves or arrange for others to care for them when they can no longer care for themselves. Thus, this is a modern pragmatic adaptation of the filial script in which many adult children in Hong Kong today are not necessarily the ones directly serving their parents, but they use various means to arrange that someone takes care of them. Ultimately, filial caregiving is now achieved through "open exchanges of care needs and care capacities between parents and children for establishing a compromised commitment to care" (Lum et al. 2015: 9) through dialogue and negotiation.

In consequence, it is clear that the family is still the bedrock for the provision of care for the majority of the elderly in Hong Kong, but the role of the family has been transformed in accordance with the modern ethics of filial piety. Although the details vary from place to place and time to time, this general theme resonates with examples provided by Ikels (2004) and colleagues who contributed to that edited volume for mainland China, Japan, and Korea for earlier decades. Hong Kong's new policy direction should expand the current CCS to enable the family and community to possess the necessary skills and resources, consonant with the contemporary trends in family composition and modern lifestyles, to provide caregiving to its elders. The government should also encourage the private market to join in more vigorously in community-based service provision, to generate a more viable choice of services to complement informal care. A new family/community shared care approach that places elderly people and their informal caregivers at the center of attention, interacting with a mix of private and public funding and services, is needed. Specialist services would be at the periphery, matched and provided only when elderly people truly need them (Association of Directors of Social Services and Local Government Association 2003). It is possible that a charismatic official similar to the one Tang and Shea describe in China's Jiangxiang (chap. 1), is needed in Hong Kong to shake the area out of the bureaucratic inertia that is still privileging RCS, although dependence on charisma engenders concerns about sustainability over time even when institutional changes are made in response.

This solution is also suitable for mainland China, since the population there is also confronting the same challenge to the traditional social contract for the provision of care for the elderly. Demographic and socioeconomic changes there pose the same crisis—the inability of China's traditional bedrock, the family, to care for the elderly. It is cause for concern that in recent years the Chinese government has relied to an unprecedented extent on RCS homes to provide care for the elderly, in partnership with a large number of private enterprises. Over the past decade an average annual growth of 10 percent in the number of nursing-home beds in China has been achieved, reaching 4.3 million in 2013. The latest national five-year plan has set a target ratio of 30:1,000 (30 nursing-home beds to every 1,000 people). This policy initiative, backed by a revision of national laws and the passing of new rules, shows the extent of the Chinese government's efforts to regulate the RCS system (Shum, Ho, et al. 2015; Shum, Lou, et al. 2015). Although there was a clear dearth of needed residential slots, there is a danger that this trend may go too far as it did in Hong Kong.

The Recent Revamp in Hong Kong's Policy for Care of the Elderly

In recent years, the government of the HKSAR has gradually been expanding its policy options to include an empowerment approach in providing care for the elderly by adopting the money-follows-the-older-person model for LTC. Between 2009 and 2011 the Hong Kong government commissioned the University of Hong Kong to conduct two studies to assess the feasibility of implementing a money-follows-the-older-person scheme for RCS and CCS in Hong Kong. The consulting team concluded that Hong Kong is more ready to implement the new funding mode in CCS than in RCS. Since 2013 the government has implemented a new pilot scheme on CCS vouchers for the elderly. This pilot scheme allows 1,200 elderly people waiting for RCS to receive service vouchers equivalent to about US$770 per month. They can then use the voucher to purchase care services for themselves from designated providers. At present, these designated providers are NGOs or social enterprises that are already providing care services for the elderly. The initial evaluation of the pilot program is positive. The elderly people involved and their families are enjoying the new flexibility. Since the money goes directly to the service users instead of to the service providers, service users can negotiate with service providers for care that better meets their needs. The pilot scheme provides care similar to the participant-directed care in North America or the personalized social care in the United Kingdom. The government plans to extend the voucher program to RCS in 2016. It is hoped that if expanded in the future, this care financing approach can reduce perverse incentives for pushing elders and their families into resorting to RCS that could be avoided with adequate supports.

In 2014 the government of the HKSAR introduced a new pilot scheme on a living allowance for caregivers of elderly persons from low-income families. This pilot program provides a monthly allowance of about US$250 to 2,000 caregivers of elderly persons from low-income families to help supplement their living expenses so that elderly persons in need of LTC services can, with the help of their caregivers, receive proper care that enables them to remain in the community. In this pilot scheme a low-income family is defined as one having an income less than 75 percent of the city's median income. Caregivers and care recipients cannot have any employment relationship (e.g., between an elderly person and their paid domestic helper) and each caregiver can receive up to about US$500 per month for providing care to two elderly people. With this pilot scheme, the Hong Kong government has for the first time provided cash support to caregivers of frail elderly people. The scheme was well received by the participants. It is also hoped that this can be scaled up to further reduce the push forces that have sent elders into unnecessary RCS.

Conclusion

Hong Kong has grown from a small fishing and trading port in south China after World War II to being a major financial center of the world. During the same period, its population swelled from less than 1 million immediately after the war to more than 7 million in 2014. Most of Hong Kong's residents are either immigrants or refugees from mainland China as well as their children and grandchildren. The migration, industrialization, and ultra-low birth rate over the past few decades have weakened the traditional family function of providing care to its young, old, and sick members. To meet the increasing welfare needs of its swelling population and, at the same time, to not overburden the private sector, the Hong Kong government has adopted a familist residual approach as its welfare ideology. Formal care services for the elderly have been provided as a last resort to individuals who do not have the resources to take care of themselves or those who do not have family members to take care of them. Otherwise, the family has been largely left to provide support and care on its own.

Because of its residual welfare ideology, the Hong Kong government has been focusing on building nursing homes and providing subsidized RCS for frail elderly people, even though its stated policy priority has been on aging in place since the mid-1970s. Frail seniors aging in place and family caregivers have been left largely unsupported in the current system. The imbalance between RCS and CCS has led to a vicious cycle of overreliance on RCS, leading to one of the highest nursing-home use rates in the developed countries and the highest in Asia.

Having recognized the imminent silver tsunami, the government of the HKSAR recently changed its policy strategy, piloting the money-follows-the-older-person model in its CCS. The initial pilot scheme, conducted between 2013 and 2015, was largely successful. The government of the HKSAR is in the process of expanding the program to cover more people and piloting a new program to apply the same principle to RCS. The government also, for the first time, provides a cash allowance to low-income caregivers who are taking care of frail elderly people.

We believe these are steps in the right direction. Hong Kong is aging very rapidly. By 2041 one in three Hong Kong residents will be elderly (Government of the HKSAR 2013). The ratio of the number of elderly people to the number of working-age people will have increased from 1:5.3 in 2011 to 1:1.8 by 2041 (Government of the HKSAR 2013). The number of elderly people will have increased from about 1 million people in 2014 to about 2.5 million in 2041 (Government of the HKSAR 2013). By 2039, the number of people with dementia aged sixty and above will have increased from about 103,000 in 2009 to more than 332,000 (Yu et al. 2012). Even though Hong Kong is blessed with a conservative fiscal policy and is able to provide a large number of financial services, in the near future it will not have enough labor power to take care of the large number of elderly people through its formal care services. Hong Kong urgently needs a new approach that empowers family and community members to participate more directly in caring for the elderly.

Michelle Shum (沈希恩) is assistant professor in the Department of Social Work at Hong Kong Baptist University. She is an experienced registered social worker who has wide exposure to a range of social work practices. Her research incorporates legal and institutional analysis into studies of social policy, governance, public administration, nonprofit and social service management, and macro social work practice. Previously, she has also published on policy directions for safeguarding human rights of older persons in nursing homes.

Terry Lum is the Henry G. Leong Professor in social work and social administration at the University of Hong Kong. His research focuses on elderly services and policies. He was elected as a Fellow by the Gerontological Society of America in 2011 and was awarded the Career Leadership Award by the Association of Gerontology Education in Social Work (AGESW) in the United States in 2016. Dr. Lum's research has been featured in many scholarly journals and edited volumes.

Glossary

ren	仁	Benevolence or "human-heartedness," having a kind disposition toward and taking care of others who are in need of care, a Confucian value.
zijia ren	自家人	My own people, people who are in my family or so close that they are considered to be a part of my family.

Notes

1. According to Census and Statistics Department of Hong Kong (2012b: FA3), the term "domestic household" means people who are living under the same roof, whether related or not, and sharing food and expenses. This excludes those nondomestic households that consist of people living in institutions and mobile residents (as defined under the resident population concept).
2. The Special Scheme for Families with Elderly Persons was originally for provision of special treatment for public rental housing applicants willing to take care of their parents but preferring to have separate flats allocated in two public housing units within the same vicinity.
3. With reference to Chui et al (2009), the institutionalization rate in Hong Kong is the percentage of the older persons aged sixty-five or above residing in institutions that provide residential care. This calculation is compatible with the OECD Health Policies studies by Colombo et al. (2011: 301) about LTC service. Please refer to Chui et al (2009: 10) for the comparison of the institutionalization rate of other countries.

References

Association of Directors of Social Services and Local Government Association (ADSS and LGA). 2003. *All Our Tomorrows: Inverting the Triangle of Care.* London: ADSS and LGA.

Bartlett, Helen. 2009. "Growing Old in a Global City: The Challenge of Urbanization for Active Aging in Hong Kong." In *Aging in Asia,* ed. Jason L. Powell and Ian G. Cook, 41–65. New York: Nova Science.

Census and Statistics Department of Hong Kong (C&SD). 1975. *Births, Deaths & Marriage 1970–1973.* Hong Kong: Hong Kong Government Press.

————. 2009. *Thematic Household Survey Report—Report No. 40: Socio-Demographic Profile, Health Status and Self-Care Capability of Older Persons.* Hong Kong: Hong Kong Census and Statistics Department. Retrieved 28 July 2015 from http.censtatd.gov .hk/hkstat/sub/sp160.jsp?productCode=C0000071.

————. 2012a. *Demographic Trends in Hong Kong 1981–2011.* Hong Kong: Hong Kong Census and Statistics Department. Retrieved 28 July 2015 from http.statistics.gov. hk/pub/B1120017032012XXXXB0100.pdf

————. 2012b. *Trends in Population and Domestic Households in Hong Kong.* Hong Kong: Hong Kong Census and Statistics Department. Retrieved 28 July 2015 from http. censtatd.gov.hk/hkstat/sub/sp160.jsp?productCode=FA100119.

————. 2012c. *2011 Population Census Summary Results.* Hong Kong: Hong Kong Census and Statistics Department. Retrieved 28 July 2015 from http.census2011.gov .hk/pdf/summary-results.pdf.

————. 2013a. *The Profile of the Population in One-Person Households in 2011.* Hong Kong: Hong Kong Census and Statistics Department. Retrieved 28 July 2015 from http.censtatd.gov.hk/hkstat/sub/sp170.jsp?productCode=FA100266.

————. 2013b. *Thematic Report: Older Persons.* Hong Kong: Hong Kong Census and Statistics Department. Retrieved 28 July 2015 from http.census2011.gov.hk/pdf/ older-persons.pdf.

————. 2013c. *Hong Kong Population Projections: 2012–2041.* Hong Kong: Demographic Statistics Section, Census and Statistics Department. Retrieved 28 July 2015 from http.statistics.gov.hk/pub/B1120015052012XXXXB0100.pdf.

————. 2018. *Fertility Trend in Hong Kong, 1981 to 2017.* Hong Kong: Demographic Statistics Section, Census and Statistics Department. Retrieved 25 October 2019 from https.statistics.gov.hk/pub/B71812FA2018XXXXB0100.pdf

Chi, Iris, and Nelson Chow. 1997. "Housing and Family Care for the Elderly in Hong Kong." *Ageing International* 23 (3): 65–77. Retrieved 30 July 2015 from doi: 10.1007/s12126-997-1005-2.

Chiu, Sammy, and Victor Wong. 2005. "Hong Kong: From Familistic to Confucian Welfare." In *East Asian Welfare Regimes in Transition: From Confucianism to Globalization,* ed. Alan Walker and Chack-kie Wong, 73–94. Bristol, UK: Policy Press.

Chiu, Stephen Wing-kai. 2005. *A Stranger in the House: Foreign Domestic Helpers in Hong Kong.* Hong Kong: Hong Kong Institute of Asia-Pacific Studies, Chinese University of Hong Kong.

Chow, Nelson. 1999. "Diminishing Filial Piety and the Changing Role and Status of the Elders in Hong Kong." *Hallym International Journal of Aging* 1 (1): 67–77.

————. 2007. "Aging and the Family in Hong Kong." *International Journal of Sociology of the Family* 33 (1): 145–55.

Chow, Nelson, and Terry Lum. 2008. *Trends in Family Attitudes and Values in Hong Kong.* Hong Kong: Department of Social Work and Social Administration, University of Hong Kong.

Chui, Ernest. 2003. "Unmasking the 'Naturalness' of 'Community Eclipse:' The Case of Hong Kong." *Community Development Journal* 38 (2): 151–63.

————. 2007. "Changing Norms and Pragmatics of Co-Residence in East Asian Countries." *International Journal of Sociology of the Family* 33 (1): 1–24.

Chui, Ernest, Kin-sun Chan, Alice Chong, Lisanne Ko, Stephen Law, Chi-kwan Law, Edward Leung, Angela Leung, Vivian Lou, and Silvia Ng. 2009. *Elderly Commission's Study on Residential Care Services for the Elderly Final Report.* Hong Kong: Elderly

Commission. Retrieved 30 July 2015 from https://www.elderlycommission.gov
.hk/en/download/library/Residential%20Care%20Services%20-%20Final%20
Report(eng).pdf.

Colombo, Francesca, Llena-Nozal, Ana, Mercier Jérôme, and Tjadens Frits. 2011. *Help
Wanted? Providing and Paying for Long-Term Care: Providing and Paying for Long-Term
Care.* Organisation for Economic Co-operation and Development Health Policy
Studies. Paris: Organisation for Economic Co-operation and Development.

Department of Health of Hong Kong. 2016. "Life Expectancy at Birth (Male and
Female), 1971–2014." Retrieved 24 April 2020 from http.chp.gov.hk/en/
data/4/10/27/111.html. Currently available at https://www.healthyhk.gov.hk/
phisweb/en/healthy_facts/health_indicators/life_exp/.

Fei, Hsiao-tùng. 1992. *From the Soil, the Foundations of Chinese Society: A Translation of
Fei Xiaotong's Xiangtu Zhongguo, with an Introduction and Epilogue,* trans. Gary G.
Hamilton and Wang Zheng. Berkeley: University of California Press.

Fung, Kwok-kin. 2014. "Financial Crisis and the Developmental States: A Case Study of
Hong Kong." *International Journal of Social Welfare* 23: 321–32.

Gough, Ian. 2004. "East Asia: The Limits of Productivist Regimes." In *Insecurity and
Welfare Regimes in Asia, Africa and Latin America: Social Policy in Development Contexts,* ed. Ian Gough, Geof Wood, Philippa Bevan, Armando Barrientos, Peter Davis, and Graham Room, 69–201. Cambridge, UK: Cambridge University Press.

Government of the HKSAR. 2013. "The 2013–14 Budget: Budget Speech." Retrieved
20 July 2015 from http.budget.gov.hk/2013/eng/budget27.html.

———. 2014. "Head 170: Social Welfare Department." Retrieved 4 January 2016
from http://budget.gov.hk/2014/eng/pdf/head170.pdf.

Holliday, Ian. 2005. "East Asian Social Policy in the Wake of the Financial Crisis: Fare-
well to Productivism?" *Policy and Politics* 33: 145–62.

———. 2000. "Productivist Welfare Capitalism: Social Policy in East Asia." *Political
Studies* 48: 706–23.

Hong Kong Government. 1965. *Aims and Policy of Social Welfare in Hong Kong.* Hong
Kong: Hong Kong Government Printer.

———. 1991. *Social Welfare into the 1990s and Beyond.* Hong Kong: Hong Kong Government Printer.

Hong Kong Housing Authority. 2018. "Harmonious Families Priority Scheme." Last
revision 3 August 2018. Retrieved 24 March 2020 fromhttps://www.housing
authority.gov.hk/en/flat-application/harmonious-families-priority-scheme/index.
html.

Ikels, Charlotte, ed. 2004. *Filial Piety: Practice and Discourse in Contemporary East Asia.*
Stanford, CA: Stanford University Press.

Lai, Daniel. 2013. "Support and Care for Aging Chinese: A Comparison of Guangzhou, Hong Kong and Taipei." In *International Handbook of Chinese Families,* ed.
Chan Kwok-bun, 289–303. New York: Springer. Retrieved 23 July 2015 from doi:
10.1007/978-1-4614-0266-4_17.

Lee, Jik Jeon, and Iris Chi. 1999. "Determinants of Life Satisfaction among the Chinese
Elderly in Hong Kong." *Hong Kong Journal of Gerontology* 4 (1): 29–39.

Legislative Council of HKSAR. 2013. *Support Services for Carers of the Elderly and Persons with Disabilities.* Retrieved 20 May 2015 from http://legco.gov.hk/yr12-13/
english/panels/ltcp/papers/ltcp0528cb2-1178-1-e.pdf.

Lou, Vivian, Chi Wai Kwan, Angela Leung, and Iris Chi. 2011. "Psychological Distress among Chinese Adult-Child Caregivers: The Effects of Behavioral and Cognitive Components of Care." *Home Health Care Services Quarterly* 30 (3): 133–46.

Lubben, James E, and Iris Chi. 1993. "Cross-National Comparison of Social Support among the Elderly Chinese and Chinese Americans." Paper presented at the 14th World Congress of Gerontology, Budapest, Hungary.

Lum, Terry, Elsie Yan, Andy Ho, Michelle Shum, Gloria Wong, Mandy Lau, and Junfang Wang. 2015. "Measuring Filial Piety in the Twenty-First Century: Development, Factor Structure and Reliability of the 10-Item Contemporary Filial Piety Scale (CFPS-10)." *Journal of Applied Gerontology* 35 (11): 1235–47.

Mulvey, Thomas J. 2005. "Hong Kong Families in the Twenty-First Century." In *Social Development in Hong Kong: The Unfinished Agenda*, ed. Richard J. Estes, 225–36. New York: Oxford University Press.

Ngan, Man-hung. 1990. "The Informal Caring Networks among Chinese Families in Hong Kong." PhD dissertation, University of Hong Kong, Hong Kong.

Shum, Michelle, Andy Ho, Hao Luo, Ying Wang, Junfang Wang, and Terry Lum. 2015. "Protecting the Rights of Chinese Older Persons in Need of Residential Care: The Social Justice and Health Equity Dilemma in the People's Republic of China." In *Towards Human Rights in Residential Care for Older Persons: International Perspectives*, ed. Helen Meenan, Nicola Rees, and Israel Doron, 66–84. London: Routledge.

Shum, Michelle, Vivian Lou, Kelly He, Coco Chan, and Junfang Wang. 2015. "The 'Leap Forward' in Nursing Home Development in Urban China: Future Policy Directions." *Journal of the American Medical Directors Association* 16 (9): 784–89.

Social Welfare Department of Hong Kong (SWD). 2015. "Overview of Residential Care Services for Elders." Retrieved 2 January 2016 from http://swd.gov.hk/en/index/site_pubsvc/page_elderly/sub_residentia/id_overviewon/.

———. 2018. "Waiting List for Subsidised Residential Care Services for the Elderly" Retrieved 22 January 2019 from https://swd.gov.hk/storage/asset/section/632/en/LTC_statistics_HP-Eng(201809).pdf.

Tönnies, Ferdinand. 1957. *Community and Society: Gemeinschaft und Gesellschaft.* transl. and ed. by Charles P. Loomis. East Lansing: Michigan State University Press.

United Nations (UN). 2015. *United Nations World Population Prospects: 2015 Revision.* Department of Economic and Social Affairs. New York: United Nations.

Wang, Pin. 2016. "Fighting For or Against a Long-Term Care Insurance in Taiwan: NGOs' Divide." Society for East Asian Anthropology Conference, Chinese University of Hong Kong, Hong Kong, 19–22 June.

Weber, Max. 1921. *Economy and Society.* München: Drei Masken Verlag.

Wilding, Paul. 1997. "Social Policy and Social Development in Hong Kong." *Asian Journal of Public Administration* 19 (2): 244–75.

Wong, Chack Kie. 2008. "Squaring the Welfare Circle in Hong Kong: Lessons for Governance in Social Policy." *Asian Survey* 48 (2): 323–42.

Working Party on the Future Needs of the Elderly. 1973. *Services for the Elderly.* Hong Kong: Hong Kong Government Printer.

Yu, Ruby, Pui Hing Chau, Sarah M. McGhee, Wai Ling Cheung. Kam Che Chan, Sai Hei Cheung, and Jean Woo. 2012. "Trends in Prevalence and Mortality of Dementia in Elderly Hong Kong Population: Projections, Disease Burden, and Implications for Long-Term Care." *International Journal of Alzheimer's Disease*, article # 406852.

5 TEACH ME TO BE FILIAL

Intergenerational Care in Singapore Families

Leng Leng Thang and Kalyani Mehta

Introduction: A Commercial to Promote Filial Piety

INTO CONTEMPORARY TIMES, ATTEMPTS TO cultivate the value of filial piety (for definition, see Introduction) starts young in many East Asian settings, including Singapore. In June 2010, as part of the ThinkFamily campaign initiated by National Family Council under the Ministry of Community Development, Youth and Sports (MCYS), a public service announcement was released on television aimed at promoting the value of filial piety to the young in Singapore.[1] More commonly known as a short film on filial piety, it is entitled *Father and Son.*[2] The story in the film revolves around a boy's realization about the unfailing parent and child bond manifested through his father's filial care of his grandmother. In the film, the young teenage son was shown watching his father tenderly care for his dying grandmother and wondering why his father would feel sad about a woman who has given the family a difficult time in her old age. His grandmother has moved in with them since she was widowed, but has apparently suffered from dementia that has adversely affected her behavior. The reason was shown in a flashback to a scene in 1960s Singapore when the grandmother—a young mother, then—was drenched in the rain rushing her sick son to the hospital. In the waiting room, she cradled her son in her arms singing the old Hokkien classic "Dark Skies" (*ti o o*). Toward the end of the film, the scene cuts back to the hospital bedside, where the father is seen singing the same Hokkien classic to his unconscious aged mother. His son looks on with tears in his eyes and seems to understand now. Here the tag line came on to capture the essence: "How one generation loves, the next generation learns." This widely known three-minute public service announcement, which will be an important touchstone for this chapter, can be seen on YouTube at https://www.youtube.com/watch?v=ybxNkpS5q-g&t=7s.

Eventually winning the Viewers' Choice 2010 Singapore commercial award, this short film was successful in raising awareness on filial piety. Popularity of the film rose very rapidly, garnering a mixture of both praise and criticism from the public (Nazeer and Heng 2010). Upon its launch, the "Myfilialpiety" Facebook page, which was set up as a companion to the TV commercial, was liked by 15,000 fans in just a few days. Examination of a blog site sheds light on what kinds of attitudes and sentiments underlie both positive and negative responses to the film. At the time there was a blog site, which no longer exists, that was an important blog space to which mainly youths and young adults posted responses to the film: http://sg.yfitopost blog.com/. On that site, 756 responses were posted in the first few days of the release of the film. The responses that were positive focused on how viewers were deeply touched by the film and on how the film brought awareness to the need to bond with one's family. The critical responses argued that the film belittled the contributions and significance of daughters-in-law in the family and stereotyped elderly people as unreasonably demanding. There were also many people posting who complained that the government was responsible for the problems surrounding eldercare, due to hefty medical costs, the high cost of living, and the heavy workload that together have left young people in Singapore with little time to care and provide for aging parents.

The widespread popularity of the film and the controversy that it generated signal the need to reevaluate the common societal notion that filial piety is quietly declining among the young in Singapore.[3] Contrary to that notion, the issues surrounding the tradition of filial piety and the dilemma of caring for older members at home in a rapidly aging modern society are a heated concern for many Singaporeans. Not only are middle-aged adult children and their parents moved by these issues, but so too are youths who are the grandchildren of today's elderly in Singapore.

The film suggested to Singaporeans that to *teach* filial piety to the young, parents should lead by example through their filial acts toward the older generation. There have been various studies examining filial piety in the Asian context, looking at, for example, perceptions of filial piety by older adults in China (e.g., Mao and Chi 2011) and redefinitions of the meaning of filial piety in contemporary socioeconomic realities (Ikels 2004b). However, there is no study found focusing on understanding how children perceive the practices of filial piety as displayed by their parents toward their grandparents.

In order to make sense of social responses to the widely discussed *Father and Son* short film and to contribute to filling in the previously discussed gap in the scholarly literature, in this chapter we address the following set of questions: In what ways does the older generation serve as a role model for the next generation in filial responsibility? Will filial piety practices manifested as coresidential living be sustained over time? Do the children see their parents' path as caregivers as something that is both desirable and feasible for themselves? What do youths regard as possible strategies that will enable them to assume caregiving of their parents?

To answer these research questions, in the pages that follow we examine the voices of grandchildren mostly in their twenties to understand how Chinese Singaporean youths and young adults view their parents' acts of caregiving for their grandparents, as well as their role as grandchildren in helping with grandparent care. We argue that, in contrast to notions that Singaporeans are becoming less filial and are abandoning their parents, they are instead very concerned as to how they can realize their values in the face of considerable challenges. Such challenges include financial constraints, lack of time, lack of sibling support and other external factors that hinder their ability to carry out their ideals in reality. Set against the backdrop of life-course and demographic changes, the findings suggest that caregiving for the elderly is gradually undergoing transformation in Singapore, and this is, in turn, leading to perceived changes in the performance of filial practices manifested through emerging changes in living arrangements and care roles related to support for elderly family members.

Filial Piety in Contemporary Singapore

In an ethnographic study of Chinese intergenerational relations in modern Singapore, Goransson (2009) quotes her respondent's (a female Singaporeans in her mid-twenties) definition of filial piety: "What do I mean by filial piety? Basically, to take care of your parents when they grow old and are not able to take care of themselves. Then you will basically respect and honor them." This quote does indeed spell out the essence of filial piety as respect and care for older persons. In Singapore filial piety is intimately linked with intergenerational relationships in the family, where intergenerational coresidence is regarded to be an outward display of filial piety (Phua and Loh 2008: 669).

Singapore is a multicultural society with Chinese as the majority population. Among its population of 5.64 million people in 2018, resident population (citizen and permanent residents) comprised 3.99 million, of whom 74.3 percent are of Chinese origin, with the other two major ethnic groups—the Malays and Indians—making up 13.4 percent and 9 percent, respectively (Singapore Department of Statistics 2019). Confucian philosophy underlies the foundation of Chinese culture in Singapore. Among the

Chinese, a variety of faiths are practiced with the majority affiliated to Buddhism and Taoism and about 20 percent identifying as Christian (Phua and Loh 2008).

Originating from the Chinese word *xiao* (see Introduction), filial piety began among the Chinese as a Confucian value. In recent decades changes in demography, modernization, and other social forces have influenced the translation of filial concepts into daily reality (Ikels 2004b; Thang 2010). Jernigan and Jernigan (1992) raise the point that "historic and classical meanings . . . need to be examined in terms of the ethical situation in the contemporary family as it interacts with the modern world" (97). Phua and Loh's (2008) study of filial piety and intergenerational coresidence among Chinese Singaporeans has highlighted filial piety as a dynamic concept open to multiple interpretations. Symbolic expression of ideals can be contrasted with the actual practice of filial piety, with the understanding that symbolic expression still plays a part in maintaining the well-being of both elders and younger generations (674). The changing interpretation of what counts as filial piety among Singaporeans as they attempt to retain the essence of filial values within challenging circumstances has also been documented (Mehta and Ko 2004).

With occasional media reports on the abandonment of elderly parents by their unfilial children, laments surrounding concerns about the weakening norms and practices of filial piety are not uncommon in Singapore. This trend is similar to public discourses on filial piety in other Confucian-influenced societies (see Introduction). Such societal concerns, especially worries that filial values have declined among the younger generation, have led to various governmental measures attempting to uphold the practice of filial piety. In 1994 the Singapore government introduced the Family Values campaign to promote five core family values deemed as important for the well-being of families and as underpinning the social progress of Singapore: (1) love, care, and concern; (2) mutual respect; (3) filial responsibility; (4) commitment; and (5) communication (Tambyah and Tan 2013: 80). While a 2010 survey commissioned by the National Family Council has indicated a general positive climate toward sustaining filial responsibility and other family values, concerns for its decline remains, as articulated in the interview of an MCYS spokesman, "Singapore's population is rapidly ageing and the traditional value of filial piety may be lost in an increasingly globalized society." (Nazeer and Heng 2010). Such awareness of the challenges to these values also led to the aforementioned 2010 ThinkFamily campaign, which featured a series of short public service announcements. The *Father and Son* film mentioned previously was the last installment of the campaign films.

By 1995 Singapore had already passed the Maintenance of Parents Act, which Goransson (2009: 159) would refer to as a contractual relationship between parents and children made concrete in legal form. This legal act enables parents sixty years old and older who are unable to support themselves to seek maintenance from their children. Similar to public responses to the short film described above, the Maintenance of Parents Act has raised questions concerning whether the act of filial piety, which should ideally be performed out of a child's heartfelt willingness, can and should be legally regulated. In 2011 the act was amended to promote a "conciliation first" approach to help parents and children resolve their differences without legal action if possible. The results were encouraging with fewer elderly parents going to court to seek maintenance from their children; the number of such cases filed in court dropped from 110 in 2011 to 84 in 2012, reflecting the positive impact of mediation (Chang 2013).

Among the practices demonstrating filial piety, intergenerational coresidence has traditionally been viewed in Chinese societies as an ideal display of filial piety (Phua and Loh 2008: 662). For example, Wang's (2004: 32) study of ritualistic coresidence performed by newly married couples in a Chinese rural village further showed the significance of coresidence as a "public statement and affirmation of one's filial piety" in the rural context.

However, it is more appropriate to regard the nuclear household type of living arrangement as a strong norm in Singapore, facilitated by public housing policies as well as changing attitudes now leaning toward a preference for privacy. The 2011 National Survey of Senior Citizens (N = 5,000 aged fifty-five years old and above) showed that living in a nuclear family household with spouse and children was already the most common living arrangement, although there was a small decline therein from 37.1 percent in 1995 to 32.6 percent in 2011. Part of that decline is related to a rise in the percentage of those living alone and living with their spouse only—together that rate more than tripled, from 8.3 percent in 1995 to 27.1 percent in 2011. The type of living arrangement seeing the largest proportional decline has been in the category of those living with spouse, children, and grandchildren; such three-generation households fell from 12.1 percent in 1995 to 6.5 percent in 2011 (Kang, Tan, and Yap 2013: 22).

While the trend toward a decline in coresidence in Singapore may be interpreted by some as a decline in filial piety, there are indeed various indicators to suggest that extended family arrangements of intergenerational support can be manifested in different forms, questioning the expectation for coresidence as a mandatory precondition for filial piety. Qualitative research has shown that within the family there are exchanges of financial, social, and instrumental help among multigenerational households and among family members living in nearby geographical proximity (Mehta

2007; Mehta and Thang 2006). Living nearby facilitates intergenerational exchanges and can be regarded as a modified extended family arrangement (Quah 1998). More married children are shown living together or within the same estate (i.e., residential complex or apartment building) as their parents. Compared with 29 percent in 1998, the 2008 Sample Household Survey of 7,902 households in the public housing estates of Singapore (where more than 85 percent of the population lives) showed an increase to 36 percent adult children and their parents living together or close by one another (Housing & Development Board [HDB] 2010: 20). In 2013, when the HDB piloted eighty-four units of new three-generation apartments with four bedrooms and three baths, responses from the public were encouraging (Au-Yong 2014). With continuing policies that provide grants for parents and children who move to live together or near each other, it is likely that figures will remain quite stable at about 30 percent among adult children who live together or near their parents.

The 2008 Sample Household Survey also showed that family ties remained strong, and the majority of residents (aged twenty-one years old and above) surveyed indicated satisfaction with their family life and placed importance on it. Similarly, the elderly scored good family relationships as the second-most important reason for their satisfaction with life. However, with the rising cost of living, financial inadequacy remains the most important cause of concern. Expected increase in the age sixty-five and older population is more than two-fold from 9 percent in 2010 to 18.7 percent by 2030. Together with perceived changes in social values, population changes raise concerns for both the state and individuals about whether and how family can continue to be a reliable form of support, and whether filial values will remain strong enough to maintain intergenerational ties and ensure informal elder support (Committee on Ageing Issues 2006: 2; Wong and Teo 2011: 2).

Methods and Data

The voices of the twenty-four young Chinese Singaporeans in this chapter are derived from a 2010 project titled "A Qualitative Study on Informal Caregiving and Its Impact on Intergenerational Relationships," commissioned by the then Ministry of Community Development, Youth and Sports (MCYS).[4] These twenty-four respondents formed part of the seventy-five interviews in the project, which also consisted of interviews with four other non-Chinese youths, thirty middle-generation caregivers (referred to here with the term "link parents" for those individuals who link the grandparents' and grandchildren's generations), two female spousal caregivers and fifteen foreign domestic workers (FDWs).[5] They were all from families that had an elderly person who required caregiving at home. Face-to-face interviews were conducted with the respondents, usually in their homes. Interviews generally lasted for one to two hours; they were voice recorded and fully transcribed and translated to English in cases where they were interviewed in another language (Mandarin, Chinese dialects, or Malay). Interviews in English were transcribed verbatim, which may account for Singlish (a variety of English spoken locally) in the transcripts. The data did not seek to be representative; however, the data illustrate some typical Singaporean families from different income backgrounds. The twenty-four Chinese grandchildren ranged from age fifteen to twenty-nine, with most of them between the ages of twenty to twenty-six (seventeen out of the twenty-four respondent grandkids were in that age range). There were thirteen females and eleven males, and all were single at the time of the interview. Voices from the link parent generation (see definition above earlier in this paragraph) are included where appropriate in the analysis.

Table 5.1 provides details on the different patterns of living arrangements among the grandchildren. More grandchildren in this group of grandchildren were living in three-generational households (nine) or used to live in three-generation households before their grandparents living with them passed away (five). The remaining ten were living with parents only. In Singapore it is common for adult children to live with their parents when they are single. All the grandchildren in this study had some experience with caring for the elderly, and/or had seen how family members care for their elderly.

Data collection from the grandchildren who were children of the link parents was most challenging. Besides the fact that the grandchildren were extremely busy since most were in secondary or tertiary education, or were working adults, we also realized that some link parents were not quite willing for us to interview their children, with reasons that they are either "not close to the grandparent who needs care" or "too busy with school work and activities." It appears that some link parents might feel apologetic to their children for affecting them (such as asking them to give up their room to the elderly, or the family finances becoming tight with the need to pay for medical and other care for the elderly). On the other hand, we were able to interview grandchildren who were willing to share their experiences with us even though their parents declined to be interviewed. To circumvent this obstacle, we extended our interviews to a small number of nieces and nephews of the link parents and included grandchildren who were not associated with the link parent caregivers. In addition, we also extended the search for grandchildren to those who were keen to share with us their experiences of caregiving for grandparents who had recently passed away.

TABLE 5.1. Profile of 24 Chinese Grandchildren.

Grandchildren Respondents	Age	Gender	Religion	Occupation	Living Arrangement (Coresiding Members)
A	18	Female	No religion	Working temp job (patient service assistant)	Three generation: Parents, siblings, FDWs, grandparent
B	19	Female	Buddhism	Undergraduate student	Three generation: Parents, siblings, uncle, grandparent
C	24	Male	Buddhism	Student (trainee teacher course)	Nuclear: Parents
D	23	Female	Christianity	Working temp job and waiting to enter art academy	Three generation: Parents, FDWs, grandparent
E	29	Male	No religion	Working as corporate gift sales executive	Nuclear: Parents, sibling
F	21	Male	Christianity	Undergraduate student	Three generation: Parents, siblings, eldest aunt, grandparent
G	24	Male	Christianity	Looking for job	Three generation: Parents, siblings, FDWs, grandparent
H	24	Male	No religion	Undergraduate student	Nuclear: Parents, sibling
I	20	Female	Taoism	Undergraduate student	Nuclear: Parents, siblings, FDWs, grandparent
J	19	Female	Christianity	Student	Nuclear: Parents, sibling
K	26	Male	Catholicism	Banker	Nuclear: Parents, sibling
L	15	Female	Buddhism	Student	Three generation: Parents, sibling, FDWs, grandparent
M	25	Female	Buddhism	Manager	Three generation: Aunt, grandparent
N	20	Female	No religion	Undergraduate student	Nuclear: Parents, sibling

Grandchildren Respondents	Age	Gender	Religion	Occupation	Living Arrangement (Coresiding Members)
O	26	Female	Catholicism	Executive	Nuclear (used to be three generation): Parents, sibling (deceased grandparent)
P	17	Female	No religion	Student	Nuclear: Parents, siblings
Q	24	Male	No religion	Undergraduate student	Nuclear (used to be three generation): Parents, sibling (paternal grandparents deceased)
R	25	Male	No religion	Graduate student	Nuclear (used to be three generation): Parents, siblings, FDWs (paternal grandmother deceased)
S	25	Female	No religion	Working as admin executive; part-time undergraduate	Nuclear: Parents, sibling
T	22	Male	No religion	Undergraduate student	Nuclear: Parents, siblings
U	29	Female	Taoism	Executive	Nuclear (used to be three generation): Mother, aunt's family (Maternal grandmother deceased)
V	23	Female	Buddhism	Civil servant	Three generation: Parents, siblings, FDWs, living with elderly
W	23	Male	No religion	Undergraduate student	Nuclear (used to be three generation): Parents, sibling (Paternal grandfather deceased)
X	21	Male	No religion	Student (admitted to Nanyang Technological University)	Nuclear: Parents, siblings

Among the grandchildren interviewed, five were grandchildren whose grandparents had passed away five months to two years before the time of interview. We note that the selection of the grandchildren respondents might be biased toward those who tended to be particularly concerned with intergenerational support, more so than their peers are. Nonetheless, it is valuable and socially significant to examine what they had to say about their views, experiences, and intentions. They represent a fast-emerging group of youths and young adults that will be faced with the caregiving needs of their grandparents with the continuing rapid aging of Singapore society. In the next section, we present a vignette of a family providing eldercare through the perspective of an eighteen-year-old granddaughter.

Family Caring for the Elderly at Home

To eighteen-year-old Cherie (pseudonym, respondent A), her notion of family has always included her grandparents, in addition to her parents and her two other siblings. Her maternal grandparents began living together with them since the birth of her eldest sibling. There was a brief period in which they had lived on their own after the family moved to the current apartment, but the separate living arrangement lasted less than a year with the need to move back when her grandmother started to show signs of deterioration in her dementia, which affected her ability to take care of herself. Cherie's mother was a full-time career woman who often needed to work late. At home, they employed an FDW who cared for the elderly (Cherie's grandmother and grandfather), and also depended on the help of the grandchildren.

Growing up, Cherie was close to her grandparents who lived with her parents and took care of Cherie and her siblings when they were little. Cherie had fond memories of the time they spent together. When her grandfather had a fall and eventually became bedridden, it was difficult for the FDW who needed to care for both of Cherie's grandparents, especially because her grandmother's condition was worsening and there were times that she would wander out and could not find her way back home. Eventually, Cherie's grandmother had to move in to a nursing home so that the FDW could better cope with caring for just Cherie's grandfather who remained at home. The nursing home that Cherie's grandmother entered was private and conveniently located; this helped to facilitate visits by the aunts and uncles, as well as other relatives such as the grand-aunts who visited her grandmother every other day. Although the grand-aunts had objected to the idea of a nursing home, her mother still thought it was a better option than the alternative of hiring another FDW and managing more people at home. Nonetheless, once her grandfather passed away two years later, her grandmother was immediately brought home, because her mother firmly believed that home care is still better than nursing-home care.

Cherie saw how her grandmother aged and changed over the years. Cherie recounted that, as her grandmother's dementia worsened, communication with her became increasingly difficult. There was a period when Cherie, busy with preparation for an important national school examination, found her grandmother's behavior disruptive.

> Cherie: She kept saying the same things over and over again. So it was like doing something unnecessary due to feeling idle [*mei shi zhao shi zuo*]. I guess she got bored watching TV, so she started talking and talking. It was quite bad.

Cherie could also feel the tension at home between her father and her grandmother because her father was an impatient person, and would get annoyed with her grandmother's behavior like moving his stuff around and so on. Cherie's father also often complained about the unfairness of relying only on his wife to shoulder the care when there were four other siblings who could help out. It was a particularly stressful time for the family when they needed to take care of both grandparents. Her grandmother was displaying aggressive behavior then; accusations and quarrels with the grandfather and others were frequent. The frequent quarrels stressed out the whole family, who often ended up arguing over how best to handle the situation.

Cherie empathized with her mother's plight as her mother put in a lot of effort to provide care for her grandmother. At the same time, Cherie also observed the positive sense of closeness and the everyday pleasures shared between her grandmother and mother, such as when her mother gently held hands with her grandmother and reminisced about the past with occasional laughter. When they were deciding whether to continue to leave her grandmother at the nursing home a few years ago, Cherie's aunts and uncles had discussed the possibility of practicing rotation of care among the siblings (compare with Jing 2004 on meal rotation). However, the aunts' and uncles' families were having difficulties accommodating an elderly person in their homes, and Cherie's mother was really concerned that the other siblings and their spouses did not know how to provide proper care. Cherie's eldest aunt had expected that the eldest uncle should take care given the norm in Chinese culture. As the eldest son, her uncle had agreed to do so. However, Cherie's mother, although the second-youngest daughter in the family, insisted that she should be the one responsible, because she saw herself as the most suitable person to provide for her mother.

Although there were stressful times, overall Cherie felt that her family was coping okay, although she hoped that her aunts and uncles could be more proactive in their support. Compared to before, she thought that her grandmother's behavior had improved, and she had been calmer. Cherie mused, "She is very cute now, although she doesn't really remember a lot of things. So when you talk to her, she will just laugh with you, it is very simple." Cherie spoke to her grandma in Teochew dialect, telling her secrets "because if I tell her now, she will forget, so it is like, there is someone to keep that secret for me." She saw her and the other family members' role as providing emotional support to her grandmother and her parents, while her mother remains the primary caregiver in charge of care provision and financial support. Cherie communicates an awareness that eldercare at home would not be possible even for her mother who was eager to take on the challenge if not for the availability of FDWs to assume the physical care.

Having watched her mother's experience in caring for her grandmother, Cherie said she and her siblings would do the same for her own parents. Cherie promised, "Should anything happen to them, we will take care of them, definitely—the three of us. . . . Everything. As long as I can do it, then I will do it." Imagining when she herself becomes a grandparent herself in the far future, Cherie said, "I hope that they [my children] will be able to let me stay with them. That's it. [But it also] depends on what illness or disease I have. Besides staying with them, maybe [they should] get a nurse—if I do need one." Cherie believed that it is best for the elderly to be taken care of by the family, "because you recognize them as part of your life already. So you will feel the love that they will give you."

Influence of the Middle Generation's Care of Their Aging Parents on the Next Generation

Cherie's family situation is not unique among Singaporean families in their efforts to care for their elderly at home instead of resorting to institutionalization. Her family story is a display of resilience and flexibility, at the same time showing the determination of a daughter (her mother) as the primary caregiver; who insisted on following what she believed to be the best care, instead of adhering to the norm of letting her mother live with the eldest son's family. It expresses the practice of filial piety as one that encompasses love, commitment, and sacrifice. For Cherie, much like the boy in *Father and Son* who had gone through the ups and downs of living with an elderly person with dementia, she was socialized to internalize the filial values learned through her mother's example.

As we will discuss below, parents play a salient role in setting forth examples of filial piety and socializing the next generation into carrying on with the value. Witnessing their parents care for their grandparents, these grandchildren have their concerns about caring for their own parents in the future.

The grandchildren in this study have all provided support to their grandparents in one way or another, although not all of them lived with their grandparents. These youths define support widely, ranging from social, emotional, and physical support to the monetary support provided by two of the granddaughters who have started working. Overall, the grandchildren that we interviewed were distinctive in that a substantial number of them lived in three-generation households, contrary to the new norm of the nuclear family living arrangement in Singapore.

All the grandchildren in the study responded firmly on their willingness to care for their parents in the future. They saw their parents as role models who have influenced and socialized them through example reinforcing the idea that it is the children's responsibility to provide support. As a result, they thought that they should thereby try all means to fulfill the role of filial caregiver.

For a twenty-three-year-old grandson Ben (Respondent W), who did not live in a three-generation household, the opportunity for his father to be seen as a role model came only when his grandfather became sick. During the period, he came to be socialized through observing how his father interacted with his grandfather in the way expected of a son in a Chinese family:

Ben: When my grandfather was ill, I spent more time at home and more time in the family. It was a chance for me to see how my father acted in his family, because I don't live with my grandparents, and my parents don't live with their parents. When I was younger, my parents were always at work, so when this whole issue came about, I had time to interact with my parents and grandparents together, so I saw how they acted as children towards my grandparents. . . . My father is a very traditional person, so he acted as how a traditional son has acted—he has done his part.

Interviewer: Do you see him as a role model?

Ben: Yes, definitely, perhaps as a kind of expectation that I have to live up to next time. . . . No [my father does not tell me that I have to take care of him next time]. My father is a very quiet person, actually. A lot of things I don't really understand, like maybe family history across decades. Then during my grandfather's funeral, my father broke down, and he cried. Then I realized what kind of man my father was.

Unlike Ben but like Cherie, a twenty-three-year-old granddaughter Sally had lived with her paternal grandparents since her birth. When her grandmother suffered a stroke, the whole family was involved with the care, as Sally indicated.

> Sally: They don't really share that they are stressed. But from the way we observe, we can see that they put in effort to take care of the elderly. So you will sort of tell yourself, next time you will take care of them the same way that they treat their parents. . . . I will take care of them like the way they take care of their parents. I will give them whatever support I can give, like emotionally, socially, and physically. (Respondent V)

Among the link-parent middle-generation interviewees who talked about how they influence their children, all of them agreed that children learn by example. They gave comments such as, "My children see, so they learn" (49-year-old mother). Another said, "You set the example, and then the next time your son will learn. If you don't [set a good example], the next time [he will say], 'you never take care of your father, why should I take care of you?' " (54-year-old father).

Some of the link parents gave examples of how they were influenced by their own parents who cared for the link parents' grandparents, and how they learned from them the duties involved in providing care for elders. One link parent (44-year-old mother) said that having witnessed the stress that her mother experienced in caring for the link parent's paternal grandmother, who had dementia, she now reads up on dementia caregiving so as to avoid her mother's fate of sinking into depression caused by caregiver burden. She further said, "I am doing this for my daughters. I don't have to teach them, I just have to do it for my children to see." It is inevitable that living in three-generation households further facilitates such transmission of role socialization for the grandchildren.

Concerns About Caring for Their Own Parents in the Future

However, despite the belief that children should care for and provide for their parents, having watched their parents' experiences in caregiving has also caused many to become concerned as to whether they are capable of doing the same in the future. The grandchildren observed that their generation is disadvantaged by having fewer siblings, if any, when compared with their parents' generation. Thus, they fear that they will need to shoulder much of the financial and care burden by themselves, as expressed by the following twenty-year-old granddaughter who lived in a nuclear family:

Tina: I'm really worried my dad is going to get dementia when he is old. It's just this fear. . . . It would be a total nightmare, because it's just my sister and I. It's not like I have a lot of siblings to share the burden. . . . They [my parents] talked about it, because they want to know what we think about it. They know that we want to do it, but they also know that in the future it's gonna be very, very expensive and very difficult for the two of us to take care of them. (Respondent N)

A twenty-three-year-old grandson Shawn, who lives with his parents, expressed similar sentiments. His grandfather used to live with them until he passed away two years ago, which made a large impression on him:

Shawn: I pray hard that they will have good health, because be it any illness, be it major or minor, it is quite taxing on all the family members. It is a totally different challenge for me and my sister, because my father has got five siblings, [and] including him, six children. But there is only me and my sister, so I cannot imagine what will happen if every other day we have to take leave to bring my parents to the hospital. (Respondent W)

Another grandson Tony, who was twenty-nine years old and working, was ready to face his position as the eldest son of the family and the expectations that came with it, but he was uncertain how he would pull it off.

Tony: I would not run away from meeting the expectations, but, imagine half of your pay is used on your parents. Moreover, these days, it is hard to find work that would be paying 4K to 5K. Imagine that, with the standard set, the eldest son has to shoulder upon himself and take on the full responsibilities of taking care of the expenses for their parents' care. I would be the one who is very stressed out, as the eldest grandchild too. People would have expectations of me. (Respondent E)

Strategies in Care Provision

As the grandchildren learned from their parents the general sense that they should care for the elderly at home, they also learned about the strategies adopted by their parents in meeting caregiving needs at home. Among them, seven of the grandchildren were explicit about needing to have an FDW to help care for their parents in the future. The Foreign Domestic Worker Scheme (FDW Scheme) was introduced in 1978 by the government as a means to facilitate women's continued employment. Today, about one in every five households employs a live-in FDW, and this labor force has become a necessary presence for many dual-income middle-class households requiring assistance in childcare, eldercare, and housework. The FDWs are usually women in their twenties and thirties from the Philippines, Indonesia, and Myanmar; they number slightly more than 200,000 in the population (Transient Workers Count Too 2011). Among the grandchildren in the study, having an FDW is particularly seen as a viable and perhaps natural and even necessary option since their parents needed to employ one to care for their grandparents at home. This trend closely tracks socioeconomic status of the care recipient. A national study on informal caregivers to care recipients aged seventy-five and above has reported that almost 50 percent of the care recipients in Singapore had employed FDWs, with a higher proportion living in housing types for lower-middle-income households and above (Chan et al. 2012: 12).

It is interesting to note that all the grandchildren who thought that they would engage FDWs to help with caregiving were female. This may imply that the males expect that their wives will be responsible for family caregiving tasks in the future, but it also suggests that, compared to younger men, younger women tend to worry and plan ahead more than younger men in anticipation of caregiving needs. The younger women compared themselves with their mothers, many of whom were housewives, and they said that they could not be full-time housewives like their mothers. Since the possibility of stopping work to care for the elderly did not seem to be a viable option for them, they regarded engaging FDW help to be the best alternative. In addition to and apart from hiring FDWs and other professional caregivers, the idea of "rotational care" surfaced quite frequently among the grandchildren. They said that siblings should share in caring for their parents. None of the grandchildren thought that going to an institution should be an option at all. As twenty-one-year-old only son Joe said,

> Joe: You cannot, like, just dump them anywhere! You must be responsible for them, because they are my parents. I must take care of them as they grow old; I cannot send them to an old folk's home.... [I] need to do my part.... [I need to] try to have them close to me.... [We need to] stay together. Because I'm the only son. It's my responsibility. (Respondent X)

Feelings about Ideal Living Arrangement after Observing Parents Caring for Elders

In Singapore, where the three-generation household living arrangements have now largely given way to nuclear arrangements, living close by has become a preferred alternative to intergenerational coresidence. As mentioned earlier, policies to promote close-proximity living between the generations have also encouraged a modified form of extended-family living across different households. For example, it is common for young dual-working couples to live close to their parents and rely on them for child-care and meals. Although living in their own homes, many young couples spend a considerable amount of time in their parents' house after work, eating dinner together and picking up their children.

When we asked the grandchildren if they would consider a three-generation living arrangement in the future, the majority were open to the possibility, although there were varying degrees of certainty, ranging from definitely willing to only willing if necessary. The grandchildren all tended to focus on the provision of eldercare when considering three-generation living arrangements.

"They Would Definitely Be Staying with Us"

The grandchildren in the study tended to focus on the provision of elder-care in considering living arrangements. More than half of them would like to live with their parents, although in varying degrees of certainty.

Among those who were certain that their parents should live with them was a twenty-one-year-old grandson John, who was explicitly unhappy with his difficult grandmother who has been living with them. However, witnessing how difficult it was caring for an elderly person at home did not deter him from wanting to live with his parents in the future:

> John: They would definitely be staying with us. Actually, my brother and I were planning to buy a house where all of us can actually stay together. Gen-erally speaking, I would definitely. If it comes to a point when my brother and I are not staying together, then definitely we would take care of our parents on a rotational basis. (Respondent F)

However, John noted that although he wanted to have everyone in the same house, "My mother said that she wants to stay alone, and I don't know why."

As we will gather from later discussion, it is not unusual for link parents to say that they want to live independently because they do not want to be a burden on their adult children. Nonetheless, the contrastive comment, "I don't know why," from the grandson implies filial piety as an internalized value that includes supporting one's elderly parents.

"If They Want to Stay with Me, They Are Welcome"

Other responses showing openness to three-generation living arrangement depending on the preference of their parents included things like the following: "If my parents are willing, I would definitely want to support them in the same house" (Respondent T). "If they want to stay with me, they are welcome" (Respondent R). "If it is necessary to stay with them, then I would do so" (Respondent S). These expressions ranged from a strong personal willingness as in the first acclamation to a somewhat reluctant form of personal willingness.

However, some stated that personal willingness of self and parents was not the only factor in determining living arrangements. For example, a twenty-four-year-old grandson Wayne was mindful that, even if he was willing, his partner might not agree to coliving:

> Wayne: If given a chance, I would love to stay with my parents. But it really depends on my partner as well, as in the future it is not just about me but my partner too. I have the thought of having my family with me, if adjustments need to be made, and then maybe I would talk it out with my [nuclear] family members. (Respondent K)

"We Require Some Space of Our Own"

Some grandchildren were concerned with having their own private space and had come up with some ideas for being filial but not living directly with their grandparents. For example, a twenty-nine-year-old grandson suggested a modified form of extended family living arrangement involving living just next door to his parents when he has his own family:

> Tony: My plan is to buy the next-door unit—my neighbor's flat—and knock down this wall. Then it would easily facilitate me taking care of them. If they were to scream or shout, we could react more easily. I don't mind living with my parents, though being an adult, we require some space of our own, and fortunately my parents are not the type to disturb us and keep us from having our own personal space. (Respondent E)

Similarly, a twenty-six-year-old working granddaughter Anna considered renting a studio apartment for her parents, together with hiring an FDW, to be the ideal solution.

> Anna: I don't mind living with my parents, but I think the most ideal situation—if both parents are still alive—would be for them to have their own little studio apartment, and with a maid who can take care of everything.... My brother and I will split the bills. (Respondent O)

Youths and their parents were not always on the same page about expectations for the future, and sometimes parents' stated expectations fluctuate over time. In discussing living arrangements with her parents, a twenty-year-old granddaughter Lily thought that her parents should probably live with her and have hired help. Her parents, however, suggested other arrangements:

> Lily: They haven't decided. . . . They said they wouldn't mind going to the old folks' home, then later on they said they would mind . . . [and] then they said they want to go and stay in those studio apartments for the elderly, and for us to just contribute financially to them. (Respondent N)

The fact that young people do discuss living arrangements with their parents shows that where and who to live with are important concerns to more than the older generation. Responses from parents such as the above show that, if possible, the parental generation would often like to have a choice and to remain independent. The availability of studio apartments for seniors built by Housing and Development Board (HDB) since the late 1990s has expanded the options available in retirement living (Thang 2014).[6] The wish on the part of many seniors to live apart from their children also shows an increasing desire for freedom in later life, as reflected in the response of a nineteen-year-old granddaughter Helen:

> Helen: They don't want to stay with me [laughs]. They want to stay alone. Maybe they were jokingly saying it. They want to enjoy life, they said. But my brother suggested that everyone stay together. (Respondent J)

Only three among the grandchildren—all males—appeared unsure about whether they would live with their parents or resolve the dilemma in another way in the future. Nonetheless all of them expressed a willingness to support their parents in old age, if not in all aspects of support (physical, emotional, and financial), then at least in the financial aspect.

Opinions about living arrangements among the grandchildren show a lingering persistence of traditional ideas among the younger population, such as the expectations that the eldest son should care for their parents. However, the three-generation living arrangement—although agreed to be the ideal situation for children to provide care and support to their parents—seems to be giving way to an expanded notion of preferred arrangements. Such expanded preferences include living closer or living separately with hired help, where the children continue to offer help in different forms, often financial. Such developments reflect ongoing modifications to and permutations in the expressions of filial practices, with tradition and modernity coexisting within new and changing contexts.

Concluding Remarks

In this chapter, we attempt a further understanding of filial piety as the values and practices are adapted and practiced by the youngest current-day generation in Singapore. Parallel with responses from the film *Father and Son*, the youngest generation seems to have internalized filial piety as a value socialized through their interactions within the family. The filial values that appear natural and incontestable to them reflect the successful transmission of values from the family, as well as the state, to the young. The open attitude about three-generation living arrangements expressed by some grandchildren is an example of some continuity in views on the practice of filial piety. Whether their fairly traditional understanding of filial piety is derived from their own internalized logic unconsciously taught to them, or from the conscious expectations expressed by their parents and others around them, the younger generation seems more concerned than their parents are about having the capacity to care. The younger generation that grew up with FDWs in the home views FDWs as having an inevitable part of the strategies that will facilitate their ability to provide care for their parents in the future.

Although the current younger generation shows a strong value commitment to caring for their parents when they grow old, they are worried about their limited capacity to do so given the reality of the significantly fewer siblings available to share the burden when compared to a generation before. Their concerns are real, and call for the need to develop a more comprehensive structure of support from the state and the community to enable families to assume filial responsibility of supporting and caring for their elderly at home. As Sokolovsky (2009) argues, familial care and state and community support for care are not alternatives; rather they are complementary systems that require each other to function effectively in providing sufficient care for older adults. It is interesting that the current younger generation seem uncertain if they can expect the same from their children when they grow old, reflecting their awareness of the larger discourse on changing social forces possibly eroding filial piety over time.

As we conclude the chapter, let us revisit the tag line of the short film, "How one generation loves, the next generation learns." In focusing on a public service announcement that features loving relationships as central to filial piety, we suggest that love should be more explicitly considered as a basis to strengthen the support of elderly parents and grandparents (Thang and Tan 2014). In the Social Orientations Survey by Tan (2011, cited in Thang and Tan 2014:63), "love for one's parents" was selected as the main reason for providing financial support to aged parents (57 percent). There were lower percentages for supporting parents out of a sense of obligation or social expectation, as in "it is expected for children to support their parents" (27 percent) and as a form of transaction shown through "a repayment for raising one from the time one was young" (17 percent). It is debatable whether "love" should replace or strengthen filial piety or a sense of duty, but another option would be for it to instead coexist to bring new motivation to the young in caring for their elderly at home. To recapitulate, whether the younger generation's willingness to care has resulted from filial obligation and reciprocity and/or love and/or law, in confronting a rapidly aging modernized society, beyond good middle-aged filial examples, eldercare by younger generations will certainly require added familial, FDW, and state support to help them in their contemporary expressions of performing filiality.

Acknowledgments

We appreciate the commissioned funding support for the project "A Qualitative Study on Informal Caregiving and Its Impact on Intergenerational Relationships," commissioned by the then Ministry of Community Development, Youth and Sports (MCYS), from which our data are derived. We are especially grateful to our respondents in the project who have kindly shared with us their life and experiences on caregiving and family relationships.

Leng Leng Thang is associate professor and head of the Department of Japanese Studies, and codirector of Next Age Institute, National University of Singapore. A sociocultural anthropologist with research interests on aging, intergenerational approaches, and relationships, gender, and family, she publishes widely in her areas of expertise with a focus on Asia, especially Japan and Singapore. Her recent works appeared in *Journal of Cross-Cultural Gerontology, Journal of Intergenerational Relationships, Social Science and Medicine,* and *Japanese Studies.*

Kalyani Mehta is professor of gerontology at the Gerontology Programme, Nathan School of Human Development, Singapore University of Social Sciences. Dr. Mehta is currently pro bono member of the board of advisers, Vulnerable Adults Act, vice president of the Singapore Anti-Narcotics Association, and justice of the peace. Her research interests revolve around caregiving issues, policies, and support for older workers, community-based networks, and environmental gerontology. She has published widely in international and regional journals on the subject of aging issues, social policies related to aging populations, retirement, technology and older workers, and gender issues.

Glossary

mei shi zhao shi zuo	没事找事做	Finding/making things to do when one has nothing to do, one need not do anything, or when nothing needs to be done.
xiao	孝	Filial piety.

Notes

1. The National Family Council changed its name in 2014 to Families for Life Council, and the Ministry of Community Development, Youth and Sports (MCYS) changed its name in 2012 to Ministry of Social and Family Development.
2. Chris Chiu, who is the creative director, art director, and copywriter at Leo Burnett Singapore, developed the film. See Macleod (2011) for more details regarding the production.
3. There is no explicit pointing to a decline in filial piety. Instead, "The State of the Family in Singapore 2004 Report", for example, has concluded, "Intergenerational ties are still positive in Singapore and filial piety remains a key moral in society" (Ministry of Community Development, Youth and Sports, 2004: 4). However, comments about the decline in filial piety are common in societal discourse found, for example, in newspapers. The launch of the Maintenance of Parents Act in 1995 and the subsequent revision in 2011 is a reflection of the state's concern with a seeming decline in willingness among the younger generation to care for aged parents.
4. The study aims to identify the key factors in intergenerational dynamics that keep the generations together or move them apart, and to provide recommendations to enhance policy and services to support families with caregiving needs, as well as to strengthen intergenerational relationships within the family.
5. The seventy-five interviews were conducted between January and July 2010. They were derived from families who were involved with caregiving of older adults at home. Twenty-one interviews were from seven families where the link parent, grandchild and FDW were all interviewed. Twenty-six interviews were from link parents and grandchildren in thirteen families (see table 5.1 for more details).
6. Studio apartments are built by Singapore's public housing authority, the Housing and Development Board (HDB), catering to the housing needs of the older population in Singapore. They are available for Singaporeans aged fifty-five and above, generally in two sizes: a studio that is thirty-five square meters and a one-room apartment that is forty-five meters square. They are high-rise apartments, built as either standalone blocks of only studio apartments or mixed with other family-type housing of two bedrooms and more. In some of these blocks, there are senior activity centers located on the ground floor or second level provided by nongovernment agencies to offer services for the older residents (Thang 2014).

References

Au-Yong, Rachel. 2014. "3-Gen Flats in Yishun Going Fast." *Straits Times,* 15 February.

Chan, Angelique, Truls Ostbye, Rahul Malhotra, and Athel J. Hu. 2012. *Report on the Survey on Informal Caregiving.* Singapore: Ministry of Social and Family Development.

Chang, Rachael. 2013. "Fewer Elderly Seeing their Children for Maintenance." *Straits Times,* 10 July.

Committee on Ageing Issues (CAI). 2006. *Report on the Ageing Population.* Retrieved 6 March 2020 from https://www.moh.gov.sg/docs/librariesprovider5/resources-statistics/reports/committee-on-ageing-issues-report-on-ageing-population.pdf.

Goransson, Kristina. 2009. *The Binding Tie: Chinese Intergenerational Relations in Modern Singapore.* Honolulu: University of Hawaii Press.

Housing & Development Board (HDB). 2010. *Public Housing in Singapore: Well-Being of Communities, Families, and the Elderly.* Singapore: Housing & Development Board.

Ikels, Charlotte, ed. 2004a. *Filial Piety: Practice and Discourse in Contemporary East Asia.* Stanford, CA: Stanford University Press.

Ikels, Charlotte. 2004b. "Introduction." In Ikels, *Filial Piety,* 1–15.

Jernigan, Homer L., and Margaret B. Jernigan. 1992. *Aging in Chinese Society: A Holistic Approach to the Experience of Aging in Taiwan and Singapore.* New York: Haworth Pastoral Press.

Jing, Jun. 2004. "Meal Rotation and Filial Piety." In Ikels, *Filial Piety,* 53–62.

Kang, Soon Hock, Ern Ser Tan, and Mui Teng Yap. 2013. *National Survey of Senior Citizens 2011.* Institute of Policy Studies Report, University of Singapore.

Macleod, Duncan. 2011 (27 March 2011). "Filial Piety in Singapore." Retrieved 5 March 2017 from http://theinspirationroom.com/daily/2011/filial-piety-in-singapore/.

Mao, Weiyu, and Iris Chi. 2011. "Filial Piety of Children as Perceived by Aging Parents in China." *International Journal of Social Welfare* 20 (1): S99–S108.

Mehta, Kalyani. 2007. "Multigenerational Relationships within the Asian family: Qualitative Evidence from Singapore." *International Journal of Sociology of the Family* 33 (1): 63–78.

Mehta, Kalyani, and Helen Ko. 2004. "Filial Piety Revisited in the Context of Modernizing Asian Societies." *Geriatrics and Gerontology International* 4 (1): 77–78.

Mehta, Kalyani, and Leng Leng Thang. 2006. "Interdependence in Asian Families: The Singapore Case." *Journal of Intergenerational Relationships: Programs, Policy and Research* 4 (1): 117–26.

Ministry of Community Development, Youth and Sports (MCYS). 2004. "State of the Family in Singapore Report." Singapore: MCYS. Retrieved 24 March 2020 from https://www.msf.gov.sg/research-and-data/Research-and-Statistics/Documents/StateOfFamily2004.zip.

Nazeer, Zubaidah, and Vivien Heng. 2010. "National Family Council on Filial Piety TV Ad—'Idea Was To Inspire Young.'" *The New Paper,* 28 June.

Phua, Voon Chin, and Jason Loh. 2008. "Filial Piety and Intergenerational Co-residence: The Case of Chinese Singaporeans." *Asian Journal of Social Science* 36 (3–4): 659–79.

Quah, Stella. 1998. *Family in Singapore: Sociological Perspective.* Singapore: Times Academic Press.

Singapore Department of Statistics (SDOS). 2019. *Yearbook of Statistics 2019*. Singapore: SDOS. Retrieved 6 March 2020 from https://www.singstat.gov.sg/-/media/files/publications/reference/yearbook_2019/yos2019.pdf.

Sokolovsky, Jay. 2009. "Introduction: Human Maturity and Global Aging in Cultural Context." In *The Cultural Context of Aging: Worldwide Perspectives*, 3rd ed., ed. Jay Sokolovsky, xv–xxxv. Westport, CT: Praeger.

Tambyah, Siok Kuan, and Soo Jiuan Tan. 2013. *Happiness and Wellbeing: The Singaporean Experience*. London: Routledge.

Transient Workers Count Too (TWC2). 2011. *Fact Sheet: Foreign Domestic Workers in Singapore (Basic Statistics)*. Retrieved 6 March 2020 from http://twc2.org.sg/2011/11/16/fact-sheet-foreign-domestic-workers-in-singapore-basic-statistics/.

Thang, Leng Leng. 2010. "Intergenerational Relations: Asian Perspectives." In *The SAGE Handbook of Social Gerontology*, ed. Dale Dannefer and Chris Phillipson, 202–214. New York: Sage.

Thang, Leng Leng. 2014. "Living Independently, Living Well: Seniors Living in Housing and Development Board Studio Apartments in Singapore." *Senri Ethnological Studies* 87: 59–78.

Thang, Leng Leng, and Ern Ser Tan. 2014. "Bonding of the Generations: Promoting Family Values and Intergenerational Solidarity in Singapore." In *Family Futures, 2014 Twentieth Anniversary of the International Year of the Family*, ed. Jacqui Griffiths, 61–63. UK: Tudor Rose.

Wang, Danyu. 2004. "Ritualistic Coresidence and the Weakening of Filial Practice in Rural China." In Ikels, *Filial Piety*, 16–33.

Wong, Yuet Mei, and Zhiwei Teo. 2011. "The Elderly in Singapore." *Statistics Singapore Newsletter* (September): 1–9.

6 CONSTRUCTING NETWORKS OF ELDERCARE ACROSS BORDERS

The Experiences of Taiwanese Immigrants in the United States and Their Parents in the Homeland

Ken Chih-Yan Sun

Introduction

OVER THE PAST DECADE, THE phenomenon of transnational families has attracted much scholarly attention (Bryceson and Vuorela 2002; Huang and Yeoh 2005; Levitt and Jaworsky 2007). Studies have documented that many migrant parents establish and use cross-border networks to care for their children left behind (Gamburd 2000; Parrenas 2000). However, migration scholarship has been slow to critically examine the role of care networks in the lives of aging nonmigrants who have children working and residing outside their homeland, with notable pioneers in this area of study including Izuhara and Shibata (2002), Lamb (2009, 2013), and Sun (2012, 2017). As a result, we still have a limited understanding of the role that cross-border care networks play in the lives of immigrants and their parents who remain in the ancestral societies.

In order to push against the limitations of current literature on transnational caregiving, this study underscores how geographically dispersed family members pragmatically and emotionally address the issues regarding eldercare in and through transnational networks of care. This issue not only serves important theoretical objectives, but also has profound practical implications since international migration is prevalent in contemporary Asia, and many expatriates still have aging parents back home in Asia.

I will begin by chronicling how parents and children divided by borders feel about and justify their decision to live far away from each other. Furthermore, I will demonstrate how immigrants construct networks of care for their aging parents in the homeland through the strategies of what I call kin transfer (i.e., recruiting relatives as helping hands) and market transfer (i.e., using migrant domestic workers, also called foreign domestic workers or FDWs, to provide direct care). As I will show, immigrants in this research reported mixed feelings and emotions about not being able to care for their parents themselves. While they sometimes felt guilty and upset, they also felt relieved since they could transfer the responsibilities of caring for their parents to other people.[1] More importantly, because many of these immigrants contracted out the physical aspect of their filial duties (for definition, see Introduction), they still needed to carefully maintain their connections to the family members who were providing care for their parents and/or carefully supervising the care provided by FDWs.

This chapter also highlights the other side of the equation, examining how parents who remain in the homeland react to the care they receive from either kin or FDWs. Many of the parents I studied were ambivalent about their relationships with their children in the United States and their caregivers in Taiwan. On the one hand, parents who remain in the homeland receiving care from some of their children or other family members in Taiwan expressed feelings of missing their emigrated child and of regret over not having (all of) their children around, while also carefully maintaining connections with the local kin on whose care they rely. On the other hand, parents who received care from FDWs said they were glad that they would not become "burdens" or "problems" that the next generation would have to handle. Unlike parents who receive care from their own family members, those who had FDWs caring for them felt empowered because they were able to receive the support they need without intruding on their children's lives too much.[2]

Background

Economic and cultural globalization pushes people to move internationally and are thus geographically separated from their family members (Carling, Menjivar, and Schmalzbauer 2012; Chee 2005; Falicov 2005; Huang and Yeoh 2005; Schmalzbauer 2004; Sun 2013). Researchers have been particularly attentive to the impact of spatial separation on the relationship between migrant parents and their children who remain in the homeland (Dreby 2010; Moran-Taylor 2008; Parrenas 2005). This body of literature demonstrates how migrant women and men assign different meanings to their responsibilities and obligations to their children. While many migrant men can fulfill their fathering responsibilities by regularly sending economic remittances home, most migrant women who provide economically for their families are still expected to be emotionally and socially available to their children left back home (Dreby 2006; Hondagneu-Sotelo and

Avila 1997; Parrenas 2001). For example, Peng and Wang (2013) reveal that many FDWs in Hong Kong use information and communication technologies to address various problems and developmental needs that their children back home may have. Likewise, Lan (2006) chronicled that in addition to their contribution to the household budget, many migrant women who worked as FDWs in Taiwan regularly mail letters, send text messages, have expensive gifts delivered, make phone calls, plan family menus, and/or supervise their children's daily activities. Doing so, these migrant mothers believe, allows their presence to be felt in their children's everyday lives and to sustain emotional connections with the next generation in the homeland (Inoue 2012).

In contrast to the relationship between migrant parents in the receiving societies and their children in the sending societies, the connections between migrant children and their aging parents back home remain understudied. Just as many migrant women and men have children left behind, they also have parents back home. With few exceptions (Mazzucato 2007; Sun 2012), the existing research has yet to carefully address the ways migrant children articulate their sense of responsibility and obligation to their parents back home. Nor do we know much about the strategies that migrant children and their parents develop to manage various needs involved in their daily lives. The role that transnational care networks play in the lives of migrant children and their parents is an example. Carling et al. (2012) commented that transnational networks of care are "elusive objects of study" because these "networks are not clearly delimited, either by geographical location or by straightforward biological kinship" (208).

To date, migration scholars have underscored the ways migrant parents mobilized their family and community members in the homeland to construct networks of support for their children (Sun 2014b). For instance, Parrenas (2005) chronicles how many Filipina migrant women transfer the responsibilities of childcare to their female relatives who remain in the homeland. Dreby (2010) uses the concept of middle women to describe the fact that Mexican migrant women and men rely on their female relatives, especially their own mothers, to be the primary caregivers who act as intermediaries in the relationship between parents and children (145). By way of contrast, the processes through which migrants and their left-behind parents negotiate the caregiving arrangement within transnational networks remain underexplored.

To fill this gap in understanding, this study uses Taiwanese immigrants and their parents in Taiwan as an example to illustrate the centrality of care networks in the arrangement of transnational eldercare. I highlight the ways in which immigrants and their parents position themselves vis-à-vis each other *and* their networks of support. I argue that immigrants and their parents pragmatically, emotionally, and symbolically negotiate the cultural ideal of family—adult children's filial duties of caring for aging parents—through the medium of larger transnational familial and social communities.

This research also shows that migrants and their parents back in the country of origin transform the cultural ideals of family in and through cross-border networks of care. Many scholars have used the concept of "filial piety" as the framework through which to understand intergenerational dynamics in Asian and Asian American families that are profoundly influenced by Confucian values and beliefs (Kibria 2002; Lan 2002; Sun 2014a). In traditional Chinese culture, filial piety is both a system of reciprocal rules through which the intergenerational exchange of resources and power within Chinese families are distributed (Greenhalgh 1988) and a cultural notion of parental authority that is passed from one generation to another through socialization (Blieszner and Hamon 1992). According to the concept of filial piety, children—especially sons and daughters-in-law—are supposed to shoulder the filial duties of physical and emotional care for their aging parents. Daughters-in-law in Chinese families typically are the primary caregivers for elderly persons, but an increasing number of daughters in Chinese and Chinese immigrant families believe themselves to be culturally obligated to take care of their aging parents as well (Gu 2006). In addition to physical and emotional care, children's respect for and deference to parental authority constitutes an important dimension of the notion of filial piety (Chen 2006). When members of older and younger generations have conflicting opinions on family affairs, adult children are usually expected to defer to their aging parents within traditional Taiwanese and Chinese families (Ikels 2004b).

In the present research, I will reveal how contemporary Taiwanese immigrants and their parents, both of whom are heavily influenced by Confucian traditions, foster new ways of thinking that (re)orient their feelings and expectations of eldercare across worlds. This research points to the complex and myriad ways in which many immigrants and their parents grapple with the complex meanings and practices of filial piety in the context of long-distance family separation. To begin with, this study will delineate how immigrants in the United States and their parents in Taiwan each make sense of family separation. Second, I will chronicle how many immigrants and their parents rely on their kin members in the homeland to arrange the networks of care they need. As I will show, the process of constructing transnational care requires my respondents, including both immigrants and their parents, to carefully devise strategies to sustain their emotional ties to their family members back home. Finally, this chapter documents how migrant workers from Southeast Asia also constitute precious resources on which my respondents draw to manage issues surrounding transnational eldercare. Immigrants and their parents in this study are often ambivalent about relying on FDWs as the primary providers of care. Yet, while these immigrants and their parents regret not being physically with one another, they also express a sense of relief about not having to shoulder or have their children shoulder the "burden" of eldercare.

In many aspects, this chapter demonstrates how immigrants and their parents who still live in the ancestral society remake what Bourdieu termed habitus (Bourdieu 1984). According to Bourdieu, habitus is a set of dispositions intimately tied to our backgrounds, generating our cultural expectations, and orienting our daily practices (Bourdieu 2001). Situating the experiences of my respondents in a transnational social field, I reveal how changing structural contexts (i.e., family dislocation) push immigrants and their parents back home to develop new worldviews that differ from the habitus that they inherited from their homeland when they were younger. Doing so requires them to reconstruct the embodied practices of intergenerational care in Taiwan (e.g., being physically close to older generations, commensality in regular reunion dinners with parents, and, most importantly, intimate bodily care when one of the parents is sick).

Methodology

This study used in-depth interviews as the method of data collection. First, twenty-four Taiwanese immigrants who live in the Greater Boston area were interviewed. Subsequently, twenty-three of the parents of these immigrants who continued to reside in Taiwan were interviewed. I gained access to my informants in Taiwan through the referral of their migrant children in the United States, and I recruited most informants through snowball sampling. Doing so has enabled me to document the continuities and gaps in parents' and children's perspectives on family relationships. In total, forty-seven informants (N = 47) were interviewed across fourteen households.

Of the Taiwanese immigrants interviewed, fourteen were male and ten were female. Thirteen of them were married, and twelve were married to each other (see table 6.1). Their ages ranged from late twenties to early forties. The average age of immigrants to the United States in this study was thirty-five years old. At the time of the interviews, ten immigrants in this study had siblings in Taiwan while fourteen did not have any sibling who lives in Taiwan. All of the immigrants in this study were American citizens. The amount of time that they have resided in the United States ranged from ten to twenty-two years. Among the parents being interviewed, eleven were

TABLE 6.1. Interview Sample: Taiwanese Immigrants and Left-Behind Aging Parents.

	Male	Female	Age Range	Average Age
Taiwanese immigrants to the United States	14	10	Late 20s–40s	35
Their aging parents left behind in Taiwan	11	12	Early 60s–80s	67

Source: Author data.

male and twelve were female. Like their children in the United States, these parents were middle class. Their ages ranged from early sixties to eighties. The average age of the parents in this study was sixty-seven years old. Six of these parents lived in rural areas in Taiwan, and seventeen of them lived in or around major metropolitan cities such as Taipei, Taichung, and Kaohsiung. Despite different birth cohorts and residential locations, systematic differences in the responses of these parents to aging and geriatric care along those parameters were not identified in this study because the sample size within those subcategories was not large enough to conduct that kind of analysis.

All of the data collected for this project were analyzed by using the general principles of grounded theory (Charmaz 2006). In the first round of coding, "open coding," concepts were labeled and grouped into categories. After categories emerged, and their characteristics and dimensions were (roughly) defined, "axial coding" enabled me to establish relationships between the different categories. By establishing a relationship between different codes of my data, I identified larger social and cultural forces that organized and shaped my informants' understanding of family relationships.

Finally, all the names of informants are pseudonyms. This chapter uses the terms "Mr." and "Mrs." as prefixes to surnames to conform to the cultural practice of addressing elders through more-formal and honorific language in Taiwan. In contrast, this chapter uses conventional American first names to address my informants in the United States in order to highlight their status as inhabitants who have settled there.

Making Sense of Family Separation

Most immigrants and their parents I interviewed struggled with physical distance from each other. Many Taiwanese immigrants worried about their parents who were halfway around the globe and felt guilty about not being able to physically be around to support their parents. Despite worries about their parents, these immigrants were reluctant to and/or had trouble relocating to Taiwan. Some immigrants asserted that staying in the United States would be more beneficial for their career than returning to Taiwan. Some immigrants reported appreciating Western lifestyles (such as living in a spacious suburban house) and sensibilities (e.g., respect for personal privacy and freedom) and had trouble readjusting themselves to Asian societies, where they thought collectivism prevailed and their individual desires might be compromised. Still, some immigrants claimed that they stayed in the United States not for themselves, but for the future of their children. According to these immigrants, the educational system in Taiwan did not encourage relational or independent thinking, but required students to memorize materials by rote. This, for many of the immigrants I interviewed, would hinder the sound development of the next generation. These immigrants also argued that having a Western college diploma would enable their children to be more competitive on the global job market than having a Taiwanese one. It is for these reasons that these immigrants preferred to stay in the United States rather than reuniting with their family in Taiwan.

At the same time, many immigrants I interviewed thought about having their parents move to the United States. However, they soon realized this plan was not ideal for either them or their parents. Some Taiwanese immigrants were particularly concerned about whether they would have the time and energy to be competent providers of care for their parents if they moved to the United States in their later lives. Most of the immigrants in this study acknowledged that moving to the United States at a later life stage would be a difficult transition both for them and for their parents. Because the parents of these immigrants had lived in Taiwan for most of their lives, they could not speak English well, could not drive, and/or had limited social connections in the United States. Given this context, immigrants with whom I talked were not only worried about the adaptability of their parents to life in the United States, but also were concerned that taking care of their parents in the United States would demand much of their time. Unlike the typical case in Taiwan, immigrants I interviewed did not have many other family members who could share the responsibility of eldercare in the United States. Jennifer, for example, clearly discussed the tension she felt when her parents-in-law traveled to visit her family in the United States. According to her,

Jennifer: My parents-in-law don't speak English. They don't drive and didn't know where to go when they visited us. My husband was very busy with his job. During the time they visited us, my in-laws very much depended on me. I had to take care of them. I had to cook for them and drove them around. But I also had two little kids and a part-time job. I was already very busy and had a tight schedule. So, I felt very stressed out when they stayed with us. I cannot imagine what would happen if they moved to the US and lived with us.

Similarly, many parents I interviewed in Taiwan were reluctant to relocate to the United States at a later life stage. To be sure, most of the parents I studied would have liked to be physically closer to their children, and hoped to see them as often as they could. However, these parents typically emphasized that living in Taiwan gave them a strong sense of agency; due to their familiarity with their homeland and hometown, they were able to plan and arrange various forms of support that they need. Some aging parents appreciated their lifestyle and communities in Taiwan and were unwilling to start over in the United States, and they echoed the concerns of their children in the United States about becoming a burden to the next generation. A seventy-eight-year-old respondent clearly explained why he thought moving to live with his children in the United States was a bad idea:

Mr. Chao: In Taiwan, we have neighbors, friends, and relatives. We have known each other for several decades. When we are bored, we can always hang out. But I did not speak English, I did not like American food, and I did not have many friends in the US. How could I live there? If I wanted to see a doctor, I did not know how to talk to my doctor about my problem. I did not want to bother my children all the time.

Such concerns about social isolation and dependence on adult children if they were to migrate to join them parallel Min Zhang's findings (chap. 3) on the disconnection and dependence felt by Chinese parents moving domestically to Shenzhen to help care for grandchildren, so even internal comigration can bear this result.

Some of these parents also maintained that they could foresee the conflicts they would have with their children or their children's spouses if they moved to the United States. Mrs. Chiang is a case in point. Mrs. Chiang had only one son, but she did not want to move to the United States to live with him, because she did not have a good relationship with her daughter-in-law. Mrs. Chiang reported that, from the beginning, she was strongly opposed to her son marrying his wife, who was both twelve years older than him and previously divorced. This caused many conflicts among Mrs. Chiang, her son, and her daughter-in-law. Her son and her daughter-in-law ended up flying off to study in the United States, where they got married without letting Mrs. Chiang know in advance. Mrs. Chiang felt betrayed and thus refused to talk with her son for years. Only after her grandchildren were born did Mrs. Chiang try to make amends with her son and daughter-in-law. However, Mrs. Chiang's daughter-in-law remained cold to her. According to Mrs. Chiang, she did not feel welcome when visiting her son's family in the United States. Her daughter-in-law did not call her "mom," was not interested in talking to her, did not allow her to spend much time with her grandchildren, and occasionally made bitter comments about why she was staying in the United States for so long (about three weeks). Against this backdrop, Mrs. Chiang believed that the idea of relying on her son and daughter-in-law in the United States would be far from ideal, since she did not think that her son's family would treat her warmly or respectfully.

While the parents of immigrants (especially those who do not have any other child in Taiwan) reported a sense of loss about having children living thousands of miles away, they also were proud about their children moving to a country that, from their perspective, is socially and culturally superior to Taiwan. This notion that the United States is a better society than Taiwan enabled parents back home not only to rationalize but also to develop positive feelings about their separation from their children. For instance, Mrs. Chen stated that she felt particularly lonely when seeing other friends and relatives gather together with their children on Chinese New Year. Mrs. Chen complained about having to travel a long distance to see her children and grandchildren. Yet, at the same time, Mrs. Chen was also happy that her children and grandchildren could move to a "better" society. By framing the United States as a nation superior to Taiwan, Mrs. Chen, like many other parents I interviewed, bragged about their children in the States. As Mrs. Chen expressed, her children's professional achievement in the United States made her feel honored and gave her face in front of her relatives and friends. This, to a certain extent, compensated for her feeling of loss that stemmed from being separated from her son's family.

> Mrs. Chen: My son was an engineer in [company's name]. It is really difficult for him to succeed in the US. He was not born in the US, and English was not his native language. The US is much bigger and more competitive than Taiwan. My son works very hard to stand out at school and in his workplace. I am really proud of him. If he stayed in Taiwan, he would not have so many precious opportunities, and it would be difficult for him to make a good income. Every time my relatives talked about my son, they always praise how good my son [in the United States] is and wish that their own kids could be the same. Some of my nephews and nieces also wanted to talk with my son to learn from his experiences. I did sometimes feel lonely, but I feel very proud of my son and know that staying in the US is a good decision for his career and for my grandchildren's future.

Kin Transfer: Immigrants and Parents Who Rely on Family Members Back Home

Many immigrants I interviewed relied on their extended families, especially their siblings, in Taiwan to look after their parents. Although it may not always be the case, the immigrants in this study typically were the ones who had initiated the construction of networks for their parents in the homeland. The health condition of immigrants' parents influenced the extent to which they needed the help of their kin in Taiwan. Immigrants whose parents suffered from disease and illness typically needed their kin in the homeland to provide more hands-on and direct care than those who did not. They also had a greater need to consult with their relatives in Taiwan in order to understand the health condition of their parents. However, even immigrants who did not have sick or ailing parents still relied on their family members in Taiwan to be their safety net, just in case anything happened to their parents. For instance, one of my respondents, Mary, recalled that one day, her mother in Taiwan tripped and fell onto the ground. This accident caused her mother a serious bone and hip fracture; for several months, her mother had trouble taking care of herself and could not walk around without crutches. Mary reported that she was stressed and guilty because she believed that she should be in Taiwan taking care of her mother. To her relief, her sister lived in Taiwan and was able to care for their mother. According to Mary, during the time when her mother was not able to walk and could not care for herself, her sister—who was married and did not cohabitate with her parents—visited, cooked, and cleaned for her parents almost every day. In addition, her sister helped her mother take a bath every other day. Without the assistance of her sister, Mary said that she would not know how to address this crisis experienced by her family.

Like Mary, other immigrants I interviewed expressed a wide range of feelings and emotions toward the relatives who cared for their parents back home. Most of my respondents felt grateful to the kin to whom they entrusted their parents. Their sense of gratitude was typically coupled with feelings such as guilt and indebtedness. In order to make sure that their relatives back home will continue to support their parents, the immigrants I interviewed fostered several strategies to maintain their connections with the family who offered timely support when their parents were in need. Some immigrants regularly sent economic remittances to their family members who took care of their parents in Taiwan. For instance, Felix stated that he regularly wrote checks to his brother and sister-in-law, who handled most of the responsibilities of caring for his parents in Taiwan. For Felix, the money he sent to his sibling and sister-in-law did not completely compensate for the fact that he could not participate in the processes of providing care for his parents. Felix said that he believed that time and energy were far more important than money in taking care of the older generation because the time and energy demanded were enormous and his monetary contributions paled in comparison. However, the money that Felix sent to his sibling served an important symbolic purpose; these economic remittances showed that he still cared about his family, including both his parents and his brother's family, even though he was on the other side of the Pacific Ocean.

In addition to money, immigrants strived to carefully sustain the affective connections with their relatives who were looking after their parents in Taiwan. To illustrate, on top of the money he sent home, Felix reported that he also regularly called his brother in Taiwan to ask about how their parents were doing, as well as how his brother and sister-in-law were coping. Felix maintained that calling his brother is different from calling his parents. Felix asserted that he could get more-correct information about the health condition of his parents from his brother than from his parents, since his parents usually held back information about their problems, because they did not want him to worry. More importantly, making regular phone calls allowed Felix to share with his brother the struggles, feelings, and emotions that his brother had in the process of caring for their parents. While Felix could not participate in the caregiving processes, he still wanted to share some of the emotional burdens carried by his brother and brother's wife:

> Felix: I am very grateful to my brother. He is busy with his own career, but he still manages to spend time with my parents. You know, older people can be stubborn and like to nag. . . . For example, my parents and my brother have different political views. They sometimes argue about the political events or candidates [for the election] and end up fighting or even yelling. I am not in Taiwan, so I don't have to deal with this situation. But my brother does, and he sometimes has complaints. What I can do is to listen and be supportive of him.

Some immigrants I studied strategically mobilized various social conventions—especially gender and kin status—to justify why they relied on their family members in Taiwan to care for their aging parents rather than moving back themselves. For instance, one of my respondents, Jessica, had one brother in the United States and one sister in Taiwan. Even though she cared about her parents, she believed that, in line with tradition, her brother should be more responsible for her parents than she or her sister. According to Jessica, her brother as the only son in the family should be the primary provider of care for her parents and should be more stressed out than her and her sister.

> Jessica: Of course, I worry about my parents. And I wonder what might happen in ten years. But I think my brother should be more worried than my sister and me since he is the only son in the family. And my brother knows that he has responsibilities for my parents too. I will also help my parents, but I think my parents expect me to play the supporting role.

In a related vein, several respondents emphasized the conflicts between their responsibilities as parents and those as adult children, framing their decision of leaving parents behind as painful but inevitable. For instance, Jonathan said that he and his wife brought their two children to the United States as he decided to pursue his doctoral degree in an elite university on the East Coast. Initially, Jonathan never thought about settling in the United States, but he and his wife had trouble moving back to Taiwan after he graduated because his children—one was in the sixth grade and the other was in junior high school at the time of interview—could barely speak Mandarin and could not read Chinese at all. Given this situation, Jonathan talked to his siblings in Taiwan and made them understand why he decided to stay in the United States. For Jonathan, his social role as a father gave him a legitimate reason to transfer the responsibilities of eldercare to his brothers and sisters in Taiwan. According to him, at least, his siblings understood his dilemma and were supportive of his decision.

Although immigrants I interviewed tried hard to maintain positive relationships with the family members who took care of their parents in Taiwan, some of them mentioned conflicts with their kin that arose in the processes of negotiating eldercare transnationally. These conflicts often arose when immigrants disagreed with how their family members took care of the parents. These disagreements, according to immigrants I interviewed, were often related to the advice that they gave to their family members back in Taiwan. Even though my respondents claimed that they were just trying to help, their kin sometimes sensed that they were being given directives on how to care for the older generations, or, even worse, were being indirectly criticized.

Long-distance conflicts with caregiving kin back home provoked negative emotions and feelings among immigrants in this study, sometimes jeopardizing the relationships that immigrants attempted to maintain with their relatives in Taiwan. This sometimes happened when kin in the homeland made important decisions about the immigrant's parents' affairs without first consulting the immigrant child. To illustrate, one of my respondents, Joshua, reported that he was upset that his brother and sister in Taiwan persuaded his parents to sell their ancestral land. He asserted that his siblings did so without consulting with him in advance and believed that his brother and sister did so for their own benefit. Joshua told me that after his siblings sold the land without his permission, he rarely talked with them and did not plan to make amends with them in the foreseeable future. Another respondent, Marissa, similarly disliked the decision of her siblings in Taiwan to send her mother—who suffered from mild dementia—to a nursing home; she thought that hiring a domestic caregiver for her mother would have been a better choice. However, unlike Joshua, Marissa chose to suppress her discontent. She did not argue with her siblings, in large part because she was not the primary care provider for her mother, and she did not feel she had the right to say anything. In addition, Marissa thought that since she would still need to rely on her brother and sister to know about her mother's situation, she wanted to sustain a good relationship with them, so it was best to keep quiet. Although Joshua and Marissa took different approaches to handling family conflicts, both of their cases suggested the various emotions that immigrants needed to negotiate when establishing networks of care from afar.

Like their children in the United States, parents back home were also careful about how to maintain relationships with relatives in Taiwan who helped them manage their daily lives. This was particularly the case with the parents who relied for help on some of their children still living in Taiwan, as opposed to those who relied on other types of relatives on the island. Specifically, these parents often deliberated and negotiated the boundaries between what they should ask for and what they should not (on similar deliberations, see chap. 11), because they did not want to become or be perceived as a "burden" (*fudan*) for the children back home. Many of these parents emphasized that their children in Taiwan also had their own families and careers to attend to. Therefore, they did not want to create additional work for their children in Taiwan to handle.

For these parents who relied on their children, the last thing they want to see is for the next generation to be burnt out or overwhelmed, wherever they were living. One example comes from my interview with Mr. Wei when I asked him about his relationship with his children during the time after his wife's stroke. He told me that even if his son and daughter-in-law had lived in Taiwan, they would still have had difficulty providing care for his wife, since even his left-behind children in Taiwan found it hard to come back home to help out:

> Mr. Wei: Basically, I don't think that living in Taiwan makes much difference compared with living in America. . . . A lot of children whose family is in South Taiwan are working in North Taiwan. How often can you come back

to look after parents? Living in America is just farther away. . . . I have a son and a daughter in Taiwan, but they don't live in [the county where I live]. I cannot ask them to come back often to take care of their mom. If I did, they would soon be burnt out and could not concentrate on their work. I don't want to ruin their lives.

Similarly, Mr. Sun tried his best to be fair to all of his children—no matter where they lived—when seeking help from the next generation. Mr. Sun had three daughters, two of whom were in the United States while one was in Taiwan. According to Mr. Sun, he and his wife were careful about the support that they asked from their daughter in Taiwan and tried not to be intrusive in their daughter's life. According to Mr. Sun, his daughter—who was married and had two little children—had her own life to be busy with. Expecting too much from his daughter in Taiwan was not only stressful but also unfair. Mr. Sun did not want his daughter in Taiwan to think that because she was the only child in Taiwan, she had to take over all the caregiving responsibilities that her sisters in the United States left behind. For parents like Mr. Sun, receiving the care from the next generation was no longer the taken-for-granted privilege and entitlement that tradition had once claimed it to be. Rather, for aging parents in Taiwan nowadays, it took much deliberation to decide when and how to ask for or accept help from one's children, and it required careful management to apportion requests fairly among one's children.

The character of the particular relationships that senior parents had with their children and their children's spouses also influenced their willingness to seek support from the younger generation in the homeland. Parents who had conflicts with their children and children's spouses were typically more reluctant to turn to their children in Taiwan for help than those who did not have such conflicts. For instance, Mrs. Chen reported having a stormy relationship with her daughter-in-law. Mrs. Chen described her daughter-in-law as self-centered and unappreciative. She recalled purchasing a new washing machine and refrigerator for her son and daughter-in-law when they moved into their new apartment. However, Mrs. Chen's daughter-in-law did not acknowledge her good intention; instead, she complained that she did not purchase the brand and model she liked. Also, Mrs. Chen reported that she used to help care for her grandchildren when her son and daughter-in-law were busy with work. Yet, instead of appreciating the help Mrs. Chen provided, her daughter-in-law often blamed her for breaking the rules (such as letting her grandchildren watch too much TV or eating junk food) and spoiling the kids. Mrs. Chen's unpleasant interaction with her daughter-in-law had a negative impact on Mrs. Chen's communication with her son; because she did not want to put her son in a difficult situation, she rarely called and asked her son in Taiwan for help. For Mrs. Chen, relying on her son and daughter-in-law in Taiwan was a bad idea, because she did not believe they would care for her in the ways she liked. In order to live a dignified (*you zunyan de*) life, she preferred to stay independent and self-sufficient as long as she could.[3] Mrs. Chen also claimed that she planned to hire an FDW to assist her or move into a nursing home if she could no longer take care of herself.

Market Transfer: Immigrants and Parents Who Hire Foreign Domestic Workers

While the majority of immigrants I interviewed chose to entrust the care of their parents to their family members in Taiwan, some of them decided to transfer the responsibilities of eldercare to FDWs they hired. These immigrants did so in part because the health condition of their parents had deteriorated to the point that self-care was nearly impossible and in part because their family members in Taiwan could not provide or were overwhelmed by the care their parents back home needed. Given this situation, some immigrants resorted to the market mechanism (i.e., hiring FDWs) to address the care crisis they encountered in their transnational familial situation. For these immigrants, hiring Southeast Asian migrant women workers as domestics back home in Taiwan was much more affordable than moving their parents to the United States and hiring Taiwanese immigrant women as paid helpers in the States. Several immigrants I interviewed had already thought about the possibility of sending their parents to an old age home in Taiwan at some point in the future, but none of them had actually done so at the time of interview.

Immigrants who hired FDWs—typically Southeast Asian FDWs from places including the Philippines, Indonesia, and Vietnam—to care for their parents back home in Taiwan typically reported mixed feelings about doing so. On the one hand, immigrants I studied were upset about not being able to take care of their parents themselves. In comparison with immigrants who relied on their family members to take care of their parents, those who relied on FDWs felt uncertain and insecure about this practice and the response of their parents. At the same time that they were concerned about the quality of the care that their aging parents received, they were also worried that their neighbors, relatives, and friends might think of them as people who abandon their aging parents. Yet, those with paid helpers worried less about other things. Unlike immigrants who relied on their family members in Taiwan to look after their aging parents, those who contracted out their caregiving responsibilities did not worry about whether the caregivers they hired would be exhausted or burnt out. Nor did they feel socially and morally indebted to the FDWs who cared for their aging parents who remained in Taiwan. Monetary payment, and in many cases, live-in room and board, were seen as sufficient recompense.

Shirley was a case in point. Shirley lived on the East Coast of the United States and her parents lived in Taiwan. Shirley reported that her mother, who was in her late eighties at the time of the interview, was experiencing deterioration of her vision and hearing and was increasingly unable to walk steadily. Because Shirley did not have any family members who were able to provide hands-on or direct care for her mother, she hired a migrant woman from Indonesia to help her mother manage daily life. Shirley felt sorry and even guilty about not being able to care for her mother herself. Yet, Shirley asserted that relying on family members as the primary care providers for her mother would also be stressful, because she would not know how to reciprocate for them. For Shirley, purchasing care from FDWs did not impose similar reciprocal or moral responsibility on her, thus reducing the social pressure on her. After all, Shirley did not see FDWs they hired as her family members, and thus did not have to worry about how providing care around the clock might impact their well-being as caregivers. In addition, Shirley discussed the difficulties of caring for older people and talked about how her female friends in Taiwan were overwhelmed by taking care of the older members of their families. By contrast, employing an FDW to care for her mother prevented her and her family members from similar mental and physical exhaustion.

It is worth noting that even when immigrants transferred the duties of caring for elder parents to FDWs in Taiwan, they still needed their family members or friends to supervise the practices of the hired help to ensure that their parents were cared for appropriately. For instance, although Shirley relied on FDWs to care for her parents in Taiwan, she still asked her cousins and friends to check in with her mother regularly to make sure that the FDW that she hired treated her mother well. A couple of immigrants who relied on hired help for everyday parental care and who did not have reliable family members in Taiwan to check in on the hired help were much more anxious than their peers with reliable family back home who could oversee the help. They were also more likely than other immigrants to consider the possibility of moving back to Taiwan for their parents.

As their children described, parents who relied on FDWs were generally not in good health. Several of the parents I interviewed had difficulty managing their daily lives or could not walk without assistance. Like their children in the United States, parents in the homeland also were ambivalent about being cared for by FDWs rather than by their own children. These parents often expressed regret about not being able to have their own children attend to their daily needs. A couple of them were envious of their friends who cohabitated with or lived close to their children. At the same time, while these parents struggled with the difficulties that arose due to biological aging and illness and being separated from their children, they still did appreciate receiving various forms of care from the FDWs their children employed. More importantly, aging parents who employed paid caregivers felt empowered, because they could straightforwardly give orders or directives to the FDWs, and they did not believe they could do so with their own children or their children's spouses.

For instance, Mrs. Lin echoed the perspective of her daughter, Shirley—whom we met earlier in this chapter—and emphasized that she was satisfied with the care she received from the FDW that her daughter hired. Mrs. Lin maintained that she was more content receiving the hands-on and physical care from the FDW than from her own children. Specifically, Mrs. Lin emphasized that the migrant women who cared for her would not argue with her as her children would have done. As a result, Mrs. Lin felt that she had more control over the caregiving process because, unlike her children, the paid caregiver generally deferred to her wishes.

> Mrs. Lin: Wise parents should not rely too heavily on their children. . . . Our children have a lot to be busy with—their work, their own family, and their own career. They do not have much time for you. If you ask too much from them, they feel stressed. Then your relationships become difficult, and we feel unhappy too. . . . The Indonesian woman I have is very attentive to me. She cleans my house. She cooks for me. She shops for groceries for me. She accompanies me for a walk every morning. She is a good woman. Unlike my children, she always follows my instruction. And she never answers back or complains.

Mrs. Lin, similar to other parents who relied on FDWs for various forms of care, also maintained that purchasing care from FDWs prevented them from exhausting their children with their various needs or having conflicts with family members caring for them. While these parents back home thought carefully about the impact of eldercare on their children's career and family lives, they were generally silent about the physical, psychological, and social well-being of the FDWs who cared for them on a daily basis. A couple of them even expressed relief because they did not have to burden their children with the care they needed or desired. In this sense, parents I interviewed defined a clear boundary of who belonged to their family: their children are the ones who they should care about while the migrant women on whom they depended constituted the labor that they paid for and had no moral or social obligation to do so. This made market-based domestic care less encumbering to left-behind parents because it was relationally simpler than local kin care and lacked feelings of indebtedness.[4]

Discussion and Conclusion

This chapter has examined transnational Taiwanese families in which migrant children and their parents were separated from each other in order to explore how globally dispersed family members manage their connections to each other and to their left-behind family members who support their parents physically, socially, and emotionally. While most studies of transnational caregiving focus on migrant children and their children left behind, this research throws a new light on the relationships between migrant children and their aging parents back home. Specifically, this study demonstrated how internationally migrating children and their parents not only find ways to get the support that they need from their left-behind family members or by hiring FDWs back home, but also have to negotiate complex feelings and emotions in and through cross-border networks of care. At the same time, this study also unpacked the impact of spatial dislocation on family solidarity. I have shown that when migrant children and their parents cannot practice filial piety in a conventional fashion, given physical separation, they developed new thinking and strategies to justify their situations, to acquire the support they need, and to manage the multiple relationships involved in the caregiving process. As Ikels (2004b: 3) pointed out, "continuing the family line" is an essential component of filial piety in addition to just taking care of aging parents. By this logic, many of the left-behind parents agree with their children that the United States is a better place to raise grandchildren; this belief justifies transnational family arrangement.

This research also attests to how the notion of filial piety is negotiated and transformed in contexts of international family separation. With economic and cultural globalization, more and more people in contemporary Asia move across different geographic locations and are separated from their family members. In other words, even though this case study focuses on Taiwanese migrants and their parents back home, it has profound implications for other Asian and Asian American families who rethink the meaning and practice of eldercare in the context of long-distance family dispersal. While many Taiwanese expatriates and their parents are heavily influenced by the Confucian notion of intergenerational reciprocity, they have to remake their understanding of responsibility and obligation to each other given the structural constraints they encounter (see also chap. 5).[5] Many migrants throughout the world actively grapple with how to support the older generation in this transnational setting. Similarly, their parents back in the homeland are also generating strategies, both concrete and discursive, to rationalize the fact that their children are on the other side of Pacific Ocean and to acquire various forms of support they need at home.

More importantly, I have underscored that migrants in the United States and their parents in Taiwan did not just negotiate their reciprocal relationships with each other at the household, or even the family, level. They have done so within a larger cross-border community. I used the concepts of kin transfer and market transfer to describe how they used family networks and commercial forces to construct networks of eldercare transnationally. Migrants in this study were typically anxious about how to construct networks of support for their parents. Specifically, immigrants in this research transferred their responsibility to care for parents to their family members back in the homeland (especially siblings) or to the hired FDWs based in Taiwan. I have shown how doing so involved complex emotional and relational work. Immigrants who relied on their family members to care for their parents consistently deliberated about how they could sustain the connections to their kin in the homeland. In some cases where migrants failed to maintain good relationships with their siblings who were taking care of their parents back home, they tended to be more anxious than those who were on good terms with their siblings. By contrast, immigrants who depended on FDWs to care for their parents did not spend anywhere near as much time and energy managing their emotional connections to their employees. For them, relationships with these FDWs are mostly instrumental and business-like. What they needed to do is to find ways to monitor that the migrant care-providers that they hired worked hard to meet the needs of their parents.

Like their children, parents who remained in Taiwan also grappled with their relationship to their care providers in the homeland. Parents who relied on other children or relatives in Taiwan were often careful to discern the boundary between what they could ask for and what they should not ask for. In doing so, parents I interviewed sought to not become too much of a burden for the family members who provided hands-on and direct care for them. In contrast, parents who relied on FDWs did not share those kinds of worries. While these parents at times regretted not having their children around and looking after them, they also were relieved that they were not causing great inconvenience to their children's daily lives (on positives of nonfamilial options, see also chap. 1). This finding also suggests that left-behind parents are not always constrained or conditioned by traditional belief systems, at least to the degree sometimes intimated in the literature. Rather, despite their age and remaining behind in the homeland, they too operate as social actors who initiate or support new ideas and practices in response to changes in various structural realities in the world around them.

It is worthwhile to stress that this research might unintentionally select out families with communication failures or serious conflicts. Migration might actually exacerbate the potential for some children to feel unfairly put upon. Will migrant children's lower ability to help their parents turn their local kin members into reluctant caregivers (at least sometimes)? How do migrant children, parents left behind, and their local relatives respond to this situation? And what are the factors (such as preexisting sibling relationships) that mediate and influence the ways transnational family conflicts are addressed? It is my hope that future research can further explore the questions unanswered in this research.

Acknowledgments

I greatly appreciate the insightful feedback of Jeanne L. Shea and meticulous editing of Nathaniel Tuohy.

Ken Chih-Yan Sun is assistant professor of sociology and criminology at Villanova University in the United States. His research interests include migration, families, inequalities, race/ethnicity, gender, life-course issues, youth and aging, and globalization studies. His publications have appeared in many journals, including *Journal of Marriage and Family, Global Networks, Sociological Forum, Current Sociology, Ethnic and Racial Studies, Journal of Family Issues, Journal of Ethnic and Migration Studies, Symbolic Interaction, Qualitative Sociology, Identities,* and *Sociology Compass.* His new book on aging and migration will be published by Cornell University Press in 2021.

Glossary

you zunyan de	有尊严的	Dignified.

Notes

1. On guilt, see also chap. 10.
2. On hired domestic helpers, see also chap. 4.
3. On independence and self-reliance, see also chap. 7.
4. See also Lamb (2013: 179) on nursing homes in South Asia today providing independence from their children for some Indian elders.
5. This case is also interesting in that Whyte (2004: 123–24) argued that despite earlier modernization in many respects in Taiwan compared with mainland China, in terms of the filial support system, Taiwan remained much more traditional.

References

Blieszner, Rosemary, and Raeann Hamon. 1992. "Filial Responsibility: Attitudes, Obligations, and Roles." In *Gender, Families, and Elder Care*, ed. Jeffrey Dwyer and Raymond Coward, 105–19. Newbury Park, CA: Sage.

Bourdieu, Pierre. 1984. *Distinction: A Social Critique of the Judgement of Taste*. Cambridge, MA: Harvard University Press.

———. 2001. *Masculine Domination*. Stanford, CA: Stanford University Press.

Bryceson, Deborah, and Ulla Vuorela. 2002. "Transnational Families in the Twentieth-first Century." In *The Transnational Families: New European Frontiers and Global Networks*, ed. Deborah Bryceson and Ulla Vuorela, 3–30. New York: Berg.

Carling, Jørgen, Cecilia Menjivar, and Leah Schmalzbauer. 2012. "Central Themes in the Study of Transnational Parenthood." *Journal of Ethnic and Migration Studies* 38 (2): 191–217.

Charmaz, Kathy. 2006. *Constructing Grounded Theory: A Practical Guide Through Qualitative Analysis*. Thousand Oaks, CA: Sage.

Chee, Maria W. L. 2005. *Taiwanese American Transnational Families: Women and Kin Work*. New York: Routledge.

Chen, Carolyn. 2006. "From Filial Piety to Religious Piety: Evangelical Christianity Reconstructing Taiwanese Immigrant Families in the United States." *International Migration Review* 40 (3): 573–602.

Dreby, Joanna. 2006. "Honor and Virtue: Mexican Parenting in the Transnational Context." *Gender & Society* 26 (1): 32–59.

———. 2010. *Divided by Borders: Mexican Migrants and their Children*. Berkeley: University of California Press.

Falicov, Celia. 2005. "Emotional Transnationalism and Family Identities." *Family Process* 44 (4): 399–406.

Gamburd, Michele Ruth. 2000. *The Kitchen Spoon's Handle: Transnationalism and Sri Lanka's Migrant Housemaids*. Ithaca, NY: Cornell University Press.

Greenhalgh, Susan. 1988. "Intergenerational Contracts: Familial Roots of Sexual Stratification in Taiwan." In *A Home Divided: Women and Income in the Third World*, ed. Daisy Dwyer and Judith Bruce, 39–70. Stanford, CA: Stanford University Press.

Gu, Chien-juh 2006. *Mental Health Among Taiwanese Americans: Gender, Immigration, and Transnational Struggles*. New York: LFB Scholarly.

Hondagneu-Sotelo, Pierrette, and Ernestine Avila. 1997. "'I'm Here, But I Am There': The Meanings of Latina Transnational Motherhood." *Gender & Society* 11 (5): 548–71.

Huang, Shirlena, and Brenda S. A. Yeoh. 2005. "Transnational Families and their Children's Education: China's 'Study Mothers' in Singapore." *Global Networks* 5 (4): 379–400.

Ikels, Charlotte, ed. 2004a. *Filial Piety: Practice and Discourse in Contemporary East Asia*. Stanford, CA: Stanford University Press.

———, ed. 2004b. "Introduction." In Ikels, *Filial Piety*, 1–15.

Inoue, Chiho Sunakawa. 2012. *Virtual "ie" Household: Transnational Family Interactions in Japan and the United States*. PhD dissertation, University of Texas, Austin.

Izuhara, Misa, and Hiroshi Shibata. 2002. "Breaking the Generational Contract? Japanese Migration and Old-Age Care in Britain." In *The Transnational Family: New*

European Frontiers and Global Networks, ed. Deborah Bryceson and Ulla Vuorela, 155–69. Oxford: Berg.

Kibria, Nazli. 2002. *Becoming Asian Americans: Second-Generation Chinese and Korean American Identities.* Baltimore, MD: John Hopkins University Press.

Lamb, Sarah. 2009. *Aging and the Indian Diaspora: Cosmopolitan Families in India and Abroad.* Bloomington: Indiana University Press.

———. 2013. "Personhood, Appropriate Dependence, and the Rise of Eldercare Institutions in India." In *Transitions and Transformations: Cultural Perspectives on Aging and the Lifecourse,* ed. Caitrin Lynch and Jason Danely, 171–87. New York: Berghahn.

Lan, Pei-chia. 2002. "Subcontracting Filial Piety: Elder Care in Ethnic Chinese Immigrant Families in California." *Journal of Family Issues* 23 (7): 812–35.

———. 2006. *Global Cinderella: Migrant Domestics and Newly Rich Employers in Taiwan.* Durham, NC: Duke University Press.

Levitt, Peggy, and B. Nadya Jaworsky. 2007. "Transnational Migration Studies: Past Developments and Future Trends." *Annual Review of Sociology* 33 (April): 129–56.

Mazzucato, Valentina. 2007. "Transnational Reciprocity: Ghanaian Migrants and the Care of their Parents Back Home." In *Generations in Africa: Connections and Conflicts,* ed. Erdmute Alber, Sjaak van der Geest, and Susan R. Whyte, 91–109. Münster, Germany: LIT Verlag.

Moran-Taylor, Michelle. 2008. "When Mothers and Fathers Migrate North: Caretakers, Children, ad Child Rearing in Guatemala." *Latin American Perspectives* 35 (4): 79–95.

Parrenas, Rhacel Salazar. 2000. "Migrant Filipina Domestic Workers and the International Division of Reproductive Labor." *Gender and Society* 14 (4): 560–81.

———. 2001. "Mothering from a Distance: Emotions, Gender, and Intergenerational Relations in Filipino Transnational Families." *Feminist Studies* 27 (2): 361–87.

———. 2005. *Children of Globalization: Transnational Families and Gendered Woes.* Stanford, CA: Stanford University Press.

Peng, Yinni, and Odalia M. H. Wang. 2013. "Diversified Transnational Mothering via Telecommunication: Intensive, Collaborative, and Passive." *Gender and Society* 27 (4): 491–513.

Schmalzbauer, Leah. 2004. "Searching for Wages and Mothering from Afar: The Case of Honduran Transnational Families." *Journal of Marriage and Family* 66 (5): 1317–31.

Sun, Ken Chih-Yan. 2012. "Fashioning Reciprocal Norms of Elder Care: A Case of Immigrants in the U.S. and their Parents in Taiwan." *Journal of Family Issues* 33 (9): 1240–71.

———. 2013. "Rethinking Migrant Families from a Transnational Perspective: Experiences of Parents and Their Children." *Sociology Compass* 7 (6): 445–58.

———. 2014a. "Reconfigured Reciprocity: How Aging Taiwanese Immigrants Transform Cultural Logics of Elder Care." *Journal of Marriage and Family* 76 (4): 875–89.

———. 2014b. "Transnational Kinscription: A Case of Parachute Kids and Their Parents in Taiwan." *Journal of Ethnic and Migration Studies* 40 (9): 1431–49.

———. 2017. "Managing Transnational Ambivalence: How Stay-behind Parents Grapple with Family Separation Across Time." *Identities* 24 (5): 509–605.

Whyte, Martin King. 2004. "Filial Obligations in Chinese Families: Paradoxes of Modernization." In Ikels, *Filial Piety,* 106–27.

PART II
Aging and Caregiving in Japanese Contexts

7 WHO CARES FOR THE ELDERS?
Aging, Independence, and Interdependence in Contemporary Japan

Katrina Moore

Introduction

THIS CHAPTER EXAMINES HOW JAPANESE elders negotiate personhood within kin-based and non-kin-based care relationships, focusing on independence and self-reliance as key new values that are in frequent conflict with coexisting older values of dependence and interdependence. The chapter begins by reviewing scholarly literature on the historical and social context regarding aging and eldercare, and the values of dependence, interdependence, and independence in old age in Japan. Then it provides examples from my ethnographic work on-site of how elders negotiate these values within various emerging eldercare situations in contemporary Japan, including at-home care by coresident people who are family by choice and who volunteer, or technological assistance to elders living in the community. The analysis argues that ambivalence toward aging is not entirely a novel condition in Japanese culture and that discourses on dependence, interdependence, and independence in old age are all found in both past and present Japan. However, their precise social meanings and the balance between the practice of dependence, interdependence, and independence are changing in light of present-day demographics, policies, and social and material conditions. In contrast to stereotypical visions of the laid-back comfort of life for elders in East Asia, the analysis shows the earnest involvement and humorous episodes of good old elders caring for fellow elders in contemporary Japan.

Historical and Social Context:
Review of Related Scholarly Literature

In this review of the scholarly literature on old age and elder dependence and independence in Japan, I examine three main topics: (1) aging-related demographic, social, and policy changes in post–World War II Japan; (2) historical ambivalence toward old age and elder dependence in Japan; and (3) later life self-reliance and self-responsibility in contemporary Japan.

Aging-Related Demographic, Social, and Policy Changes in Post–World War II Japan

In the latter part of the twentieth century, Japan experienced population aging based on a fall in fertility and a rise in longevity. Between 1945 and 1974 fertility rates fell, from about three children per woman to two children per woman, largely in response to improvement in infant and child survival rates (see Introduction). Death rates fell as hygiene and nutrition levels improved, diseases such as tuberculosis and polio were eradicated, and medical ability to treat chronic diseases like diabetes and heart disease progressed. Life expectancy went from 62.8 years old in the early 1950s to 77.01 in the early 1980s (see Introduction). The confluence of these trends combined to produce rapid population aging. By 1995 over 14 percent of Japan's population was age sixty-five and above, and by 2015, 26 percent was elderly (see Introduction).

Japanese governmental stances concerning who should be primarily responsible for eldercare have changed over time, first evolving in terms of kin-based expectations. The government has not always stressed the eldest son and his wife as responsible for eldercare. That idea was established in the Civil Code of 1898 (Mackie 2003). In the decade following World War II, however, laws were enacted reducing the eldercare obligation of the eldest son and his wife. Under the new family registration law of 1948, in order to increase equity and resources, care for aging parents became the responsibility of all children (Mackie 2003).

Over time, it became clear that the large family unit (*ie*) on which the state had based its expectation of support and care was rapidly changing (Jenike 2004). After falling to two children per woman in the 1970s, the fertility rate continued to decline. From the 1980s onward, Japanese women and men were increasingly delaying marriage, and a growing number began to forgo marriage. By 2018 fertility had fallen to 1.4, far below replacement level (see Introduction). This meant both few offspring across whom to spread eldercare responsibilities and few young workers to contribute to social security and pension systems (Ezawa 2011: 105).

Within this changing demography, expectations and preferences about eldercare in Japan have shifted from the 1980s to the present in relation to residential preferences, kin versus non-kin care, and gendering of care. Surveys in the 1980s showed that 58 percent of seniors preferred to reside with their children (Prime Minister's Office 1987, cited in Lock 1993), whereas 2015 surveys revealed that the majority of single elders preferred to live apart from their children (Campbell and Kurokawa 2016). Increasingly, independent living has been framed as a virtue by government and society, and many Japanese elders prefer the ease and familiarity of living in their own home and neighborhood. By international standards, the level of cohabitation of elders with their adult children is still very high in Japan, with 50 percent in Japan compared with 1 percent in the United Kingdom and in Denmark (International Longevity Center [ILC] 2015). Still, there is a rising incidence of Japanese elders choosing to live on their own or with just their spouse, with just a paid live-in caregiver, or in group homes, rather than with their children (see Stickland 2014).

Expectations and preferences in Japan have also changed around preference for care by children or other kin versus by non-kin. In the 1980s the majority of people age sixty and above reported that they preferred to be cared for by their children rather than by paid helpers (Lock 1993). At that time, policymakers responded to population aging with a relatively short-lived campaign advocating a Japanese-style welfare state, arguing for a distinct Japanese ethos in which caregiving and eldercare were primarily familial concerns (Lock 1993). The state insisted that since elders had contributed to the country's wealth and prosperity, they deserved to rely on their children for care in old age. Today, such expectations about family-based care arrangements no longer prevail. Robertson notes that surveys tracking elder preferences have shown increased openness to nonfamilial care and to roboticization (Robertson 2017). Both nonfamilial and robotized measures have been expanded in recent years with the argument from government and care industry stakeholders that they can help to protect the Japanese family by removing undue strain (Robertson 2017). As the needs of modern family life in Japan have changed, reliance on caregivers who are not part of the nuclear family or the kin network has grown, with Japanese seniors and their families increasingly turning to paid caregivers, institutions of care, and volunteers for assistance (Danely 2014).

Gendered expectations regarding eldercare have also changed. In the 1980s the Japanese government encouraged women to prioritize caregiving for seniors. They urged women to work part time as caregivers in the few available nursing-home facilities to gain some on-the-job experience before shifting to take care of their own elders in their homes when the time came (Lock 1993). While women remain central to providing care, their increased full- and part-time labor force participation before and after childbirth (Ezawa 2011: 109), as well as shifting attitudes to who provides care, mean that they are no longer the default caregivers for elders. Today, in fact, one in three caregivers for the elderly in Japan is a male family member (Amano 2014). There is more social acceptance of men providing care for their wives who, for example, develop dementia. I met elders where the husbands provided care. Also, as Japan aged, young brides have sometimes been enjoined to become the full-time caregivers of their grandparent-in-law upon tying the knot. Because their spouses' grandparents are alive at the time of nuptials, the new bride's role becomes that of full-time caregiver to an elderly grandfather.

Since the 1980s the state has changed its strategy regarding eldercare when three things became clear. Those are (1) the realization that the family could no longer be the one social unit to care for the aged, (2) middle-aged family members should no longer be so unfairly overburdened with eldercare (Schoppa 2006), and (3) former stop-gap social-welfare-based safety nets for indigent or disabled elders were insufficient and unsustainable (Campbell 1992). Even the Gold Plan, a ten-year strategy to double the scope of old age, health, and welfare services, was insufficient to cover emerging long-term care needs (Schoppa 2006).

With that realization, following lengthy deliberations by special councils (*shingikai*) composed of stakeholders such as municipal governments and welfare agencies under the Japanese Ministry of Health, Labor, and Welfare, the state introduced the long-term care insurance (LTCI) system in the 1990s. The LTCI asked people to pay insurance premiums into the fund, seeking to redistribute the risk of aging to individuals and society and away from the family unit. Financial management plans and pensions were also introduced with the expectation that individuals would demonstrate self-responsibility in joining them (Danely 2014). Individuals were thus enjoined to take initiative in being a productive, autonomous, and self-governing member of society responsible for preparing their own old age through enrolling in these forms of social pooling of risk (see Hook and Takeda 2007).

Analysts observe that, in recent decades, the Japanese state has frequently emphasized its responsibility for the elderly and has prioritized government spending in that direction (Campbell, Ikegami, and Gibson 2010). Successive tax reforms, including the revision of the consumption tax, have been enacted under the rationale that more funds are needed to cope with the aging of society. The government's creation of the expansive

Gold Plan and LTCI system clearly indicate its commitment to use public funds for aged care. In the context of overall government spending in Japan, spending on eldercare has become a far higher priority than spending on many other sectors of the population, such as households headed by single mothers (Akaishi 2011: 121) or households with full-time housewives, from whom subsidies were pulled in 2005.

The structure of Japan's LTCI has inadvertently disadvantaged family elder caregivers, two-thirds of whom are still women (Amano 2014), thus neglecting a real-time gendered life-course vision of people's eventual lot in old age. Unlike some other LTCI systems such as Germany's and Taiwan's (Wang Pin 2016: 6), the Japanese system stipulated that family members could not be paid cash allowances for their eldercare services. In Japan, the *shingikai* came to believe that stipends to family caregivers would stifle development of paid care services. Influential here was the Japanese women's not-for-profit organization known as the Women's Association for a Better Aging Society or WABAS (*Kōrei shakai o yokusuru josei no kai*). The group pointed out that labor conditions underpinning part-time work for women but full-time work for men were tied to government welfare arrangements that placed eldercare expectations on women (Mackie 2003: 190). They argued that the living conditions of elders, including female elders, could be improved by mitigating the eldercare burden placed on women kin. As a result, in order to incentivize a shift away from female kin-based care to nonfamilial care, Japan's LTCI system disallowed family caregiver stipends, hoping over the long run to nudge care away from sole reliance on family and toward individual insurance-based provisioning, societal pooling, and nonfamilial care (ILC 2015). However, in the short term, more female than male middle-aged eldercare caregivers provide kin-based care, as do single mothers and housewives, each without subsidies, detracting from those women's lot in later life.

Historical Ambivalence toward Old Age and Elder Dependence in Japan

It is common to hear that in Japan elders are respected, revered, and gladly cared for at home by their adult children based on their tradition of Confucian filial piety (for definition, see Introduction). Along similar sanguine lines, Takeo Doi (1973) has argued that, traditionally, the kind of loving dependent relationship of an infant on its mother (*amae*) was a key part of emotional life throughout the life course in Japan. This meant that, when an older person becomes frail or sick, culturally they and their family caregivers can accept their dependency and devotedly support and care for them as long as the elder lives.

Archaeological records show that people who were disabled or were incapacitated were not always maltreated (Schrenk and Tilley 2018). Archaeologists have found, for example, evidence of villagers' extension of support to people who lacked the capacity to live on their own. Similarly, in Japan the actual records of abandonment were few, and yet stories of elder abandonment proliferated, perhaps revealing wishes of wanting to gain some space from family members. Moore and Campbell (2009) assert that an entirely rosy view of old age and elder dependence in Japan, as an idyllic period of filial piety and veneration by others does not, in fact, bear careful scrutiny. Stories circulated of elder abandonment on mountaintops. For example, literary sources from the Middle Ages show a history of elder abandonment: Villagers abandoned elders who were thought to be on the verge of death because they were frail or had dementia (Formanek and Linhart 1997: 18). Based on the contemporaneous novel by Fukuzawa Shichiro, the film *Ballad of Narayama* (1957), according to Danely, recalls this history by depicting a seventy-year-old woman, Orin, who accepts her abandonment on the mountain as village custom, and, in fact, demands to be taken there as her ethical obligation, to "avoid the shame of being a burden" (Danely 2012: 11). Older males living in agrarian regions of Japan that historically upheld the practice of retirement of the household head (*inkyo*) usually had to live on the small marginal portion of property that he and his spouse were entitled to retain for themselves, as stipulated by the retirement contract. Old age was a precarious time for many elders. Elders with no children risked being abused by caregivers or being rotated from one nonlineal relative to the next. While some remained well-to-do and powerful, many became disenfranchised (Otake in Formanek and Linhart 1997: 18).

Thus, in spite of general notions involving filial piety (*oya kōkō*) and respect and support for the aged in Japan, there is evidence that historically dependent Japanese elders were not unconditionally socially embraced. Instead, elders were enjoined to embody and manifest certain life principles to accord with values of respected elderhood, which resemble a kind of ideal of self-reliance. Scheid (1997) elaborates that this ideal has strong affinities to the Buddhist concept of nonattachment and world renunciation (98–99). Such a state was difficult to achieve, since many elders remained attached to their memories of earlier times in their lives, recalling them with fondness or nostalgia. This emphasis on world renunciation came from the perception that elders should exercise self-restraint and know when to let go, transitioning to new states of seclusion and social detachment appropriate to their stage in life (see, for India, Lamb 2013). As the twelfth-century poet Saigyo said, old age was a time for cool reflection and acceptance of mortality (Tsuji 1997: 202). Scheid argued that exhibition of self-restraint and withdrawal in old age were important in winning others' admiration as a proper old person. Similarly, Tu Wei-Ming argued that, in traditional Confucian settings, old age was not a condition for respect from the young. Rather, the elder needed to "foster within themselves an inner drive to . . . [undergo] a dynamic process of self-transformation" if they were to gain respect (Moore and Campbell 2009: 223). For the caregiver, caring involves an ongoing process of transformation.

Later Life Self-Reliance and Self-Responsibility in Contemporary Japan

While we find some evidence of valuing self-reliance in seniors historically in Japan, the priority placed on related values has ballooned in recent decades. Part of a social trend affecting postindustrial societies around the world, including Japan, is the rising emphasis on independence, stressing self-reliance among older persons and responsibility for the self (see also chap. 9). These new values stand in tension with the value of mutual reliability, a very strong value in Japanese society but one that critics observe has become attenuated in an information technology society (see Robertson 2014: 583). The value of self-reliance manifests in the push to encourage older people to remain independent and not become dependent. Independence generally refers to "the ability to perform functions related to daily living: that is, the capacity of living independently in the community with no or little help from others" (Kalache 2007: 38). It may involve physical, mental, emotional, moral, and/or financial issues.

The modern discourse of a life founded on independence (*jiritsu shita seikatsu*) aims to make elders more self-reliant. The state has introduced policies intended to reduce dependence, and thus reduce the cost of social welfare (Danely 2014: 4). These policies encourage people to work longer, to stay active physically and socially, and to bear more of the cost of their long-term care by increasing their copayments (see also chap. 8). In my own work on-site, I have seen governmental bodies providing advice to elders on how to stave off becoming frail and dependent through responsible aging practices involving healthy diet and exercise, and encouraging elders to be less reliant on hospitalization and institutionalization. The mass media and organizations that support healthy longevity actively feature news stories of healthy elders and athletics events such as the Senior Olympics (Nenrinpics) to showcase the athletic feats of fit elders. Those who do not participate are encouraged to make a strong effort (*gambaru*) and stay well. In pamphlets and brochures produced by municipal governments, there is increased affirmation and recognition of the merits of independence. As the population is reminded of the burden of aging, they are encouraged to play their part in reducing their need for nursing care. There is an effort to delay dependence. If, previously, growing into maturity involved acceptance of mortality, including frailty and hence acceptance of change, now what is emphasized is spiritual, emotional, and moral maturation in responsibly taking care of the self for as long as possible, even if physical decline occurs.

While there is a counter-discourse encouraging acceptance of mortality and dependence in contemporary Japan, there is even stronger pressure to embody self-reliance and independence as an act of consideration to the community, thoughtfulness to family, and awareness of their social role in a rapidly aging society, on the other. John Traphagan (2010) has shown that being a burden on others is discouraged. James Wright (2018) and Susan Long (2013) have discussed how elders are taught to embrace independent living as part of what it means to be a globally minded, successful elder who is keen to demonstrate how Japanese are embracing technological aids that promote independence in old age. The embrace of active aging is thus framed prosocially, in terms of conveying consideration for others, or as not being a burden on others, in line with a Japanese notion of the self as interpersonal and contextual (Kondo 1990).

Self-responsibility has arisen as another strong related value in contemporary Japan, applying not only to elders but also to all citizens. It involves a redefinition of the relationship between the citizen and the state (Hook and Takeda 2007: 93). Scholars of Japan generally trace this rise to the 1990s, when so-called neoliberal values of responsibility and individualism became dominant in Japan after the collapse of the economic bubble.[3] Economic decline came to be seen as a person's own responsibility. In the media, the concept of self-responsibility (*jiko sekinin*) became widespread. The support of strong individuals (*tsuyoi kojin*) introduced by Prime Minister Junichiro Koizumi (2001–5) was subsequently passed on to the Shinzo Abe Cabinet (2006–7, 2012–20). Self-responsibility in the name of greater freedom (*jiyū*) became the new value, and deregulation occurred. Deregulation involved privatization. Amano observes that these deregulation moves contributed to the emergence of an unequal society (*kakusa shakai*) and growing numbers of vulnerable populations, whether they be homeless elders or retrenched workers or temp workers and even children from single-parent households.

With the collapse of the bubble economy in the 1990s, zero growth became the norm. The aging population combined with the low birth rate created what is sometimes known as the mature society. The mature society is characterized by a new value centering on the conserving of limited resources (Amano 2011: 193). For some seniors, this has involved pursuing simple thrifty lifestyles and preventive self-care. Some people, young and old, began to explore alternative values and lifestyles, such as pursuing more-informal networks of mutual aid in place of more-official structures. The hope is that people will find fulfillment in their day-to-day lives (*jujitsushita hibi*) in a low-growth society, rather than assuming that economic growth will continue. Retirees who take it upon themselves to care for disabled and elders in their local communities have emerged as well (194). I will return to this point later.

In terms of mutual aid and families of choice, Leonie Stickland (2014) has presented an interesting example. Stickland's analysis demonstrates the advocacy work of people seeking to develop an inclusive society. She shows how noticing a gap in eldercare provisions for nonheterosexual people, Japanese elder activists Komashaku and Konishi lobbied to create group homes that were friendly to elders of diverse sexualities. They created a living space called Village of Friends (Tomodachi-Mura) based on the concept of family of friends, so that nondependent people of different generations, genders, and sexualities could coreside in homes in a spirit of mutual assistance and affection, and take care of each other (Stickland 2014: 34). A successful innovation, the village has a tofu-making facility and a foot spa to help sustain itself; these services have been a boon for local residents who purchase the tofu and use the spa. Stickland reminds us that almost 39 percent of elder Japanese women in 2009 lived with nonfamily members, which includes institutional living or mutual-aid family of choice arrangements.

Some scholars of aging have begun to critique the groundswell of senior independence discourse in Japan. Some ask why Japanese seniors are being asked to be independent at the same time as having paid into the LTCI system; it is within their right to access nonfamilial care (Amano 2014). Some argue that elders have a right to be dependent, meaning that social acceptance of the changes that come with aging is the mark of a humane society. For example, sociologist Amano Masako (Amano 2014) asserts that only a society that advocates a survival-of-the-fittest mentality would deny elders the right to be dependent (115–16). She calls for active mutual coreliance, reminiscent of the Village of Friends, as a more realistic way to live within a society experiencing rapid aging. Sociologist Ueno Chizuko (2007) criticizes the successful aging movement in Japan known as the *pin pin korori* movement, which upholds the ideal of remaining active and healthy until the end of one's life and then dying a swift death, as discussed below. Ueno argues that this movement is ageist in rejecting the reality of declining health associated with aging.

Methodology for Ethnographic Research

I offer insights from interviews I conducted in Japan that touch on the issues of dependence and emotions surrounding caregiving. This chapter contains an analysis of texts and ethnographic interviews. I have performed research in Japan on aging during the past fourteen years, concentrating on urban-dwelling elders. My informants come from diverse educational backgrounds and professions. They range in age from fifty-five to a hundred, and all have considered themselves suitable participants in a study of aging, in which I include both involvement in formal lifelong learning in classes (such as music and theater classes), and learning to provide care for aging members of society, both blood kin and other. The interviews focus on their experience of aging, attitudes to living a meaningful life as they grow older, daily life practices and social relations, and caregiving experiences. I took a narrative analysis approach in analyzing recorded and transcribed interviews and other notes. My research examined the emotions and affects that people experience when they engage in care. Through interviews and observations in the field, I sought to elicit caregiver commentaries on their enactment of care.

This chapter focuses primarily on care examples from my work in a Zen temple, which I present as a form of innovative home-based care. In the pages that follow, I also examine the ways elders embrace the ideal of thoughtfulness through independence in later life, and how many elders struggled emotionally with their efforts to provide care for kin. Ethics approval was obtained from the University of New South Wales's low-risk research ethics committee, and the work was carried out in 2016 and 2017. The study used participant observation and semistructured interviews. All persons in this chapter have been assigned pseudonyms in order to protect their privacy.

Ethnographic Examples of Caregiving

In this section I explore some ethnographic case examples of at-home care by coresidents and assistance by local neighborhood volunteers who help elders living in their own homes. Care involves three aspects of interaction between caregiver and cared-for, including physical attention to the everyday needs of the patient; social care, which includes advice from professional caregivers and support networks; and spiritual care, which includes the emotional aspects of care. My discussion addresses all three aspects with most attention to emotional aspects. In each case, discourse and practices related to dependence, interdependence, and independence are examined. Following these two cases, the oft-cited issue of technological and robotic aids in Japan is considered.

At-Home Care by Family of Choice

Our first example shows a form of at-home aging in place in which the care recipient can sustain living outside an institutional context due to the support of LTCI, and in which the care recipient is very dependent in a physical sense, but cares for her caregiver in an emotional sense, which shows interdependence. Some people in Japan, as elsewhere, renovate their homes so that they can provide care at home instead of institutionalizing family members: they believe that their relatives will be happier at home. For some in Japan, a Buddhist temple serves as a long-term communal home for nuns where, with some home modifications, they can age in place with care by younger, healthier coresidents. Although a temple nunnery is not a conventional family home, fellow nuns become a kind of family for each other, and living in the nunnery is considered living at home, not institutional living and not a nursing home. Koei, the abbess of Sanko-in temple in Tokyo, is an example of one such nun aging in place in her temple home. Sanko-in is a nunnery of the Rinzai sect of Zen. Up to 100 Rinzai Zen nunneries exist, along with 77,000 temples in Japan (Ministry of Cultural Affairs 2014, 26). In religious institutions such as Zen temples, where there are no blood kin, fellow nuns look after the abbess. Sanko-in's origins stem back to a woman who wanted to contribute to women's education and so built Sanko-in in the 1920s. She invited a nun named Soei from Kyoto's Imperial Convent nunnery, Donke-in, to be the resident nun. Today, it is Soei's disciple Koei, age eighty-five, who is the abbess. I conducted interviews and extended participant observation at Sanko-in, conversing and interacting with its members. I observed the relationships in the temple, and I was involved in assisting with the care of the abbess, for example by conversing with her about Australia or serving cups of water to keep her hydrated.

Kōshun, the deputy abbess of the temple, is the abbess's main caregiver. Twenty years ago, when she was in her fifties, Kōshun moved into the temple, initially to become the sous chef or understudy to the abbess. Kōshun elected to keep the abbess in the temple and to re-form the temple building into a place of care, rather than place the abbess in an institution. Not all aged nuns take the approach that Abbess Koei did, with Kōshun's help. Other nuns have elected to step down from their roles as abbesses by passing on the responsibilities of the temple to the sub-abbess, and moving into an assisted living facility from which they commute to the temple to carry out certain limited duties.

TABLE 7.1. Benefits Used by Care Recipient in the Home Context, Including Those Subsidized and Not Subsidized by Long-Term Care Insurance System.

Services	Subsidized by LTCI	Not Subsidized
Dental	X	
Showering and bathing	X	
Music therapy		X
Physical therapy	X	
Full-body massage	X	
Facial massage		X

Source: Author data.

Abbess Koei is in a state of requiring full-time care. She is bedridden in a state of Level 5; under the Japanese LTCI classification system, Level 5 is the level requiring most care. She has a full-time schedule of caregivers coming to the temple, including dentists, bathers, music therapists, rehabilitation doctors trained in physiotherapy, and masseurs who do facial massages. The caregivers are both male and female. Only some of these visits are subsidized by the LTCI system (see table 7.1). Under LTCI, the abbess has an allowance of US$2,700 of long-term care services per month.

The abbess's main caregiver, Kōshun, says, "It's not like the abbess can go out to the movies or do anything 'fun,' so I think it's important to schedule these services." Kōshun says that these services will slow or prevent the development of Alzheimer's. Without social interaction, she would become less alert. Kōshun was particularly concerned to rehabilitate the abbess after she suffered a stroke and lost her capacity for speech and facial movement.

Kōshun is also the deputy abbess and director of cooking of the Zen temple. When we met, she had just turned seventy-two. Her energy was boundless. She prepared meals for the temple guests most days a week. In this temple, the abbess's designated heir, who inherited and carries on the work of the temple, which is the cooking of the food of the temple, is not ordained as a nun. She has taken charge of keeping the tradition of temple food alive. This food, which is a form of income for the temple as well, is a living tradition, inherited from generation to generation over the past 600 years.

Kōshun had also turned her attention to restoring the legacy of her teacher, Abbess Koei, by collecting all the documents she could find related to Abbess Koei and compiled a biography of her. She had enlisted her journalist friend, Suzuki Taro, to be her scribe to write down the stories of Koei's life as the abbess had told them to her. Suzuki compiled a manuscript of chapters, documenting the abbess's life from her early childhood as an adoptee to her discovery of the glorious world of the nunneries on a chance visit to the Imperial Convent nunnery in Kyoto to her entry into the life of the Sanko-in temple and her various activities there (see Fister 2009: 74).

I interviewed Kōshun in the main hall of the temple while we waited for the abbess's music therapist to arrive. Kōshun was new to the process of caregiving. Kōshun said, "I have never really experienced caring for anyone in my own family. I have very few kin. My mother died when I was 14 from diabetes, she was just skin and bones and was injecting herself with insulin each day when she died. My father died of a heart attack when I was a teen-ager. So caring for the abbess is the first real caring relationship I've had."

We discussed aspects of Kōshun's interactions and relationship with the abbess. Kōshun described how she becomes frustrated when the abbess wakes up often during the night, but how the abbess herself says and does things to help Kōshun manage her feelings.

Kōshun: She wakes me up at 10 p.m., then 12 a.m., then 2 in the morning. I want to sleep so I feel like going "aaaarghh!" But the person who softens these feelings of "aaarghh" is the abbess. She often says "I am sorry." And when she puts her hands together in prayer facing toward me [Kōshun starts to chuckle], I have to give in. The abbess does that to me, yes. And she always praises people, including me. Even when I say these terrible things because I'm so frustrated, she praises me.

Katrina: Do you ever feel anger?

Kōshun: Yes, I let that out a lot. I do a lot of "GAAA" [expression that denotes making noise]. So when I shut the door, I slam it. The abbess accepts everything. She doesn't react at all. So I get no reaction from her when I do these things.

Katrina: What explains her patience?

Kōshun: It is the long years of meditation. I am sure she learned a lot of perseverance [*gaman*] by accepting things that might irritate other people.

Kōshun framed her caregiving for the Abbess in the language of *ongaeshi*. "*Ongaeshi*" is the term that people use to describe feelings of gratitude. They want to return gifts they have received. Gifts can sometimes be understood as debts they have incurred, as disciples, in receiving tutelage from a superior.

I came away from the temple feeling that the abbess provides a great deal of care to the persons who are providing her with care. As illustrated above, Kōshun, for example, felt inspired, humbled, and cared for by the abbess's capacity to *accept* everything and everyone, including Kōshun's own irritation and feelings of frustration. When asked about the relevance of the Buddhist concept of compassion (*jihi*), she invoked the terms "forgive" (*yurusu*) and "accept" (*ukeireru*) to explain the abbess's way of relating to her. "Accept" refers to two things: One is the abbess submitting to her own situation of having to stay all day in bed. The abbess acknowledged her situation of needing to be confined to bed and of having to put up with what she sometimes said, with a smile, "It's pretty boring having to stay like this the whole day." The second is the abbess yielding to the people around her who provide care, including Kōshun and the outbursts of frustration that Kōshun had.

Acceptance of Things Just as They Are

The acts of yielding and of submission can be construed as something passive, meaning to condone, to not fight. But acceptance—or allowing, letting be—can also be an agentive act, an act of strength. To suffer can mean to put up with, to bear, to endure, and to tolerate. It is *both* passive and active. There is strength in that suffering. This tolerating draws on strength, and is also strength generating. I dare say it is strength generating for the one who is enduring, and it is also that way for the people caring. By allowing, the abbess's heart is calm, in spite of her physical challenges.

Compassion: Receiving Care from the Cared For

Caring involves empathy, perception, and a sense of shared connection (John Archer, 2017, personal communication). Nishino, Buddhist researcher at Taisho University, states that *jihi* involves two interrelated acts. One is for the caregiver to alleviate the discomfort of the person they are caring for. Another is to remove the suffering of the person they are caring for. He observes that caring as a lived practice is like a training ground (*shugyō no dōjō*) (Nishino 2007). The spirit of *jihi* means to consider the position of the other and to remove the suffering that the other may be going through. It is a space to grow the spirit of compassion.

In my conversations with the abbess, she never complained about her situation. Not being able to toilet by herself was a source of frustration. She disliked wearing diapers and having to use them. Often in the night she would wake Kōshun, because she wanted to go to the bathroom. Kōshun would explain that she could not go, and she would have to rely on her diapers.

What forms the basis of the abbess's capacity to accept what she does not like? According to Kōshun, it is the abbess's extended training in Zen, together with her feelings of thoughtfulness (*omoiyari*) that saves them both. Kōshun says, "The abbess tries hard in her rehabilitation exercises to move her body even if it's painful, because she wishes to not be a further burden to me. I think that her wish to not become any worse is an expression of the *omoiyari* that the abbess feels for me. She has a concern to not be a bother (*meiwaku*) on me." Kōshun said this in relation to the abbess's recovery from her stroke and improvement in her current situation.

The Role of Volunteers Who Care for the Disabled and the Elderly

What is seen as community mutual aid in the form of volunteer services for the disabled and the elderly in neighborhoods in Japan is a form of interdependence that allows disabled or frail elders to maintain independent living in their own home, rather than being forced into dependence on an institution. Municipal governments in Japan support this voluntary assistance by neighbors to help prevent high rates of institutionalization. Here I offer an illustrative case.

Kayoko-san is a retiree from a film company. She has worked her whole life. In retirement she helps those who are in need of assistance. She visits their homes, takes them bread from the local bakery, and does their gardening. A soft-spoken person with few words and not liking much attention, she is always thinking a lot about other people, and resisting receiving help herself. Kayoko-san helps people who hardly have any money to make ends meet. She says, "I do what I can to help out." I ask if she does this as part of a formal group involved in aiding elders at home, she says "no," that she just calls on her neighbors to see if anybody needs a hand (on neighborly assistance, compare with chap. 4). Retirees who have taken on the care of the elderly and disabled have emerged in Japan. Sociologist Amano contends that some are trying to form groups of mutual aid.

Lynne Nakano (2004) observes that in Tokyo home services offered by volunteers allow the middle-class disabled elderly to continue to live in their own homes rather than in institutions or with family members. Nakano claims that doing so gives them "pride and comfort in their ability to remain self-reliant" (155). Nitta, a strong advocate of volunteering, has created a program of mutual aid where volunteers can help fellow elders to remain in their homes. Nitta saw gaps in the services that could be filled by volunteers (144). Many participated in the program expecting that, one day, they also may rely on volunteers because their children lived in distant locales. This can be contrasted with the relations between the abbess and her caregiver.

Nakano recounts the case of a retiree who used public and nonprofit care services to maintain a sense of personal dignity after he became ill (Nakano 2004: 156). He had worked as a white-collar worker within a large bureaucratic organization for many years and had no meaningful friendships at work or in the neighborhood while he had been healthy. Despite living there for more than three decades, he knew his neighbors only enough to greet them when he saw them on the street. After he became ill, he relied on those neighbors who were community volunteers to help him take out the trash.

Care managers play a very important role in the industry today (Yamagishi, 2016, personal communication). They visit the homes of elders to establish the level of living assistance that they require and develop an overall plan. They then assign a monetary value to the services the elder may get through the insurance system. As the cases of Kōshun and the abbess demonstrate, care by older people for older people has become increasingly common in Japan. It is a topic of debate and concern in Japan. Aids to assist caregivers have become popular. It is to this topic that I turn next.

Optimism and Debates about Technological Aids and Robotics for Eldercare in Japan

Technological aids and robotics are another means that seniors and their caregivers in Japan are using more and more to allow elders to maintain independent living and avoid or at least delay institutionalization, and to reduce the difficulty of caregiving. Such usage is not seen as being dependent on technology, but as being independent of institutions and in many cases as being less dependent on family than they would otherwise need to be (compare with chaps. 1–2, 9). The cost of some technological aids such as wheelchairs is subsidized by LTCI.

Many devices are available to make the lives of caregivers easier. These include tools like walkers, wheelchairs, and motorized scooters to help elders to move around. To allay the concerns of children who live apart from their elderly parents, manufacturers of kitchen devices have made electric kettles that send a text message to the adult children each time the elder uses the kettle to boil water. Meanwhile, gas companies have installed devices in homes so that a signal is sent to the gas company if, in a twenty-four-hour-period, there is no evidence of the use of gas in the home (Nikkei Newspapers 2017). Such innovations have been created to support the care of elders from a distance.[1]

Technological aids to reduce the weight burden of elders have become very popular for use at home. One is the Hoyer lift, which I observed in the field. The caregiver places a netted cloth about one-meter square underneath the bedridden elder, and then wraps it around her. Then the two ends of the cloth are connected to an overhanging hook, and a pulley lifts up the person and maneuvers her onto a wheelchair. The lift enables the caregiver to transfer the elder without lifting them in their arms. Robotics research aims to eliminate the risk of injury to caregivers stemming from the weight of carrying the elderly (Chuo Rôsai 2017; Marshall 2016: 29).

Scientists in Japan have been advancing robotics technology to assist seniors, including in their own homes. Humanoid robots such as Softbank's Pepper have been created to serve as companions for elders. A robot may accompany Alzheimer's patients and help them find their way back to their bedrooms. It is hoped that a robot will enable elders to live independently in their homes for three to four years, delaying the time when they will need institutionalization (Pasick 2014).

Prime Minister Abe announced in June 2013 that his administration was earmarking US$24 million toward the development of "urgently needed nursing and elder-caregiving robots" (Robertson 2014: 578). These robots are considered an integral part of a plan to address the shortfall of caregivers in the country, as well as to spark new spin-off industries. The absence of debate about the shortage of caregivers is conspicuous, contends Robertson. Low pay for caregivers makes it unattractive to Japanese workers, and Japanese language exams for foreign domestic workers (FDWs) from Indonesia and the Philippines allegedly make it challenging for FDWs to secure full-time employment in the field (Switek 2014: 266). Some surveys show that elders are more comfortable being cared for by robots than by FDWs because of the language and cultural difficulties with the latter (Robertson 2014: 578) Some elders prefer robots to FDWs because robots do not spark memories of the war. Such surveys show that among care recipients, 65 percent prefer to be assisted by robots. The National Robot Strategy wishes to see this figure increase to 80 percent by 2020 (Marshall 2016: 29). State representatives who advocate for robots, including Prime Minister Shinzo Abe, argue that robots may also keep the Japanese family system intact by "[relieving] women from household chores and responsibilities" (see Robertson 2014: 578). It is claimed that robots will reduce the strain on women to support their families both in the domestic realm and in the paid workforce. Robots may fulfill their role by serving as live-in nannies or housekeepers who will care for children and stretch their minds or do domestic tasks like cooking and paying the bill for cable television. In doing so, the argument goes, women and men as parents will have more opportunities to embrace and play with their children.

While historically some elsewhere see such robotic measures as possibly leading to a dehumanized brave new world, some elders in Japan see advantages in eldercare by robots in freeing care recipients from the emotional shortcomings of human caregivers and the embarrassment of carrying out intimate bodily functions in their presence. For example, one elder saw some advantages in robots: she thought that robots would be better able to accommodate the volatile emotions of elders, especially those who were suffering from dementia. She had witnessed her elderly aunt treat her caregivers with spite. In turn, her caregivers were sometimes cool and detached to this aunt. She thought robots would not be curt, or, worse, retaliate to patients who are aggressive or ill tempered. They would maintain a neutral stance. They would be unable to offer respect or recognition (see Sparrow 2015) or empathy (Airenti 2015), but neither would they be rude or willfully withdraw emotional care. This elder also said that robots would show patience when assisting elders who took a long time to go to the bathroom. They would show more consideration than human caregivers, who in a facility where staff shortages and low wages placed pressures on staff to rush may not show the same kind of patience or tolerance for the resident elders.

A related hope about robots was expressed by another informant of mine. Chisan, who is involved in palliative care, reacted with glee when she heard about the role of robots in care. Chisan claimed that robots reduce the emotional turmoil of older persons having to receive support for toileting and other personal needs. In regard to social obligation in care, nobody wants to offend the other person. Robots have the ability to lessen the emotional complexity involved in caring and being cared for. Elders do not want to offend the goodwill of their child, especially when the child is extending an invitation to do something, such as live together. Many elders claim to be more at ease living on their own in places where they have lived for many years. Uprooting their lives to live with their children is not that appealing, especially if it entails navigating new kinds of transportation, new spaces, a different dialect or language, and different social relations. There is also the reluctance, among elders, of being controlled or managed by children who are the heads of their households. Elders know they are entering someone else's house. For women who are married, they did this once when they moved to their patrilineal household and came under the authority of the husband's family and oftentimes their mother-in-law. To move again, this time to their child's household, would involve another adjustment, this time to the ways of the child and spouse of their child, as well as to the ways of the in-law. In such a situation, a robot companion may be preferable.

Yet, mixed feelings arise in regard to robots in relation to human feelings and connection and with regard to social class and jobs and the very need for humanity. Human connection is valued, and that may be why robots, despite Prime Minister Abe's keen support, will not be the ultimate solution to Japan's eldercare problem. Observers state that humanoid robots cannot reciprocate the human feeling that adults can pour into robots (Airenti 2015). They can perform tasks. They can simulate emotion and stimulate emotional responses, but there is no one home inside the machine. Not all Japanese sources have portrayed robots in a positive light. For example, Japanese robot fiction of the 1930s focuses on the disturbing relationship between humans and robots. Discussion of robots was often mixed with discussion of social class. In fictional accounts of robots, there was a fear that robots, and mechanization and industrialization more generally, would take over the jobs that humans had. Literary scholar Rebecca Suter observes that Japanese robot fiction has discussed incidents of robots stealing jobs, causing rising unemployment, and invading the streets (Suter 2011: 274). Characters in these accounts held a fear that robots might rebel against oppression and overtake their masters. More contemporary popular culture shows on robots include the drama *Real Humans* about human-robot relations. The show raises questions such as, "Should a sentient machine have human rights? What if robots do to us what we did to them?" In the show, these synths are employed as servants, caregivers, and tram drivers. They have cognitive abilities but no free will. The humans on the show wonder "how much longer they themselves will have a purpose" (Poniewozik 2017: C5).

Given these questions, what exactly do we make of the use of caregiver robots? Since 2007 the Japanese state has sought to promote a robot-dependent society (Robertson 2014: 578). It is currently debating whether to confer citizenship rights to robots, akin to rights conferred to human beings (Robertson 2014). This has profound implications for human rights, since robots are gaining citizenship rights before certain ethnic minorities do. Robertson contends that Japanese have pursued this strategy of pursuing automation over replacement migration since the 1960s. Robertson interprets these moves to use robots as a way to create gated communities. She refers to this trend as technological national isolation, reminding readers of Japan's policy of national isolationism during the Tokugawa period (1600–1867). It is curious that robots are being promoted as a form of independence from other humans, ignoring the danger of overdependence on robots and technology for tasks like emotional support to which they may not be as well-suited either in a technical sense or in a moral sense.

Robertson also states that the introduction of humanoid robots is, in her view, a form of reactionary postmodernism. The robots are being introduced in order for the patriarchal family to remain intact and for Japan's reluctance to accept FDWs to go unchallenged. The humanoid robots that do housework are meant to help women to distribute their agency so that they may continue to do housework in collaboration with humanoids. Such humanoid robots were introduced to supposedly offset the extreme reliance on the Internet and hyper-technologization of Japanese society, and the resulting feelings of loneliness.

What if elders are happy with their robot companions? Should we consider the argument of bioethicist Robert Sparrow (2015), who claims that robots will not succeed in providing humans with two things that are more important than happiness: recognition and respect? Recognition consists of "the enjoyment of social relations that acknowledge us in our particularity and as valued members of a community" (7). Respect consists of "social and political relationships wherein our ends are granted equal weight to those of others in the community" (7.) Sparrow argues that engineers who design robots may not expect this, but robots will end up detracting from, rather than enhancing, humans' quality of life. Both Sparrow and Sheila Jasanoff (2016) warn that interpersonal tensions arise from such innovations. While a positive side exists, human technologies like robotics and artificial intelligence are likely, at least to some extent, to undermine human dignity and compromise core values of being human.

Conclusion

What does the aging of Japan portend? Japan's population is shrinking while the proportion of elders is increasing. Care of elders in Japan has become an urgent issue because of rapid changes in Japan's demographic structure (Switek 2014: 264). Demographic changes that led to a precipitous decline in fertility are one factor. Another is the increased longevity of the population due to enhanced medical services. Limited levels of migration also play their part in this demographic structure. Major considerations driving discussion of caregiving policy include the shortfall of labor, and labor's impact on the social security system. Japan's workforce declined to 77.2 million in 2015 from a peak of 87.2 million in 1995. By 2065 it is expected to drop to just 45.2 million (Reuters in Asahi 2017). To help mitigate the situation, the state wishes to keep women in the workforce for longer and to provide forms of socialized care when older people are no longer able to live in their own homes and live independently for extended periods of time.

Elders are responding increasingly to this situation with innovative ideas of their own. Despite the state at least beginning to share some of the responsibility for eldercare with the family by providing LTCI since 2000, the risks of aging are increasingly being moved away from the state and the family toward the aging individual. To address this situation of demographic aging, many initiatives have been offered.

A diversity of coliving and care options has emerged in Japan in the wake of the development of the LTCI system. As we saw, one such option is aging in place for coliving nuns with a high level of care need since LTCI provides the funds to remodel nunnery rooms for such care. We also saw how LTCI helps to incentivize neighborhood volunteers to support ordinary elders living in their homes. Technology and robotics are increasingly being used to help avoid or delay institutionalization. Live-in hired home caregivers, commuting hired caregivers, and residential nursing homes are among some of the other care options available, though not described above. The coliving arrangements for seniors of a nonheterosexual orientation described earlier attest to the diversification of eldercare living options. The state has kept the notion of the family intact through the household registration system, but a diversity of kinship relationships exists to accommodate the reality that not all people are biologically related or live in nuclear households.

The twin values of personal responsibility and independence have emerged, influencing social perceptions of desirable aging. Not imposing unduly on the other is valued. The general trend is to aim toward reducing dependence on family and promoting adaptation to change in later life. Health maintenance is undoubtedly a major aspect of what it means to be a responsible elder, and importance is placed on diet and exercise such as walking. Use of LTCI benefits, volunteer services, and robotics is not necessarily considered forms of excessive dependence on the state, the community, or technology. At the same time, forms of inter-human dependence and interdependence can, of course, still be seen. Expectations about living arrangements are evolving. We see a shift from residing with family to more elders living on their own. Based on surveys of elder residential preferences, we expect more elders in the future to be living in the community on their own rather than in institutions, and for those living in institutions to be cared for by robot companions—if the facilities can afford them.

How to age gracefully is a question that has entered the public sphere in a prominent way. Many discussions focus on lifestyle habits that promote responsible living. For elders, responsible living involves engaging in mutual aid and helping each other live well. It includes attaining optimum well-being in later life through increased activity levels and exercise. Other philosophies of responsible living that have not been addressed here but that are worth mentioning briefly include the implementation of advance care directives (NHK Radio 2017) and downsizing in a timely manner by getting rid of personal belongings. Elders aim to value life in the present, while being cognizant of their mortality and taking steps to address the implications of their mortality for their family members.

I have sought to show how Japanese models of sociocentric personhood emphasize a strong interpersonal orientation. Remaining aware of others is important. As the well-publicized case of Takagi Boo attests, seniors showing consideration for family and for others in society is framed as a virtue. How older people show care for others is to adapt to changing circumstances. This involves attention to younger members' needs and being open to new technology and devices. It is hoped that by embracing change new configurations of family can be sustained. The purported aim is to keep the experiences of family and human connection alive, oftentimes with the aid of technology.[2]

Drawing on the ethics of care developed by Eva Kittay (1999), Rosemarie Tong (2014) argues that the state should pay more attention to the needs of caregivers and address these needs in policy and programs. I think that she is right that such needs include education, counseling, and respite time. Caregivers also need structural reforms in the workplace such as job sharing, flex time, family leave policies, and on-site eldercare. It is important not to focus so much on technological solutions that we lose sight of these more basic needs.

Growing older can be construed in an ambivalent light. With age comes wisdom stemming from experience, and also physical debility. In contrast to popular stereotypes of Japanese society as a place where elders can be wholeheartedly dependent without reservation, elders in Japan historically were encouraged to embody self-restraint and to realize that their presence could be an imposition on the communal resources. What is different today is the scale of self-reliance discourse (see also Introduction) due to the percentage of elders in the population, which now is far higher than it was in the eighteenth century. Consequently, an aging population has come to be a biopolitical problem for the state—that is, as something that requires shaping and managing by the state's institutional arms. As a pioneer in addressing population aging, Japan is one important model for social welfare policies and gerontechnological innovation. While Japan is far from having all the answers, it will be fascinating to see how sentiments about aging and caregiving, and strategies for healthy longevity and managing eldercare needs, evolve as new challenges and opportunities arise.

Acknowledgments

Supported by a Special Studies Program grant from the University of New South Wales, the fieldwork was conducted in Tokyo. I would like to thank Hugh de Ferranti of the Tokyo University of Technology for his hospitality as my academic sponsor during my stay. I would also like to thank my fellow coeditors and Alison Hope for invaluable suggestions on earlier drafts of this chapter. I gratefully acknowledge the caregivers who participated in this research and thank Tsutsumi Yumiko, Lisa Moore, Sotomi Takashi, and Priscilla Song.

Katrina Moore is an honorary associate in Japanese Studies, Faculty of Arts and Social Sciences, the University of Sydney. She is the author of *Joy of Noh: Embodied Learning and Discipline in Urban Japan* (SUNY Press 2014). She contributed chapters to Vera Mackie and Mark McLelland (eds.), *Routledge Handbook of Sexuality Studies in East Asia* (Routledge 2015); Maren Godzik (ed.), *Altern in Japan* (Verlag 2009); and articles in *Aging and Anthropology* (2017), *Japanese Studies* (2013), *Asian Anthropology* (2010), and *Journal of Cross-Cultural Gerontology* (2010). She currently researches conservation practices as well as family and household relationships.

Glossary

gaman	我慢	Perseverance.
gambaru	頑張る	Put in effort.
ie	家	Japanese household.
jiko sekinin	自己責任	Personal responsibility.
jiritsushita seikatsu	自立した生活	Life of self-reliance.
jiyū	自由	Self-responsibility in the name of greater freedom.
jūjitsushita hibi	充実した日々	Fulfilled days.
Nenrinpics	ねんりんピック	Senior Olympics.
omoiyari	思いやり	Thoughtfulness.
ongaeshi	恩返し	Make a return on a debt.
oya kōkō	親孝行	Filial piety.
pin pin korori	ぴんぴんころり	Being active until death.
shugyō no dōjō	修行の道場	Training ground.
Tomodachi-Mura	ともだち村	Village of Friends.
tsuyoi kojin	強い個人	Strong individual.

ukeireru	受け入れる	Accept.
yurusu	許す	Allow, forgive.

Notes

1. Thoughtful adult children also install automated garden watering systems with the goal of helping their parents see their gardens flourish.
2. Proponents believe that technology, used appropriately in support of national goals, promises hope: Robots and humans can coexist and aid elders. Robertson notes in her study of robotics in Japan that they have to be understood through Japanese Shintoist beliefs and animistic ideas about the coexistence of diverse life forms and mutual reliability. Since robots are seen as living things and not machines, they can be incorporated into social units of interdependence (Robertson 2014: 583).
3. For discussion of shifting notions of responsibility arising during this period, see Gluck 2009.

References

Airenti, Gabriella. 2015. "The Cognitive Bases of Anthropomorphism: From Relatedness to Empathy." *International Journal of Social Robotics* 7 (1): 117–27.

Akaishi, Chieko. 2011. "Single Mothers." Trans. Minata Hara. In Fujimura-Fanselow, *Transforming Japan*, 121–30.

Amano, Masako. 2011. *In Pursuit of the Seikatsusha: A Genealogy of the Autonomous Citizen in Japan*. Trans. Leonie Stickland. Melbourne: Transpacific Press.

———. 2014. *Oigai no Jidai: Nihon eiga kara mita Kōreisha* [An era worth aging in: Elders portrayed in Japanese film.] Tokyo: Iwanami Shoten.

Campbell, John C. 1992. "How Policies Change." Berkeley: University of California Press.

Campbell, John C., Naoki Ikegami, and Mary Jo Gibson. 2010. "Lessons from Public Insurance in Germany and Japan." *Health Affairs* 29 (1): 87–95.

Campbell, Ruth, and Yukiko Kurokawa. 2016. *Ichiban Mirai no Idea Book: Futsu no Koreisha no Minasan ga Kangaemashita* [The idea book for the best future: Ideas conceptualized by ordinary seniors]. Tokyo: Dai Nihon Insatsu Gaisha.

Chuo Rōsai, Bōshi Kyōkai. 2017. "Kaigo Kakaeage Gensoku Kinshi o: Kyōzai o Sakusei, Shokuin no Kega ga Zoukade" [Lifting of nursing patients banned in principle: Creation of educational materials to educate caring professionals after increase in injuries]. *Nihon Keizai Shimbun*, 12 April.

Danely, Jason. 2012. "Aging and Abandonment: Obasute Narratives in Contemporary Japan." Paper presented at the annual meeting of the Asian Studies Association. Toronto, Canada, 13–20 March 2012.

———. 2014. *Aging and Loss: Mourning and Maturity in Contemporary Japan*. New Brunswick, NJ: Rutgers University Press.

Doi, Takeo. 1973. *The Anatomy of Dependence*, trans. John Bester. Tokyo: Kodansha.

Ezawa, Aya. 2011. "Changing Patterns of Marriage and Motherhood." In Fujimura-Fanselow, *Transforming Japan*, 105–120.

Fister, Patricia. 2009. "Hōkyōji Imperial Convent." In *Amamonzeki, A Hidden Heritage: Treasures of the Japanese Imperial Convents*, ed. Patricia Fister and Monica Bethe. Tokyo: Sankei.

Formanek, Susanne, and Sepp Linhart. 1997. *Aging: Asian Concepts and Experiences Past and Present*, Vienna: Austrian Academy of Sciences.

Fujimura-Fanselow, Kumiko, ed. 2011. *Transforming Japan: How Feminism and Diversity Are Making a Difference*. New York: The Feminist Press at the City University of New York.

Gluck, Carol. 2009. "Sekinin/Responsibility in Modern Japan." In *Words in Motion: Toward a Global Lexicon*, ed. Carol Gluck and Anna Tsing, 83–108. Durham, NC: Duke University Press.

Hook, Glenn D., and Hiroko Takeda. 2007. "'Self-Responsibility' and the Nature of the Postwar Japanese State: Risk through the Looking Glass." *Journal of Japanese Studies*. 33(1): 93–123.

International Longevity Center (ILC). 2015. "Towards a Sustainable Aging Society: International Comparative Study on Productive Aging 2012–2015." Presentation made at the North-East Asian Forum on Population Aging, 6 November.

Jasanoff, Sheila. 2016. *The Ethics of Invention: Technology and the Human Future*. New York: W. W. Norton.

Jenike, Brenda Robb. 2004. "Alone in the Family: Great Grandparenthood in Urban Japan." In *Filial Piety: Practice and Discourse in Contemporary East Asia*, ed. Charlotte Ikels, 217–44. Stanford, CA: Stanford University Press.

Kalache, Alex. 2007. "The World Health Organization and Global Aging." In *Global Health and Global Aging*, ed. Mary Robinson, William Novelli, Clarence Pearson, and Laurie Norris, 31–46. San Francisco: Jossey Bass.

Kittay, Eva. 1999. *Love's Labor: Essays on Women, Equality, and Dependency*. New York: Routledge.

Kondo, Dorinne. 1990. *Crafting Selves: Power, Gender, and Discourses of Identity in a Japanese Workplace*. Chicago: University of Chicago Press.

Lamb, Sarah. 2013. "Personhood, Appropriate Dependence, and the Rise of Eldercare Institutions in India." In *Transitions and Transformations: Cultural Perspectives on Aging and the Life-Course*, ed. Caitrin Lynch and Jason Danely, 171–87. New York: Berghahn.

Lock, Margaret M. 1993. *Encounters with Aging: Mythologies of Menopause in Japan and North America*. Berkeley: University of California Press.

Long, Susan Orpett. 2013. "Bodies, Technologies and Aging Japan: Thinking About Old People and their Silver Products." *Journal of Cross-Cultural Gerontology* 27: 119–37.

Mackie, Vera. 2003. *Feminism in Modern Japan: Citizenship, Embodiment, and Sexuality*. Cambridge, UK: Cambridge University Press.

Marshall, R. C. 2016. "What Doraemon, the Earless Blue Robot Cat from the 22nd Century, Can Teach Us about How Japan's Elderly and their Human Caregivers Might Live with Emotional Care Robots." *Anthropology and Aging* 37 (1): 27–40.

Ministry of Cultural Affairs. 2014. *Buddhism Bulletin (Bukkyô Nenpyô)*. Tokyo: Ministry of Cultural Affairs.

Moore, Katrina, and Ruth Campbell. 2009. "Mastery with Age: The Appeal of the Traditional Arts to Senior Citizens in Japan." In *Aging in Japan* [Altern in Japan], ed. Maren Godzik, 223–252. Vienna: Verlag.

Nakano, Lynne. 2004. *Community Volunteers in Japan: Everyday Stories of Social Change.* London: Routledge.

NHK Radio. 2017. *Island Relay News.* Retrieved 29 March 2017 from http://www.nhk .or.jp/radionews/.

Nikkei Newspaper. 2017. "Hanareta Rōshin no Mimamorikata, Tatsujin Nakamura Sumiko-san ni Kiku: Kaeru tabi Ie no Ihen o Chekku suru" [How do we care for older relatives who live apart from their families: we ask expert Nakamura Sumiko: Checking for accidents on each home visit], 12 April.

Nishino, T. 2007. "Rōjin Kaigo ni Okeru Bukkyōteki Shiten" [Eldercare from the viewpoint of Buddhism]. *Bukkyō Bunka Gakkai Kiyo* 17: 28–51.

Pasick, Adam. 2014. "Softbank's Humanoid Robot Will Be Great for Tending to Japan's Elderly." *Quartz.* Retrieved 20 May 2017 from https://qz.com/217199/soft banks-humanoid-robot-will-be-great-for-tending-to-japans-elderly/.

Poniewozik, James. 2017. "A Plea for Robot Rights, Filled with Feeling." *New York Times,* 13 February.

Reuters in Asahi. 2017. "Labor Shortage a Stress Test for Japan's 24/7 'Combinis.'" Retrieved 25 April 2017 from https://fr.reuters.com/article/businessNews/ idUSKBN17Q2FR.

Robertson, Jennifer. 2014. "Human Rights vs Robot Rights: Forecast from Japan." *Critical Asian Studies* 46 (4): 571–98.

Robertson, Jennifer. 2017. *Robosapiens Japanicus: Robots, Gender, Family, and the Japanese Nation.* Berkeley, CA: University of California Press.

Scheid, Bernard. 1997. "An Old Tree in Bloom: Zeami and the Ambivalent Perspectives on Old Age." In Formanek and Linhart, *Aging,* 97–106.

Schoppa, Leonard. 2006. *Race for the Exits: The Unraveling of Japan's System of Social Protection.* Ithaca, NY: Cornell University Press.

Schrenk, A., and L. Tilley. 2018. "Caring in Ancient Times. In Health and Well-Being." *Anthropology News* 59 (1): 57–63.

Sparrow, Robert. 2015. "Robots in Aged Care: A Dystopian Future?" *AI and Society.* Published online 10 November 2015. Retrieved 25 April 2017 from doi:10.1007/ s00146-015-0625-4.

Stickland, Leonie. 2014. "Accommodating Japan's Aging Sexual Minorities: The Family of Friends Concept in LGBTI Seniors' Residential Care." In *Configurations of Family in Contemporary Japan,* ed. Tomoko Aoyama, Laura Dales, and Romit Dasgupta, 33–45. London: Routledge.

Suter, Rebecca. 2011. "Science Fiction as Subversive Hypothesis: Henkaku Tantei Shōsetsu between Entertainment and Enlightenment." *Japanese Studies* 31 (2): 267–77.

Switek, Beata. 2014. "Representing the Alternative: Demographic Change, Migrant Eldercare Workers, and National Imagination in Japan." *Contemporary Japan* 26 (2): 263–80.

Tong, Rosemary. 2014. "Vulnerability and Aging in the Context of Care." In *New Essays in Vulnerability,* ed. C. Mackenzie, W. Rogers, and S. Dodds, 288–307. Oxford: Oxford University Press.

Traphagan, John. 2010 *Taming Oblivion: Aging Bodies and the Fear of Senility in Japan*. Albany, NY: State University of New York Press.

Tsuji, Yohko. 1997. "Continuities and Changes in Conceptions of Old Age in Japan." In Formanek and Linhart, *Aging*, 195–208.

Ueno, Chizuko. 2007. *Ohitorisama no* Rōgo [Old age of the single elder]. Tokyo: Hōken.

Wang Pin. 2016. "Fighting For or Against a Long-Term Care Insurance in Taiwan: NGOs' Divide." Paper presented at the Society for East Asian Anthropology (SEAA) Conference, The Chinese University of Hong Kong, 19–22 June.

Wright, James. 2018. "Tactile Care, Mechanical Hugs: Japanese Caregivers and Robotic Lifting Devices." *Asian Anthropology* 17: 1, 24–39.

8 "SON, I'VE ALREADY DIED AND BECOME A MUMMY"

The Sociocultural Contexts of Missing Centenarians in Super-Aging Japan

Heekyoung Kim

Introduction

ON WEDNESDAY, 23 FEBRUARY 2011, I was drinking tea as usual with Koyama-san and Hanazato-san. Koyama-san had been widowed at sixty years of age and for the past ten years had been living alone. She had a son and a daughter, both of them married and living in Tokyo and Nagano, respectively. Hanazato-san had two sons and one daughter. Hanazato-san had been widowed when she was seventy-five years old after caregiving for her husband who had suffered from thirty years of a chronic illness. She lived alone for a while but had been living with her daughter and son-in-law for the past seven years. We had tea every Wednesday and talked about various things, including family. That day, we were talking about what the two women would want their funerals to be like and who would take care of the Buddhist family altar (*butsudan*) to deceased family members.

> Koyama: I could regret it later, but I feel fortunate to have built this house before my husband died.

> Hanazato: Good job. It's okay while you're alive, It may be a problem when it becomes empty.

> Koyama: Do you know what my son said? He came home during New Year's and said, "What will you do with this house later?" So I said, "I will give it to someone who takes care of me, whether it's a relative or non-relative." [laughter] Then my son says, "Oh, then brother-in-law can take care of you and inherit this house." My son-in-law is also the oldest son in his family. Does that even make sense? Listening to what he said, I don't think my son has even the slightest inclination to come home.

Hanazato: I've already written my will and shown it to my son. It mainly says that even after my death, the *butsudan* should be well-kept. Second, a funeral ceremony should be carried out even if it's only with family. That's all I asked. My son saw it [my will] and said, "Mother, we have the *butsudan* in mind, too." So I said, "Please keep it well." Well, they will give a proper funeral.

Koyama: So I told my son during a [rare] phone call a while ago, "If I die, it would be a bit weird to just leave me like that, so just give me a cremation and then do what you like" [laughter]. He wouldn't just leave me at home like that, unless I became a mummy [laughter]. I called him before, but he was so busy that we couldn't talk. So my son-in-law must have told him to at least call me. Then my son called me and asked, "Are you well?" so I said "How would I be well? Son, I've died and become a mummy. I've saved the pension in the bank." Then my son said, "Ah, I know where you've saved it, so I'll just withdraw the money myself" [laughter]. The children don't help and are good for nothing. It's such a worry.

Both of these women are daughters-in-law who took care of parents-in-law before they passed away, but they were not living with their eldest sons as tradition holds. Thus, Hanazato-san and Koyama-san feared that the traditions of keeping the Buddhist altar and the practice of the oldest son coming to live in his parents' house after they pass away to maintain the family homestead would not be performed after their death. Rather than seeing a death as the termination of a person's social existence, it has long been seen as a transitional point, beyond which the deceased enters a new state of existence through the ritual efforts of those left behind in the Japanese social universe (Kawano 2010: 1). Koyama-san was especially worried about who would manage her house and the altar if she were to pass away suddenly, because she was living alone. Teasing her about her fears that he would not keep with tradition, Koyama-san's son often joked that her son-in-law should inherit the house. He (her son) would then withdraw the pension money himself from Koyama-san's bank account and not take care of his obligations. Given these jokes and her son's apathy about what Koyama-san felt was proper decorum and attention to his mother, she smiled bitterly, recalling how she greeted his call with dark humor: "How would I be well? Son, I've died and become a mummy."

Koyama-san's joke of saying "I've become a mummy" alludes to a widely reported incident involving the discovery of an elderly man in Japan in 2010 who actually had become a mummy (Kim 2017). On a hot summer day in 2010, Kato, purportedly 111 years of age and Tokyo's oldest reported man, was found to have been dead at home for more than thirty years. It came to light in talking with family members that thirty-two years ago he had said that he was ready to die and that he was determined to die at home. So he went into his bedroom, locked his door, lay down, and refused to eat or open his door. The media impact of the news of the incident grew to larger proportions when it was found that Kato's death had never been officially reported, and his oldest daughter, an eighty-one-year-old in 2010, and his grandson, a fifty-three-year-old, had for decades been withdrawing part of the widower pension that was accumulating in Kato's account. The police arrested them for corpse abandonment and illegal embezzlement of pension funds (McCurry 2010).

This was not the only incident of a mummified centenarian being passed off as alive in order for descendants to cash in. Around the same time, a corpse that had been dead for five years was found wrapped in plastic in Osaka. The dead person was an old man who would have been ninety-one years old if he had still been alive. At first foul play was suspected, but it turned out that the criminal who had stashed away the corpse was his oldest daughter, a woman in her fifties, who had hidden her father's body after he died of natural causes. The daughter confessed that her father died about five years ago and she put him in a plastic bag and put him in the closet. She withdrew her father's pension from his account and used it. The police determined that she had withdrawn about 300,000 yen of his pension every two months, and received 30,000 yen from the city for celebration of her father's longevity (Masatoshi 2013).[1]

The reaction of the larger Japanese society was shock. It was feared that these incidents might not be confined to only a few irrational and bizarre families. After the discoveries just noted, the government and the press carried out research, and the results revealed further shocking cases. In August 2010 it was found that the oldest woman in Tokyo, Huruya-san, could not be located. The district office employees visited her eldest daughter (aged seventy-nine) who said she had moved her mother into the Suginami District of Tokyo in 1986. This daughter claimed that her mother had only moved her residential records but she did not move then, so she did not know whether her mother is alive or dead. The employee then visited the Huruya-san's son's registered address in Chiba, but the address was uninhabited and they could not find a forwarding address. The district office got in touch with a second daughter, but the second daughter also indicated that she did not know where her mother was.

Beyond Suginami district, other incidents were exposed in other places. According to announcements by the Ministry of Health, Labour and Welfare (MHLW), as verified based on resident registers as of 1 September 2010, the number of elders reported to be living at age 100 or more was 44,449, but among them only 23,269 had been verified as to their whereabouts and actually being alive. Ten people were found to be lost and the remaining people amounting to about 20,000 had not been verified. Actually, practical registration for passing away is completed only when a family files a report of death with the government (*Yonhab News* 2010). Among families who have not submitted notices of death, other than those who simply forgot, cases continued to emerge showing families not keeping in touch for decades and adult children ignorant of whether their parents were alive or dead.[2] The MHLW has officially announced that 3 percent of those receiving pensions appear to be receiving the funds unlawfully (MHLW 2011). In addition, as a result of the government survey, 572 elderly people whose living conditions were not confirmed were further suspended from pension payments (MHLW 2011). In other words, in many of these cases it has been demonstrated that adult children deliberately hid their parents' dead bodies and/or did not report the death to the district office so that they could take advantage of continuance of the deceased elders' pension funds.

This pattern of missing elderly amply demonstrates a wide gap between the image of Japan as paradise for the elderly and the reality in which filial piety (for definition, see Introduction) cannot be assumed. Many early Western scholars interested in aging in Japanese society considered Japanese society to be one where the aged are free of all duties, and where the elderly are still respected and cared for (Benedict 1946; Doi 1962; Lebra 1984; Palmore 1975; Plath 1964). Yet, the reality is not so sanguine for all Japanese elders.

Anthropological research conducted more recently has paid attention to the gap between ideal and reality, and scholars argue that the actual ways in which Japanese people treat the elderly do not always realize the ideal. Specifically, much of this research criticizes an emphasis on the culture of respecting elders as a unique Japanese virtue, pointing out that this ideology places the burden of caring for elders on family (Campbell 2000; Jenike 1997; Kelly 1993; Lock 1993; Long 1996; Maeda and Shimizu 1992). Moreover, many studies show that unlike the description of paradise for the elderly, many people are anxious about their lives after retirement, and families are unsure how to deal with the problem of eldercare (Danely 2014; Kiefer 1987; Kinoshita and Kiefer 1992; Traphagan 1998; Wöss 1993; Young and Ireuchi 1997).

The present study entails mixed methods research. I examine the literature to explore why the missing centenarians incident took place in a society like Japan where the popular image has been that of a paradise for the elderly. For this purpose, I look into how eldercare needs to transform as family and economic situations change by analyzing statistics and primary data from the Japanese media. Second, I show that the value that the Japanese government places on the tradition of family care for elders does not correspond to the actual situations of contemporary families by examining the welfare policies for the elderly and elder families contrasted with actual living conditions. The governmental policy focus on families acts as an ideology that obscures the need for change. Thus, families and government, the latter of which desperately needs to overhaul out-of-date policies, should share responsibility for the eldercare crisis more equally. Last, I ethnographically investigate the case of Saku City in Nagano Prefecture to reveal how community members created volunteer services for the elderly in order to fill in for the limitations of current government assistance. I conclude by recommending broad-based community and family studies to establish foundations for future policy reform in the area of eldercare.

Research Methods

I collected and analyzed articles and commentaries from newspapers and magazines that dealt with the cases of the missing centenarians. Moreover, I collected statistical resources that summarize the situations in which Japanese families find themselves. I also collected studies that examine Japanese society with special attention to aging. To complement this critical literature review I conducted anthropological field study in Saku City, Nagano Prefecture, from January to February and from June to September 2009, and from June 2010 to May 2011. During these periods I directly participated in and observed the activities of Dousin (eastern part of Nagano Prefecture) Cooperative for the Aged, and carried out in-depth interviews with union members. I also participated in and observed the activities of volunteers who strive to solve the so-called problem of elders, and conducted in-depth interviews with them and with family members. All interviews and archival material were originally in Japanese, and are translated here by me. The names of all interviewees are pseudonyms.

Economic Difficulties in the Postmillennial Generation and Single Caregivers

In the 2000s in Japan, struggles to care for the elderly in the context of the family created economic hardship for the younger generation.[3] Job availability was low in the early 2000s, and as a result, young adults often went without work and many were unable to form independent households. Many young and middle-aged adults went from having full-time work to piecing together irregular work including part-time jobs, contract work, and nonregular work. Table 8.1 shows that it became difficult to secure stable jobs, the number of so-called NEET (Not in Employment, Education or Training, aged fifteen to thirty-four) who have de facto given up employment has risen from 1.9 percent in 1992 to 3.0 percent in 2012 (Japan Institute for Labor Policy and Training [JILPT] 2014: 11).

As a result, it is difficult for many in younger generations today to form households. Statistics show that in 1960 1.26 percent of men and 1.88 percent for women were unmarried (and most were resigned not to marry during their lifetimes). By contrast, 2010 statistics show increases to 20.14 percent for men and 10.61 percent for women (Statistics Bureau of Japan 2013).

Among this postmillennial population are many unmarried adults who care for their parents. However, when children have not formed new households and their parents are in need of care, a number of problems arise. Hiroshi-san's situation, Case 1, illustrates problems that arise in these situations. This case was introduced in NHK's (Japan Broadcasting Corporation) program *Shades of Muen Shakai*, a society in which individuals are

TABLE 8.1. Employment Situation in Japan, 1992–2012.

	% (thousand)				
	1992	1997	2002	2007	2012
Job Seekers	4.6 (1,150)	6.2 (1,1613)	7.7 (1,923)	6.0 (1,342)	6.2 (1,180)
NEET: Not in Education, Employment, or Training	1.9 (479)	2.0 (525)	2.6 (647)	2.6 (577)	3.0 (564)
Single domestic workers	0.6 (153)	0.6 (157)	0.8 (206)	0.8 (182)	1.0 (190)
Housewives	11.6 (2,875)	10.9 (2,875)	10.1 (2,543)	8.7 (1,934)	7.2 (1,375)
Remaining unemployed persons	0.9 (217)	0.8 (217)	0.7 (182)	0.5 (122)	0.6 (124)
Employed persons	80.4 (19,998)	79.5 (20,527)	78.1 (19,627)	81.3 (18,105)	82.0 (15,650)
Total	100.0 (24,872)	100.0 (25,832)	100.0 (25,128)	100.0 (22,262)	100.0 (19,082)

Source: JILPT 2014.

isolated and have weak personal links between each other. It demonstrates the hardships of unmarried adult child caregivers.

Case 1

The corpse of an elderly individual was hidden for seven months in a room on the second floor of a house in a newly constructed residential area near Tokyo. The son, who was arrested by the police, had hidden his father's death and had been falsely receiving his pension. The convicted thirty-nine-year-old man (pseudonym Hiroshi-san) was on probation. Hiroshi's father had worked as a regional government officer until retirement and Hiroshi-san worked in a construction company near his home. Their routines started to change when his mother became ill. Hiroshi-san had to take up nursing for his mother and housekeeping for his parents, so that he had to quit work when he was about twenty-eight years old. This was necessary because his father could not quit work, since his salary was the basis for mortgage payments for the house. After three years Hiroshi-san's father retired and received severance pay but used it up within three years for his wife's medical needs. From then on, the three of them lived on the father's pension. Afterward, the mother passed away and the sister, who had participated in care for their parents together with Hiroshi-san, also suddenly died from heart disease. Hiroshi-san's father was greatly shocked and distracted; he was hit by a car while riding a bicycle. After that, he could not use his legs well, and he stopped going outside and eventually showed signs of dementia. Hiroshi-san thought of going out to work, but he could not leave his disoriented father alone. He thought of a care service but could not even pay the 10 percent of payment required from the service user of government subsidized eldercare. He applied for livelihood protection assistance (a government plan, which guarantees a minimum standard of living for people whose income is low because of illness, accident, and unemployment, or who have a difficult life because of medical costs). However, Hiroshi-san's application was rejected due to his level of assets since he was listed as an owner, along with his father, of the house in which they lived.[4] Hiroshi-san did not have anyone to ask for help. After significant debating of the issues, when his father silently passed away at one evening last February, Hiroshi-san moved his father's body to a room on the second floor and continued to live on his pension for seven months.

This incident, as is true for many other incidents of missing elderly persons, illustrates the difficulties of single caregivers such as Hiroshi-san. Similar to Hiroshi-san's case, many people who had to give up jobs in order to care for their parents ended up depending on one or more parents' pensions for basic living expenses. According to the results of reports by Japan National Health Insurance Clinics and Hospitals Association (2012: 141), 30.2 percent of female caregivers were unemployed in 2011.

Change in Caregiver Models and Diffusion of *Rōrōkaigo*

As the generation of children whose parents became elderly near the turn of the twenty-first century began to find it extremely difficult to form households themselves or to afford to care for their parents, their elders became less likely to expect their children to take care of them, at least to the extent that they had for their parents. In fact, more than half of the elderly in Japan living alone or with their spouse do not expect their children to care for them, despite the fact that they had taken care of their own parents. As a result, aged spouses frequently care for their spouses, and children or sons- and daughters-in-law care for their parents less often.

The results of the MHLW (2013) study show that caregivers are mostly spouses and children of the elderly, at 48.0 percent, and they rarely include the daughters-in-law or sons-in-law, at 11.2 percent in 2013. This differs from the situations in 1960s, when the major responsibility for eldercare was put on daughters-in-law, who constituted 49.8 percent of elder caregivers according to one source of statistics for that decade. At that time, spousal elder caregivers consisted of 25.1 percent of elder caregivers due to declining percentage of elderly persons living with their children and increasing in the number of working women (Masatoshi 2013: 22).

As the caregiver model changed from relying mostly on daughters-in-law to leaning primarily on spousal caregivers (on spousal caregiving, see also chap. 2), the age of the main caregiver also significantly increased, leading to the social category of elderly persons aged sixty or older who provide care for other elderly persons (*rōrōkaigo*). In fact, *rōrōkaigo* is now the prevalent elder caregiving arrangement, because the age distribution of cohabitant caregivers shows that the percentage of the elderly people aged sixty-five to sixty-nine providing care to those aged sixty-five to sixty-nine is the highest among caregivers at 52.6 percent (see table 8.2). Additionally, the percentage of the elderly people aged seventy to seventy-nine providing care to those aged seventy to seventy-nine is the highest among caregivers at 50.6 percent (MHLW 2013: 33).

This means that the most common situations are, first, those in which aged individuals are caring for their spouses; this is especially true for couples in their sixties or seventies. Second, aging children are caring for their parents particularly when those parents are eighty years old or older (MHLW 2013: 33). This reliance on the *rōrōkaigo* creates many social problems. Elderly caregivers may die before their care recipients do, since they are also aged and weak themselves. As one elderly caregiver dies, the other often becomes secluded and might end up dying alone (on death and dying, see also chaps. 2, 9, 12). Elderly children who have been caregivers resort to postmodern embezzlement of parents' pensions when destitution leaves them desperate.

TABLE 8.2. Ages of Caregivers and Care Recipients in Japan.

Age of Caregiver	Age of Care Recipient				
	< 40 years old and younger	Age 65–69	Age 70–79	Age 80–89	> 90 years old and older
< 40 years old and younger	7.8	4.1	2.3	1.5	1.2
Aged 40–49	9.2	11.9	14.4	6.2	2.3
Aged 50–59	28.7	5.7	10.0	29.9	18.1
Aged 60–69	34.2	52.6	13.7	26.1	59.2
Aged 70–79	9.6	24.4	50.6	16.4	14.6
> 80 years old and older	10.5	1.3	9.0	19.8	4.6
Total	100.0	100.0	100.0	100.0	100.0

Source: MHLW 2013: 33.

Critical Examination of Japanese Government Actions

Despite its established social welfare system and recent reforms, current Japanese government efforts to support eldercare are insufficient to meet the changing needs of society described above. During the postwar period Japan drastically modified its senior welfare system, as well as the medical and social security systems, building a welfare state as their number one priority. The portion of responsibility for eldercare held by the government has changed over time, however. In 1973, the first year of welfare, the cost of care for those older than seventy was fully supported by public funds and this lasted several years thereafter. But after the second oil shock in 1978 the government began to promote a new Japanese-style welfare society model that limits governmental spending on eldercare by emphasizing individuals' self-help efforts and the solidarity of family, neighborhood, and the community. This Japanese-style welfare society model is based on a theory about the national character of Japanese called the Nihonjinron. The Nihonjinron interprets the past positively, giving new meaning to family and filial piety when elderly parents get support from their offspring while living with them, reevaluating the family-centered system, and reevaluating social values recently considered old-fashioned. It argues that such traditional values are central to Japanese culture and are key in giving the Japanese nation strength and stability.

However, as the population of Japan ages, the welfare model cannot keep up with the demands for eldercare. The percentage of the people older than sixty-five years old has increased from 5.7 percent in 1960 to 17.3 percent in 2000 (UN 2017). As society ages, needs for long-term care have been increasing because of more elderly persons requiring long-term care and the lengthening of care period. Meanwhile, due to factors such as the trend toward nuclear families and the aging of caregivers in families, environment surrounding families has been changed. In 2000 the Japanese government enforced a long-term care insurance system (LTCI, or Kaigo Hoken) (JHPN n.d.). Users pay 10 percent (20 percent for persons with income above certain level after August 2015) of long-term care services in principle, but must pay the actual costs for residence and meals in addition. This system adheres to the existing position that the family and the community are responsible for the care of the elderly. By giving preference to housewives over working or single women in the tax system the government encourages an environment in which a family member, especially an adult wife, cares for the elderly.[5] Additionally, caregiving by family members is not remunerated by the state, as it is in Germany (Olivares-Tirado and Tamiya 2014; Nakatani 2019).

The high cost of professional caregivers frequently precludes outside assistance. Ochiai and colleagues argue that, with the LTCI system, "many people have been granted care service, but on the other hand, services available to low-income class have in fact decreased" (Ochiai et al. 2010: 13). With the introduction of Japan's LTCI system in 2000, anyone receiving services must pay 10 percent regardless of their income levels. As a result, it has become harder for people in difficult economic situations who cannot pay the 10 percent to use the services, and the burdens on families taking care of elders have become heavier.

Additionally, the Japanese government introduced a system centered on prevention. The government not only supports leisure activities such as singing but also operates classes for elders to learn techniques and knowledge about managing their aging bodies. What the elders are eating, how they are taking care of their teeth, and whether they are getting enough exercise are becoming some of the important duties that civil servants of the region have had to promote and manage among their citizenry. It was the ultimate goal of this general education policy to decrease the number of care recipients by including as subjects of government management not only those in need of care but also those who might need care in the future.

The most significant reason that the Japanese government introduced a prevention-first system was indeed financial. After the LTCI system was established, it was initially used at a drastically higher rate than expected by the government, and government outlays for eldercare soon became unmanageable. There were many elders, and their family members mostly wanted "living assistance" or *seikatsushien* services. *Seikatsushien* is the service that provides not only care but also housework such as cooking, laundry and cleaning, advice for living, and general attention to those in need of care if they live alone or if they live with family members who cannot carry out housework due to disability or disease. However, the government then revised the system so that only single-person households could use the livelihood support service, arguing, "If people with relatively low necessity for help start leaving housework to helpers, their living functions will decline" (Sankeiweb 2006). By doing this, the government pushed the burden for eldercare onto cohabiting elderly spouses or onto non-coresident children. Thus, single caregivers who care for their parents alone have had to give up jobs or switch to part-time jobs, as I mentioned above.

Japan's LTCI system categorizes elders' levels of need for support or care into eight levels, ranging from no need for assistance, to needing some support or care, to needing support and care in nearly all areas of life. The categorization is formed on the basis of assessment of elders' abilities in activities of daily living (ADLs) and instrumental activities of daily living (IADLs), with ADLs involving the skills needed for basic daily functioning and self-care, and IADLs involving more advanced skills. ADLs include using the toilet; moving from bed to chair; and feeding, bathing, and dressing oneself. IADLs are more complex skills associated with independent living in the community. IADLs include the ability to prepare meals, do laundry and housekeeping, use the telephone, manage money, do the shopping, navigate transportation in the community, and take medications correctly. As table 8.3 shows, Japan's LCTI system classifies people as in need of "support level" 1 or 2 services if they require a relatively low level of help with some IADLs but have only a little or no need for help with ADLs. For those with more needs, the system has "care levels" 1 through 5. At care level 1, the person needs some moderate assistance with IADLs. At care level 5, the highest level of need, the person requires full assistance with all ADLs and IADLs.

Moreover, as the financial goal of the LTCI program became clear, the government imposed limitations on the number of LTCI recipients. While the number of recipients requiring support is dramatically increasing, the number of elderly receiving care level 1 decreased by a huge amount in 2007. For care level 2, the number increased in that same year but only by a small amount. This is because the Japanese government readjusted the care level evaluation tool such that recipients formerly classified as requiring a light level of care were reclassified down to the level of only requiring support, not care. In this way, the government has strictly controlled access so that the number of recipients in the "requiring care" levels does not increase significantly (table 8.4).

Moreover, the many local governments imposed limitations on the number of affordable eldercare facilities in order to avoid raising taxes. The rest of those in need of facilities were left to market logic. On that account, the

TABLE 8.3. Categorization of Levels of Care Need under Japan's LTCI System.

Level of Care Need Category	Mental and Physical State	Specific Example	Care Time (mins.)
Self-help persons	Person who has no problem in performing ADLs and IADLs by oneself		
Support required 1	Person who can perform ADL by oneself but needs support for IADL		25–32
Support required 2	Person who is a little bit less able in ADL than those in necessary support required 1		25–32
Care level 1	Person needing partial care due to lower ability to perform IADL compared to support required groups	Specifically needs care from neighbors and requires help when moving around, or shows a little bit of problematic behavior or falling behind in comprehension	33–50
Care level 2	Person needing partial care in ADL in addition to the care level 1	Specifically in need of help when feeding or going to bathroom	51–70
Care level 3	Person needing overall care due to substantially low abilities for both ADL and IADL		71–90
Care level 4	Person with difficulty in ADLs without care due to lower motor abilities compared to care level 3		91–110
Care level 5	Person who is unable or finds it nearly impossible to carry out ADLs without care due to further reduction in motor abilities	Nearly impossible to feed self, showing many problematic behaviors and falling behind in overall comprehensive abilities	111 and more

Source: MHLW (n.d.).

TABLE 8.4. Annual Number of Japanese Aged Sixty-Five and Above Acknowledged as Requiring Care.

Year	Requiring Support	Advancing to Requiring Care	Requiring Care Level 1	Requiring Care Level 2	Requiring Care Level 3	Requiring Care Level 4	Requiring Care Level 5	Total
2000	318,019	–	680,066	460,804	340,593	350,699	320,801	2,470,982
2003	584,088	–	1,198,091	567,306	465,669	456,852	432,089	3,704,095
2005	705,834	–	1,373,823	616,016	531,036	503,574	445,012	4,175,295
2007	1,146,980	1,681	747,647	767,752	678,973	556,199	478,908	3,231,160
2009	1,221,822	–	825,021	815,541	688,398	607,432	538,170	3,474,562

Source: MHLW 2009.

vast majority of paid-care facilities are established in accordance with economic priorities rather than family needs. The case of Nagano is typical, showing that the facility with the highest demand among the elderly and their families was the nursing home. Yet the city office strictly limited the construction of such facilities because the nursing home would put a heavier burden on the residents' taxes. As a result, in the most popular nursing homes in the Nagano area 910 people were waiting for open spots in 2020 (Kaigodb n.d.). In contrast, private facilities such as paid nursing homes or paid residential nursing homes for the elderly had more availability than demand, to such an extent that responsible employees had to take part in direct promotional activities. These discrepancies between the public and private sector nursing homes occur due to a situation in which private facilities largely choose users, rather than users choosing facilities. Private facilities screen out those unable to pay or whose level of need is too great to make them a profitable client.

The missing centenarian crisis was triggered by the combination of changing family relationships, rising unemployment in the younger generation, and limits of the social security system. Nevertheless, the Japanese government has so far failed to address the governmental responsibilities here and instead has responded only by making motions to catalogue and monitor its citizens and by making prevention and care demands on families with elderly members.

In Nagano Prefecture, for example, a set of strategies were established and continue to be used to monitor the elder population. The local government announced a new provision offering a list of elderly residents, together with the identity of their close relatives and contact information, to "community representatives (*minsei-iin*)."[6] The community representatives visited a household of any size where at least one resident is an elder and checked on families who have refused to provide full personal information on those elders. In addition, after identifying pensioners seventy-six years old and older in government records who had not used medical insurance or LTCI for more than one year as of July 2010, the government began to solicit information on their status or visit their homes in order to stop support for pensioners found to be deceased or missing.

Elders who live alone in Nagano, as a result, experience a new type of anxiety about whether they or their families may appear as "problematic elders" or "problematic families" (*mondai kazoku*) if they should die alone unexpectedly. To prevent troublesome situations, neighbors are often asked to serve as emergency contacts so that their family members who may live at a distance will receive news of their parents' death via their neighbors immediately.

Responses of the Community in Nagano

While it was shocking to find cases of bodies long dead or of missing unidentified people who had lost contact even with their families, such cases were neither occurring for the first time in Japanese history nor happening only to the elderly. According to Kotsuji and Kobayashi (2011: 121–30), cases that can be called lonely death (*kodokushi*) can be documented from the end of the Meiji era to the war period, although the term was not used. Analysis of Asahi Shinbun's database indicates that the term "*kodokushi*" was first used on 16 April 1970, when introducing the incident of a twenty-year-old man who died from disease in his apartment. In 1977 the concept started to draw attention as a major social issue when an old man died by himself on the high-speed train (*sinkansen*) (Kotsuji and Kobayashi 2011).

In January 2010 the *Muen Shakai* project team at NHK produced and aired a program showing that the number of isolated or lonely deaths in forms such as the unidentified, those seemingly dead by suicide, or those who die away from home reached 32,000 annually. This aroused a great sensation in society, and the term "*muen shakai*," meaning a society in which individuals are isolated and have weak personal links between each other, was selected as the most popular 2010s catch-phrase in Japan. However, it is inaccurate to argue that isolated death is a problem exclusively of modern society or one that is confined to elders.[7] Rather than a crisis of the morals of the populace, the more important issue is the lack of a governmental social security system to prevent such isolated deaths.

Therefore, missing centenarian incidents are not only demonstrative of a moral problem in the family, but also and even more so they reflect the limitations of the Japanese welfare system that largely depends on self-help, family, and local community, largely independent of the national government. There were in fact many who sympathized with cases of hiding parents' deaths to receive pension income, saying, "I can see how it could easily happen," rather than criticizing the perpetrators' moral hazard. They were acknowledging the background of such incidents to be the lack of an effective social security system that might save the increasing number of people in dire economic hardships.

Citizens, who realized the anxiety of the elderly and the limitations of government policies, came to share the idea that eldercare should not be regarded as a private matter. Many Japanese people started to think that the community should come forward to solve the problems. Even if the government neglects the situation and shifts the responsibility onto families and neighbors, there are people who try to help others in need, thus trying to construct a new form of affectionate relationship that cannot be easily severed (*kizuna*). The literal meaning of *kizuna* is the leash used to hold beloved pets, such as horses, dogs, or hawks. *Kizuna* became a buzzword in 2011, particularly following the aftermath of the 3.11 triple disaster in Fukushima. In 2011 *kizuna* was even selected as the Japanese word of the year occurring in Japanese character form (*kanji*). It can thus be seen that the missing centenarian incident became an instrument to expand awareness that new forms of community other than the existing family or regional society are needed and are emerging.

My own ethnographic research shows how the will of the citizenry has been actualized for eldercare support in the rural Nagano area. Residents of Nagano are trying to improve their community so that anyone can live a decent life and face their last breath in comfort. Rejecting the government's view of the missing centenarians as reflective of criminal families, the community members face the matter as something that could strike anyone and offer a series of options. First, they help old people live decently until the end in the village where they had been living. The activities of the Cooperative for the Aged in Nagano and various elderly self-help groups are carrying out various volunteer activities, mainly consisting of solving daily problems of the elderly living alone that are not covered by the LTCI.

The Cooperative for the Aged in Nagano Prefecture includes several branches: Nagano Prefecture Hokushin branch (northern part of Nagano, Nagano city), Tyushin branch (middle of Nagano, Matsumoto city), Tôshin branch (eastern part of Nagano, Saku city). I mainly participated in and observed the activities of the Cooperative for the Aged in Tôshin. In the case of the Tôshin Cooperative for the Aged, the main agents were people with experiences of working in the National Welfare Association, which was established within the Japanese Agriculture Cooperative to increase farmers' medical care and welfare. There had been a circle of people considering and studying how to improve the medical care and welfare services for regional residents, and since aging was rapidly progressing in the rural areas, they had naturally become interested in the issue of the elders. Thus, they were taking the stance that they must improve and fix sociocultural environments so that all residents living in their regional society can live humane lives, an approach quite different from the government's partial solutions to the problems of problematic elders who simply need help.[8]

According to Ichikawa-san (male, aged fifty), who is participating as a member of the Cooperative for the Aged in Nagano, government-led welfare programs for the elderly provide only part of the services that elders actually need in order to lead decent lives. He argues that government policy limits elders to particular kinds of care and thus does not reach its original purpose—enabling independent living (on independence, see chap. 7), which, by definition, requires that people be given a wide range of choices.

Case 2

Ichikawa-san: In the past, Japanese families supported their elders. But as nuclear families appeared, families became insufficient as settings for the care of elders. That's why the state implemented care insurance in 2000. On the surface this measure constitutes socialization of care, meaning the state acknowledges the problem of care as a social issue. But the insurance system has many problems. For example, in the case of elders who actually may need level 5 care for living, the government may only provide assistance at level 1 or 2. Since 2000 the care insurance [LTCI] has provided service to many elders. But the standards have become stricter and stricter through revision every three years. For financial reasons the standards became increasingly rigid as well, so that elders who need services seldom receive the care they require. There are also limitations in the care insurance system from the administrative perspective. For example, even if the elderly are under care, they will want to shop and they have to throw away garbage. But the administrative service does not provide assistance for these needs. Thus the elderly often cannot go out nor can they keep their homes clean; their conditions worsen so that their care levels escalate, creating a vicious circle. This is tending in a direction like that taken in Germany, such that the Japanese system will provide partial service.

Heekyoung: But isn't the city office also carrying out preventive health activities?

Ichikawa-san: For prevention activities, they should be full-fledged, but they are not sufficient. They start to provide care service only after the conditions of the elderly have become sufficiently severe to demand necessary support [*yōshien*]. The activities of the cooperative are to fill up those insufficient parts to support the residents.

Heekyoung: Does the cooperative stop at fulfilling the insufficient parts of the state care insurance service, or is it also critically pointing out the problems of care insurance itself and calling for [government] measures to fix them?

Ichikawa-san: Currently we are stopping at filling in the gaps in the national service. That is the reality. But what we are ultimately trying to do is point out the flaws of the national policy and [show the need for] revising it. If your house leaks water, you can put a cup underneath the dripping but that cannot be a long-term solution. You need to make a roof that fundamentally prevents leakage. Likewise, we must fundamentally solve the problems of the policy itself.

Heekyoung: There must be many problems of the LTCI system. Which point is the cooperative focusing on?

Ichikawa-san: As I have said earlier, there is a need for total, full-fledged prevention activities. This means that service should be provided not after people need care but should be offered to maintain a livable condition before problems arise, and it should not just stop at the surface, but actually provide help. Next is supporting necessary services to people regardless of their care levels. I don't think that the livelihood of people under care should be different from that of those not receiving care. Whether the elder people are admitted as long-term care beneficiaries or not, I think we need to fulfill various needs of elder people for basic living [i.e., housekeeping, grocery shopping]. So it is our goal to equip cooperative institutions with the right to provide the services for a fee and be supported for them by the government to take care of some parts if the government cannot do [it].

The Cooperative for the Aged in Nagano was running various projects in order to overcome the limitations of government-led welfare projects for the elderly. For example, the cooperative in turn prioritized at-home meal delivery and construction of a small day-time eldercare service facility. One of the difficulties for aged people in Nagano, which is a mountain area, was transportation. It is difficult for them to even go grocery shopping.[9] Moreover, since more elderly people lived only in couples or alone due to changes in family structure, and more elderly found it difficult to prepare all three meals every day, the meal delivery project was greatly welcomed.

In addition to the activism of the middle-aged and the young-old volunteers, Nagano elder cooperatives trained youths to examine and solve matters from a local perspective. One elderly cooperative opened a class for unemployed young adults who wished to take a qualifying examination to become certified eldercare workers. The classes were taught by volunteer professionals in charge of the health and welfare of the elderly in Nagano, such as doctors, civil servants, and care managers. They delivered professional knowledge, as well as passing on know-how already established by seasoned adults in the area, by teaching younger community members how to apply relevant knowledge in the local context.

In Nagano, various activities were in practice not only through large institutions such as the cooperative, but also through smaller initiatives by individuals with awareness of particular local problems. After retirement, Yoda-san (male, aged seventy), who is the community representative, wanted to see what he could do in the local community. For two years he took classes in leadership at the district university for the aged, but he complained that those classes were university in name but mainly gave light instruction on mere hobbies. Eventually, Yoda-san founded a small volunteer group called Life Support for You (LSY). He identified local elderly needing help in daily activities such as fixing electronic devices, gardening, cleaning, cooking, shopping, painting, driving, babysitting, or taking out the trash. Simultaneously he called for volunteers from the elderly who wanted to help, and connected the two parties (Kim 2020).

One important message the elderly convey through the practices of Yoda-san is their will to define themselves as people who can do something themselves, instead of dependent people who always ask for help. In the document to ask regional residents to join the volunteer group, Yoda-san suggests that they think what they can do, rather than requesting the administration to do something (see Case 3).

Case 3

As the aging of Japanese society and family nuclearization rapidly progress, various welfare policies are being implemented. But the people who need support are also varied, and the public system has limitations in supporting them. I think informal services, in addition to LTCI systems or various welfare facilities, are more necessary now. Therefore, I came to think what we can do, rather than requesting the administration to do something. I suggest that we make a small volunteer group. Support is not to be given, as care insurance and welfare facilities do, to people who are nearly hitting their limits, but rather should be given by healthy seniors to all seniors who need it. Through these activities, the supporters can gain experience and knowledge and will be thankful that their activities are needed. So, they find satisfaction in interacting within the region, and enlarge their wheel of communication, which connects to maintenance of health and rewards of living.

Furthermore, it should be noted that Yoda-san's practice is derived from a critical acknowledgment of public welfare policy for elders, such as the LTCI. He explained that he thought of alternative organizations, since public systems cannot solve the various needs of the regional residents. As a means to overcome the limitations of the system, he suggests establishing small regional welfare communities. To Yoda-san, this means identifying needs and practicing what he can do to help.

Conclusion

In July 2010 police found the body of a 111-year-old, nominally Japan's oldest man, lying in bed. The problem was that he had died thirty years earlier. Subsequent investigations showed that this was not an isolated incident. The missing centenarian crisis has been triggered by the combination of changing family relationships, rising unemployment in the younger generation, and limits of the social security system. Nevertheless, the Japanese government has so far failed to address the governmental responsibilities and instead has responded only by making motions to catalogue and monitor its citizens and by making prevention and care demands on families with elderly members. Therefore, the more important issue is the lack of a social security system that prevents such isolated deaths.

In this study, through analysis of existing literature and research on site, I examined the situations of the elderly and their families in super-aging Japanese society and investigated how the Japanese government has responded by contextualizing the missing centenarian crisis. With changes in family structure and economic opportunities there has been a transition from family care for the elderly to eldercare for the elderly. Also, youths in financial difficulty have been found to rely on their parents' pension in exchange for providing care for them. As for community members, those who noticed the limitations of the government are creatively forming various volunteer organizations and activities to forestall isolation of the elderly living alone.

The government has been practicing a policy that minimizes governmental responsibility by underlining the crisis of population aging as a problem primarily for families and communities to tackle. The government has emphasized the responsibility of families and communities by establishing a Japanese Welfare Society Model that rests on the tradition of filial piety, in which elderly parents are dependent on and live with their children. In other words, the government has been using a traditional moral call to familial duty as an ideological device to minimize governmental responsibility. However, this approach fails to demonstrate understanding of the social and familial economies.

Rather than blaming individuals for what at first appear to be shocking cases of hidden deaths, to account for the crisis of missing centenarians one needs to recognize changes in family relationships, rising unemployment, and the limits of the Japanese social security system. The way the Japanese government is coping with this situation exacerbates the problems by wasting resources and surveilling the elderly and their families, rather than by helping them.

Local community members have stepped in to fill the gaps, rather than passively succumbing to the dark future the government foresees. Middle-aged and able elderly citizens are endeavoring to prevent the isolation and decline of the elderly by carrying out various volunteer activities when government policy cannot cover the needs of seniors. Furthermore, these citizens are training local youths to resolve problems, which could be a solution to young people's unemployment in addition to mitigating the problems of the elderly.

Japanese society long has been considered an ideal society that cares for the old people, and it is maintaining that reputation with the activation of LTCI. However, many anthropological studies, including my own recent ethnographic research, have explored the mismatch between cultural ideals and reality, and raise the need to review the romantic stereotype critically. In this research, by investigating the sociocultural context of the incident of missing centenarians, I argue that the issue of eldercare should not be only the responsibility of the elderly themselves or their families, but also the duty of both the local community and the national government. A holistic approach is needed to fully understand the various situations of the elderly, their families, their communities, and the government in order to design and implement policy and programs that will suit Japanese elderly citizens' diverse and changing needs.

Heekyoung Kim is assistant professor in the Department of Archaeology and Anthropology at Kyungpook National University, South Korea. Her recent works include "Underground Strongman: Silver Seats, Fare-Exempt Status, the Struggles for Recognition on the Seoul Subway" (*Korea Journal*, 2017); and "Irony and the Sociocultural Construction of Old Age in South Korea: Perspectives from Government, the Medical Profession, and the Aged" (*Care Management Journals*, 2010).

Glossary

butsudan	仏壇	Buddhist family altar to deceased family members.
jiko sekinin	自己責任	Self-responsibility.
kaigo	介護	Long-term care system benefits category of care required.
Kaigo Hoken	介護保険	Long-term care insurance (LTCI) system.
kizuna	きずな	A new form of affectionate relationship or bond that cannot be easily severed.
kodokushi	孤独死	Lonely death or someone dying alone.
Kokumin Seikatsu Kiso Chousa	国民生活基礎調査	National Basic Livelihood Research Study.
mondai kazoku	問題家族	Problematic or dysfunctional families.
muen shakai	無縁社会	Society in which individuals are isolated.
rōrōkaigo	老老介護	People aged sixty and older who provide care for other elderly persons.
seikatsushien	生活支援	Living assistance that provides not only care but also housework, advice for living, and general attention to elders in need of care, if they live alone or if they live with family members who cannot carry out housework due to disability or disease.
yōshien	要支援	Long-term care system benefits category of support required.

Notes

1. Regulations regarding congratulatory money for the aged are different in each regional government.
2. Some have questioned the credibility of average longevity data, throwing into doubt whether Japan really is a "long-living" nation. Thus the MHLW explained that average longevity is not based on calculations from administrative records but rather on regularly performed vital population statistics research.
3. Unmarried adults who care for their parents are referred to as single caregivers (*singuru kaigosya*) in Japan.
4. In Japan's social security system, families have first responsibility in taking care of elders, and in the case of having a family member to provide care, one cannot be selected as a livelihood protection recipient. In the case of Hiroshi-san's father, he could not be selected for protection service because on paper he not only owned a house but also had a son in his thirties.
5. In the case of housewives, for those aged forty to sixty-five, if a husband is paying the insurance fee his wife does not need to pay separately (for those aged over sixty-five, the welfare insurance fee is charged individually). Housewives also receive income tax exemption privileges along with a pension. Such policy privileging housewives was started in 1960 with the aim of acknowledging the efforts of housewives who dedicate themselves to household support including eldercare. However, critics note that these policies do not reflect the reality in which households with housewives (7,040,000 households) are now (2014) those with two working spouses (10,770,000 households). As a result, it is argued that current system that overly privileges housewives should be revised accordingly (J-cast News 2015).
6. The community representatives are volunteer workers who are taking the role of helping the performance of researches by regional governments, selected through recommendations from regional community's organizations for community representatives, and finally from appointment by the Minister of Health and Labor. Their office term is four years and they can serve consecutive terms.
7. According to Allison (2013: 152), many Japanese people are choosing to limit (or eliminate) their dependency on others by living alone and embracing an ethos of self-responsibility (*jiko sekinin*).
8. In the case of Tôshin Cooperative for the Aged, they had established a nonprofit corporation to carry out business that operates within a small multifunctional facility. The nonprofit making corporation can receive some subsidy from central and prefectural governments. Other than that, the organization operates on profits made from an autonomous business, delivering packed meals to elders who live alone.
9. Many elders were at risk of not being able to drive at all, or no longer being able to drive due to aging. Moreover, with large-scale department stores being built in central parts of the region, the small grocery stores near the elders' residences had gone bankrupt, making it impossible for the elders to go shopping on foot. They are in danger of becoming the "shopping weak," a term that refers to people who are experiencing difficulties in buying living goods including groceries, due to the changes in distribution and transportation. The Ministry of Economy, Trade and

Industry is estimating the shopping weak to be nearly 6 million nationwide. Nagano's Department of Commerce, Industry and Labor has defined the shopping weak to be those who find it is difficult to buy things, who have shops more than 500 meters away from home, who cannot go shopping by foot or bicycle, or who cannot or do not drive. This number has estimated them to be about 140,000 (22.7 percent of the total population) in Nagano (Shinano Mainichi Shimbun 2018).

References

Allison, Anne. 2013. *Precarious Japan*. Durham, NC: Duke University Press.

Benedict, Ruth. 1946. *The Chrysanthemum and the Sword: Patterns of Japanese Culture*. Boston: Houghton Mifflin.

Campbell, John Creighton. 2000. "Changing Meanings of Frail Old People and the Japanese Welfare State." In *Caring for the Elderly in Japan and the U.S.: Practices and Policies*, ed. Susan Orpett Long, 82–97. London: Routledge.

Danely, Jason. 2014. *Aging and Loss: Mourning and Maturity in Contemporary Japan*. New Brunswick, NJ: Rutgers University Press.

Doi, L. Takeo. 1962. "Amae: A Key Concept for Understanding Japanese Personality Structure." In *Japanese Culture and Behavior: Selected Readings*, ed. Takie Lebra and William P. Lebra, 132–39. Honolulu: University Press of Hawaii.

Japan Institute for Labor Policy and Training (JILPT). 2014. *Shūgyō-kōzō kihon-chōsa – Rōdō-seisaku-kenkyū Kenshū-kikō* [Basic survey on employment-structure labor policy research and training organization]. Retrieved 1 June 2015 from https://www.jil.go.jp/institute/siryo/2014/documents/0144.pdf.

Japan National Health Insurance Clinics and Hospitals Association. 2012. *Kazoku-kaigo-sha no Jittai-to-shienhōsaku-ni Kansuru Chōsa-kenkyū-jigyō Hōkoku-sho* [Report on the status of family caregivers and support measures]. Retrieved 1 June 2015 from https://www.kokushinkyo.or.jp › Report-houkokusyo/H23/H23家族介護_報告書.pdf.

J-cast News. 2015. "Sengyō-shufu-wa Yūgūsaresugiteiru! Zeiseikaiseirongi Sutāto [Housewives are being treated too favorably: Debate on tax reform begins]," 14 July. Retrieved 18 August 2016 from https://www.j-cast.com/2015/07/14239939.html.

Jenike, Brenda Robb. 1997. "Gender and Duty in Japan's Aged Society: The Experience of Family Caregivers." In *The Cultural Context of Aging*, 2nd ed., ed. Jay Sokolovsky, 218–38. London: Bergin & Garvey.

JHPN. N.d. "Long-Term Care Insurance." Japan Health Policy Now. Retrieved 24 May 2020 from http://japanhpn.org/en/longtermcare/.

Kaigodb. N.d. *"Nagano-ken-no Tokubetsu-yōgorōjin-hōmu Hikaku* [Comparison of the number of waiting people of nursing homes in Nagano]." Kaigodb Data Repository. Retrieved 8 March 2020 from https://kaigodb.com/ranking/status_over-capacity_people/kaigo_service/103/20/.

Kawano, Satsuki. 2010. *Nature's Embrace: Japan's Aging Urbanities and New Death Rites*. Honolulu: University of Hawaii Press.

Kelly, William W. 1993. "Japan's Debates about an Aging Society: The Later Years in the Land of the Rising Sun." In *Justice across Generations: What Does It Mean*, ed. Lee M. Cohen, 153–68. Washington, DC: American Association of Retired Persons.

Kiefer, Christie W. 1987. "Care of the Aged in Japan." In *Health, Illness and Medical Care in Japan: Cultural and Social Dimensions*, ed. Edward Norbeck and Margaret Lock, 89–109. Honolulu: University of Hawaii Press.

Kim, Heekyoung, 2020, "Place and Placelessness of Old Age: The Politics of Aging in Place in Rural Japan." *Korean Anthropology Review* 4: 149–175.

Bigyomunhwayeongu [Cross-cultural studies] 22: 259–89.

———. 2017. "Yulyeong-golyeongja Sageon-gwa Han-yeoleum-bam-ui Sichwi: Ilbon-ui Geundaehwa-wa Noin-bogji-cheje-ui Mosun [Missing centenarians and the smell of dead bodies: Contradictions between modernization and the welfare system for the elderly in Japan]." In *Uilyo, Asia-ui Geundae-leul Ilgneun Chang* [Medicine and modernities in Asia: Anthropological perspectives], ed. Hyeon-jung Lee and Tawoo Kim, 141–64. Seoul: Seoul National University Press.

Kinoshita, Yasuhito, and Christie W. Kiefer. 1992. *Refuge of the Honored: Social Organization in a Japanese Retirement Community*. Berkeley: University of California Press.

Kotsuji, Hisanori, and Muneyuki Kobayashi. 2011. "Kodokushi no Houdou [The history of reports on Kodokushi]." *Core Ethics* 7: 121–30.

Lebra, Takie Sugiyama. 1984. *Japanese Women: Constraint and Fulfillment*. Honolulu: University of Hawaii Press.

Lock, Margaret. 1993. *Encounters with Aging: Mythologies of Menopause in Japan and North America*. Berkeley: University of California Press.

Long, Susan Orpett. 1996. "Nurturing and Femininity: The Ideal of Caregiving in Postwar Japan." In *Re-imaging Japanese Women*, ed. Anne Imamura, 156–76. Berkeley: University of California Press.

Maeda, Daisaku, and Yutaka Shimizu. 1992. "Family Support for Elderly People in Japan." In *Family Support for the Elderly*, ed. Hal Kendig, Akiko Hashimoto, and Larry C. Coppard, 235–49. Oxford: Oxford University Press.

Masatoshi, Tsudome. 2013. *Kea-man o Ikiru-Dansei Kaigo-sha Hyaku-man-nin-e-no Eru* [Living as a caregiving male: supportive messages for the one million male caregivers]. Kyōto: Kurieitsu-kamogawa.

McCurry, Jusin. 2010. "Centenarians 'Missing' ahead of Japanese Day Honouring Elderly." *The Guardian*, 12 August. Retrieved 1 March 2014 from https://www.theguardian.com/world/2010/aug/12/japan-missing-elderly-centenarians.

Ministry of Health, Labour and Welfare (MHLW). N.d. "Yōkaigonintei-wa Donoyōni Okonawa-reru-ka [How level of care need is measured under Japan's LTCI System]." Retrieved 20 August 2014. https://www.mhlw.go.jp/topics/kaigo/nintei/gaiyo2.html.

———. 2009. *Kaigo-hoken-jigyō-jōkyō-hōkoku: Kekka-no-gaiyō* [Business status report on long-term care insurance]. Retrieved 1 March 2014 from https://www.mhlw.go.jp/topics/kaigo/toukei/joukyou.html.

———. 2011. "Shozai-fumei Kōrei-sha-ni-kakaru Nenkin-no-sashidome-ni-tsuite [Implementing pension suspension for missing elderly people]." Retrieved 20 August 2014. https://www.mhlw.go.jp/stf/houdou/2r9852000001lew6.html.

———. 2013. *Kokumin Seikatsu Kiso Chousa* [National Basic Livelihood Research Study]. Retrieved 20 August 2014. https://www.mhlw.go.jp/toukei/saikin/hw/k-tyosa/k-tyosa13/.

Nakatani, Hiroki. 2019. "Population Aging in Japan: Policy Transformation, Sustainable Development Goals, Universal Health Coverage, and Social Determinants of Health." *Global Health and Medicine* 1(1): 3–10.

Ochiai, Emiko, Aya Abe, Takafumi Urabashi, Yuko Tamiya, and Rihito Yomo. 2010. "Nihon-ni Okeru Kea Daiamondo no Sai Hensei: Kaigo Hoken-wa 'Kazoku Shugi'o Kaetaka [Reorganization of care diamond in Japan: Has nursing-care insurance changed familism?]." *Kaigai Shakai Hoshō Kenkyū* [Overseas social security studies] 170: 4–19.

Olivares-Tirado, Pedro, and Nanako Tamiya. 2014. *Trends and Factors in Japan's Long-Term Care Insurance System: Japan's 10-Year Experience*. New York: Springer.

Palmore, Erdman Ballagh. 1975. *The Honorable Elders*. Durham, NC: Duke University Press.

Plath, David. 1964. "Where the Family of God Is the Family: The Role of the Dead in Japanese Households." *American Anthropologist* 66 (2): 300–17.

Sankeiweb. 2006. "Hōmon Herupā-ga Konai [Visiting helpers are not coming]," 9 October. Retrieved 20 August 2014 from http://www.sankei.co.jp/yuyulife/kaigo/200610/kig061009005.htm.

Shinano Mainichi Shimbun. 2018. "Kaimono-jakushao Sasaeru Chiiki-no-jijō-ni Yorisotte [Assisting the 'shopping weak' by considering local circumstances]," 1 July.

Statistics Bureau of Japan. 2013. "Shogai-mikon-ritsu [Lifetime unmarried rate]." Retrieved 20 August 2014 from https://www.stat.go.jp/library/faq/faq02/faq02a05.html.

Traphagan, John W. 1998. "Contesting the Transition to Old Age in Japan." *Ethnology* 37 (4): 333–51.

United Nations (UN). 2017. *World Population Prospects: The 2017 Revision*. United Nations Department of Economic and Social Affairs, Population Division. Retrieved 1 June 2018 from https://population.un.org/wpp/DataQuery/.

Wöss, Fleur. 1993. "*Pokkuri*-Temples and Aging: Rituals for Approaching Death." In *Religion and Society in Modern Japan: Selected Readings*, ed. Mark R. Mullins, Shimazono Susumu, and Paul L. Swanson, 191–202. Berkeley, California: Asian Humanities Press.

Yonhab News. 2010. "Hojeogsang 149sekkaji: Il tto 'Yulyeong-golyeongja' Sodong [Up to 149 years on the Family Register: Japanese issue of 'Ghost Elderly']," 24 August. Retrieved 12 January 2013 from https://www.yna.co.kr/view/AKR201 00824224200073.

Young, Richard, and Fuki Ireuchi. 1997. "Religion in 'the Hateful Age': Reflections on Pokkuri and Other Geriatric Rituals in Japan's Aging Society." In *Aging: Asian Concepts and Experiences, Past and Present*, ed. Susanne Formanek and Sepp Linhart, 229–55. Vienna: Austrian Academy of Sciences.

9 RETHINKING BURDEN
Japanese Eldercare Careers from Helping to Grieving

Susan Long and Ruth Campbell

Introduction

THIS VOLUME ATTESTS TO DRAMATIC changes in the configurations and cultures of East Asian societies in recent decades in association with demographic trends. With over a quarter of its population aged sixty-five or older as of 2015, Japan has been a pioneer, if a reluctant one, in these trends. It has the largest proportion of its population sixty-five years and older, one of the lowest birth rates, and the highest life expectancy of any country in the world. Illustrating the extreme aging of society in 2013, a 116-year-old Japanese man became the world's oldest living person in 2013 and, remarkably, was cared for by his grandson's sixty-year-old wife (Kyodo News Service 2014).

As the number of old people, especially those older than eighty, increases, so too does the number who now or in the future will need assistance in daily living—including help with transportation, preparing meals, and even taking care of personal hygiene. Since the 1980s Japanese government bureaucrats, politicians, welfare organizations, and the general public have all wrestled with the question of how such assistance should be provided, and by whom. A significant policy breakthrough occurred with the 2000 establishment of a national system of long-term care insurance (LTCI) designed to partially relieve the burden of eldercare on family members and to provide a safety net for those living without family to care for them. Despite the integration of components of professional services into care routines, familial care remains central to meeting the daily needs of frail old people.

This chapter focuses on the experiences of such family caregivers after the establishment of the national long-term insurance care (LTCI) system, and explores the patterns of activities and meanings in relation to different stages in their caregiving "careers" (Aneshensel et al. 1995). What daily tasks do they undertake, and what are their options for assistance from professional care workers? How do the affective elements of caregiving change over time? How do the caregiver's past and current family relationships, as well as the condition of the elderly relative, shape the caregiving experience? We first present background factors in Japanese caregiving for the elderly, including the structure of the LTCI system and historical expectations for eldercare, both of which impact today's caregivers. Using data from a qualitative, five-year longitudinal study of eldercare in Japan in the first decade of the twenty-first century, we introduce styles of caregiving and patterns of caregiving careers that we have identified. Finally, we observe the significant transitions from caring for a relative with a chronic health problem to one who is dying, and to the work that remains for the caregiver after the death. We find that recognizing the changes in caregiving through a trajectory of the elder's illness and frailty, suggests that labeling the act of caregiving as a burden is overly simplistic. We also discover that there are important continuities in relationships and care work that transcend a definition that sees eldercare ending with the care recipient's death.

Common Gerontological Notions of the "Burden" of Eldercare and Filial Piety

Most of the gerontological literature on burden focuses on caregivers of people with dementia. It also deals with the subjective burden in the current caregiving situation such as coping with problem behaviors and deteriorating health, deciding on nursing-home placement, and the unavailability of respite services (Zarit, Todd, and Zarit 1986). Studies have found no relationship between time spent on activities of daily living (ADLs) and stress or relationship burden (Savundranayagam, Montgomery, and Kosloski 2011) and the authors conclude that it is not the workload that causes burden but rather the interpretation that caregivers apply to the caregiving activities. Our study goes beyond the concept of burden during the actual caregiving process and reflects the prior history of the relationship between caregiver and care recipient, changing cultural ideas about giving and receiving care, and adapting to collaboration with a variety of LTCI services offered to both relieve caregiver stress and enrich the lives of care recipients. Caregiving in the Japanese context is changing structurally and psychologically and has to be viewed in a historical and multidimensional framework.

Tendency to Separate Caregiving from End of Life and Mourning

Another concern that we address in this chapter is the gap between the perspectives of scholars of death and dying and those of gerontologists. For the most part, the field of death studies focuses on bereavement and mourning as the response to the death of an intimate. Many scholars and clinicians see the task of a person whose family member or partner has died as one of a journey that must be taken, a journey with an end point of returning to normal. Clinically, this might be assisted with medication, and to wallow too long in one's loss may result in a diagnosis of prolonged grief disorder (World Health Organization 2019).[1] In this literature, there does not seem to be consideration of the nature of the relationship and the loss of elements of that relationship prior to death, but rather the disruption is seen as beginning with the death.

On the other hand, the gerontology literature has paid scant attention to the caregiver once the care recipient dies. Caregiving is what is done to and for a living person who needs assistance. Some research addresses bereavement, and there is recognition of the person's loss. In particular, there has been interest in the relationship between caregiver stress prior to the care recipient's death and the adjustment of the former caregiver afterwards (see, e.g., Schulz et al. 2003; Bass, Bowman, and Noelker 1991). Yet in their review of a range of empirical studies, Schulz and his colleagues (1997) found only limited support for a causal relationship between stress and later adjustment for U.S. caregivers.

Our approach in this chapter is rather to see the stages of the care recipient's situation as a continuous "career" for the caregiver as well. We bring together the traditional concerns of the two disciplines as we try to understand the subjectively integrated experiences of a sample of Japanese caregivers in the first decade of the twenty-first century. We follow them as they provide assistance in daily living to a frail or ill older person in the home, to more-intensive medical care in an institution, through the beginning stages of their incorporation of their loss, and their own altered status into their post-caregiving selves.

Population Aging and Policy Response in Japan

The end of World War II brought rapid demographic, social, and political change to Japan. In 1950 the average family had 3.65 children (Coulmas 2007), and the majority of older people lived with an adult child.[2] By the twenty-first century, changes in the economy and in the legal definition of family had led to smaller and more-mobile families, and expanded participation of married women in work outside of the home. By 2010, 42 percent of people sixty-five and older lived with a family member, while 37 percent lived as couples and 17 percent lived alone. In 1950 the population of citizens aged sixty-five and older constituted less than 5 percent of the Japanese population; in 2015 that proportion was 26.3 percent (calculated from Statistics Bureau 2015).

By the 1980s these trends were already clear at a personal level to family members struggling to provide care for a frail relative, often for many years, since people were less likely than in previous generations to die quickly from an infectious disease and more likely to suffer years of chronic illness. Government bureaucrats recognized the trends as well. Local government welfare offices were providing services to some frail seniors, generally limited to those living alone or with only a spouse, and the need was growing rapidly. At the national level, policymakers developed the 1989 Gold Plan that set goals for a significant increase in the number of facilities providing LTCI and the services available for those living at home, but provided little funding to achieve these goals.

After revising the targets for facilities construction and service providers upward in 1994, the government determined that a new approach to the growing problems of eldercare was needed. Politicians, aware of the increasing proportion of voters who were themselves old or facing the need to care for someone, supported the proposal to establish a public LTCI program. This program relied on a combination of new tax money and premiums to be paid by everyone age forty and older. The mandatory premiums not only raise revenue to fund the benefits to be paid, but also destigmatize the use of services. Since everyone pays into the system, receiving benefits is an entitlement rather than a handout, much as Social Security is perceived in the United States. The bill establishing the new program was passed in 1997, and the program began operating in 2000.

Under this system, people older than age sixty-five with disabilities and those older than age forty with age-related illnesses such as having had a stroke or having Alzheimer's disease, may be certified for benefits by the local government welfare office and their physician. The certified care needs level determines the value of benefits received each month; services up to that amount are paid not in cash to the person or family, but directly to service providers. Those with the most severe needs are eligible for residential care, but even those with lighter needs may take advantage of some other services. These include adult day care, respite care for short stays in nursing homes, home helper services, rental or purchase of assistive equipment such as walkers and wheelchairs, and/or one-time payments for minor home modifications, such as installing grab bars or replacing a toilet with one easier for an elderly person to use. The program ideally maximizes choice of services, ranging from in-home assistance to community services to residential facilities, depending on the care level for which the person is qualified. Prevention programs are available to those with mild impairment.

Service providers may be for-profit companies, government agencies, or not-for-profit groups, although not all options are available in all areas, and some residential services have substantial waiting lists. Certified care managers help navigate and coordinate the services for those eligible (Campbell and Ikegami 2003; Tamiya et al. 2011; Tsutsui 2014; Tsutsui and Muramatsu 2005).

The Continuing Presence of Earlier Meanings of Caregiving for the Elderly

The cultural meaning of caregiving in Japan has been based on an early twentieth-century stem family model in which one child, ideally the eldest son, was designated as heir and remained in the household through adulthood. In this traditional ideal scenario based on ideals of family continuity and Confucian ethics of filial piety, the head of his household was the individual culturally designated as responsible for the welfare of all members of the household, including frail relatives and aging parents (see also Traphagan 2004: 204–5). This son's wife, who married into the family, had responsibilities not only to assist with the family farm or business, but also to attend to the bodily needs of the household members. This included tasks such as cooking, feeding, bathing, doing laundry, and nursing those members who might be ill, frail, or disabled (Jenike 1997; Jenike 2004: 221–4; see also Wallhagen and Yamamoto-Mitani 2006). Thus, although Confucian norms of filial piety made her husband (the heir) the person with ultimate obligation for decisions, the day-to-day tasks of eldercare were seen as his wife's responsibility. Noninheriting children, grandchildren, and their spouses maintained relationships with parents or in-laws, but they did not have the level of responsibility of the coresiding couple for the well-being of the elders (Ikels 2004a: 4–6).

With the decline in the number of older adults and younger couples continuously living together, the remaining coresiding female, the wife, has also become a common caregiver for an elderly man. In recent decades, demographic and social changes have created additional challenges to the assumptions of birth order and gender. Wives of younger sons, daughters, sons, and husbands have increasingly become caregivers to a frail parent or spouse, although coresidence remains the assumed means of fulfilling the role, and female gender remains the default criterion. However, the percentage of male caregivers is steadily increasing. In 2010 just over 30 percent of primary caregivers who lived with elderly care recipients were male, primarily husbands and sons (Ministry of Health, Labour, and Welfare [MHLW] 2010). Regarding the increasing role of elders' spouses in their care, this is similar to what Shea has found in contemporary China (see chap. 2).

The historical model of caregiving carried assumptions not only about who should be responsible, but also about the tasks to be done and how. Hands-on care work (*kaigo*) emphasized meeting physical needs and providing physical comfort, but there was no expectation of verbal communication as a form of emotional support. Rather, concerns and insecurities of an ill or frail household member could be alleviated by the caregiver's successful efforts to take them on herself and to create an atmosphere in the home that was calm and restful. This meant maintaining a cheerful countenance and avoiding open expression of conflict regardless of the tensions that might exist in the household. The continuous presence in the house of the caregiver was also a key element of that nonverbal reassurance. In serious circumstances, the caregiver would give priority to attending to the needs of a sick or dying family member to the point of sanctioned neglect of other obligations to family members and the community. Time off for the caregiver to relax and care for herself was not part of this model and would have been judged harshly.

This ideal of caregiving that accompanied the early twentieth-century family system was of course extremely onerous and unlikely to be fully achieved. However, it remains significant today because, to varying degrees, caregivers continue to judge themselves and be judged by others according to its standards. In post–World War II reforms, the legal basis for the stem family was eliminated and equal inheritance of all children after the death of both parents was instituted, undermining the rationale and reward for unequal caregiving responsibilities among sibling households. In recent years, although the meaning of providing care has evolved to include an increased use of professional service providers, changes in the meaning of caregiving are always understood in relation to past assumptions regarding who should be *the* caregiver and the importance of physical comfort, calm environment, and total commitment (Long 1997; see also Tsukada and Saito 2006). Japanese daughters-in-law may, in an era of changing expectations and new services, have more "room for maneuver" (Pyysiainen 2007), a bit of flexibility in day-to-day caregiving such as using LTCI services or asking a husband for help. Who will be the primary caregiver may now be negotiated, rather than assumed. Daughters-in-law may set limits on what they will tolerate in abusive demands or language from the care recipient by the very threat, even if unspoken, of refusing to take on the caregiver role at all. Yet many still feel the heavy weight of past expectations, some wanting to do their best in the sole caregiver role and some rejecting its assumptions and criticism from others. The historical understanding of filial piety and what it means to be a caregiver thus continues to frame the experience for caregivers, whether they embrace, tolerate, or fight against its assumptions and standards, as we illustrate in the pages that follow.

Methods and Participants

Our collaboration in writing this chapter derives from our participation in a Japanese research team studying a sample of clients who were using the services of the LTCI program and their family caregivers over five years from 2003–2007.[3] We draw on our many years of conducting interviews and observing practices in Japan, but in particular we focus on the series of semi-structured interviews conducted as part of the five-year team project in two geographical areas—urban Tokyo and a small city and surrounding villages in the northern prefecture of Akita. In each area, fifteen families participated for as long as they were willing to speak to us each year. The interview sample was selected to include both men and women as care recipients, and a range of insurance system care levels, which often changed over the course of the study. During the research period, fourteen out of the thirty care recipients we interviewed died. The average age of the deceased care recipients was 81.57 (ages ranging from sixty-seven to ninety-four) and the average age of the caregivers was 67.28 (ages ranging from forty-two to eighty-four). Of the caregivers, we interviewed ten daughters-in-law, four daughters, three sons, seven wives, and six husbands.

Teams of at least two researchers visited the homes and spoke with both care recipient and caregiver, separately when possible, using an interview guide but encouraging free conversation. Sessions lasted from one to two and a half hours. Informed consent was obtained for all interviews, which were audiotaped and later transcribed with permission. Interview topics included the nature of the care recipient's health and daily living problems, daily life for the care recipient and caregiver, decisions about the use of medical and social services, family relationships, and the concerns and sources of pleasure for both caregiver and care recipient. We conducted follow-up interviews each year through 2007 for as long as the families were willing and able to participate, to track changes of status, learn about decision-making in conjunction with these changes, and hear about the participants' experiences in greater depth. As often as possible, the research team interviewed the caregivers within a year after the death, allowing us to hear their reflections looking back on their caregiving experiences. Data from this time period offer an important lens into the caregiving and grieving experiences of Japanese older adults soon after the establishment of national LTCI, with important implications for both the present and the future.

Caregiving Approaches in Early Twenty-First-Century Japan

Just as eldercare policy and changing ideals of caregiving responsibilities impact contemporary caregivers, so too do models of *how* to provide care. Dependency and independence are two existing cultural frameworks through which caregivers make sense of their work. One approach begins with the assumption of the elder relative's dependency. The other approach acknowledges that some degree of dependency is necessary but tries to maximize the older person's independence. In our study, which approach an individual caregiver adopted related to personal inclination, family relationships prior to illness, and family members' openness to professional advice or government messaging about the best way to assist an elderly person.

Assuming Dependency

The approach that sees the caregiver taking on total care for the person fits with historical expectations described above. Japanese psychiatrist Takeo Doi (1973, 1986) has attempted to explain the differences in the emotional life of Japanese and non-Japanese as grounded in *amae,* glossed as passive love or dependency (see also chap. 7). In his view, the dependency of an infant and the indulgence of the child by the mother was the prototypical relationship that continued to affect patterns of interpersonal behavior throughout life. The issue of dependency requires that we consider the increasing need for reliance on others both as a universal feature of old age, and as a feature to be understood in cultural context.

Among the caregivers we interviewed, we observed different expressions of and responses to the physical and emotional needs of the frail relative. We saw many examples of caregivers reaching out to help the care recipient do something that they might have been able to do on their own. The sense that caregivers should always be doing more than they were, or could be doing was sometimes reinforced by demands from the older person (often a mother-in-law) or by criticism from sisters-in-law (i.e., the daughters of the care recipient) that the caregiver was paying insufficient attention to the care recipient's needs. In one case, a vocal sister-in-law who lived close by complained that the daughter-in-law caregiver did not cook the things her mother liked for breakfast, but instead was only making what the daughter-in-law and her husband wanted to eat. The caregiver and the sister-in-law may have had different models of dependency and response to frailty in mind.

The emotional stress experienced from taking on another's desire or need for dependency should ideally be counterbalanced in eldercare by a transfer of interpersonal power such that the care recipient trusts the caregiver and assumes a dependent role (Pyke 1999). Some of the daughter-in-law caregivers noted that, with increased frailty, the mothers-in-law had become more dependent on them and the relationship had become less stressful than it had been earlier in their marital history. One daughter-in-law explained the relationship: "Relations with my mother-in-law were hard over the years, but they were probably still better than most. We didn't actually argue, but a lot of things were unpleasant. I was working, and then when I got home, I was busy with laundry and cooking, so there was really no time to fight. But in contrast, now that my mother-in-law can't do anything [due to dementia and difficulty walking], the relationship is better. We don't fight. I realize that when she does something, it's because she doesn't understand." In fact, the greatest anger we saw from caregivers was where that anticipated transfer had not occurred as expected in the mother-in-law's old age.

The past relationship between the caregiver and care recipient greatly impacts the way that caregiving is done within this framework, providing different caregiver motivations and leading to two quite different ways of carrying out caregiving tasks.[4] For some, being the caregiver feels like the natural result of a parent–child or spousal relationship, often drawing on cultural notions of "returning the favor" (*okaeshi*), here referring to paying back past care when the need arises. In an interview in an earlier study in the mid-1990s, a husband talked lovingly about the way his wife had taken care of him all the years that he was working, even meeting him with an umbrella at the bus stop if it unexpectedly began to rain. For him caring for her when she needed it was a way to express his gratitude. A wife told us, "I think I did my best in the nursing care of my husband. At the same time, however, I wanted to do more things for my husband. I feel that I was meant to take care of him. It was my destiny." Even daughters-in-law who had a good relationship with their mother-in-law over the years, viewing the mother-in-law as a mentor or substitute parent, thought that caregiving now was a payback for earlier kindness or that it was "natural" to care for a person with whom they had lived for many decades. These caregivers built their commitment around a positive long-standing relationship that seemed to lead to less of a sense of burden compared with other caregiving situations. In these cases, the obligation was more embraced than merely tolerated.

When the past relationship was weak or the caregiver felt resentment over years of poor treatment (most often expressed by the care recipients' wives and daughters-in-law who had married in to the husband's household), caregivers might still accept the framework of what should be done, but subvert it because of their anger or resentment. Some caregivers chose to do the minimum for the relative, such as a wife whose husband had spent most of their married life working as a day laborer in other parts of the country, not doing all he could to provide financially for the family, such as not applying for a pension from his company. Her husband had lost his right arm in a work accident, and had an artificial joint that later became infected and had to be removed. He then retired at age fifty-eight and returned home. His wife complained that he was drunk on sake, all day and every day. "Having only one arm is an inconvenient thing, but he manages doing most things by himself. But his drinking is bad. I understand he can't move like he wants to, but still he could do a little more." For financial reasons, she explained, she took a job at a hot springs resort, coming home only once a week. While she was gone he was alone, and when she returned the refrigerator was empty. She saw his dependency as inappropriate but intractable, so provided only minimal support, staying at a distance to make her sense of burden more tolerable by gaining a sense of revenge.

Several daughters-in-law described the exclusion, bullying, and unreasonable demands they experienced when they came in to the family as a new bride and the continued refusal of their mother-in-law to accept them as a daughter, referring to them as an outsider even after thirty or forty years of marriage and coresidence. One recounted that her mother-in-law "never once said anything nice to me. Whatever I did, she found something to nag me about. And that wasn't enough for her. She had to tell neighbors or other people." She often thought of running away in those days. She added that her husband did not support her, but that "I am one of them now, but these people don't even realize what they did to me. I will never forget what I had to go through." She took care of her mother-in-law "because I have to. I don't have sincere feelings about wanting to take care of her." Because of their past relationship, the daughter-in-law had trouble mustering up the will to care for her graciously, but did the bare minimum required of her kinship role, perhaps as a way to avoid the perceived moral censure of the community if she did not.

Maximizing Independence

Such personal resistance, however, does not challenge the cultural frame-work of ideal caregiving. In contrast, professionals and government agencies now emphasize a new approach that maximizes independence (see also chap. 7). Older people are encouraged to maintain their health by eating and sleeping well and by exercising, participating in rehabilitation programs if they experience a health problem, and staying engaged in the social world, for example at senior centers and day-care centers. In this new model, reliance on care professionals who are experts is designed to relieve some of the burden experienced by family caregivers. Ideal caregiving in this framework thus looks quite different from the approach that assumes dependence. A caregiver should do only what is necessary for the person, and encourage them to do as much as possible on their own. A daughter caregiver learned from a teacher of an eldercare class she took at a local nursing home to "watch but not do" (*me o kakeru ga te o kakenai*). A daughter-in-law explained, "I let her wash dishes even if she doesn't do a good job. We can always go back and wash them again." She had learned this approach through classes that she took as a community welfare volunteer (*minsei-iin*).

This new caregiving style is becoming better known as more professionally trained caregivers interact with family because of the LTCI system, and many of those we interviewed had incorporated elements of that style into their caregiving decisions. One family, concerned that their grandmother would become bedridden if she stayed a week in the hospital, brought her back the same day the ambulance took her there for an acute problem. The entire family worked to activate her brain, working together with her on elementary school math books and limiting the period that she could wear diapers to just two months. Another example is a daughter-in-law caregiver who lives in a rural area where the family owns a small plot of land on which they grow vegetables for themselves. She had always worked outside the home, but quit her job when her mother-in-law needed care due to dementia, difficulty walking, and incontinence. Initially, she was the sole caregiver, with some support from her husband. She had been getting up several times a night to help her mother-in-law go to the toilet, and the lack of sleep affected her own health. They began using day care and respite care services under the LTCI system, reporting, "At first, I worried a lot and felt that I needed to be at home so I could be contacted if something happened." But, she continued, "Now even though I still worry, I realize that worrying won't accomplish anything." She began to use the time her mother-in-law was away to pursue her own interests—although those interests included caregiving for her own mother who lived about an hour and a half away by bus.[5] Taking time for yourself to refresh is supposed to be good for caregivers in the approach to care that emphasizes independence in contrast to the ideal of 24/7 care in the dependency model.

What happens when family members advocate different styles of caregiving? In one family we observed there was tension between the son Hiroshi and daughter-in-law Chizuko about the care for his eighty-seven-year-old mother who had diabetes and difficulty walking. When we began our study, Hiroshi was identified as the primary caregiver, but it turned out that Chizuko, a nurse, had started out as the caregiver, but disagreement in the family led to Hiroshi taking on the designation of family caregiver for his mother. His mother desired a dependent style of care, and Hiroshi felt that whatever his mother wanted should be provided. But as a professional nurse, Chizuko believed that it was best if people do more on their own to the extent they are able. She also favored the use of the LTCI services available to them. The mother tried day care twice but did not want to go back, a decision Hiroshi supported. Chizuko said, "Families who take care of the person completely [on their own] until the end receive praise, but at a cost to the caregivers." She pointed out that if her mother-in-law used day care it would make it easier for them to schedule respite care for a few days if they needed it. After several arguments, Chizuko finally said to her husband that he could do it his way, but that he would have to be the one to be the caregiver. Although the daughter-in-law continued doing household tasks that benefited the mother-in-law, Hiroshi provided the majority of the hands-on care his mother required until her admission to the hospital shortly before her death. Thus, the stories of the caregivers we interviewed demonstrate that caregivers come to the job with a variety of motivations and interpersonal histories, which affects the ways they cope with their obligations (Steadman, Tremont, and Davis 2007).

Caregiving Careers and Changes over Time

Our interviews showed that the demands, relations, and experiences of caregiving varied considerably based on a range of factors and changed often markedly over time as the ailing elder's condition progressed and in relation to proximity to death. In the previous section, we described frameworks for thinking about how best to care for an older relative, but the activities and emotions of caregiving are neither static nor random. Rather, they change in response to changes in the care recipient's condition, which require new forms of assistance and caregiver adjustments. New skills or resources may change the subjective sense of burden the caregiver experiences. Such new circumstances may further the kind of power shift discussed earlier, or other changes in the relationship between the caregiver and care recipient. Patterned activities punctuated by transitions that lead to new sets of activities might be considered a sort of caregiver career (Aneshensel et al. 1995). The caregiving career might begin at very different points depending on the cause of the need for care, the relationship of those involved, and the motivation of the caregiver to take on the job. Common elements of the beginning stage might be diagnosing the problems, psychological adjustment, and surveying and marshalling resources. This initial stage may be long or short, might develop into a relatively smooth routine, or might improve or worsen. Two very significant changes that many people we interviewed identified as major transitions were worsening dementia and incontinence, both of which dramatically increase the work and unpleasant aspects of the job for the caregiver.

Changes as the Care Recipient's Condition Worsens

One factor that alters the caregiving career is the changing condition of the care recipient. Although in a few cases there were improvements in the elder's condition during our study, most of the changes were those of increasing frailty and worsening disease symptoms. A common theme was that, paradoxically, as care continues and the old person's condition worsens, caregivers often find their attitudes changing. With increased frailty and accompanying loss of control of the old person, the caregiver may be able to stand back and view the care recipient's situation with greater empathy. One told us, "When she was healthy, my mother-in-law had a sharp tongue. But from last year, I decided to forget about all the bad things." A wife caregiver told us she has stopped speaking harshly to her husband. "When I see him [lying there] on his back, I become so emotional and stop saying [critical] things to him." She often feels sorry for him. "I often watch him as he leaves for the day-care center. I remember when he was healthy. Seeing him like that I think, How could a man like him become so weak?" Noriko, the woman who had trouble with her sister-in-law's criticism (discussed earlier in this chapter) told us, "Now I can almost forget about [how badly I was treated as a newcomer to the family] and feel sorry [*kawaisou*] for [my mother-in-law]. But I can't forget my anger over what her daughter has done to me. I can't forgive *her.*"

Another aspect of change is that it may be easier to care for a person confined to bed or relatively immobile than to care for someone wandering around. An eighty-one-year-old woman had been caring for her husband for several years. He had dementia from a stroke and was often agitated, wandering out on the street, talking loudly. Now that he was bedridden with colon cancer, she said that she rarely loses her temper anymore. "My husband is now bedridden. He can't sit up or walk." Increased immobility over time made his care far easier than it had been. Thus, some caregivers found themselves able to forgive those who were suffering weakness or pain despite past mistreatment, their anger replaced with pity.

The most visible change occurs when a care recipient moves from home to institutional care; this is not just a geophysical alteration, however, but rather a synecdoche for deeper transformations. The family caregiver loses the status of designated caregiver, often much to their relief. In the past, the tradition of a single caregiver and its heavy burden led to what many considered abandonment to institutional care. In the 1980s and 1990s numerous nursing-home administrators complained that family members rarely visited their residents, a situation that may have resulted in one daughter-in-law in our study receiving an encouraging thank-you letter from the nursing home each time she visited. Among those we interviewed in the 2000s, family members continued to feel responsible, regardless of how often they visited. When they went to the nursing home, they often brought items back and forth from home and did the care recipient's laundry. Clearly, the change of residence is at the very least a move to a model of shared caregiving, if not a total shifting of the burden.

Changes in Caregiving as Death Nears

Whereas Heekyoung Kim (chap. 8) wrote of the phenomenon of seniors in Japan dying alone at home unnoticed and uncared for, in our research the situation was one of being tended to closely near the approach of death, but not necessarily at home. While diapers and dementia are obvious markers of transitions for those involved, another transition is more gradual and recognized more readily in retrospect—the transition from caring for someone with a chronic illness or frailty to caring for someone in their final weeks or hours of life. In the past, whether an older person was living at home or in a care facility, they were nearly always taken to a hospital when death appeared close. Statistically, close to 80 percent of deaths in Japan take place in a hospital or clinic, although the proportion of deaths at eldercare facilities has increased from 1.5 percent in 1995 when this category of death was first recorded to over 6 percent in 2012. Still, in contrast to the ideal of home-based caregiving for the elderly, home deaths, and even nursing-home deaths, are relatively rare in Japan, as compared with hospital- or clinic-based deaths. In our survey, nine of the fourteen people who died were in hospitals, even if just for a night or two. Four died in eldercare facilities, and one died at home but was taken to the hospital where his death was certified by a doctor. Another caregiver explained,

"My son said that in the very end he wanted to have the doctor take care of her. Even if she was at home. The reason is . . . we didn't want anyone to say, 'Ah, they didn't even take her to the doctor,' so even if it was for a night, even if it was for an hour, we wanted to have a doctor see her" (see also Long 2013). Thus, the physical transfer of the dying to a clinic or hospital was not regarded as burden-shifting from the family to the professional sphere, but rather as fulfilling familial obligations to do everything possible for the ill person.[6]

End-of-life care in a hospital thus does not absolve the family caregiver of caregiving obligations, although the nature of the tasks changes and the tasks themselves become more widely dispersed. Hospitals are staffed with nurses around the clock, but it is common for a family member to remain overnight in the hospital room with a seriously ill or terminal patient. They bring requested items to the hospital and take dirty laundry home, and they help keep the patient as comfortable as possible. One family member is charged with being the liaison between the family and the medical staff for the purpose of conveying information and making decisions. But mostly the job is to be present. The expectation that all family members be in the room at the moment of death (*shinime ni au*) is so strong that the realization of a good death nearly depends on it (Long 2005, chap. 4). Hospital staff will call if no one is there and tell them to come, and they will sometimes keep people alive until the necessary family members can assemble (Fetters and Danis 2002). But the timing of the call is not always perfect; thus it is better to have a family member already there. Several caregivers we interviewed described family members, including those who had previously been only marginal to the home caregiving process, taking turns staying at the hospital in the days or weeks leading up to the death. Since most deaths take place at hospitals, this expectation that many relatives are there means that there is less physical labor involved since the nurses do much of the care. For the primary family caregiver, the expectation that a wider group now share in the work of supporting the dying person and the reprieve from the more physically demanding tasks provides relief from the intensity of the single-caregiver experience of many of those we interviewed, and allows that caregiver to approach the care recipient with a new attitude.

Some of the interviews suggest that a change in affect may occur near the end of life. When the care recipient's condition takes a serious turn for the worse, they may experience both a huge sense of relief as well as guilt that perhaps they did not do enough. One caregiver of her mother-in-law told us that although the care recipient was a gentle person who had experienced a difficult life with an alcoholic husband, she never totally accepted her (the daughter-in-law) into the family despite years of living together.

The mother-in-law had developed dementia and suffered from hallucinations. Around the time our study began, she had become bedridden and required a catheter. The caregiver was clearly tired and stressed, worried about finances, and feeling resentment at having to care for someone who did not accept her. During one interview, she expressed that, despite the wonderful help and support from the LTCI service providers, "it gets too much for me sometimes. . . . I'm not a good daughter-in-law, so when it goes on and on, I burst!" The care recipient was later moved to a nursing home, and during a visit there the nurses told the family that she had blood in her stool and needed to be transferred to a hospital. She died there two days later. As death came, the daughter-in-law's orientation toward her mother-in-law underwent a transformation involving multiple contradictory feelings. She explained that when her mother-in-law was first admitted to the nursing home, "I was really happy when we received notice that she would be able to enter [the nursing home]. I felt that I still had my life left to spend for myself. I felt truly liberated. [But then] after that, I sincerely wished for her to have a long life."

Along with the sense of relief, final days often allow the caregiver the rare experience of feeling that their hard work has been appreciated. One element of a good death in Japanese culture is that the dying person expresses thanks to the family and others for what they have done for them over the years, and for the relationship. The two most common features of caregivers' narratives about the death were whether they and other family members were present at the time of the person's last breath and whether there had been thanks from the care recipient. The expression of gratitude might take a variety of forms, from calling out "thank you" from another room to one man's acknowledging his dependency on his wife by telling her that he did not want her to leave, to go home to get some needed items. Such direct expression would not be expected in ordinary family life, but it appears to be a culturally scripted and widely understood means for the dying to say good-bye, to acknowledge what the person has done for them over the long course of their relationship as well as recent caregiving (Long 2005: 61). In our interviews we found that, when care recipients expressed appreciation, caregivers were able to have positive emotions about the death, and, later, about the caregiving experience.

Caregivers after the Death of the Care Recipient

Caregiving and bereavement have generally been considered separately by different groups of experts rather than seen as a continuous caregiving career as we conceptualize it for Japan.[7] In research in the United States, Bernard and Guarnaccia (2003) recognize that rather than two points in time (pre-death and post-death) caregiving can be seen as a continuous experience through the illness, dying, and mourning periods. They argue that family caregiving and bereavement are not separate, but rather are parts of a single stressor, with cumulative effects on the caregiver. Opening the discussion beyond concern for caregiver stress from a clinical perspective, Orzeck and Silverman (2008) place this continuity more explicitly within a life-course perspective. Their discussion of post-caregiving acknowledges the subjective continuity of the caregiver's experience; although they recognize the continuity of stress and loss, they also note that the rebuilding of an identity after the care recipient's death is part of the caregiving experience. Our interviews suggest that these factors are relevant to understanding continuities and transitions in the lives of Japanese caregivers as well. Just as the tasks, routines, and relationships of the caregiver change over time and with the care recipient's condition (Long et al. 2010), so too do these things continue to change through the process of dying, mortuary ritual, and daily life after the death. Although the death of the care recipient certainly alters some aspects of their lives dramatically, in other ways caregiving continues to be part of their lives, representing a more gradual and incomplete transition.

We argue in particular that although the work of caregiving is seemingly over when the care recipient dies, it is useful to think about some indefinite period, from weeks to years, being a final stage in the caregiver career. A number of instrumental, emotional, and spiritual tasks remain to be done, and the experience of caregiving continues to be incorporated at least selectively in the memory and identity of the caregiver. Many of the instrumental tasks are common responses to death in other societies, but the tasks take on specific cultural forms and carry with them particular social expectations in different contexts. In this section of the chapter, we explore the experiences of those caregivers in our study who experienced the death of their relative and, following this, the continuing trajectories of caregiving careers in mortuary practices, maintaining bonds with the deceased, dealing with loneliness, and reconstructing their lives and identities.

Mortuary Ritual

In the past, a Buddhist funeral conducted by the priest of the family's affiliated temple and burial in the family tomb would have been assumed in rural areas. In cities, however, that may no longer be practical or desirable. Increasingly common are decisions about burial made individually or jointly by a couple prior to need, often based on the availability and desirability of burial in the family tomb versus purchasing their own gravesite

(Danely 2014, 2015; Kawano 2010). Some of the people we spoke with in this and earlier studies indicated that they saw this decision as an obligation to avoid burdening children later, and they felt a sense of accomplishment once arrangements were in place. But when death was unexpected or the decision had not been made in advance, the caregiver (sometimes in consultation with other family members) might need to make such a choice quickly after the death. In one of the families we interviewed, for example, the caregiver wife decided that after her husband's death, apparently without challenge to her authority to make the decision, the burial should be nearby rather than in the family grave, the assumed site. The family grave was located hours away in another prefecture, so she arranged to have his ashes buried locally so that she could visit frequently.[8] Furthermore, the caregiver, especially if a woman, is likely to be responsible for the practical tasks of not only the funeral, but also subsequent memorial services. This work includes hosting and feeding participants in these rituals.[9] Caregivers also selected and saw to the delivery of a small return gift to those who contributed monetary funeral offerings. In recent years, hospital staff wash the body, and funeral homes offer packages of services that take on most of the other jobs (Suzuki 2000), requiring a single set of decisions and relieving much of the work of the mourning caregiver. Yet in some communities these services are less available, or the social pressure to conform to traditional practices remains strong.

Continuity of personal care in this stage of the caregiver's career exists in the form of maintenance of the grave as well as, often, a home altar. Although few Japanese take traditional beliefs at a literal level, there remains a sense in which the spirit of the deceased remains around the home and grave for an extended period, needing the care of surviving family to rest peacefully as an ancestor. Historically, it was the responsibility of the senior woman in the household to offer fresh flowers, food, and drink at the altar, although anyone with a relationship to the deceased could light incense and recite sutras. The wife and daughter-in-law caregivers of their elderly relative often transitioned to this new role.

There is great variation in contemporary mortuary practices. While some contemporary households have ornate altars, in others there may be nothing but a formal photograph of the deceased on a shelf without any accompanying ritual. Similarly, care of the family graves is often done by the senior woman of the household, who was the person who was most likely the primary caregiver before death. Some older women in our study visited the family grave regularly, sometimes daily, washing the grave and bringing flowers, food, and drink; other graves are visited and washed only around the summer memorial holiday of Obon or not at all. One wife visited her husband's grave daily but eventually reduced her visits to once a week, saying, "Everyone joked that my husband could not rest in peace if I visited him so often." This might partially reflect concerns of her family and friends that she was exhausted from caregiving. She had fallen while her husband was in the hospital, injuring her knee, and seemed depressed. She had worked hard organizing her husband's things until the forty-ninth day after his death, a ritual marking point, and then she said, "Every morning I ask myself whether it was all right or not, whether I've become lazy or not."

We noted earlier that the interpersonal relationship between the caregiver and care recipient prior to illness affected the way caregiving was perceived and carried out. When a caregiver's relationship with the care recipient was poor, caregiving tasks might be done with resentment, perhaps doing the bare minimum, arguing (instead of keeping a calm environment as in ideal caregiving), or ignoring requests. The sharing of the caregiving burden with nursing homes or hospitals at the end of life led some caregivers to be able to see the care recipient objectively as a frail old person who had lost the ability to make decisions about their own life or impose their will on others. This sometimes resulted in better relationships, the caregiver's acceptance of the situation, and forgiveness for the care recipient's earlier mistreatment. Yet hard feelings might remain, leading to a continuation of the resentful caregiving style after death. In one family in our study, the daughter-in-law was still angry when we spoke to her after her mother-in-law died. There were withered flowers at the household altar. She spoke of her long-term resentment, saying that she was "tricked" when she came into the household in marriage, with the presence not only of her mother-in-law but also the mother-in-law's mother-in-law. Even after becoming ill and needing care, her mother-in-law refused to relinquish power over her, the daughter-in-law caregiver. Despite being subjected to highly demanding orders from her mother-in-law, she received no expression of support or appreciation for her efforts from her husband. She felt as if she had lost ten years of her life taking care of the mother-in-law, adding, "I do not offer her incense. I take revenge on her." Sometimes poor relationships carry through caregiving and beyond to characterize relationships between the living and the dead. In a previous study of older couples, we found that several daughters-in-law still carried strong resentments about the bad treatment they had received, even many years after their mothers-in-law had died (see also Zeserson 2001).

Maintaining Bonds with the Deceased

Other work of the caregiver after a death involves establishing the place of the deceased care recipient in the family, or as Klass et al. (1996) put it, maintaining continuing bonds with the dead. Photographs help to maintain the deceased's presence as a part of the family, and we saw many in the homes we visited. Gardens may be maintained or habits continued, such as the son who, after his mother died, started going to the mountains to collect vegetables, one of her favorite activities (see Richardson 2014). Records of funeral offerings and the return gifts are maintained across generations, helping people keep track of relations between families and thus determine the amount the family should give when someone else dies. The deceased also continues to have a presence in the household and in the lives of its members through continuing talk about the departed. The caregiver may also continue to talk to the deceased, sometimes at first as though the person was still there, as one wife told us: "Every day I would talk this and that to him, but then I felt I would lose my mind, because I would say something, and he often did not respond. But I would just ask him, 'Did you hear me, did you hear me?' And he responded, 'Yes I can hear.'"

Less literal talk with the deceased may take place indefinitely through reporting at the altar the daily and special events in the lives of family members, offering thanks to the ancestors or asking for their help and protection. The way the caregiver also talks *about* the deceased to others, what is emphasized and what is forgotten, contributes to the creation of the memory of who that person was in the household and community. The deceased may be the symbol of extended family who gather at Obon, or may serve as a moral guide, such as in the case of the wife caregiver who decided not to have her dying husband put on a ventilator based on an earlier discussion with her mother-in-law who had expressed a desire to not have her life extended with such technological interventions. The caregiver role thus extends to care for the memory of the person who had been in her charge.

Although there may be a sense of relief and freedom, the response of many caregivers we interviewed after the death of the care recipient was loneliness. A daughter-in-law caregiver had been living in a traditional, four-generation rural household consisting of her mother-in-law, herself, her adult son, his wife, and their children. She explained that she had felt angry when her husband died fifteen years earlier. She was bitter because he should have taken better care of himself to prevent him from dying so young. Her mother-in-law's death was different. Their relationship had been close, and her mother-in-law had been very kind to her, teaching her everything about farming when she came into the household as a young bride. "Baasan [my mother-in-law] and I would be sitting here, and we'd talk about this and that. I feel lonely that she passed away." It helped her to talk to her family about her mother-in-law's death, but she sensed that the younger family members had things they would like to discuss with each other in private, so after dinner she would say thank you for dinner and leave the table before everyone else. "After I ate, I used to leave the table and talk to Baasan [in the other room], but she's not here anymore so now I come [to the other room], watch TV, and laugh to myself." The lingering presence of the deceased was sought in the time and place the two women used to chat together after dinner.

Several wife caregivers said that their husband's death left a large void in their lives. One said, "I don't have a companion now. I talk about the TV programs, but no one replies. I sometimes forget to eat." Another wife missed her team—the doctor, visiting nurse, and day-care staff with whom she had been in constant contact during her husband's illness. "If they had followed up on me properly for a while, I may not have been at such a loss. [While my husband was still alive,] these people visited my house more than my relatives. I felt lonely losing all contact with them."[10] If the care providers had been able to follow up after the death with the bereaved they might have helped to provide a more gradual transition to widowhood and eased the loneliness of the early days and weeks following the husband's death. She really wanted the care team to visit her and share memories of her husband. It is interesting to consider how this sense of emptiness might be different where caregiving responsibilities are less centered on a single individual expected to make that the center of their life.

Reconstruction of a Post-Caregiving Life

A final caregiving task of this stage of the caregiver career is that of re-creating the caregiver's own life after the often near-single-minded focus on caregiving. Kellehear (2009: 393) writes that people do not give up on their losses, but rather renegotiate a new way to relate to them, incorporating them into new identities and social roles. Given the emphasis on the sole caregiver responsibilities they had experienced before the death of the care recipient, it is not surprising that they went through a period of adjustment after the death and funeral. Many incorporated their caregiving experience into their new sense of self.

Although our post-death interviews took place about a year after the death of the care recipient and it is thus difficult to evaluate the ways people moved on with their lives, we are able to identify several ways that people responded to their new post-caregiving situation. One major transition was how they spent their days without their previous duties. One daughter-in-law caregiver had earlier complained about the burden of caring for his mother to her husband, pleading that he not allow her own life (*jin-*

sei) to end with the caregiving. As her burden eased following her moth-er-in-law's death, she turned to her husband to look to the future, telling us that the previous New Year's they had decided just to toast each other. Other couples went on trips together, which they had not been able to do during caregiving. One wife in her early sixties, the youngest of the wives we talked to, went back to work the day after her husband died. She said she learned from her mother-in-law, who was widowed when she was fifty-two, that she should look ahead, be healthy, and pursue hobbies. She continued her hobby of hip-hop dancing and began to play the piano, to play the *koto*, a large stringed instrument in the zither family, and to study Buddhism. But perhaps the most effective intervention for her was when her son who lived nearby bought her a puppy named Shin. Her own dog had died shortly be-fore her husband died. She said she used to come home from work and cry, but after her son brought Shin to her house during the day, taking care of the dog made a big difference in her life. Her son had also recently married, and she enjoyed talking and going out with his young wife. Her new life seemed to be fulfilling and varied.

The wife who complained about losing her caregiving team, after a year began reconnecting with old friends and had more time to spend visiting her daughter who worked in a hospital in another city. She also began play-ing the *koto* and writing Japanese poetry. These traditional arts are often pursued by elderly people, and the settings in which they occur provide good places to make new friendships (Moore and Campbell 2009).

Another wife planned to rebuild her house so that all three of her sons could live there together. Whether that was something they wanted was uncertain, but she took it on as her special project after the death of her husband. Several of the caregivers found comfort in talking to Buddhist priests about their complicated feelings after the death of their relatives. The wife who had tried and failed to stop her husband from drinking went on the famous Shikoku temple pilgrimage (*henro*) with a friend after his death, prayed, and set out incense. She remembers that, as she departed, a temple priest had encouraged her to stay healthy and return next year. "It's a good memory," she said.

Looking to the future also involved reflecting on the caregiving experi-ence that was now the past. What did I sacrifice? What did I learn? How do I want things to be when I need care? It seemed natural to regard the caregiving experience as a rite of passage. A few caregivers told us they had regrets about their caregiving. One reflected that she was mostly happy with what she had done but regretted that she had not been more kind to her mother-in-law. Another was sad that her husband had been able to live in their new house only a short time, and that retirement dreams had never been realized. A son regretted that he had not asked his mother more about where she gathered wild vegetables and how to prepare them.

When we spoke with people during the caregiving period few expressed any personal satisfaction with what they were doing. Yet the predominant feeling in the post-death interviews was that most caregivers were proud of what they had accomplished. Our colleagues who conducted the survey portion of our research project that formed the basis of our interview sample (see note 3) report that there was deterioration in caregivers' mental health immediately after the death, but after a year respondents felt a sense of achievement that contributed to an increased sense of well-being and fulfillment (Nishimura et al. 2010). The daughter-in-law who told us that she at times almost burst from the stress of caregiving, now a year after the death said, "It was not some ordinary task, but I did it. It's like the feeling of receiving a medal. I had the opportunity to gain that experience, so there is something to be proud of." A wife echoed that sentiment, saying, "It's a good feeling to do something you're good at. It's happiness to take care of someone." Often they used their expertise in helping friends and family with their caregiving issues, and several decided to get training to become home helpers or official community volunteers (*minsei-iin*) in order to use their new skills to assist other family caregivers. Although caregiving is usually depicted in the Japanese media as a grim, unending burden, it appeared that many of the caregivers after the death of their relatives took pride in their hard-won skills and felt they had grown in the process. "It's good to know that I can take care of others in a very deep sense," one daughter said. "I've accomplished a lot," another daughter-in-law said, adding, "I've become broadminded."

This sense of satisfaction was often reflected in their feelings about how they wanted to be cared for themselves in the future. The wife with the daughter who is a doctor was happy her daughter could observe how she cared for her father. She thought this would help her daughter with her patients, but she also implied that her daughter would take care of her mother when she needed care. The daughter-in-law who had been so close to her mother-in-law hoped that her daughter-in-law would do the same for her. She was happy that her son told his wife, "You are going to take good care of your mother-in-law, otherwise your daughter won't take good care of you." He reinforced the notion that the reciprocity chain continued through the women of the household across the generations. In this case, she was living with her son and daughter-in-law, her grandson and his wife, and their children so that continuity through the generations was certainly plausible. Indeed, several of the caregivers believed that their devotion would be reciprocated by their daughters or daughters-in-law. One wife said, "I can't [bear to] live in a nursing home, so I won't quarrel with my daughter-in-law."

However, some caregivers, especially those who had difficult times with their mothers-in-law over the years, stressed that an eldercare facility would be better because, as one woman said, "There would be no burden on the family." She told her husband, "I have strong feelings about that." Another said she did not want her daughter-in-law to take care of her and that she would feel more comfortable in a nursing home. The woman who was very angry about her own situation wanted her own later-life care to be outside of the family entirely, and she raged against the government for changing the rules for long-term hospitalization for chronic illness in hospitals. The government is trying to reduce the use of hospitals and nursing homes and to encourage people to use services to "age in place." Whether this "aging in place" exhortation from the government will reduce the demand for institutionalization—there are now long waiting lists—remains to be seen. It is also clear that the reluctance of some older women to have their daughters-in-law be their caregivers reflects the daughter-in-law's signaled hesitance to assume this role.

We also saw ambivalence on the part of some. One woman said she wanted to stay at home as long as possible, but if she became weak she would want to go to her oldest son's house. However, she worried about living with her daughter-in-law because they might have to be very careful around each other, psychologically burdened—like walking on egg shells (*ki o tsukau*). Since her husband's death, she has discussed moving in with them, but in the same interview also said, "If I am frail and can't move on my own I would like to put myself somewhere [in a nursing home]."

What was universally acknowledged by the caregivers whom we interviewed was the value of the LTCI-sponsored services that they all had used to one degree or another. Many caregivers thought that the best style of care was to be able to draw on some combination of both family care and professional services. A large survey of Japanese adults aged twenty and older conducted in 1995 and 2003 asked, "What kind of nursing care do you want?" The percentage who replied, "family only" decreased from 25 percent in 1995 to 12 percent in 2003, and those preferring some combination of family and services increased from 65 percent in 1995 to 74 percent in 2003 (Cabinet Office 2003). As one woman who had cared for her husband remarked, "I want services for myself, not only family care." She thought that it was best to live separately from her children, and her experience caring for her husband and mother-in-law reinforced the importance of using various services. Some of the caregivers worried about the sustainability of the system, however, and hoped it would still be there when they needed it.

Discussion and Conclusion

In this chapter we have described what it is like to be a caregiver for an elderly relative who needs assistance with daily activities in early twenty-first-century Japan. As in other rapidly aging and affluent societies, many of the eldercare and mortuary duties formerly performed only by family are becoming increasingly professionalized and often commercialized (see Suzuki 2000 regarding mortuary ritual). Governmental policy and historical cultural patterns are important factors setting the stage for caregiving careers that span years and decades of changing bodies and changing relationships. In this chapter we have pointed to a range of personal circumstances and cultural models that influence the ways each caregiver acts, and that create both variation and commonality in the caregiving experience. Family relationships, especially the history of the relationship between the caregiver and the care recipient, were the most significant factors influencing the way in which the caregiver provided care and in how they viewed their experience before and after the death of the family member. Social pressure from other relatives or from the larger community in the case of the Akita caregivers, and the extent to which the caregiver felt empowered to make caregiving decisions, also impacted the caregiver experience, as did the sharing of the job with other family members or LTCI service providers. In a general sense, these factors may be applicable in any setting as people deal with aging and frailty. But to understand caregiving in Japan, or in any other specific place, we need to understand the policy-generated options, cultural models, and specific histories of interpersonal relationships of the situation that shape the choices and meanings of a caregiving experience.

In this chapter we further argue that we can better understand that experience if we view caregiving as a career that spans the illness, dying, and death of the family member. In the midst of daily stresses of the most difficult period of caregiving, many of the caregivers we interviewed expressed the feeling that it will never change or end. Yet it does change, allowing many to step back from the sense of burden to also experience empathy, believe that their work has been appreciated, and forgive past mistreatment. Caring for the deceased as an ancestor through mortuary ritual and the continued (selective) inclusion of the person in the daily life of the family and community provides a culturally meaningful path from the anger and frustration of caring for an elderly relative. As caregivers restart life without the onerous responsibilities of daily care, they do not put the caregiving experience behind them; rather its memory becomes part of who they are. Regrets and lingering anger may accompany their recollections of the last stages of the relative's life as they consider their own old age. They have learned new practical skills and have developed new abilities and competencies. For some caregivers, at least, these can be the basis of a sense of satisfaction and accomplishment to exist side by side with the memories of the pain, stress, and regret of the caregiving experience.

Unlike most studies of caregiving, a longer-term approach allows us to identify not only changes in the care recipient's status, but also changes in the caregiver's. Some of the transitions the caregiver experiences are immediate, such as the specific tasks to be done when someone is admitted to the hospital or dies. Yet even after death caregiving continues in the form of ritual, caring for the grave, retaining and transmitting the memory of who the person was, and dealing with the material things that mattered to the person while alive. Just as changes in the medical and social condition of the care recipient, such as increased dementia or incontinence, necessitated adaptation of caregiving routines and led to both desirable changes in power dynamics and to new challenges, the caregiver may also experience desirable changes and confront new tasks during the last stages of life and after the death. There may be increased autonomy or increased family support. The caregiver may be thanked for the first time by the care recipient as they are dying. After the death, the caregiver may gain a sense of accomplishment not possible while the care recipient was alive. Viewing such changes as part of a caregiving career is not only consistent with the understanding of the Japanese caregivers we met of the changes over time, but also helps us better understand caregiving as a social and interpersonal process requiring continuous adjustments. A longer-term view that uses a life-course approach focused on transitions and continuities, leads to deeper appreciation of the cultural meanings, personal regrets, and reconstruction of identity that are part of what it means within a person's life history to have assumed the responsibility for caring for a frail older person.

Such a perspective means supplementing common research methods in the field. Along with cross-sectional surveys and retrospective life reviews, we need longitudinal research designs that provide timely accounts to track transitions and offer in-depth personal data to better understand both general cultural patterns and individual variation in the meaning of the caregiving experience over time. Our own study offers a hint of the richness of such data, but an even longer view would have allowed us to follow caregivers as they continue to adapt after the death of the relative.

In addition, we need future studies that explore in greater depth some of the significant elements of the caregiving career. For Japan, the notion of burden found so frequently in both the gerontology literature and the popular media seems to be deeply embedded in concepts of social relationships more generally. It might also be useful to compare the Japanese concept of burden to other relationships such as the decision to marry and have children where the financial and emotional burden of raising children is often portrayed in the media as a reason for the low birth rate. Caregiver interviews suggest that the discourse of burden could be beneficially expanded to include the longer caregiving career represented in this chapter by consideration of the pre-caregiving relationships in the family and the work of end-of-life and post-death care. We know little about personal experiences of bereavement and how they are related to the types of care activities we have described in this chapter. This could be beneficially explored for Japan, and cross-culturally. Another topic that deserves systematic investigation is that of control, autonomy, and decision-making across the caregiver career. How might we best make sense of the changes and the variations within the same cultural framework and cross-culturally? We might also ask whether, as newer models of caregiving take hold more widely in Japan, and in particular as more husbands and sons become caregivers, whether caregiving will remain a solo career or will be more intertwined with the contributions of other family members and professional service providers. As gender roles change, will the continuity, which we have perceived as grounded in assumptions of female nurturance, decrease across the transition from caring for a living elder to caring for a deceased ancestor?

Not only scholars and the media, but also Japanese policy discourse has focused on the rhetoric of caregiver burden, which the public LTCI system intended to address. We do not deny that the standards to which family caregivers are held are often unattainably high, or that tasks and stresses are physically and emotionally exhausting and impact the caregiver's own health. Unpleasant tasks are sometimes made worse by criticism by others and by unreasonable demands for personal sacrifice. However, when that emphasis is the only framework used, some things are left out of the discussion. Service availability *does* provide relief, but not only by sharing the physical and emotional work, which has historically fallen on a single person in the household, but also by introducing new skills and validating alternative approaches to caregiving. Policymakers and service providers are also beginning to take the longer-term view of caregiving that we are advocating to identify unmet needs, considering in particular the possibility of greater continuity of support for caregivers of the dying and the newly dead. The complex and changing relationships at the basis of caregiving, however, cannot be standardized. The flexibility of the design of the LTCI system is one of its greatest strengths in providing assistance for a range of family situations. We hope that in light of ongoing concerns for the financial sustainability of the LTCI system going forward, policy and programs continue to offer creative, culturally sensitive ways to assist frail older adults and their caregivers. The ultimate truth about caregiving is that someone has to do it. How each society defines this process in the era of aging societies is of great significance and interest to all.

Acknowledgments

We are grateful to those who shared their experiences, thoughts, and feelings with us. This work would not have been possible without the collaboration of the interview team of Asakawa Noriko, Asano Yūko, Izumo Yūji, Kodama Hiroko, Muraoka Kōko, Nishida Masumi, Nishimura Chie, Shimmei Masaya, Suda Yuko, Takahashi Ryutaro, and Yamada Yoshiko. Financial support for the entire project came from the Japanese MHLW; the Ministry of Science; the Ministry of Education, Culture, Sports, Science and Technology; and the Univers Foundation. The coprincipal investigators were Takahashi Ryutaro and Suda Yuko. John Carroll University provided additional support for writing to Long.

Susan Long is professor emerita of Anthropology at John Carroll University and founding director of its East Asian Studies program. She authored *Final Days: Japanese Culture and Choice at the End of Life* (University of Hawaii Press 2005). She edited *Caring for the Elderly in Japan and the US: Practices and Policies* (Routledge 2000) and *Lives in Motion: Composing Circles of Self and Community in Japan* (Cornell East Asia Series 1999), and coedited *Death in the Early Twenty-First Century: Authority, Innovation and Mortuary Rites* (Palgrave 2017).

Ruth Campbell retired in 2006 as associate director for Social Work and Community Programs at the University of Michigan Geriatrics Center in the United States. She was also adjunct professor at the University of Michigan, School of Social Work. After retirement, she was associated with gerontology institutes in Tokyo for ten years. Her research and publications have centered on U.S.–Japan comparative studies on caregiving and family relationships, reminiscence, and community programs for the elderly in both Japan and the United States.

Glossary

henro	遍路	Famous Buddhist pilgrimage of eighty-eight temples on the Japanese island of Shikoku.
jinsei	人生	Human life.
kaigo	介護	Care (of the sick); nursing (an invalid); looking after an elderly relative.
Obon	お盆	Summer memorial holiday.

| *okaeshi* | お返し | To return the favor. |
| *minsei-iin* | 民生委員 | Community welfare volunteer. |

Notes

1. This was included for the first time in ICD-11 (World Health Organization 2019).
2. The fertility rate during Japan's Pacific War (also known as World War II, although the Pacific War began for Japan with the occupation of Manchuria in 1931) was much higher due to government pressure and encouragement of women to bear as many children as possible. That policy continues to have implications today, as today's elderly are the survivors of those children born between 1930 and 1950.
3. The study was a five-year longitudinal project with both quantitative and qualitative components. The first stage was a survey of 1,500 family caregivers and care recipients who had been certified as eligible for LTCI benefits in a largely working-class ward of Tokyo and in a small city and surrounding area in Akita, a northern prefecture that has the second-largest percentage of elderly in the country. This survey was repeated every other year with the same families, for a total of three sets of responses as long as the respondents were willing and alive. At the end of the interview the first year of the study, the respondents were asked if they would be willing to speak with someone in greater depth about their experiences at a later date. Several months after the survey, we conducted semi-structured interviews with a subset of those willing respondents, fifteen care recipient-family caregiver pairs in each area.
4. We have discussed the variety of motivations of caregivers in our study in Long et al. (2010) and the differences between daughter and daughter-in-law caregivers in Long, Campbell, and Nishimura (2009).
5. In that this rural woman was seen as having married into her husband's household and taken on the role of daughter-in-law, her primary social obligation was to take care of the members of that household, in this case her husband's mother. That she felt a personal desire to help her own mother was admirable but was secondary to the obligation she had to her household, thus constituting a free time activity. Due to the totalizing role of the caregiver in the traditional model, no one could be expected to care for more than one frail old person at a time unless they were a married couple with whom the caregiver shared a household.
6. Recently, the government has been actively trying to promote home-care teams of doctors, nurses, pharmacists, and careworkers to encourage choice, including the choice of dying at home. Two programs in 2015 on NHK, public television, featured a panel of celebrities discussing dying at home with a doctor who provided team hospice care. Vignettes showing caregivers with their relatives who were dying at home illustrated the benefits of this approach. At the beginning of each program at least one of the celebrities (one middle-aged and one older woman) endorsed dying in the hospital to avoid burdening family caregivers. By the end of the program, each of these celebrities changed her mind and said maybe dying at home was best. How influential this promotion will be on the general public is

yet to be determined. As ideal as it might be to die at home, it also seems likely that home deaths will increase the workload of family caregivers.

7. We are unaware of any literature in Japanese that ties together the caregiving experience with the care of the dying or post-death responsibilities and mourning.

8. From the early twentieth century, nearly all corpses are cremated in Japan. There has been increased interest in recent years in alternatives to family graves to which the ashes of the newly deceased are added, decisions intended to reflect the personhood of the deceased, such as ash scattering, natural cemeteries, or individual graves. However, family graves remain the default.

9. The timing of these vary but are commonly held at the seventh, forty-ninth, and hundredth day after the death and then annually until either the thirty-third or fiftieth anniversary. For further details and a discussion of the significance of these for the living, see Smith (1974).

10. Analysis of the quantitative survey data from our research team found that fatigue decreased after the death of the care recipient, but that grief the first year made mental health recovery difficult. When surveyed two years later, however, more caregivers replied that they had a sense of accomplishment, which correlated with a lower rate of depression (Nishimura et al. 2010).

References

Aneshensel, Carol S., Leonard I. Pearlin, Joseph T. Mullan, Steven H. Zarit, and Carol J. Whitlatch. 1995. *Profiles in Caregiving: The Unexpected Career.* San Diego, CA: Academic Press.

Bass, David, Karen Bowman, and Linda S. Noelker. 1991. "The Influence of Caregiving and Bereavement Support on Adjusting to an Older Relative's Death." *Gerontologist* 31 (1): 32–42.

Bernard, Lori L., and Charles A. Guarnaccia. 2003. "Two Models of Caregiver Strain and Bereavement Adjustment: A Comparison of Husband and Daughter Caregivers of Breast Cancer Hospice Patients." *Gerontologist* 43 (6): 808–16.

Cabinet Office. 2003. "Koureisha Kaigo ni kan suru Yoronchousa" [Public opinion survey on old age care]. Retrieved 30 January 2014 from http8.cao.go.jp/surveyj15h 15-kourei/.

Campbell, John C., and Naoki Ikegami. 2003. "Japan's Radical Reform of Long-Term Care." *Social Policy and Administration* 37 (1): 21–34.

Coulmas, Florian. 2007. *Population Decline and Ageing in Japan: The Social Consequences.* London: Routledge.

Danely, Jason. 2014. *Aging and Loss: Mourning and Maturity in Contemporary Japan.* New Brunswick, NJ: Rutgers University Press.

———. 2015. "Temporality, Spirituality, and the Life Course in an Aging Japan." In *Transitions and Transformations: Cultural Perspectives on Aging and the Lifecourse,* ed. Caitrin Lynch and Jason Danely, 107–22. New York: Berghahn.

Doi, Takeo. 1973. *The Anatomy of Dependence.* Trans. John Bester. New York: Kodansha.

Doi, Takeo. 1986. *The Anatomy of Self: The Individual versus Society.* Trans. Mark A. Harbison. New York: Kodansha.

Fetters, Michael D., and Marion Danis. 2002. "Death with Dignity: Perspectives on Cardiopulmonary Resuscitation in the United States and Japan." In *Bioethics and Moral*

Content: National Traditions of Health Care Morality: Papers Dedicated in Tribute to Kazumasa Hoshino, ed. J. Tristram Engelhardt Jr. and Lisa M. Rasmussen, 145–64. Dordrecht, Netherlands: Kluwer Academic.

Ikels, Charlotte, ed. 2004a. *Filial Piety: Practice and Discourse in Contemporary East Asia.* Stanford, CA: Stanford University Press.

———, ed. 2004b. "Introduction." In Ikels, *Filial Piety,* 1–15.

Jenike, Brenda Robb. 1997. "Home-Based Health Care for the Elderly in Japan: A Silent System of Gender and Duty." In *Aging: Asian Experiences Past and Present,* ed. Susanne Formanek and Sepp Linhart, 323–42. Vienna: Verlag der Österreichischen Akademie der Wissenschaften.

———. 2004. "Alone in the Family: Great-Grandparenthood in Urban Japan." In Ikels, *Filial Piety,* 217–42.

Kawano, Satsuki. 2010. *Nature's Embrace: Japan's Aging Urbanites and New Death Rites.* Honolulu: University of Hawaii Press.

Kellehear, Allan. 2009. "On Dying and Human Suffering." *Palliative Medicine* 23 (5): 388–97.

Klass, Dennis, Phyllis R. Silverman, and Steven L. Nickman, eds. 1996. *Continuing Bonds: New Understandings of Grief.* Washington, D.C.: Taylor & Francis.

Kyodo News Service. 2014. "World's Oldest Living Man, 113-Year-Old Nonaka from Japan Dies," January 20. Retrieved 30 August 2014 from https://english .kyodonews.net/news/2019/01/4ca97adc2634-worlds-oldest-living-man-113-year-old-nonaka-from-japan-dies.html.

Long, Susan Orpett. 1997. "Risōteki na Kaigo to wa? Amerika kara mita Nihon no Rinen to Genjitsu" [What is ideal caregiving? Japanese ideals and reality from an American's perspective]. *Hosupisu to Zaitaku Kea* [Hospice care and home care] 5 (1): 37–43.

———. 2005. *Final Days: Japanese Culture and Choice at the End of Life.* Honolulu: University of Hawaii Press.

———. 2013. "Dying in Japan: Into the Hospital and Out Again?" In *Death and Dying in Contemporary Japan,* ed. Hikaru Suzuki, 49–63. London: Routledge.

Long, Susan Orpett, Ruth Campbell, and Chie Nishimura. 2009. "Daughter-in-law and Daughter Elder Care in Japan: Is There Really a Difference?" *Social Science Japan Journal* 12 (1): 1–21.

Long, Susan Orpett, Ruth Campbell, Chie Nakamura, and Hiroko Kodama. 2010. "Nihon no Kōreisha Kaigo: Jikan, Henka, soshite Kaigosha no Shutaisei no Shiten kara" [Time, change, and agency in Japanese eldercare]. In *Zaitaku Kaigo ni okeru Kōreisha to Kazoku: Tōshi to Nōson Chiiki ni okeru Chōsa Bunseki kara* [The frail elderly and their families: A research study of those living at home in urban and rural communities], ed. Takahashi Ryūtaro and Suda Yūko, 200–29. Tokyo: Minerva.

Ministry of Health, Labour, and Welfare (MHLW). 2010. "Primary Caregivers who Live with Elderly Care Recipients by Age Group (per 100,000 Care Recipients)." *Comprehensive Survey of Living Conditions of the People on Health and Welfare.* Tokyo: Ministry of Health, Labor, and Welfare. Retrieved 30 August 2015 from https.mhlw. go.jp/english/database/daccessb-hss/dl/report_gaikyo_2010.pdf.

Moore, Katrina M., and Ruth Campbell. 2009. "Mastery with Age: The Appeal of the Traditional Arts to Senior Citizens in Contemporary Japan." *Japanstudien, Yearbook of the German Institute for Japanese Studies: Ageing in Japan* 21 (1): 223–51.

Nishimura, Masanori, Ryutaro Takahashi, Yuko Suda, Yuji Izumo, and Masumi Nishida. 2010. "Fulfillment of Caregiving (2): The Effect of Sense of Achievement and Tired

Feeling on the Mental Health of Caregivers Following the Death of the Care Recipient." *Japanese Journal of Gerontology* 32 (2): 225.

Orzeck, Pam, and Marjorie Silverman. 2008. "Recognizing Post-Caregiving as Part of the Caregiving Career: Implications for Practice." *Journal of Social Work Practice* 22 (2): 211–20.

Pyke, Karen. 1999. "The Micropolitics of Care in Relationships between Aging Parents and Adult Children: Individualism, Collectivism, and Power." *Journal of Marriage and Family* 61 (3): 661–72.

Pyysiainen, Jaana. 2007. "Negotiations and Room for Maneuver in Caring for an Elderly Parent." In *Family Caregiving for Older Disabled People*, ed. Isabella Paoletti, 103–26. New York: Nova Science.

Richardson, Therese. 2014. "Spousal Bereavement in Later Life: A Material Culture Perspective." *Mortality* 19 (1): 61–79.

Savundranayagam, M. Y., R. J. Montgomery, and K. Kosloski. 2011. "A Dimensional Analysis of Caregiver Burden among Spouses and Adult Children." *Gerontologist* 51 (3): 321–31.

Schulz, Richard, Aaron B. Mendelsohn, William E. Haley, Diane Mahoney, Rebecca S. Allen, Song Zhang, Larry Thompson, and Steven H. Belle. 2003. "End-of-Life Care and the Effects of Bereavement on Family Caregivers of Persons with Dementia." *New England Journal of Medicine* 349 (20): 1936–42.

Schulz, Richard, Jason T. Newsom, K. Fleissner, A. R. Decamp, and Anna Petra Nieboer. 1997. "The Effects of Bereavement after Family Caregiving." *Aging and Mental Health* 82 (3): 269–82.

Smith, Robert J. 1974. *Ancestor Worship in Contemporary Japan*. Stanford, CA: Stanford University Press.

Statistics Bureau. 2015. *Population Estimates Monthly Report*. Retrieved 30 August 2015 from http.stat.go.jp/English/data/jinsui/tsuki/.

Steadman, Pamela Lea, Geoffrey Tremont, and Jennifer Duncan Davis. 2007. "Premorbid Relationship Satisfaction and Caregiver Burden in Dementia Caregivers." *Journal of Geriatric Psychiatry and Neurology* 20 (2): 115–19.

Suzuki, Hikaru. 2000. *The Price of Death: The Funeral Industry in Contemporary Japan*. Stanford, CA: Stanford University Press.

Tamiya, Nanako, Haruko Noguchi, Akihiro Nishi, Michael R. Reich, Naoki Ikegami, Hideki Hashimoto, Kenji Shibuya, Ichiro Kawachi, and John Creighton Campbell. 2011. "Population Ageing and Wellbeing: Lessons from Japan's Long-Term Care Insurance Policy." *The Lancet* 378 (9797): 1183–92.

Traphagan, John. 2004. "Curse of the Successor: Filial Piety vs. Marriage Among Rural Japanese." In Ikels, *Filial Piety*, 198–216.

Tsukada, Noriko, and Yasuhiko Saito. 2006. "Factors that Affect Older Japanese People's Reluctance to Use Home Help Care and Adult Day Care Services." *Journal of Cross-Cultural Gerontology* 21 (3–4): 121–37.

Tsutsui, Takako. 2014. "Implementation Process and Challenges for the Community-Based Integrated Care System in Japan." *International Journal of Integrated Care* 14 (Jan–Mar), published online 20 January, PMCID: PMC3905786.

Tsutsui, Takako, and Naoko Muramatsu. 2005. "Care Needs Certification in the Long-Term Care Insurance System of Japan." *Journal of the American Geriatrics Society* 53 (3): 522–27.

Wallhagen, Margaret I., and Noriko Yamamoto-Mitani. 2006. "The Meaning of Family Caregiving in Japan and the United States: A Qualitative Comparative Study." *Journal of Transcultural Nursing* 17 (1): 65–73.

World Health Organization. 2019. "6B42 Prolonged Grief Disorder." In *ICD-11 for Mortality and Morbidity Statistics.* Retrieved 3 March 2020 from https://icd.who.int/ browse11/l-m/en#/http://id.who.int/icd/entity/1183832314.

Zarit, Steven H., P. A. Todd, and J. M. Zarit. 1986. "Subjective Burden of Husbands and Wives as Caregivers: A Longitudinal Study." *Gerontologist* 26 (3): 260–66.

Zeserson, Jan M. 2001. "*Chi no Michi* as Metaphor: Conversations with Japanese Women about Menopause." *Anthropology & Medicine* 8 (2/3): 177–99.

PART III
Aging and Caregiving in Korean Contexts

10 "WITHOUT FEELING GUILTY"

Filial Piety and Eldercare in Twenty-First-Century Korea

Hyun Ji Lee and Kyong Hee Chee

Introduction

THE REPUBLIC OF KOREA HAS been undergoing dramatic social and demographic changes, including modernization and population aging, and accompanying institutional and cultural transformations. The traditional family system of Korea was founded on Confucian filial piety (for definition, see Introduction), and the lifestyles of Koreans today continue to reflect some dimensions of that traditional value. For Koreans who care for their aging parents, filial piety represents familial duties expected of adult children. Within a Confucian culture built on patriarchy and a gendered division of labor, women have typically performed more familial roles than men do, disproportionately serving as primary caregivers of older family members as well as young children (Jung 2013). Industrialization and modernization have transformed the family system, resulting in fewer extended families and more nuclear families, with greater variability with regard to who assumes caregiving responsibilities. Going forward, the long-term care insurance (LTCI) program, instituted in 2008, may instigate further changes in the care of Korean elders. It is, therefore, important to investigate what filial piety means to Koreans today, who they believe should provide elder support and care and how, and what they see as the positive and negative outcomes of the LTCI program.

The purpose of this chapter is to contribute to the body of knowledge on filial piety, eldercare, and long-term care (LTC) through a review of recent Korean scholarly literature on these issues and a small exploratory qualitative pilot study we conducted in Korea. In exploring these materials, we pose these questions: What does filial piety mean to Koreans today? Who do Koreans believe should provide elder support and care and how? What do they see as the positive and negative outcomes of the LTCI program? Our main thesis is that the idea of filial piety is being reconstructed in today's Korea as its meaning and practice are now less bound by the context of family hierarchy and are increasingly being replaced by a nonfamilial society-based concept and practice of eldercare. These themes arose strongly in both our review of the scholarly literature and our own qualitative research in Korea. These sources show that the sense of responsibility for eldercare is increasingly being shifted from families onto society and the state (on this shift, see also chaps. 1, 4, 7). They demonstrate how this is being done such that adult children can stray from traditional filial expectations without feeling guilty about it (on guilt, see also chaps. 6, 9). For instance, the practice of filial piety used to be carried out by adult children who took care of their parents in the same household. These days, however, people tend to accept whatever form of eldercare is perceived to be the best care for their elderly parents (Lee 2015: 184). It means that one can still practice filial piety while leaving one's parents in a residential care facility if that choice is considered the best for parental care. The story here is one of a shifting collaboration between families and the state and changing notions of what constitutes filiality and care that is good enough. Since most research on filial piety in contemporary Korea has been largely quantitative, our qualitative evidence provides a valuable focus on the ways in which ordinary Koreans talk about these issues.

Studies of filial piety and eldercare in South Korea vary considerably in their findings largely because of different research questions, definitions, methods, and samples. This chapter provides a review of recent studies on these topics published in Korea in the Korean language, which are not widely known to readers around the globe. We also discuss findings from our own qualitative pilot study designed to identify current perceptions in Korea on these aging and caregiving issues to inform a large-scale study that we plan to carry out in the future. The chapter is organized as follows. The first section is a brief overview of Korea's historical background, followed by a section on demographic trends and population aging in Korea. The third section summarizes our literature review, and reports on our pilot study. Finally, in the fourth section we discuss how the findings relate and contribute to the broader scholarly literature on eldercare in Korea.

Historical Background

Like most sources, the Ikels (2004) volume emphasized the roots of filial piety (for definition, see Introduction) in East Asia in Confucianism; however, some Korean scholars have suggested additional wellsprings in Korea from both before and after Confucianism arose in China in the sixth century BCE. Some Korean scholars argue that the origin of filial piety in Korea can actually be traced back to the culture of dolmens megalithic tombs in the prehistoric era (Ahn 2005)[1] in which descendants honored their senior dead. Others believe that after Confucius, Buddhism made significant contributions to filial piety in Korea, where it had traveled via China from India and prevailed in Korea's Three Kingdoms era and Goryo Dynasty (918–1392 CE). At that time, a natural law of expressing gratitude toward parents was emphasized (Jung 2011), flowing out of Buddhist principles of mutuality, fairness, and reciprocity in daily life, which also called for parental benevolence toward children and expanding affection for everyone (Ahn 2005). More in line with orthodox genealogies of filial piety, Korean scholars most strongly, of course, connect filial piety with Confucianism, which had entered Korea from China by the fourth century CE. By the Joseon Dynasty (1392–1910), Korean society considered filial piety as understood in Confucianism as the basis for familial and social relations and as the foundation for ethics and morality. It stressed children's obligatory duties and responsibilities toward parents, enforced by hierarchy (Ahn 2005), rather than parents' and children's equal obligations to each other. In this Confucian sense, to practice filial piety was to respect and care for, and not burden, parents. When adult children could not provide care for their aging parents in the same household for whatever reason, they felt guilt or shame for not practicing filial piety (Lee 2015: 181).

Traditional Korean norms expected eldest sons and their wives to care for their aging parents, but modern Korea has been undergoing changes in family values (Yoon and Ryu 2005). As we will show below, the scholarly literature indicates important transformations in how Korean people today characterize filial piety and good eldercare and their orientation to guilt. Before 2008 it was considered acceptable for older adults to stay in nursing homes only in those cases in which seniors had no adult children to care for them. Still, in the decades preceding 2008 many adult children taking care of aging parents with chronic conditions such as dementia at home had ambivalent feelings about the situation, often feeling burdened (Lee 2015: 185). Since the 2008 implementation of the LTCI program, many Koreans have come to think that caring for elders with dementia or other serious chronic illnesses at home might not be best for either adult children or the elderly. There is increasing recognition that professional care workers can provide better services than family members can, and a rising sense that it is okay for adult children to consider residential care for their elderly parents as a viable option, without the need for guilt.

Demographic Trends and Population Aging in Korea

After the war (1950–53), the Republic of Korea's population expanded dramatically, from 25 million in 1960 to 48 million in 2010 (Choi et al. 2013; Statistics Korea 2019a). The South Korean population is projected to peak at 51.9 million in 2030, after which it will decline to 48 million by 2050 (Statistics Korea 2019a), to be followed by ongoing gradual decline (Yoon 2013). With the fastest-aging population in the world today, the proportion of people age sixty-five and above was just 5.1 percent in 1990, but had soared to 11.0 percent by 2010, is projected to be 15.7 percent in 2020, and could reach as high as 43.9 in 2060 (Statistics Korea 2019b; see table 10.1).

Whereas there was one adult aged sixty-five and above for every child aged fourteen years old and below in 2010, there will be almost four older adults per child in 2050. The fastest-growing age group will be the old-old, with those aged eighty and above expected to increase tenfold in number between 2010 and 2050.

The trend of population aging is partly attributable to low fertility rates, resulting in an increased old age dependency ratio. This ratio—the number of the old age population (age sixty-five and above) divided by the number of the working-age group (fourteen to sixty-four years old)—rose from 5.3 percent in 1960 to 10.1 percent in 2000, and is projected to rise to 21.7 percent in 2020 and jump to 77.6 percent in 2050 (Statistics Korea 2019a). In other words, only 1.3 workers are expected to support each older adult in 2050 whereas 10 workers supported each older adult in 2000 (Statistics Korea 2019a). The increase in life expectancy has also contributed to the rapid growth of the older adult population. As shown in table 10.2, the country's life expectancy increased by 9.5 years from 71.3 years in 1990 to 80.8 years in 2010, and is expected to continue to increase to 89.4 years by 2060 (Statistics Korea 2019b).

Considering the longer life expectancy of women, who are more likely to be widowed than men are, the proportion of older women living alone is likely to grow significantly (Statistics Korea 2019b). Implications include a much larger number of older adults living in poverty, hence a greater need

TABLE 10.1. Trends of Population Aging in the Republic of Korea.

	1990	2000	2010	2020	2030	2040	2050	2060
% 65+ years old	5.1	7.2	11.0	15.7	25.0	33.9	39.8	43.9

Source: Statistics Korea 2019b.

TABLE 10.2. Trends of Life Expectancy in the Republic of Korea.

	1990	2000	2010	2020	2030	2040	2050	2060
Male	67.3	72.3	77.2	80.3	82.6	84.6	86.2	87.7
Female	75.5	79.6	84.1	86.1	87.7	89.0	90.1	91.0
Total	71.3	76.0	80.8	83.2	85.2	86.8	88.2	89.4

Source: Statistics Korea 2019b.

for government assistance. These demographic changes may engender generational and familial conflict in a society that has long considered filial piety as the most important virtue (Kwon 2013). Below is a summary of patterns in recent research findings concerning filial piety, eldercare, and the LTCI program in Korea. We also delve into issues of any systematic differences or similarities across different disciplines and methodologies.

Literature Review

This section provides a review of Korean literature on topics related to the care of frail elders. Using the Korean Studies Information System (KISS n.d.), our initial search parameters included (1) documents published in Korea and in the Korean language from 2000 on, and (2) documents that focus on filial piety (*hyo*), eldercare (*noinbuyang, noindolbom*), or eldercare perception (*noinbuyanguisik*).[2]

Our search revealed that research on eldercare in Korea exists in diverse fields, namely, social work, sociology, gerontology, religious studies, nursing, community studies, consumer science, human development, family studies, public health, and early childhood education. The disciplines of social welfare/social work, sociology, and nursing have generated most of the existing studies on eldercare. Social workers tend to publish most frequently on the topic, and about 40 percent of the studies used for the current review are from that field. Overall, we reviewed more than fifty Korean studies, the most notable of which are included in the references.

Methodologically, six out of every ten studies relied on a quantitative approach, analyzing survey data collected from sizable samples. Two out of ten studies represented qualitative research, predominantly based on in-depth interviews, and rarely based on ethnography. Between one out of ten and two out of ten studies used mixed methods, one of which analyzed quantitative and qualitative data collected from focus group interviews. Remaining works were either conceptual papers or literature reviews.

Both the quantitative and qualitative studies reviewed here indicate that eldercare mostly occurs within a family context in contemporary Korea and has therefore been associated with the notions of filial piety, caregiving consciousness, and caregiving burden for family members. Qualitative studies have added the importance of additional notions and factors, including community-based eldercare in the rural area, how family eldercare is organized, caregiving experiences of husbands, types of burden involved with dementia care, and family caregivers' use of institutional care.

One major theme emerging from the literature review is that the meaning and practice of filial piety are undergoing some changes. Traditionally, providing care for elderly parents was the responsibility of the oldest son and his wife, but today caregiving duties tend to be considered the responsibility of all adult children who should share such duties equally. Today there is also a growing belief that older Koreans should prepare for old age themselves, rather than simply relying on their children. There also exist beliefs that the society as a whole, including the government, must be held responsible for the older population, not just families (Yoon and Ryu 2005). At the same time, some older adults are now selecting their own caregivers, and some caregivers are choosing whom to care for based on the contingent relationships between the two parties, rather than on pre-set kinship obligations (Yoon and Ryu 2005).

Filial Piety in Korea

In Korea, recently published studies on filial piety and family eldercare have relied heavily on quantitative research methods, attempting to quantify filial piety to measure its levels among people, and to identify various factors associated with it. Multiple scales have been developed to operationalize filial piety, with each displaying considerable variation from the others. Some studies have based their measures on foundations clearly divergent from filial piety in a traditional sense. For example, Yoon and Ryu (2005) adopted Seelbach's (1978) scale of caregiving expectation to study factors associated with filial piety. The scale consists of six questions, each with a five-point Likert scale, about living close by, providing care, visits, financial support, telephone calls or letters, and responsibility. Jeon (2006) studied family caregivers using a scale by Gallois and colleagues (1999). That scale has six subscales, which measure caring, respect, financial support, listening, creating happiness, and contact with elders.

Other studies have worked to develop scales with better cultural fidelity. Based on a review of Korean literature on traditional filial piety, Ahn (2005) developed a scale for filial piety as understood and practiced in the Korean family relationship context. The scale includes thirty questions, broken down into two subscales: one for filial piety toward living parents and the other for filial piety toward dead parents. Lee, Shin, and Lee (2005) created another scale on the basis of review of the Korean literature. A total of fifty questions were designed to measure filial piety, which had the components of filial piety and consciousness of filial piety.

Benefits of using existing scales to measure filial piety include potential comparability across different studies. Benefits of updated scales are that indicators or items in scales developed years ago may no longer apply in current cultural contexts. However, existing variation in measurement means that it is difficult to compare across quantitative studies of filial piety, because they are using the same term to stand for a wide variety of underlying measures. Such diversity in measurements of filial piety illustrates the complex nature of the concept, a lack of consensus among ordinary Koreans, and the absence of agreement among researchers about how to measure it.

Quantitative studies have also tended to look for factors that correlate with filial piety. Such studies have identified factors that correlate with individuals' filial piety in Korea. These have showed that sociodemographic factors such as age, gender, education, income, and family structure were significantly associated with the level of filial piety (Ahn 2005; Lee et al. 2005; Shin, Park, and Kim 2009; Yoon and Ryu 2005). More specifically, men and older adults were more aware of filial piety than were women or younger adults (Ahn 2005; Yoon and Ryu 2005), and individuals who had lower levels of educational attainment or were living in a larger household were found to possess a greater level of filial piety (Ahn 2005). Studies of filial piety consciousness and practice among children revealed significant differences based on gender (Lee et al. 2005; Shin et al. 2009). One study showed various differences between boys and girls in elementary school regarding their beliefs and practices related to filial piety (Shin et al. 2009). Another showed boys to be more aware of filial piety in middle school than same-age girls (Lee et al. 2005), which is a phenomenon in need of further research.

Anthropological studies on filial piety in Korea add to the literature on filial piety by allowing for different kinds of research questions, for instance by identifying new or changing patterns and contextualizing such patterns in greater detail. For example, referring back to chapters in Ikels (2004), we can see two examples of this. Through their work in the field from 1970s to 1990s, Janelli and Yim (2004) documented a shift in filial piety over time in an agricultural village transforming into an industrialized community. They found new practices that young people considered "filial piety," including daughters' greater involvement in the care of their natal parents, something that elders did not necessarily recognize at the time as filiality. The researchers also observed that, overall, elderly residents seemed to receive less care than their own parents had received (Janelli and Yim 2004: 150). In a study in an urban community involving interviews with forty-seven informants, Sorensen and Kim (2004) found that filial piety did not disappear, but rather there was variation, with some adult children still willingly performing the moral norms of filial obligation in terms of financial support and/or coresidence.

Family Eldercare in Korea

A majority of the empirical literature on the topic of eldercare in Korea also used a quantitative approach. Similar to studies of filial piety, these studies attempted to quantify caregiving in order to identify factors associated with it. They most frequently refer to two different dimensions of care, both of them in a family context: caregiving consciousness (sometimes described as consciousness of care or consciousness of support), and the other is caregiving burden. Although there are few qualitative studies on filial piety or eldercare in Korea, those that exist both deepen and broaden the scope of research on eldercare.

Conceptualized as individual attitude and consciousness toward eldercare in terms of physical, financial, and emotional dimensions, caregiving consciousness seems to be operationalized in a relatively uniform manner (Ha and Hong 2002). Several studies measured consciousness about eldercare by using the same instrument with questions about aspects of financial, emotional, and physical care (Cho and Kim 2011; Choi et al. 2009; Kwon and Lee 2009; Y. Yang 2013). The concept of caregiving consciousness seems to be closer to filial piety than the concept of caregiving burden. Interestingly, many recent studies concerning eldercare in Korea tended to focus on caregiving stress and burden (on burden see also chaps. 2, 9, 11), as opposed to filial piety. Studies trace how caregiving stress and burden have risen with modernization and changes in family structure and function that increasingly made it difficult for families to provide eldercare at home. They also relate added caregiving stress and burden to fewer adult child siblings to share the load of eldercare and to more Koreans living longer into old-old age, with increasing years of infirmity. A higher level of filial piety or caregiving consciousness is related to a lower level of caregiving burden (Jeon 2006; Kim and Choi 2011). Although this may reflect the benefits of cultural beliefs buffering the potential negative effects of lack of resources, it is difficult to say with certainty if filial piety or caregiving consciousness is associated with more-positive or more-negative outcomes.

Overall, a higher level of caregiving consciousness was found among people who have a good relationship with their parents (Kwon and Lee 2009; Lee 2007; Y. Yang 2013) and those with a sense of filial obligation or intention to provide care for their own parents or the parents of their spouse (Lee 2007; Y. Yang 2013). Similar to the findings on filial piety, men were more likely to report caregiving consciousness (as defined above) than women were (Choi et al. 2009; Y. Yang 2013). This is interesting because it appears that women do more of the actual work of intimate care for elders than men. For spouses involved in caregiving, the couple's marital intimacy appears to affect their caregiving consciousness (Cho and Kim 2011). According to the recent studies of college students in Korea, consciousness of eldercare in society in general is significantly associated with the level of satisfaction from youths' participation in volunteer activity in the service of older adults outside the family (Choi et al. 2009; Kwon and Lee 2009). It is also linked with their attitudes toward older adults such as cognitive and emotional trust and reactions (Choi et al. 2009), and knowledge about experiences of physical, psychological, and social aging (Kwon and Lee 2009).

Compared to caregiving consciousness, there is more variability in the operationalization of caregiving burden (see also chaps. 2, 9). The variability in the assessment of caregiving burden is due to the varying circumstances in which caregivers find themselves, whereas caregiving consciousness is attitudinal and is not contingent on the environment. Researchers have assessed caregiving burden in multiple ways (Baek and Kwon 2008; Chung and Yu 2009; Kim 2006; Lee 2006; Lim, Hong, and Lee 2010; Song 2004; Song and Kim 2003; Song and Choi 2007; Yoon and Ryu 2005). Some studies used the cost of caregiving index developed by Kosberg and Cairl (1986), which comprises both objective and subjective caregiving burden (Song 2004; Song and Kim 2003). Kim (2006) used a modified version of the instrument developed by Seo and Lee (1991), which has the dimensions of constraints, change in family relationships, and economic burden. Many other researchers assessed caregiving burden on the basis of physical, emotional, social, and economic burden, and negative changes in family relationships (Baek and Kwon 2008; Chung and Yu 2009; Lee 2006; Song and Choi 2007; Yoon and Ryu 2005).

Quantitative studies have uncovered a number of factors that tend to influence caregiving burden involved with family eldercare. Recent findings include significant effects of family caregivers' health condition (Chung and Yu 2009; Song 2004; Song and Kim 2003; Song and Choi 2007), cognitive impairment (Song and Choi 2007), and physical impairment

(Lee 2006; Song and Choi 2007; Yoon and Ryu 2007) on their caregiving burden. The number of older adults in the family (Song and Kim 2003) and the number of hours a day that are spent on caregiving (Song 2004; Song and Kim 2003; Yoon and Ryu 2007) mattered as well (compare with chap. 9). Caregiving burden was also found to increase with the presence of economic constraints (Lee 2007; Song 2004; Song and Kim 2003) and emotional conflict with care recipients (Chung and Yu 2009; Lee 2007; Park and Song 2008; Song 2004; Song and Kim 2003). Family support (Park and Song 2008; Song and Choi 2007) and eldercare-related familism or filial obligation (Chung and Yu 2009; Lee 2007; Song 2004; Song and Kim 2003; Yoon and Ryu 2007) were related with lower levels of caregiving burden for family caregivers of elders. Research about caregiving for elderly partners indicates that caregiving burden was significantly influenced by a caregiver's health condition (Han and Lee 2009), level of activities of daily living (Han and Lee 2009; Lee 2006; Yoon and Ryu 2007), and cognitive impairment (Yoon and Ryu 2007). The duration of caregiving is also known to affect the partner's caregiving burden (Yoon and Ryu 2007), which is found to decrease with family support (Han and Lee 2009) and quality relationship with the partner (Lee 2006).

Some quantitative researchers investigated caregiving burden as an independent variable and found that it was significantly related with caregivers' psychological well-being (Baek and Kwon 2008; Lee and Park 2007) or their quality of life (Joo and Kim 2008; Lee and Kim 2009; Oh and Sok 2009). The emotional burden of caregiving was found likely to have a negative impact on caregivers' overall psychological well-being (Baek and Kwon 2008) and family relationships (Kim and Choi 2011). Research also suggests that caregiving burden leads to caregivers' burnout (Joo and Kim 2008; Yun 2010), fatigue (Lee and Park 2007), depression (Lee and Kim 2009; Lee and Park 2007), and guilt (Yun 2010). According to a study of 220 caregivers of frail elders, those who had placed their family members in a nursing home appeared to have more guilty feelings (Yun 2010). Yet both groups had guilt. For these caregivers who had placed their family member in a nursing home, the sense of guilt was influenced by lack of control, burnout, and worry about norms, whereas those who took care of the elderly at home felt guilty owing to lack of resources and burnout (Yun 2010).

Qualitative studies help to uncover important aspects of filial piety and eldercare orientations and practices from the perspective of elders themselves, a dimension inadequately addressed in quantitative studies, which tend to focus on caregivers rather than on care recipients. Qualitative studies raised a variety of research questions related to processes or changes in eldercare, or different types of caregiving experiences, documenting diverse lived experiences among different subgroups of caregivers. For instance, Yang's (2009) research used Schütze's (1983) autobiographical-narrative interview method to study the process by which changes in elder support take place in Korea's rural areas, where family-based caregiving underwent a "dual structural shift" as a result of modernization. On the one hand, there has been an internal shift from family care based on intergenerational mutual support to family care based on intragenerational self-support. On the other hand, a structural shift has occurred involving increased reliance on nonfamilial support as part of a family's caregiving repertoire. This finding was not reflected in the quantitative studies. From their case study in rural Korea, Yoon and Che (2008) explored potential problems involved in community-based eldercare performed by elderly neighbors, who helped complement the formal service system, caring for those in very poor and unsafe housing conditions. Most of these care recipients experienced financial difficulties and therefore preferred material help to immaterial support such as companionship or safety checking (Yoon and Che 2008). We did not find comparable qualitative studies conducted in urban areas.

Qualitative studies have also examined gender in eldercare. Most studies focused on daughters-in-law's and wives' experiences with eldercare (Jung and Suh 2014; Lee 2006), for example by focusing on caregiving burden in eldercare or how eldercare arrangements were organized, as discussed below. Lee (2005) provided a rare examination of husbands' experiences of eldercare. Lee used Giorgi's (1985) phenomenological approach to delve into caregiving experiences of husbands caring for wives with Alzheimer's disease. From interviews with five caregiving husbands, the researcher identified seven themes with twenty-three sub elements. The seven themes were (1) a late discovery of the disease because of ignorance, (2) repentance for neglecting the wife, (3) transition from husband to caregiver role, (4) experience of both physical and mental crises because of troublesome behaviors, (5) recovery from suffering using various resources, (6) adaption of oneself to caregiving roles, and (7) change and growth.

Qualitative studies examine different experiences of caregiving depending on other types of kinship relationships. Jung and Suh (2014) used grounded theory to focus on the experiences of daughters-in-law by observing the patterns of organizing familial eldercare. Results from interviews with sixteen primary caregiving daughters-in-law showed that crucial determinants of how familial care was organized included perceived fairness, birth order of siblings, degree of parental dependency, parental wishes and expectations, and perceived traditional norms for allocating duties. Important contextual factors were the kinds of values and attitudes held toward eldercare in one's husband's family, whether the family was financially secure, and whether a house would be inherited by the caregiver's husband.

Jung and Suh found that the key factor to a stable family support system for eldercare was whether a real consensus had been built among family members. When daughters-in-law reluctantly accepted or were pressured into complying with other family members' proposed solutions, rather than being a full partner in consensus-building, family conflict and poor caregiving resulted.

Sons as caregivers were another focus of qualitative research on eldercare in Korea. Exploratory research by Choi (2012) examined six case studies of sons serving as primary caregivers who used in-home services. Choi (2012) found that the son's sense of filial obligation was an important factor. They took charge of caregiving roles through a task-oriented approach by using public services and managing diverse tasks. While they did express happiness over their caregiving roles, they also reported the experience of caregiving burden and problems with caregiving skills and communication. These sons endured the difficulties rather than expressing them, in part because they believed that their caretaking alleviated family conflict entangled with the issue of caregiving.

Qualitative research has also focused on emic notions of different kinds of burden among caregivers managing care for family members with various different kinds of medical conditions. One study used Q-methodology, described below, to find out the types of burden experienced by primary caregivers of elders with dementia (Kang, Yeun, and Jeon 2014). Q-methodology classifies individuals' attitudes, convictions, perceptions, or values in order to increase an understanding and explain a particular phenomenon. It uses open-ended questions to develop Q statements and can thus identify participants' subjectivity. This methodology helped identify four types of burden experienced among thirty-two primary caregivers of elders with dementia: (1) optimistic dutiful type, (2) ambivalent type, (3) exhausted, devoted son and spouse type, and (4) selfish evasive type (Kang et al. 2014).

Differences in caregiving experiences by locus of care are another area explored by qualitative research in Korea. For instance, one study looked into the experiences of family caregivers whose elderly family members stayed in a nursing home (Hong and Son 2007). The researchers interviewed ten caregivers to learn about the transition to a nursing home, using Strauss and Corbin's (1998) grounded theory. According to Hong and Son's analysis, "finding a way to live together" was the main theme, and the social process of finding a way to live together occurred in three phases: (1) recognizing the problems, (2) finding solutions to the problems, and (3) accepting changes in their surroundings. The family caregivers reflected on problems such as lack of privacy, family troubles, extreme distress, and unavailable caregivers. The process of finding solutions concerned making a decision, obtaining family consent, choosing the best nursing home, and enduring financial burden. Possible outcomes included peace of mind or continued conflict.

Overall, the results of these qualitative studies demonstrate a considerable variability in the changing experiences of caregivers, both positive and negative, and expose a myriad of issues involved with eldercare, beyond the variables of caregiving consciousness and caregiving burden. The sample sizes are small, however, so more research needs to be done in order to determine how widely distributed this variation is and whether it would be wise to retool quantitative instruments to reflect these findings.

The Korean Long-Term Care Insurance Program and Its Outcomes

Attempts to socialize eldercare through government programs may transform the culture of eldercare, which may affect, in turn, the well-being of elders and their family caregivers. The Korean government started providing financial assistance and services to older members in need in 1981 when the Welfare for Senior Citizens Act was passed with the intention of alleviating poverty, illness, loneliness, and isolation in old age. The following is a brief overview of the country's LTCI program, followed by a review of studies on various outcomes of the program.

The Korean government currently offers three health-care programs: the National Health Insurance Program, the Medical Aid Program, and the LTCI program (National Health Insurance 2010). Funded by individual contributions from the insured and by government subsidy, National Health Insurance provides universal health care to the entire population living in the Republic of Korea. Medical Aid, however, is a program that is a form of public assistance designed to secure minimum livelihood for low-income households and to assist low-income individuals' self-help efforts by providing medical services. Implemented in 2008, the LTCI program draws on the principle of social solidarity in which both the nation and the family bear responsibility for eldercare.

As a form of social insurance for the entire Korean population, the LTCI program offers care services to those older adults who are diagnosed with disabilities related to old age or illnesses. More specifically, this program is designed to assist elders who cannot independently take care of themselves for at least six months because of geriatric illnesses such as dementia or cardiovascular diseases. Eligibility is determined by the health condition of older adults according to the assessment of their LTC needs. Services include assistance with their daily activities and housework at home, care provided at an LTC facility, and special cash benefits (National Health Insurance 2010). Those who are sixty-five years old and above or those with geriatric diseases are qualified to apply for services, although their ultimate

LTC needs are based on program measurement of disability status level. The extent and distribution of actual use of services within this system varies by family, but a majority of caregiving continues to occur within a family (Jung and Suh 2014). It appears that elders with a bone fracture or cognitive deficits tend to opt for institutionalization through the LTCI program (Han, Kang, and Kwon 2011). Below is a review of empirical studies that have examined the outcomes of this new LTCI in Korea on their beneficiaries (compare Japanese LTCI program in chap. 9).

Regarding the effects of the LTCI program thus far, findings from quantitative research suggest a significant improvement in the functional status of elder beneficiaries of the program (Hyun and Lee 2012). When elders used institutional services through the program, for instance, they showed significant improvement in the areas of activities of daily living and rehabilitation (Hyun and Lee 2012). Those who used home care services showed improvement in their activities of daily living, cognitive function, and behavioral changes (Hyun and Lee 2012). Other studies have found LTCI program participation to be associated with better physical and mental functioning (Kim et al. 2010), and enhanced quality of life among frail elders (Kwon et al. 2011). Research also shows that family caregivers, after the inception of the LTCI program, tend to experience reduced caregiving burden (Han et al. 2015). Mo and Choi (2013) found, however, that the level of physical, psychological, and social burden varied significantly depending on whether a service was provided at home or in an institutional setting. Study results were inconsistent concerning the effects of LTCI on quality of family relationships. Mo and Choi (2013) found that family relationships were better after using LTC services, but Han and associates (2015) found that family relationships deteriorated.

There have also been a few qualitative studies on the relationship between the LTCI program and eldercare, exploring what happens to family relationships and how caregiving patterns change. One study found that relationships between elders and their adult children and spouse are reorganized in the process of resolving the increase of elders' physical, mental, and economic dependence (Jung 2013). Some families experience improvement in their familial relationships following their use of these social services, but other families' experiences are more negative with intensified conflict or even the severance of a relationship when there is a lack of consensus about using public programs or institutional care for frail parents (Jung 2013). Another study found that the government's LTC services reduced caregiving burden for family caregivers, although their perceptions varied by type of service (Yang and Choi 2013).

One distinctive aspect of Korea's LTCI program lies in the certified family care worker (CFCW) program. This program involves a kind of hybrid between informal and formal eldercare, placing eldercare between the private and public domain. In this program, informal family caregivers can become certified as CFCWs to care for their own elderly family members at home and get paid for that care work (Yang and Choi 2013). Through in-depth interviews with CFCWs, a qualitative research study identified the main reasons for choosing the CFCW option (N. Yang 2013). First, it was an inevitable choice for family members who faced a dual burden of caregiving and earning a living. Second, the choice was simply an additional duty as part of caring for family elders, and, finally, being a CFCW was a way of fulfilling service needs that were not available within the system (N. Yang 2013). Furthermore, focus group interviews with CFCWs, social workers, and nurses (Kim et al. 2012) uncovered additional dimensions of the experiences of CFCWs. These included (1) the process of obtaining a care worker certification for employment, (2) taking care of elders in their homes, (3) difficulties involved with life style changes, (4) difficulties caused by a reduction in pay, and (5) dissatisfaction with the LTCI program. These findings suggest that CFCWs within the LTCI program face many challenges in providing care for their family elders in their homes.

This review of Korean literature on filial piety, eldercare, and the LTCI program in Korea points to a few gaps. First, there is a gap in a qualitative understanding of how contemporary Koreans conceptualize filial piety. There is a need for complementing and updating the quantitative findings on filial piety. Second, the existing literature does not adequately examine the relationship between people's thoughts about the ideal of filial piety and the actual real-life practice of eldercare. This gap could be filled in part by finding out what kind of eldercare people consider ideal as opposed to good enough or inadequate. Finally, there remains a lack of understanding about what ordinary people see as the main benefits and problems of the LTCI program growing out of their own observations and lived experiences.

Korean Perceptions of Filial Piety, Eldercare, and Long-Term Care

We hope to help contribute to addressing the aforementioned gap, first through a modest qualitative pilot study, and then building toward a large-scale mixed methods study in the future. In our pilot research, we examined Korean adults' perceptions of filial piety, eldercare, and the Korean government's support for LTC care in a small convenience sample. Specific research questions were (1) How is the tradition of filial piety changing in South Korea? (2) What do today's Koreans perceive to be good eldercare?

FIGURE 10.1. Photo of a Three-Generational Korean Family. Photo provided by Kyong Hee Chee.

(3) What do Koreans say about the effectiveness of the LTCI program? This small-scale exploratory study was based on a focus group interview with seven Korean adults in the fall of 2014, all of whom were enrolled in a social work graduate course. Two of the participants were male, and all but two were married. The participants' ages ranged from twenty-three to sixty-one years old, with the median age of forty-seven. All identified as middle to upper class. Six were Christian, and one was a Buddhist. Half had had some eldercare experience.

The participants were asked about their opinions on what filial piety constitutes, how to care for frail elders, and the benefits and shortcomings of the LTCI program. While the sample is small and limited by the high socioeconomic status and graduate course enrollment of the participants, the upside to a pilot sample is the participants' ability to clearly articulate their views and observations. Despite the small sample size, the interviews added useful information on contemporary lived experiences regarding changing beliefs about filial piety, the conceptualization of ideal eldercare, and perceptions about the LTCI program that complement and supplement the scholarly literature. This and the literature review will inform the design of our future research. Figure 10.1 shows a three-generation family in Korea on a family outing. The photo does not include participants in the study, but it provides an illustration of an example of family life in South Korea today. Following are the findings from our pilot research.

Supporting Independence

The traditional concept of filial piety in Korea appears to be closely tied to multigenerational coresidence with aging parents whereas today's conception might focus more on respect and support for the independence of aging parents. A female study participant in her 50s with caregiving experience said, "Living together is not the only form of filial piety. It is a good idea to offer institutional care and visit often, rather than sharing the same space with mutual stress." An unmarried, younger woman believed filial piety to involve "making parents proud of their children" and "making frequent contact with parents who should live independently." A married, middle-aged woman echoed this sentiment by saying, "Children now think they are filial to their parents by growing up well and becoming independent themselves." According to a middle-aged woman from an upper-class family, with no caregiving experience, people may believe they should take care of their parents, but, realistically speaking, they face a lot of difficulty in carrying out their sense of duty. She herself thought that filial piety constitutes frequent visits to one's parents when adult children do not support the parents in a coresidential setting.

As this volume has shown for other parts of East Asia, our study participants attributed these changes in the perception of filial duties to industrialization, capitalism, individualism, women's labor force participation, prevalence of nuclear families as opposed to extended families, and financial burden for eldercare. These social changes have resulted in generational differences and even conflict at times as middle-aged people prepare for their own old age and some of their older parents persist in the traditional idea of dependence on their adult children and living together. Nevertheless, the new conception of filial piety represents greater emphasis on the individuality of not only younger generations but also aging parents. Many of today's Koreans, both young and old, may assume independence as a hallmark of well-being and accommodate or accept individualism much more than before (on independence, see also chaps. 1–2, 7, 9, 11).

Eldercare by Family and Society

Ambivalence seems to characterize people's attitudes toward who should provide eldercare and how. "Today's young people do not want to take care of their parents while parents hate to burden their children," said a young woman, who added that nonetheless younger people should help out their aging parents more because the Korean government cannot continue to fund eldercare with taxes and current community programs do not suffice. Considering "who can provide eldercare and how," several study participants talked about their actual caregiving experiences, and how stressful it was to care for their parents-in-law or their own parents, especially when they had dementia. They also discussed resorting to or considering institutional care. One person mentioned the need for more government assistance and for old-age preparation at the individual level. Others voiced that children should both respect their parents' opinions and discuss care issues together, and that all siblings should contribute financially with one of them living with the parent. Of course, these latter suggestions do not consider Korea's years of extremely low fertility.

When asked to differentiate among ideal, good enough, and inadequate eldercare, most of the study participants assumed eldercare in a family context rather than an institutional setting, and considered situations for both parents and adult children—a slight departure from traditional Confucian ways. Ideal eldercare was typically conceptualized as a positive outcome for not only parents but also adult children. One person explained ideal eldercare as producing mutual satisfaction for parents and children in terms of financial and emotional aspects, adding that inadequate eldercare results from unhappy parents and children whose levels of financial and emotional stress run high. Another participant considered it ideal for parents to "live separately from children who pay respect to their parents by visiting or calling while providing economic support." An older participant who was the eldest son in the family, however, expressed a different opinion. He thought that an ideal situation would be one in which "adult children live with aging parents and take care of them according to the wishes of the parents as long as elders take into consideration their children's circumstances and are not authoritarian." One man in his fifties argued that ideal eldercare would occur when and if the government would eventually take full responsibility for eldercare, and that good eldercare is possible when the government and adult children share care responsibilities. He said that inadequate eldercare occurs when all care responsibilities fall into the hands of children and other family members.

Room for Improvement

Given the usual difficulties with eldercare in a family setting and greater acceptance of institutional care, the LTCI program seems to be viewed as helping ease the stresses of family caregivers. Study participants were clearly positive about this new support. A middle-aged, married, female participant thought that the program reduced personal burden of caring for elderly parents and that individuals' sense of guilt for not being able to provide adequate care decreased as the society shared responsibilities for care. A married woman in her fifties, who had experienced much stress as a caregiver for both of her parents-in-law, assessed the LTCI program favorably. She said that, in the past, some low-income families had faced crises during their care of vulnerable elders, especially those with dementia, but the new system greatly lightened their load. She further believed that the Korean government helped meet the majority of such caregiving needs, either in institutional settings or through professional care workers who would visit homes. Some respondents talked about the benefits of Korea's CFCW system in which family caregivers can qualify to be paid for taking care of elderly family members. In contrast with the Japanese situation in which family caregivers cannot be paid (see chap. 7), the idea here is to ease the financial stress of caregiving among low-income families with eldercare needs. According to a female study participant in her forties with no prior caregiving experience, the CFCW system is perceived to lessen the guilty feelings that other family members have when they themselves could not participate in caregiving. Another participant added that the system could also reduce family conflict caused by eldercare demands.

At the same time, however, study participants talked about problems with the LTCI program, citing the alleged misuse and overuse of the system and recommending closer oversight and more-severe punishment for such violations. They typically held the view that services could improve by expanding benefits to others in need. In addition, people were acutely aware of several potential problems with the aforementioned CFCW system, which also had been misused and allowed some CFCW to provide much less care than what nonfamilial homecare workers do, sometimes to the point of neglect and/or abuse. Another unintended outcome of using CFCWs mentioned by a couple of participants concerns the weakening of collective eldercare responsibilities in families, and reliance on one family member solely hired to provide care.

Discussion and Conclusion

Filial piety is a complex and relatively fluid concept as suggested by a variety of scales that social scientists have developed in an attempt to measure it and the variety of Korean research findings, qualitative and quantitative, with regard to it. Our review of recent published literature in Korea has suggested that social and demographic change over time and various sociodemographic variables may affect notions or levels of filial piety. Qualitative studies, including our pilot research, suggest that the notion of filial piety has changed over the years in Korea, beginning with the expectation of support and care to parents through coresidence with eldest sons and their wives, moving to mutual respect for the individuality of aging parents and their adult children. These findings accord with the anthropological studies by Janelli and Yim (2004) and by Sorensen and Kim (2004) from Ikels's volume, while also offering updated material following the 2008 implementation of Korea's LTCI program, which has deepened reliance on the state for assistance with elder support and care.

Eldercare remains closely related to filial piety and still tends to occur in the context of family, but not without difficulties. Most studies reviewed here focused on either caregiving consciousness or caregiving burden involved with eldercare. Studies of filial piety were conducted mostly during the major financial crises of the 1990s that contributed to the transformation of the Korean family and its culture. Since 2000, however, studies have focused more on the notion of familial eldercare than on that of filial piety. This trend reflects the state and society's growing interest in the care of its older members today compared with the past. At the same time, the fact that caregiving burden surfaced as a notable research topic stems in part from the increased challenges for familial eldercare in a context marked by decreasing conceptual parameters and levels of filial piety at the individual level. According to the results of qualitative research, including our pilot study, most contemporary Koreans do not tend to believe that living together with parents while supporting and caring for them is the ideal form of eldercare. A small proportion of Koreans even state that government support and/or care for elders is the ideal (see also chaps. 11–12).

As implied above, people in Korea today value individuality more than before, especially younger cohorts. Pyke and Bengtson (1996: 390) speculated that individualist families in the United States would be more affected by increased caregiving demands than collectivist families, viewing eldercare less as their sole responsibility and more as a political issue. Their prediction seems to apply to Korean families that are becoming more individualistic. Furthermore, much like many baby boomers in Canada who expect more formal services for caregiving than preceding generations (Guberman et al. 2012), Koreans increasingly opt for using institutional care with government support for eldercare, without feeling guilty.

While the meaning, significance, and function of family in Korea have diminished in comparison to the past (Min 2011), filial piety has not disappeared altogether. Rather, filial piety persists in Korea, albeit in different forms and manifestations, one of which we would argue is a so-cietized form of filiality. The decreased functions of the family coupled with low fertility rates and the expanding older adult population alerted people that eldercare had to be not just a family responsibility but also a societal responsibility. This, in turn, led to more research on eldercare issues, culminating in the implementation of new policies and systems for its older members and their family caregivers in order to help them maintain their quality of life. The LTCI program, in spite of its limitations underscores eldercare as a major public policy area, reflective of the tradi-tional value of respect for elders. The present study and a few other stud-ies on the effects of the LTCI program found some perceived benefits for elders, their quality of life, and their family caregivers. Family caregivers may no longer feel guilty about leaving their elderly family members in a nursing home as the number of LTC facilities have increased and more elders receive formal care since the implementation of the LTCI program. Family caregivers are aware that trained and certified nonfamilial LTC workers may provide better care than they can. Even though it is still too early to tell, such positive outcomes could alleviate caregiving burdens to some degree and possibly help restore family relationships. Korea's LTCI program, however, needs improvements in the CFCW system, including better management and oversight. More mixed methods research on ex-periences of the LTCI program with a much larger and more represen-tative sample size is necessary in order to expand knowledge about the relationships among filial piety, eldercare, and the well-being of both care recipients and caregivers.

Generally speaking, the older the people are, the greater their depen-dence on their families, relatives, the government, and society, although this varies from person to person, and is differentiated by gender, cohort, assets, savings, and family make-up. Older women in comparison to older men are more likely to depend on the assistance of children and relatives, since they had fewer asset-generation opportunities when younger. In spite of government programs and services, those who are currently sixty-five or older in Korea continue to rely heavily on informal social support net-works comprised of family and friends, having come up through times that offered little preparation for old age and no public welfare system for older adults. Many family members primarily responsible for caring for their aging parents are currently experiencing various forms of difficulty, confusion, and conflict within a dualistic culture in which the tradition of familism and the realities of modernity coexist. On the one hand, Koreans continue to believe that at some level filial piety and familial eldercare are a social good. On the other hand, they are burdened with caregiving duties in a modern capitalist society that places little value on familial caregiving. CFCWs within the LTCI program are an example of an innovative adaptation trying to bring together these two regimes of value by paying family members to take on familial eldercare.

This comprehensive review of the literature on filial piety and eldercare published in Korea since 2000 exposed a need for studies from a greater variety of disciplines and less reliance on purely quantitative methods. Currently, social work perspectives and quantitative methods dominate the literature. Methodologically, a majority have used a quantitative approach, although qualitative and mixed methods studies are emerging. More anthropological and sociological studies are needed to generate more socioculturally sensitive research questions. We need more research that uses a qualitative or mixed methods approach to gain a more context-rich understanding of filial piety and eldercare, given the multifaceted nature of both.

Finally, as one of our interviewees said, good eldercare is possible when the government and adult children share care responsibilities, whereas inadequate eldercare occurs when all care responsibilities fall into the hands of children or other family members. It is difficult to speculate on the future of eldercare in Korea, but the LTCI program is likely to have some unintended consequences, one of which may be increasing medicalization of eldercare, thus reducing elders to patients (see also chap. 12). Korea needs more socioculturally informed mixed methods research to see how the value of filial piety and practices associated with eldercare evolve and what kinds of positive and negative effects LTCI may have.

Hyun Ji Lee is professor and head of the Department of Social Welfare at Daegu Catholic University, South Korea. Her research interests include aging, especially familial caregiving, community care, long-term care, issues of death, and end-of-life care. She has published in many journals including *Death Studies, Journal of the Korean Gerontological Society, Korean Journal of Community Welfare, Korean Journal of Family Social Work, Korean Journal of Gerontological Social Welfare,* and other scholarly venues.

Kyong Hee Chee is professor in the Department of Sociology at Texas State University in the United States, where she serves as a graduate coordinator for the Master of Science in Dementia and Aging Studies Program. She is a fellow of the Gerontological Society of America (GSA) and a recipient of the GSA Civic Engagement in an Older America Project Senior Scholar Award. Her publications have appeared in many journals, including *Geriatrics and Gerontology International, Aging and Mental Health, Journal of Aging and Health, Sociology Compass, International Journal of Sociology of the Family, Hallym International Journal of Aging,* and *Death Studies,* among others.

Glossary

hyo	효	Filial piety.
noinbuyang	노인부양	Eldercare.
noinbuyanguisik	노인부양의식	Eldercare perception.
noindolbom	노인 돌봄	Eldercare.

Notes

1. Scholars, however, disagree about whether or not Buddhism inherently emphasizes filial piety in this way, with some arguing that reference to filial piety in Buddhist texts was added in China before Buddhism reached Korea (Jung 2011).
2. For the transliteration of these Korean words, we followed the basic rules established by the National Institute of Korean Language in the Republic of Korea (n.d.).

References

Ahn, Hei Sook. 2005. "Relationship between Urban Married People's Normative Sense of the Traditional Filial Piety and their Affiliation with Relatives." *Journal of Korean Home Economic Association* 43 (5): 183–98.

Baek, Kyung-Sook, and Yong-Shin Kwon. 2008. "A Study of the Effects of the Psychological Well-being for the Caregiving Burden of the Major Caregivers of Elderly with Dementia." *Journal of Welfare for the Aged* 39, 33–52.

Cho, Seong-Hee, and Yun-Jeong Kim. 2011. "Influence of Elderly Marital Intimacy on their Consciousness of Caregiving for Their Partner." *Journal of Agricultural Extension and Community Development* 18 (4): 765–91.

Choi, Hee-Kyung. 2012. "An Exploratory Study on Caregiving Sons." *Journal of Welfare for the Aged* 55: 7–32.

Choi, Sung-Jae, Jae-Nem Bae, Kyung-Jin Min, and Yong-Kyun Roh, eds. 2013. *Ageing in Korea: Today and Tomorrow*, 3rd ed. Korea: Federation of Korean Gerontological Societies.

Choi, Seung-Ah, Ji-Hong Cheong, Seung-Jong Cho, and Sun-Mi Jin. 2009. "Effects of University Students' Voluntary Activities Serving the Elderly: Mediating Effects of the Attitude toward the Elderly." *Journal of Welfare for the Aged* 46: 239–62.

Chung, Soon Dool, and Jung Ye Yu. 2009. "Relationship between Perceived Family Belief System and Caregiver Burden among Family Caregivers of Frail Elderly." *Journal of Welfare for the Aged* 45: 67–88.

Gallois, Cindy, Howard Giles, Hiroshi Ota, Herbert Pierson, Sik Hung Ng, Tae-Seop Lim, John Maher, Lilnabeth Somera, Ellen Ryan, and Jake Harwood. 1999. "Intergenerational Communication across the Pacific Rim: The Impact of Filial Piety." In *Latest Contributions to Cross-Cultural Psychology: Selected Papers from the Thirteenth International Congress of the International Association for Cross-Cultural Psychology*, ed. J. Lasry, J. Adair, and K. Dion, 192–211. Lisse, The Netherlands: Swets and Zeitlinger.

Giorgi, Amedeo. 1985. *Phenomenology and Psychological Research.* Pittsburgh, PA: Duquesne University Press.

Guberman, Nancy, Jean-Pierre Lavoie, Laure Blein, and Ignace Olazabal. 2012. "Baby Boom Caregivers: Care in the Age of Individualization." *The Gerontologist,* 52 (2): 210–18.

Ha, Keun Young, and Dal Ahgi Hong. 2002. "Effect of Grandchildren's Solidarity with Their Grandparents on Caring Attitude for the Elderly." *Korean Journal of Human Ecology* 11 (2): 107–21.

Han, Eun-Jeong, Im-Ok Kang, and Jin Hee Kown. 2011. "Study of Dementia on Institutionalization of Elderly Using Home Care Services." *Journal of the Korean Gerontological Society* 31 (2): 259–276.

Han, Eun-Jeong, Kyung-Hee Na, Jung-Myun Lee, and Jin-Hee Kwon. 2015. "Factors Influencing Family Caregivers' Burden in Community Dwelling Elderly under Long-Term Care Insurance System: Comparison among Sub-Dimensions." *Korea Social Policy Review* 22 (2): 61–96.

Han, Gyoung-Hae, and Seo-Youn Lee. 2009. "The Effect of Motivation and Social Support on Burden of Spouse Caregivers: Focused on Gender Differences." *Journal of the Korean Gerontological Society,* 29 (2): 683–699.

Hong, Sun-Woo, and Hang-Mi Son. 2007. "Family Caregivers' Experiences Utilizing a Nursing Home for Their Elderly Family Members." *Journal of Korean Academy of Nursing* 37 (5): 724–35.

Hyun, Kyung-Rae, and Sun-Mi Lee. 2012. "Effects on Functional Status of Long-Term Care Services." *Journal of the Korean Gerontological Society* 32 (2): 593–609.

Ikels, Charlotte, ed. 2004. *Filial Piety: Practices and Discourse in Contemporary East Asia.* Stanford, CA: Stanford University Press.

Janelli, Roger L., and Dawnhee Yim. 2004. "The Transformation of Filial Piety in Contemporary South Korea." In *Filial Piety: Practice and Discourse in Contemporary East Asia,* ed. Charlotte Ikels, 128–52. Palo Alto, CA: Stanford University Press.

Jeon, Mi Ae. 2006. "Effects of Filial Piety Values on the Coping Styles in Family Caregiver Burden and Depression." *Journal of the Korean Geronotological Society* 26 (4): 665–80.

Joo, Kyung-Bock, and Kwyu-Bun Kim. 2008. "A Study of Care Burden, Burnout, and Quality of Life among Family Caregivers for the Elderly." *Korean Journal of Women Health Nursing* 14 (4): 278–89.

Jung, Soo Dong. 2011. "Hyo Thought of Confucianism and the Buddhism." *Journal of Eastern Asian Buddhist Culture* 7: 259–87.

Jung, Yun Tae. 2013. "Study on Familial Relationships in Connection with Caring for the Elderly: Focus on Female Main Caregivers Who Utilize Long-Term Care Insurance." *Journal of Korean Family Relations* 8 (3): 207–31.

Jung, Yun Tae, and Yong Sung Suh. 2014. "An Approach to Patterns of Organizing Family Caregiving for Elderly According to Grounded Theory: Focusing on Daughter-in-law's Experience." *Journal of Korean Family Relations* 19 (2): 29–53.

Kang, Tae Wha, Eun Ja Yeun, and Mi Soon Jeon. 2014. "Burden Types of Primary Caregivers for Elders with Dementia Using Q Methodology." *Journal of Human KSSSS* 28: 57–74.

Kim, Eun-Young, Ga Eon Lee, Sam-Sook Kim, and Chun Yee Lee. 2012. "Experience of Family Caregivers under Long-Term Care Insurance." *Journal of Korean Academy Community Health Nursing* 23 (4): 347–57.

Kim, Hyeong-Seon, Jae-Young Park, In-Sun Kwon, and Yong-Chae Cho. 2010. "Quality of Life and Its Association with Physical and Mental Function in Elderly People Affiliated with Long-Term Care Insurance Services." *Journal of the Korea Academia–Industrial Cooperation Society* 11 (10): 3808–19.

Kim, Jae Yop, and Jang Won Choi. 2011. "Study of the Influences of Filial Responsibility Attitude and Care Burden of Families with Elders with Dementia on Changes in Family Relations." *Korean Thought and Culture* 60: 495–525.

Kim, Yun-Jeong. 2006. "Verification of the Effectiveness of Caregiving Model on Caregiving Stress." *Korean Association of Family Relations* 11 (1): 79–101.

Korean Studies Information System (KISS). N.d. "Daegu Catholic University Library Login Page for Accessing KISS." Retrieved 14 September 2014 from http://libproxy.cu.ac.kr/bbd64ed/_Lib_proxy_Url/kiss.kstudy.com/cscenter/faq.asp.

Kosberg, Jordan, and Richard Cairl. 1986. "The Cost of Care Index: A Case Management Tool for Screening Informal Care Providers." *The Gerontologist* 26 (3): 273–78.

Kwon, Gi Gab, and Jae Mo Lee, 2009. "A Study on Undergraduates' Consciousness of Support for the Elderly." *Korean Journal of Regional Innovation* 4 (2): 1–17.

Kwon, Hyun-Jung, Yong-Un Cho, and Ji-Young Ko. 2011. "The Effects of Long-Term Care Insurance on Life Satisfaction and Satisfaction in Family Relationships: The DD Method Combined with Propensity Score Matching." *Korean Journal of Social Welfare* 63 (4): 301–28.

Kwon, Jong Don. 2013. *Welfare for the Aged.* Seoul, Korea: Hakjisa.

Lee, Duk-Sik. 2015. "A Study of Hyo and Caregiving in Relation to Familism in Korea." *Social Science Research Review* 32 (2): 173–209.

Lee, Hyun Joo. 2005. "Caregiving Experience and Adaptation Process of the Husbands Who Are Caring for Wives with Alzheimer's: Focusing on the Elderly Couple Household." *Journal of the Korean Gerontological Society* 26 (1): 45–62.

Lee, Hyun Ji. 2007. "Impact of Family Caregivers' Filial Obligation on Caregiving Burden and Future Care Willingness for the Frail Elderly." *Journal of the Korean Gerontological Society* 27 (4): 1015–30.

Lee, In-Jeong. 2006. "Comparison of the Determinants of Caregiving Burden between Wives and Daughters-in-law of the Impaired Older Persons." *Korean Journal of Social Welfare Studies* 31: 161–93.

Lee, Joo Young, and Young Ae Kim. 2009. "Relationship between Family Burden, Family Support, Depression and Satisfaction of the Elderly Caregiver." *Journal of Korean Academy Community Health Nursing* 20 (1): 41–48.

Lee, Sook-Hee, Hyo-Hik Shin, and Seon-Jeong Lee. 2005. "Study on *Hyo* Consciousness and Filial Piety of Middle School Students." *Journal of Korean Home Economics Education* 17 (2): 159–70.

Lee, Young-Whee, and Kyung Hee Park. 2007. "A Study on the Influencing Factors of Dementia Caregivers' Life Satisfaction." *Journal of Nursing Query* 16 (2): 135–56.

Lim, Jeong-Gi, Eun-Jin Hong, and Ju-Yeon Lee. 2010. "A Study on Comparison of Household Characteristics Affecting Elderly Support." *Korean Journal of Social Welfare Research* 24: 255–75.

Min, Kichae. 2011. "The Difference-in-Difference Model Analysis about the Effects of Long-Term Care Insurance on Family Relationships' Change." *Journal of the Korean Gerontological Society* 31 (4): 999–1014.

Mo, Seon Hee, and Se Yeong Choi, 2013. "Changes in Caregiving Burden of Families after Using Long-Term Care Services." *Journal of Critical Social Policy* 40: 7–31.

National Health Insurance (NHI). 2010. *National Health Insurance Service.* Retrieved 15 November 2014 from http.nhis.or.kr/static/html/wbd/g/a/wbdga0101.html.

National Institute of Korean Language in the Republic of Korea. N.d. "Korean Language." Retrieved 24 November 2019 from https://korean.go.kr/front_eng/main .do.

Oh, Hee Sok, and So Hyune Sok. 2009. "Health Condition, Burden of Caring, and the Quality of Life among Family Members of the Elderly with Senile Dementia." *Journal of Korean Academy Psychiatry Mental Health Nursing* 18 (2): 157–66.

Park, Young-Joon, and In-Uk Song 2008. "The Analysis on the Causal Model: The Burden of Family Conflict, Family Support and Caregiving Burden." *Journal of Welfare for the Aged* 39: 53–78.

Pyke, Karen D., and Vern L. Bengtson. 1996. "Caring More or Less: Individualistic and Collectivist Systems of Family Eldercare." *Journal of Marriage and Family* 58 (2): 379–392.

Republic of Korea (ROK). N.d. *National Pension Act.* Retrieved 15 November 2014 from http.nps.or.kr/jsppage/english/act/act_01.jsp.

Schütze, Fritz. 1983. "Biogranphieforschung and Narrative Interview." *Neue Praxis* 13: 283–93.

Seelbach, Wayne C. 1978. "Correlates of Aged Parents' Filial Responsibility Expectations and Realizations." *Family Coordinator* 27 (4): 343–44.

Seo, Byung-Sook, and Sin-Sook Lee, 1991. "A Study of Caregiving Perceptions and Caregiving Behavior among Married Women in Rural Areas." *Journal of the Korea Gerontological Society* 11 (2): 191–207.

Shin, Yung Yee, Yong Sin Park, and Ui Chul Kim. 2009. "Indigenous Psychological Analysis of Filial Piety towards Parents among Elementary School Children." Presented in *Korean Psychology Association* 1: 424–25.

Song, Da-Young. 2004. "The Consciousness of Family Caregiving among Women and Eldercare Policy." *Social Welfare Policy* 19: 207–33.

Song, Da-Young, and Mi-Kyung Kim. 2003. "A Study on Eldercare Burden and Role Conflict among Working Women and Housewives." *Korean Women Studies* 19 (2): 145–76.

Song, Mi-Young, and Gyung-Goo Choi. 2007. "The Decision Factor in Primary Caregiver's Burden for Senile Dementia Elderly." *Journal of Welfare for the Aged* 37: 131–60.

Sorensen, Clark, and Sung-Chul Kim. 2004. "Filial Piety in Contemporary Southeast Korea: Practices and Discourses." In Ikels, *Filial Piety,* 153–81.

Statistics Korea. 2019a. *Population Projections.* Retrieved 21 October 2019 from http:// kostat.go.kr.

———. 2019b. *2017 Statistics on the Aged.* Retrieved 21 October 2019 from http:// kostat.go.kr/portal/english/news/1/23/1/index.board.

Strauss, Anselm, and Juliet Corbin. 1998. *Basics of Qualitative Research: Grounded Theory Procedures and Techniques.* Newbury Park, CA: Sage Publications.

Yang, Nan-Joo. 2013. "A Study on the Emergence of Family Care-Worker: Why Families Choose to be Care-Worker in Korea?" *Korea Social Policy Review* 20 (2): 97–129.

Yang, Nan-Joo, and In-Hee Choi. 2013. "The Impact of the Korean Long-Term Care Insurance System on Its Family Caregivers: Focusing on Family Caregiving Arrangement." *Korean Journal of Social Welfare Studies* 44 (3): 31–56.

Yang, Yeung Ja. 2009. "A Biographical Reconstruction of the Process Involving Changes in Elderly Support: From the Perspective of the Rural Elderly." *Journal of the Korean Gerontological Society* 29 (1): 1–20.

Yang, Ya Ki. 2013. "A Study on Aging Knowledge, Attitudes and Awareness about Supporting the Aged in Undergraduates Students." *Journal of Korean Academy Society Nursing Education* 19 (4): 498–507.

Yoon, Hyun-Sook. 2013. "Korea: Balancing Economic Growth and Social Protection for Older Adults." *The Gerontologist* 53 (3): 361–68.

Yoon, Hyun-Sook, and Sam-Hee Ryu. 2005. "Factors Associated with Filial Responsibility Expectation and Preference for Sons of the Elderly in Korea." *Journal of the Korean Gerontological Society* 25 (3): 177–94.

———. 2007. "Factors Associated with Family Caregivers' Burden of Frail Elders: Comparing Spouse with Adult Children." *Journal of the Korean Gerontological Society* 27 (1): 195–211.

Yoon, Soon-Duck, and Hye-Sun Che. 2008. "Case Study on the Problems of Elderly Care by Community Elderly in Rural Korea." *Journal of Welfare for the Aged* 40: 31–54.

Yun, Eun-Kyung. 2010. "Research on the How Caregiving Burden for the Frail Elder Affect Caregiver's Guilt: Comparing between Home-Care and Nursing-Home Elderly." *Journal of Welfare for the Aged* 47: 289–308.

11 THE DYNAMICS OF CARE IN THE CONTEXT OF LIMITED REPATRIATION OF SAKHALIN KOREAN ELDERLY

Dorota Szawarska

Introduction

IN THIS CHAPTER, I WRITE about the complexities of a South Korean repatriation program that seems to defy filial piety (for definition, see Introduction) by separating seniors geographically from their descendants. The basic situation is as follows. During the Japanese occupation of Korea in the 1930s and early 1940s, Korean workers were sent to the Japanese-occupied part of Sakhalin Island to serve as labor; in some cases their wives and children were permitted to follow. Coming under the USSR after World War II, the island retained the Korean laborers as a much-needed workforce. In the late 1990s to the early 2000s, after the breakup of the Soviet Union, Sakhalin remained under Russian control, but the original Korean conscripted laborers, now elderly, were allowed to take part in a limited repatriation program back to South Korea. The catch was that their descendants were not included in the program.

In the analysis that follows I show how a group of elderly Korean repatriates from Sakhalin, with the aid of their adult children, used that repatriation program in order to try to maintain harmonious intergenerational relationships. This case is significant in that the repatriation program was restricted to the first generation of Korean Sakhalin settlers who were either elderly or approaching old age at the time of repatriation. First generation was defined as people born up to 15 August 1945. As a result, those repatriated from Sakhalin to South Korea were physically separated from their children.

The fact that the Korean state introduced this restriction and that people nonetheless chose to participate in the program goes against the logic of filial piety usually associated with the region. The case shows that intergenerational Sakhalin Korean family relationships cannot be reduced to filial piety, and that one should be careful when using the term in analyzing Korean norms and practices. Many seniors and their descendants saw limited repatriation involving intergenerational separation as a way to minimize the burden of old age care on both generations: caregiving is perceived as burdensome, but so also is being cared for. It was also seen as a way to gain greater control over assistance given to the junior generation and to take advantage of the circumstances in order to allow the seniors the dignity of boosting their own self-sufficiency as a way to enact care for their descendants.

In Ikels's (2004) classic volume on filial piety in East Asia, Janelli and Yim (2004) wrote about the "transformation of filial piety in contemporary South Korea" (128). In their analysis, they noted that, compared with the 1970s, by the 1990s there were far fewer mentions of filial piety in the village they studied. The value and norm had never been, in their experience, entirely uncontested, and the burden of elderly care was openly recognized even in the 1970s. However, while in the 1970s the elderly were more or less assured of receiving care, due to the changes resulting from industrialization and urbanization, in the 1990s that was far from obvious. This does not automatically mean that members of the junior generation did not respect their parents, but rather that filial piety, as expressed through coresidence with the eldest son and his family, for example, was difficult to practice. This meant that creative solutions had to be used in fulfilling the needs of the elders, relying on existing resources and accommodating social changes, either by the junior generations or by the elders themselves. Following Janelli and Yim (2004: 150), I argue, "Rather than pose an unanswerable question of whether or not filial piety has declined, it seems more fruitful to look for modern practices that exhibit a continuing sense of obligation towards parents."

Medical anthropologist Kleinman (2010: 100) has argued, "Living our lives is about animating and enacting values. We are constantly experiencing, negotiating, defending, and just living values." Care is precisely such a moral value that is also a social practice. It does not exist outside of a dynamic, cultural, and social context in which people have to fit it with the rest of their lives in sometimes challenging and changing circumstances. As Kleinman continues, "Our own moral life may be consistent with or in conflict with our local worlds of experience. We can collaborate with such worlds or seek to resist and transcend them by our aspiration for ethical commitment" (100). We can also use changing circumstances in order to reshape the social practice surrounding certain values, in order to remain moral people in our own eyes. Furthermore, the complexity of competing moral values and differing subject positions relative to those values means that living a moral life is a complex dance of trade-offs.

In this chapter, I draw on ethnographic data I collected in order to illustrate how Sakhalin Koreans took hold of this unexpected opportunity and made sense of it, while negotiating both complex adjustments and compromises within and among different moral values. Drawing on work I carried out in the community of Sakhalin Koreans in South Korea in 2005 and 2006, I examine how people exploited this unusual arrangement in order to maintain good family relations, in particular and somewhat counterintuitively in relation to the matter of care. I argue that the moral compass of providing optimal care within contemporary exigencies and traditional norms of filial piety may clash with other values and interests such as intergenerational solidarity and family harmony. This, in turn, creates nuanced patterns of ambivalence in everyday family life toward even the most highly esteemed values. In order to avoid family conflict amidst competing values in negotiating later-life living arrangements, intergenerational relations demand goodwill and active creative engagement on the part of both junior and senior generations. The examples provided show how a re-examination of what constitutes a good and moral way to be in an intergenerational relationship is required in circumstances like these of unexpected opportunities with a new set of trade-offs among treasured values. I demonstrate how, in order to understand the dynamics of the situation, we must factor in the efforts of seniors to live a moral life by manifesting care for younger generations, not just the filiality of the actions of younger generations toward their elders. Geographical distance could allow elders greater self-sufficiency to show care toward their children, but it could also extricate elders from caregiving obligations they no longer wished to perform for their descendants.

Sakhalin Koreans and Their Repatriation

Sakhalin Koreans, like countless others, suffered as a result of World War II and its Cold War aftermath. Unlike others, however, they as a community suffered the pain of being separated from their families twice. Their separation came first when they were forced to move to Sakhalin and, second, when a limited repatriation program was launched that permitted the return of just first-generation migrants to South Korea. This was bound to have consequences on how intergenerational relationships, and in particular matters related to caring for the elderly, were perceived and practiced. For several reasons, the situation is complex: first, because the original settlers had limited or no opportunity to care for their own parents remaining in Korea; second, because the conditions of repatriation made it extremely complicated; and third, because of the impact of Soviet and Russian culture.

The original settlement of Koreans on Sakhalin has its roots in the Japanese war effort, during the time when both the Korean Peninsula and the southern half of the Sakhalin Island, known then as Karafuto, were under Japanese control. Korean laborers on Sakhalin worked in the coalmines, construction sites, and factories; and as lumberjacks. Some Koreans settled on the island as part of Japanese labor recruitment in the late 1930s; most were forced laborers in the period from 1942 to 1945. The recruitment in 1944 and 1945 was straight-up forced labor, while the earlier periods were on a voluntary (1930s) or semi-voluntary (1942–44) basis at the point of recruitment, though not at the point of labor—the workers were commonly unpaid, and were not permitted to return to Korea following the end of their two-year contracts. However, their immediate families, in particular wives and children, from Korea were permitted to join them, and some did. At the end of the war there were approximately 43,000 Koreans remaining on Sakhalin, but that was after 100,000 Korean men were moved from Sakhalin to Japan, to work in the mines on Hokkaido while the war still raged (Choi 2004: 116). In 1998 there were 43,000 Sakhalin Koreans living on Sakhalin (Lee 2001: 122), comprising some 5 percent of the population.

Following the end of World War II in August 1945, the Soviet army took over control of the entire island. Japan evacuated its citizens, either during the withdrawal of the Japanese army or later in the 1940s, but only those who were ethnically Japanese. Koreans, despite being until then subjects of the Japanese empire, were left behind. There were two reasons for that. First, Japan claimed that Koreans lost their Japanese citizenship in accordance with the conditions of surrender, flowing from the 1945 Potsdam Declaration and the 1943 Cairo Declaration, that supported Korean independence (Choi 2004: 119). Therefore, they were no longer the responsibility of Japan. Second, the Soviet Union did not want to let go of qualified Korean workers in the resource-rich but sparsely populated island. So the Koreans were trapped—without Japanese or Korean passports, living in the Soviet Union, and yet without Soviet citizenship—stateless people dreaming of a return home. Following years of campaigning and struggle, some sixty years after the original migration to Sakhalin, this dream was set to become true in the late 1990s, but not without problems.

It is not often that a group of transnational migrants is limited to the senior generation, especially in the context of East Asia. But that was exactly the case of Sakhalin Koreans. The repatriation program organized and implemented in the late 1990s and especially in the year 2000, when the bulk of the repatriation took place was restricted to the first generation of settlers only, where first generation meant people born before the end of 1945, with the priority given to people born before 1935. The additional

FIGURE 11.1. Sakhalin Korean Seniors at a Gathering at Home Village in Ansan, Korea. Photo by Dorota Szawarska.

restriction was that the capacity of housing dedicated to the needs of the repatriates was limited. Home Village (see figure 11.1)—the purpose-built apartment complex in Ansan near Seoul, could house 978 people, though there were also some care homes, especially one in Incheon, a town close to Seoul, and one in Ansan.[1] Some apartments were made available in social housing in Incheon, Pucheon, and Seoul. The repatriation began in 1997 with eighty-two persons belonging to the most fragile group. They were settled in temporary housing, which for many proved to be permanent. Then in 2000 there came the next wave of migrants to the purpose-built Home Village and the Incheon nursing home. By the end of the year 2000, some 1,352 Sakhalin Korean elderly had been repatriated (Choi 2004: 130). During repatriation, priority was given to married couples and closely related pairs (e.g., mother and child who both met the date-of-birth criterion, or sisters) but because of the large number of widows, it was also possible for two unrelated women to come to an arrangement and choose to share an apartment. During my work in Korea in 2005 and 2006 there was still a long waiting list of elderly Sakhalin Koreans remaining in Russia who wished to return to their historical homeland.[2] Their only chance was the death of some residents of Home Village (on death in Korea, see chap. 12). The apartments remained the property of the state, and, once vacated, were quickly refilled with fresh migrants.[3] The repatriates received a living allowance from the state and were not permitted to work. This did not stop many from supplementing their income by part-time employment, however, either as cleaners or as security guards in local apartment complexes. The seniors in figure 11.1 were celebrating the fifth anniversary of this repatriate retirement community. The matching hats were given out as swag by the event sponsor.

The Burden of Care in a Challenging Place

Usually filial piety is accorded much importance by the Korean state, scholars studying Korea, and Koreans themselves (Grayson 2002; Lee 2003; Lee 1997: 35; Sung 2003: 346). Why then did the elderly, or people approaching old age, choose to participate in the repatriation? This is puzzling given that they knew that they would become increasingly fragile and that their children, grandchildren, or younger siblings would not be able to join them. Moreover, they were migrating to a country that was virtually foreign to them.

Reasons for the move were complex and mixed. There were elements of nostalgia for the mother country and the need to return to one's roots at the end of one's life. Being Korean and returning to Korea was important to many of my informants, especially the older men, who actually had some memories of the place, in contrast to their much younger wives, since a large age difference between spouses was not uncommon. Some of the women were less than enthusiastic about the migration, but felt obliged to accompany their husbands. By far the most common reason for moving was related to the matter of care and old age. "I do not want to be a burden" was the answer I heard most often when I asked why people participated in repatriation (on burden, see also chaps. 1–3, 7, 9–10).

The emphasis on not wanting to be a burden involved many considerations in relation to the problems of familial care, filial piety, and intergenerational solidarity. In part, this desire not to be a burden was an expression of care for members of the younger generation. Whereas they did not mind depending on the Korean state for repatriation, they did not want to be dependent on their children. The elderly Sakhalin Koreans reasoned that their offspring already had cares of their own: children, work, finances, and the like, so why add to them? The elders were very much aware of the hardships of living on Sakhalin, especially for people in their age group, which included the need to shovel snow for half the year or more, the risk of slipping on icy streets and breaking a leg, the need to fetch and carry coal, inadequate retirement pensions, and very high prices on the oil-rich island.

Thus, staying on Sakhalin would mean that sooner or later the elders would need help from their children or other close kin, something they wanted to avoid if at all possible for the good of the entire family.[4] This same sentiment has been expressed elsewhere with regard to contemporary South Korea (Kim and Rhee 1997: 199; Lee, Uhn, and Pilwha 2008: 78, 81; Prendergast 2005: 55), and not just Sakhalin Koreans. A Korean grandmother whose only son settled in mainland Russia had this to say on the prospect of being cared for by the junior generation:

> Anna Nikolayevna: No way. He has a family of his own—a baby daughter and a wife. They already demand a lot of effort and attention. To expect help from him, to demand it, it would be like hanging a heavy rock on his neck that would weigh him to the ground. That would be wrong. In any case, I would probably need his wife's assistance at some point and that would just be too uncomfortable. We never lived together, I hardly know her. So now that the flat is almost paid for, I will still carry on working. So that we have money to visit Russia, but also to save for the future, just in case one of us becomes sick, and there are medical bills or a hired caregiver to be paid for. But it would be wonderful if they gave me their daughter to look after, if only for a couple of years!

The elders spoke of a duty to remain fit, healthy, independent, and capable for as long as possible in order to avoid the need for care, especially from their children. Self-care was seen not just as a simple duty to oneself, but rather as an obligation toward their adult children. Actually, self-care was one of the only things that the elderly spoke of as a duty with regard to their grown children. Otherwise, once their children could support themselves, the elders felt that they had discharged their other duties toward them in contrast to what Shea observed in China (chap. 2). The need to maintain self-sufficiency through cultivating good health was important on Sakhalin and it persisted following repatriation. It was manifested in the obsession of the Sakhalin Korean elderly with maintaining good health through exercise and appropriate diet, and sometimes through visiting salons selling medical monitoring equipment such as blood pressure monitors.

An example of the duty of elders to maintain self-sufficiency in order to avoid the need for care is illustrated in the case of this seventy-three-year-old grandfather:

> Sergei: I keep telling all the guys to learn how to cook. Some don't even know how to cook rice! What will they do if their wife dies? There are some widowers here, and some don't know how to cook. Who will look after them? Will the children come over? What are they thinking of expecting the children to

come over and look after them? The children have their own lives, their own cares, their own children. They can't just drop everything and come and boil some rice!

Sergei knew what he was talking about, as he had experienced some problems when looking after his own mother. Since he was the eldest son, he and his wife looked after his mother in her old age. He was proud of the fact that after staying with each of her children in turn his mother chose to live with them, and was ultimately happy with the arrangement. At the same time, he and his wife experienced some conflict related to living in a multigenerational household. He did not want to cause similar problems to his own children, at least not until absolutely necessary, although he was seriously considering returning to Sakhalin in his extreme old age to live with his eldest son. This was so that his children would not have to face the expense and other practical problems related to looking after their parents in a foreign country. The thought of a nursing home did not appeal to him, although it did appeal to some other Sakhalin Korean repatriates (Szawarska 2013: 42). A common problem of being a potential burden on one's children had no easy solution. As Grandfather Sergei's case shows, feelings and attitudes toward care in old age were mixed and ambivalent. Care from one's children, on the one hand, was valued, but, on the other hand, thoughts of needing care from their children filled elders with apprehension.

While some scholars have questioned the traditional ubiquity of the practice of filial piety in Korea (e.g., Chung 2001: 145), caring for aging parents is an important element of filial piety, a moral norm that in the past was at least said to govern the relationship between the generations (Sung 2000; Sung 2003: 346). For the past and the present, it is important to remember that care has a multiplex meaning. Not only does it mean hands-on care and assistance, which is what worried the Sakhalin Korean elders the most, but it also means taking responsibility for arranging care, paying for care, and recognizing the need for care. In the past, it was considered the children's, and in particular the eldest son's, responsibility to look after his parents. However, ironically, it was an outsider, the daughter-in-law, who was beset with the most unpleasant of tasks associated with daily hands-on care (for examples, see Lee 1997: 55; Prendergast 2005: 74).

In the case of Sakhalin Koreans, perhaps due in part to the influence of Russian culture, the patterns of care were different. It was relatively rare for the daughter-in-law to be engaged in hands-on caregiving. The caregiver preferred by elderly parents, should the need arise, was a daughter and then a son (similar to observations for China, chap. 2). A daughter-in-law was the last resort, though a recognized source of support. To burden one's children with care unnecessarily was not only to add to their troubles, but also to risk the quality of the relationship between and within the generations, since care was recognized as a potential source of conflict among siblings as well as among parents and children. The value of family harmony was more important than filial piety expressed through practical support. There were other ways for children to show their devotion, including phone calls that were more-or-less frequent.

Care, Responsibility, and Filial Piety

The notion of filial piety in the context of eldercare in Korea focuses one's attention on the junior generation. They are the ones who have to prove their morality in appropriate conduct and on them lies the responsibility for adequate care provision and quality of life of their elders. In the case of Sakhalin Koreans, that is clearly not so. Here while children neglecting a parent would be condemned, so would the parents' thoughtless reliance on the junior generation. Their assistance should not be taken for granted.

A good parent, I was told multiple times both by the old and the young, was one who does not cause too much trouble and worry to the children, who lets them be and does not impose on them. This statement is very similar to the one associated with filial piety and family harmony, where a good child is one who does not worry a parent too much (Janelli and Yim 1993: 27).[5] Indeed, Sakhalin Korean elders, when asked to describe what they mean by a good child in the context of intergenerational relations, replied that a good child is one who lives well, breaks no laws, and does not cause worry or anxiety to his parents. The elderly tended to say that adult children do not have any obligations toward elders, now that almost everything was provided for them within Home Village. But they would be expected to attend the funeral of their parents, and to call during holidays and when parents were unwell. Ultimately, they would also be the ones expected to provide assistance to their aging parents, although the elderly did not like to think or talk about it, so much so that some of them declared that they would prefer to go into a nursing home than burden their children with care.

It is difficult to say whether the situation described above presents a major shift in everyday morality of Koreans in relation to intergenerational relations. While the Confucian value of filial piety was and is much promoted and praised, for example through state prizes for filial children (Sung 2005), voices concerning whether it was or is universally accepted by Koreans are divided.[6] What we can say is that the value is a part of the moral landscape

of Koreans of various social statuses and backgrounds. However important, it is only a part of a bigger whole. In the case of Sakhalin Koreans we
might seek an explanation for their attitude to eldercare and responsibility
in the influences of Russian culture. In Russia maximum attention tends
to be given to the youngest generations (for examples see Caldwell 2004:
86; Caldwell 2007: 73), an orientation that is interestingly also consonant
with the "boundless parental sacrifice" present in Korean discourse on intergenerational relations (Janelli and Yim 2004: 134). However, we might
also seek it in another major Confucian value, which is the maintenance of
family harmony (Lee and Linsky 2003: 272), and with which care provision based on simple filial piety may come into conflict. Finally, one might
and should take into account the longer period of old age and care that
both the elderly and their kin have to face in contemporary times, and the
awareness of which will have an impact on people's attitudes to both caregiving and care receiving.

Given the ambivalent feelings that the repatriates had about care and
family obligations it is unsurprising that some tried to use the repatriation
program in order to reshape the relations between generations and related
family values. Grandfather Vasily, a retired accountant, argued that back
on Sakhalin he and his wife would not be able to support themselves on
their retirement pensions. Moreover, their family situation was complicated
by the fact that both of them had children from previous marriages. On
the one hand, traditionally Korean women were not supposed to remarry
(even though due to the initial shortage of Korean women on Sakhalin this
did happen) and, on the other hand, Vasily's first wife was Russian, and a
cross-cultural marriage, though not unheard of, was frowned on for members of his generation. So he argued, "When we left the island, we told our
children: 'You do not owe us anything, but please do not expect any help
from us either.' It is better that way. We can manage here, and there we
would not be of any use. . . . If we shared equally among the children,
the money would be too small to be of any significance. It would make no
difference to them, and we would only grow poorer." Despite his declaration of not owing his children any assistance, in the very same breath he
told me that he assisted one of his daughters, who was suffering from a
chronic condition, by sending her some expensive Korean medicine. Thus,
as is often the case, the declared attitudes and the moral practice were not
identical.

Balance of Care

Following migration, what grew in people's minds was something that I
would call loving care without burden. Caring for members of the family

remained important, and so did keeping the relationship relatively burden free. So what came to the fore were declarations of care and concern, by both generations. The distance between South Korea and Sakhalin that made direct hands-on caregiving difficult forced Sakhalin Koreans to engage in others forms of expressing concern for each other, for example through phone calls. Importantly, both the senior and junior generations were actively engaged, but the senior generation in particular took care not to burden their children excessively with the cost, and it was they, and not the children, who tended to call. The exception was on solar New Year, which Sakhalin Koreans tended to celebrate more than the lunar one, parents' birthdays, and when parents were sick. On those days it was seen as proper for the children and grandchildren to call.

Sakhalin Koreans also relied on friends and kin traveling between Korea and Sakhalin to take small gifts to each other. It was important to show that one remembered, and this applied to both parents and children. However, in general, the elderly took care to give more than they received—whether in terms of gifts, calls, or practical assistance. Gifts were given either during family visits on Sakhalin or when their children visited them in Korea. But at the same time, they tried to keep the exchange of support in check. This meant not only avoiding receiving hands-on care, but also avoiding excessive caring themselves. Some of them were tired of looking after and supporting their families. The geographical distance between the generations was used not only to ease the life of the children, but also the lives of the elderly. Those who on Sakhalin lived close or together with their children, the latter being very uncommon, felt that they no longer had the strength to look after the grandchildren on a regular basis, cook, be on call, and not always be appreciated. A grandfather who was in his early seventies, when speaking about his decision to move back to South Korea, noted,

> Boris: But, you know, now life here is easier than on Sakhalin. My daughters don't pester me about this and that. Before, on Sakhalin, they kept asking for money. Daddy this! Daddy that! Enough I say! How long can I support them? Not that it stopped of course. Now one of my granddaughters is living with me; while she works in a factory. I wait up for her every night, so that I know she got back home safely.

While one would rarely hear people complaining about their own families, during the summer when the grandchildren were parachuted to Home Village and left there by their parents, who were busy working illegally in the nearby factories or back on Sakhalin, one would often hear the grandmothers complaining how unfair and unthoughtful that was. They complained that they no longer had the stamina, especially in this heat, to be looking after the youngsters. They had done their share of caring, and it was the children's turn now! Moreover, looking after the grandchildren was a strain on the family budget, with all the demands to go to the Internet café and so on. Boundless parental sacrifice for one's descendants, a dominant element of Sakhalin Korean discourse and practice, was clearly also a habit that some elders thought needed to be curbed.

Clearly the relationship between the senior and junior generations was not a simple one and could not be reduced either to the young cherishing the old, as the ideal of filial piety would have it, or the old cherishing the young without any thought for the consequences. Families, even much-loved ones, can be a strain, and the relationships can bring about many mixed feelings, perhaps precisely because one cannot easily escape them.

Old Age, Filial Piety, and the Matter of Memory

But escape is exactly what some of the elderly attempted to do by moving to South Korea. The desire to avoid being a burden was in part linked to the desire on the part of the elderly to be remembered well by their children and grandchildren, which I would argue is an important element in the context of filial piety. While the elderly repatriates did not really expect their children, and certainly not the grandchildren, to perform a remembrance ceremony for one's ancestors (*chesa*) for them following their death, it remained crucial for them to be remembered well. One of my elderly informants had the following to say on the matter:

> Informant: When I was a kid [still in Korea, he only moved to Sakhalin when he was 10 years old, in 1944], I had a great-uncle. He was old. I don't know how old he was, but then people aged faster and did not live long. Anyway, he was old. And the only thing that I remember about him was that he was old, sick, and that the room where he stayed stunk of urine. People would only go to his room to give him some food, maybe clean a little. I only ever went in there when I was asked to, Lunar New Year probably. So you see the only thing that us kids knew about the elderly relative, was that he stunk of piss. I don't want my grandchildren to have a similar experience. And I do not want the indignity of such weakness in front of them. In the past, it was different. If you reached sixty, you had one leg in the grave! It did not last long. But now people struggle and suffer for a long time.

Avoidance was not the only strategy for creating good memories. The other major way to make memories in which the repatriates engaged was gift giving and general assistance during visits on Sakhalin. Gifts were exchanged not only during occasional visits on Sakhalin, but also when the children and grandchildren visited South Korea. Gifts were also passed through friends traveling back to the island. Some gifts were quite substantial given the limited income of the repatriates, such as computers for the grandchildren. Both spheres of gift-giving and support were dominated by women, though not exclusively. This was because women in general were younger and more able-bodied, and more often than the men had an additional source of income, for example as cleaners. Moreover, they assisted their children and grandchildren by doing things like cooking. This creation of good memories was crucial not only in terms of future remembrance of dearly departed grandparents, but also in terms of future care that might be required from junior generations. As grandmother Nadia said,

> Nadia: I miss my children and grandchildren a lot. When my husband dies, I am thinking of moving back to Sakhalin, to be with them. To help them as much as possible, while I am still able. So that when I am fragile and need help they will care for me with love, and not just out of an obligation, and when I die, my grandchildren [will] remember something more of me than the fragile old woman that needed looking after.

Grandmother Nadia had a very loving relationship with her children and grandchildren. Her need to help them was not only a matter of future gratitude and reciprocity, but also an expression of that love. Nonetheless, she and other members of the community, through active engagement with distant children and grandchildren, strategic avoidance of care, and the creation of good memories, were building up something that I would call a moral credit, or a positive moral investment, that could be called on should the situation require it. It was apparent that for Sakhalin Korean repatriates filial care, and in particular, loving care, was not a matter of course, but had to be worked on and earned.

Caring Solutions

Despite the best efforts of the elderly repatriates there came a time when they needed daily assistance. This was a problem, since the Home Village administration employed only two personal assistants who would help the neediest of the elderly with some basic tasks, and the single nurse on call, who was of course invaluable in an emergency but not as a long-term solution. Both the elderly parents and their children had to come up with a solution that would satisfy the care needs of the elderly and be acceptable to the children. These solutions most often relied on one of the children coming over to look after their parents. Which child came and when usually depended on how flexible they were in terms of their family obligations and employment back on Sakhalin. So usually, though not exclusively, the caregiver was a daughter. Not only was a daughter, following the pattern in Russia, a preferred caregiver (Roudakova and *Ballard-Reisch* 1999: 29), but women also were often already retired or unemployed. Sometimes caregivers had to give up their jobs or take extended leave in order to come over. It also depended on whether the care required was of an intense short-term nature, for example during an illness following an operation, or long-term care, as was in the case of extreme old age and fragility, senile dementia, or following a stroke. Occasionally siblings were able to cooperate and take turns. For example, those who worked as teachers could come over during the summer, and permit the main caregiver to return to Sakhalin to rest. I also met a case in which the caregiver remained in Home Village, while her mother, with signs of early dementia, went to Sakhalin for a month to be cared for by another daughter; this might have been due to visa reasons.

Who became a caregiver was not only a question of convenience but also family negotiations. Such was the case of Losha's mother whose wake I attended. This was one of very few cases that I came across that an elderly parent was looked after by a daughter-in-law. Losha's mother was repatriated together with her son, who was born before the cut-off point for repatriation; she was a divorcée with no pending responsibilities. Following the repatriation, her son married a Sakhalin Korean woman he knew, who was not included in the repatriation program and therefore had no living allowance or right to remain in the apartment following his death. Unfortunately, he died two years before the death of his mother. So Losha's mother's many children then had to decide who should take care of the elderly, fragile lady. Ultimately, they agreed that it would be best and most convenient for all for Losha's wife to be the official caregiver. That way the mother would be cared for and Losha's wife could remain in the apartment. Losha's sister, who had also been repatriated, provided respite care, and for the last three months of Losha's mother's life, care was also provided by her younger sons and another daughter-in-law. All this allowed Losha's wife to supplement household income with earnings from a part-time job. In this case, what is often considered the traditional caring pattern in the Korean culture served as an inspiration for a satisfactory solution for all. However, this was not treated as a matter of course, but rather as an issue that required thought and negotiation.

The other remaining possibilities of care were the nursing homes run especially for the Sakhalin Korean repatriates or a return to Sakhalin. While some of the elderly repatriates were open to the idea of a care home, this was not a popular solution among their children. Nursing homes had rather negative connotations for the children, and given a choice between caring for their parents at home in Korea or in Russia, some preferred for the fragile elderly to return to Russia. This made caring easier, and had less of an impact on their own lives. Moreover, one avoided the loss of face associated with sending a parent to a nursing home.

The fact that some of the elderly did indeed return to Sakhalin in order to be cared for was something that senior members of the Ansan Kohyang-maŭl Elders' Association of Sakhalin Repatriates (Ansansi Kohyangmaŭl Yŏngchu Kwigukcha Noinhoe), the self-governing body of repatriates Home Village, did not want to discuss.[7] They dismissed it as being insignificant and discouraged me from discussing it with members of the official administration of the settlement. This was unsurprising since the fact that some people chose to return to Russia signified a failure of the repatriation program and its administration to provide adequate care for the repatriates. However, most of my informants not directly involved with the association knew of someone who returned to Sakhalin, or who was planning to return. Even I during my research came across a couple who was already packed up for the journey back. According to my informants, those who went back were usually no longer able to look after themselves, due to issues such as losing sight or problems with mobility. Return to Sakhalin was also considered by women planning to rejoin their families in Russia following the death of their much older husbands. This was as much in order to look after the grandchildren and participate in family life as it was to be looked after.

The other dimension of a return to Sakhalin was a symbolic one, namely, return of the ashes of a parent deceased in Korea to Sakhalin, in order to be buried next to their spouse. This was also a reason why some children brought a repatriated parent approaching extreme old age or death back from Korea to Sakhalin. It was important for parents to be together in death as they were in life, and it would also make tending the grave easier. While elderly repatriates had little hope for the junior generations to perform the *chesa* graveside rituals for them, after the funeral of her father in South Korea one of my informants explained, "It will be so strange to go back to Sakhalin, where there will be nothing to bow to." However, most repatriates chose for their ashes to remain in Korea, their historical home.

The Second Generation

The second generation was not a homogeneous group, but they shared one factor—elderly parents living abroad. On the one hand, they tried by various means to exploit the fact to the benefit of the family; on the other hand, there were a lot of difficult tradeoffs and family conflict, especially as the needs of the elderly grew, and care had to be provided. The second generation was caught up in a balancing game between the needs of their parents, their own needs, and the needs of the third generation. Because I carried out my research entirely in South Korea, I was not able to speak to or observe the younger Sakhalin Koreans in their home environment. Yet, even the limited access I had to them in Home Village showed that there was no single attitude toward the senior generation, matters of elderly care, or the repatriation program. The variety in attitudes and solutions demonstrate that matters of intergenerational solidarity and filial piety are not fixed and are far from obvious. Moreover, the examination of the second generation shows the impact of the needs and interests of the junior generation on how intergenerational relationships are perceived and practiced.

At least some members of the second generation were extremely glad about their parents' move, for many different reasons. For some, but especially for those who left Sakhalin to settle in mainland Russia, Home Village was an excellent solution, since it was seen as a far safer place to live in than Sakhalin. Indeed, a number of elderly repatriates recounted to me tales of being robbed at knifepoint in their own homes back on Sakhalin. However, violent crime aside, the children thought that Home Village was simply better suited for the elderly since it had elevators, constant electricity (power shortages were common on Sakhalin) and other amenities, and a nurse on call. Simply put, with parents in South Korea there was less to worry about in Russia.

The other group of juniors glad for the move were those who could directly benefit from it. Usually those were the people who were unable to find work on Sakhalin. They were not permitted to work legally in Korea, but they found illegal employment in local factories or building sites or as cleaners, while staying rent-free with their parents. The money earned was often used to benefit the youngest generation—the grandchildren, in particular. Such money was used to support grandchildren's education, but it was also spent on day-to-day living expenses. Unfortunately, occasionally some of the adult children expected their parents to support them, without any effort on their part. This led to family conflicts and elder abuse.

There were also those members of the second generation of Sakhalin Koreans that came over to Home Village in order to look after their parent. Their situation was not easy. At the time of the original repatriation, there were virtually no provisions made for them. They could obtain a three-month visa to visit a healthy parent, or a twelve-month visa if the parent was ill and required assistance. Visiting members of the junior generation had no right to legal employment, access to health care, or the use of facilities at Home Village such as the gym. Those who combined work with caring or overstayed their visas lived in fear of deportation and a five-year ban on entering South Korea.

These children were crucial in the daily lives of their fragile parents, but remained invisible to the system. This helped to maintain a façade of a successful repatriation program, but had very serious consequences for the caregivers. They often found themselves extremely isolated, bewildered by a country that was essentially foreign to them, and poor, since it was not always possible to combine caregiving with illegal employment. This, especially for long-term caregivers, led to frustration and anger directed as much against stubborn parents who point-blank refused to move back to Sakhalin, and yet demanded their children's presence. Such was the case of the following caregiver, an eldest son looking after his widowed father in his nineties:

> Caregiver: Nobody ever stopped to think what it [repatriation] would mean for us. It is not fair! There is no justice in all of this. What were they thinking of when they built these bloody houses! Who did they think about? What they should have done is give the compensation to the old. They would have been happy if they got the money, and if they could visit Korea every year. But no! They had to come back. And what the hell am I supposed to do? And others like me? Just wait a couple of years, when people become even older. Nobody ever asked me what I want, and what it will mean to me, when I have to come over here and look after my father. I am risking my company. I am risking the employment of my workers. I miss my grandchildren. And they do nothing for us here. We have to come here to care, but there is no support. Nobody tells you anything. And how am I supposed to know how all of this works? I have to guess and ask for every single thing. This is not my country, and they treat us like dirt.

While not all caregivers were as bitter about the experience as this one, they often thought that looking after a parent in Korea had a negative impact on important relationships back on Sakhalin. Not only did it cause problems within marriages, but it also disrupted intergenerational relationships. On the one hand, caregivers by being absent missed out on the relationship with their grandchildren or children. On the other hand, the youngest generation had no or extremely limited opportunity to observe what it meant to look after an elderly grandparent. It was while discussing this matter with a Sakhalin Korean activist visiting South Korea that the idea of filial piety was mentioned directly the only time during my research. The repatriation program left much to be desired, although even here the voices of Sakhalin Koreans were divided. Some repatriates thought, as the activist did, that the repatriation should have included all the Sakhalin Koreans regardless of generation, while others thought that it should have been restricted to compensation. One of my elderly informants thought that the ideal solution would have been for Home Village with all its amenities and living allowance to be built on Sakhalin, so that they could live out the rest of their days in safety and comfort, without bothering anybody, but living close to their children and grandchildren.

Discussion

In a manner of speaking, the elderly repatriates in general wanted to have their cake and eat it too, desiring both to have the loving attention of their children and grandchildren, but without receiving any familial support that could prove to be an inconvenience or a burden to the junior generations. Loving respect was one thing, but to rely on the children was another. If there was an obligation of the children to help their parents, it was to be called on only in those cases where other resources and possibilities were exhausted. The repatriation program offered a wealth of such resources, but significantly limited and disrupted the possibility of back-up in form of filial care.

This problem was addressed by a 2008 change in law that permitted repatriation of those Sakhalin Koreans of the junior generation who had a living parent or grandparent of the first generation (Ministry of Foreign Affairs and Trade 2008).[8] However, most recent research suggests that this was not done much in practice. Following the change in the law, the attitudes of the elderly regarding the repatriation of their children changed. The elderly no longer thought it would be best for the children to come over to Korea. This was in part due to the local discrimination against Sakhalin Koreans and other members of the Korean diaspora from the former Soviet Union (Koryo Saram), and also because the change in the law came too late in the lives of the children of the repatriates. Too much would have to be sacrificed. As an elderly man argued in an interview with Din (2015) around 2009,

> When I think about whether repatriation of the whole Korean community is possible, I think that it would be possible if the whole generation sacrificed themselves. They would work in really low-level jobs, have no career and live like marginal outsiders. But for the second and third generations, who were born in Korea, it would be OK if they could live like other Koreans. The problem is who would make such a sacrifice? I understand why they don't want to do it. We here are already old; we don't feel bad here, we don't work, we live here in our own community. We also understand that such conditions for our children are not acceptable.
>
> In my opinion, it is impossible to consider emigration for all of us. I, for example, do not want my sons to work here. My first son worked in Korea for two years, but there is so much nationalism. . . . This is why I do not want my sons to be here, and they have not come for eight years already. They

work in Sakhalin. . . . Earlier I thought that if my wife and I came, the children should also come. But now such thinking has changed. Now none of us wants our children to live here. (Din 2015: 190)

The Sakhalin case makes for an interesting comparison with the model Chinese village described by Tang and Shea (chap. 1). In that case, there was a much smaller systematic geographic separation of elders from their descendants by a distance of across the road. This local Chinese policy innovation of adjacent houses separated by a road, together with collective village support for elders' basic needs, was enacted as a way to have just enough distance to maintain family harmony, while keeping open the opportunity for regular interaction. In that case, the separation was designed to maintain family harmony, whereas in the Sakhalin case the salutary effects of distance were an unintended side effect. In both cases, traditional norms of filial piety and family harmony did not always go hand in hand. In addition, in the China case the village collectively showing filial respect for its elders who had lived long lives of struggle was another value that was combined with the hope that younger generations would be kind and supportive toward their parents. In the Korean Sakhalin case the repatriation program was similarly a way for the Korean nation, in a limited capacity, to show belated deference to its elderly compatriots who had suffered under Japanese occupation.

The case of the repatriated Sakhalin elders also has interesting links with Min Zhang's chapter (3) on floating grandparents in China who sojourn in the big city to help their descendants there and Sun's chapter (6) on international caregiving among Taiwanese adults who moved to the United States, leaving their parents behind in Taiwan. In each case, family members are moving long distances, in two cases internationally and in one domestically, with periodic intergenerational reunification but away from the hometown. In all of these cases, aging parents are sacrificing something in the interest of their descendants. Thus, what is happening with Sakhalin Korean families sacrificing to help and not burden their children may go beyond the influence of Russian culture to the value placed on youths and descendants in times of rapid social change, be it in Russian-influenced Korea populations or Chinese or Taiwanese groups.

Conclusion

Clearly, when thinking about the question of filial piety, intergenerational relations, and care, it is essential to bear in mind the fact that intergenerational relations are just that: a two-way relationship between children and their parents. To only consider the obligations of children toward their parents is to miss half the context. As the case of Sakhalin Korean repatriates and their children shows, care is present on both halves of the equation. The elderly are caring as much, if not more, for the children as the children care for the elderly. Care and caring can mean many things, but for Sakhalin Korean elders above all it meant pursuing what they considered in the best interest of their loved ones as a whole, not just for themselves. Given the changing circumstances, what was considered best was dynamic. Any notions of filial piety do not exist in a vacuum. This norm, like every other norm, is bound to come into conflict with other competing moral values. In the case of Sakhalin Koreans, it came into conflict with family harmony, family solidarity, and parental responsibility. It is how such conflicts are resolved or avoided that tell us the most about what is considered to be a good and moral way to live in a constantly changing world with new challenges and possibilities.

In certain contexts in East Asia, filial piety may turn into a stereotype-based slogan, which assumes certain norms and practices as given and automatic. That stereotype may prove to be an obstacle to policy planners trying to understand the everyday reality of being an elderly person requiring care (or indeed caring for others), or a junior from whom care might be expected. Filial piety is a set of practices based on a set of idealized norms, but these practices are not fixed, and the norms do not exist in a timeless, unchanging, orientalist vacuum. People are subject to moral norms, but it is also people who over time create, adapt, question, or even reject those norms. Just as one questions the orientalist image of the submissive Asian woman, one should be careful with the picture-postcard notions of filial piety, devoted sons, and benevolent and yet passive and dependent elders.

Acknowledgments

I would like to thank the inhabitants of Home Village where I did my research. Their warmth, generosity, hospitality, patience, and trust were invaluable. Korea Foundation generously provided a fellowship that enabled me to complete the research process.

Dorota Szawarska is a faculty member at the Institute of Applied Social Sciences, University of Warsaw, Poland. Her work has appeared in a variety of scholarly journals and edited volumes including *Przegląd Socjologii Jakościowej* (2018), *Roczniki Socjologii Rodziny* (2017), *Handbook of the Philosophy of Medicine* (2017), *Ethnographies of Social Support* (Schlecker and

Fleischer 2013), and in *In Vitro: Dziecko, in vitro, społeczeństwo,* (Krawczak et al. 2018), among others. Her newest, coauthored book is *Employing People with Disabilities—Good Organisational Practices and Socio-Cultural Conditions* (Giermanowska, Racław, and Szawarska 2020).

Glossary

chesa	제사 or 祭祀	Remembrance ceremony for one's ancestors following their death.
Koryo Saram	고려 사람	Reference to Korean diaspora from former Soviet Union.

Notes

1. Because this is the largest settlement of Sakhalin Koreans in South Korea, there is little point in giving it a fictitious name. Home Village is the direct translation of its Korean name, Kohyangmaŭl. I have given all the informants pseudonyms, however. In their contacts with me Sakhalin Koreans used Russian names, this is reflected in the pseudonyms I provide them with in the article. This was a habit brought over from Russia where in their daily lives, in their contacts with non-Koreans, they used Russian names that they chose for themselves, much as South Korean immigrants or students in the United Kingdom or United States today choose an English name in their contacts with non-Koreans. Interestingly, second generation Sakhalin Koreans also used Russian names between themselves, while the Korean names under which they were registered remained a formality to be used in important documents.
2. This chapter is based on research generously supported by the Korea Foundation.
3. Despite high standards, the Incheon and Ansan nursing homes were not very popular. The director of the Incheon one complained that she did not understand why she could not fill the available slots. It was probably due to two reasons. First, there was still something shameful about an elderly parent being placed in a nursing home in the eyes of first- and second-generation Sakhalin Koreans. Second, people repatriated to Home Village received a state retirement allowance, and had space to host children and grandchildren during stints of illegal labor in Korea.
4. This is a sentiment also present in contemporary South Korea. See Cheong-Seok Kim and Ka-Oak Rhee (1997: 199); Dong-Ok Lee et al. (2008: 78, 81); Prendergast (2005: 55).
5. See Janelli and Yim (1993: 27) on children keeping parents ignorant of matters that might be a cause of worry to the senior generation.
6. Scholars such as Grayson (2002) or K. Lee (1997) see Confucianism as the main principle organizing family life in Korea. But there is evidence that the spread and acceptance of Confucianism were far from uniform in the history of Korean culture and people. For examples see Hart (2003); and Yoo (1998: 129–32).

7. Oddly enough, the Korean name of the association does not contain the word Sakhalin, but the English language version of the name, taken from the business cards of the representatives of the association, does.
8. According to the Korean Ministry of Foreign Affairs and Trade (2008), from 2008 on members of the second generation of Sakhalin Koreans are permitted to move to South Korea together with their parents. The change in policy was made for humanitarian reasons.

References

Caldwell, Melissa L. 2004. *Not by Bread Alone: Social Support in the New Russia.* Berkeley: University of California Press.

———. 2007. "Elder Care in the New Russia: The Changing Face of Compassionate Social Security." *Focaal: European Journal of Anthropology* 50: 66–80.

Choi, Ki-Young. 2004. "Forced Migration of Koreans to Sakhalin and Their Repatriation." *Korea Journal* 44 (4): 111–32.

Chung, Gene-Woong. 2001. "Elders in the Family and the Strain of the Discourse of Filial Piety." *Korea Journal* 40 (4): 144–58.

Din, Yulia. 2015. "Dreams of Returning to the Homeland: Koreans in Karafuto and Sakhalin." In *Voices from the Shifting Russo-Japanese Border: Karafuto / Sakhalin,* ed. Svetlana Paichadze and Philip A. Seaton, 177–94. New York: Routledge.

Grayson, James. 2002. *Korea: A Religious History.* London: Routledge Curzon.

Hart, Dennis. 2003. *From Tradition to Consumption: Construction of a Capitalist Culture in South Korea.* Seoul, Korea: Jimoondang.

Ikels, Charlotte, ed. 2004. *Filial Piety: Practice and Discourse in Contemporary East Asia.* Stanford, CA: Stanford University Press.

Janelli, Roger L., and Dawnhee Yim. 1993. *Making Capitalism: The Social and Cultural Construction of a South Korean Conglomerate.* Stanford, CA: Stanford University Press.

———. 2004. "The Transformation of Filial Piety in Contemporary South Korea." In Ikels, *Filial Piety,* 128–52.

Kim, Cheong-Seok, and Ka-Oak Rhee. 1997. "Variations in Preferred Living Arrangements among Korean Elderly Parents." *Journal of Cross-Cultural Gerontology* 12 (2): 189–202.

Kleinman, Arthur. 2010. "Caregiving: Its Role in Medicine and Society in America and China." *Ageing International* 35 (2): 96–108.

Lee, Dong-Ok, Cho Uhn, and Chang Pilwha. 2008. "Uncomfortable Transit from Care Giving to Care Receiving: Elderly Women Encounter the Problematic Reciprocity of Caring." *Korea Journal* 48 (4): 60–92.

Lee, Jaehyuck. 2003. "Rational Rendering of Confucian Relationships in Contemporary Korea." *Korea Journal* 43 (2): 257–88.

Lee, Jeanyoung. 2001. *Ethnic Korean Migration in Northeast Asia.* Retrieved 30 April 2007 from http://gsti.miis.edu/CEAS-PUB/200108Lee.pdf.

Lee, Kwang-kyu. 1997. *Korean Family and Kinship.* Seoul, Korea: Jimoondang.

Lee, Kwang-kyu, and Joseph P. Linsky, eds. 2003. *Korean Traditional Culture.* Seoul, Korea: Jimoondang.

Ministry of Foreign Affairs and Trade, Korea (MOFAT). 2008. "Koreans in Sakhalin to Permanently Return Home in 2008." Retrieved 5 March 2020 from http://www .mofa.go.kr/eng/brd/m_5676/view.do?seq=307042#btnPrint.

Prendergast, David. 2005. *From Elder to Ancestor: Old Age, Death and Inheritance in Modern Korea*. Folkestone: Global Oriental.

Roudakova, Natalia, and Deborah S. Ballard-Reisch. 1999. "Femininity and the Double Burden: Dialogues on the Socialization of Russian Daughters into Womanhood." *Anthropology of East Europe Review* 17 (1): 21–34.

Sung, Kyu-Taik. 2000. "An Asian Perspective on Aging East and West: Filial Piety and Changing Families." In *Aging in East and West—Families, States, and the Elderly* ed. Vern L. Bengtson, Kyong-Dong Kim, George C. Myers, Ki-Soo Eun. 41–56. New York: Springer.

———. 2005. *Care and Respect for the Elderly in Korea*. Paju-si, Gyeonggido, Korea: Jimoondang.

Sung, Sirin. 2003. "Women Reconciling Paid and Unpaid Work in a Confucian Welfare State: The Case of South Korea." *Social Policy & Administration*. 37 (4): 342–60.

Szawarska, Dorota. 2013. "'Who Will Love You if They Have to Look after You': Sakhalin Koreans Caring from a Distance." In *Ethnographies of Social Support*, ed. Markus Schlecker and Friederike Fleischer, 39–58. New York: Palgrave Macmillan.

Yoo, Myung-Ki. 1998. "Community and Kinship in a Southern Korean Village." In *Anthropology of Korea: East Asian Perspectives*, eds Mutsuhiko Shima and Roger L. Janelli, 129–38. Osaka: National Museum of Ethnology.

12 EXPANSION OF END-OF-LIFE CARE SERVICES IN SOUTH KOREA

A Qualitative Analysis of the Experiences of Family Caregivers and Hospice Staff

Sooyoun Han and Jeanne Shea

Introduction

A MAJORITY OF SENIORS IN Korea today die not in their private homes, as was traditional, but in intensive care units, hospitals for acute or skilled nursing care, or long-term care (LTC) facilities, often undergoing severe suffering induced by futile and costly medical procedures (Korean Statistical Information Service [KOSIS] 2018). In this chapter, we examine the need for, promise of, and challenges for implementing hospice care in Korea from family and staff perspectives. We begin with contextual information and then analyze the results of two research studies conducted in South Korea by the first author, one on family caregivers' experiences of end-of-life (EOL) care, and the second on hospice staff experiences of hospice and patient death. Overall, the analysis finds a large need for improved and expanded EOL services in Korea and both promise and challenges for implementing the hospice model in Korea. At times, contemporary Korean interpretations of filial piety and "good care" clash with standard hospice practice. In addition, hospice discourse of patient and family EOL decision-making for a "good death" often neglects constraints beyond their control. Staff strive to achieve hospice norms and ideals, and succeed with some but struggle with others. The analysis draws on critical theory regarding biopower in EOL practices (Foucault 1991), globalization theory apropos local adoption of the international hospice model, and interpretivism regarding meanings of EOL care (for theory, see Introduction).

The chapter begins with background based on a review of the literature concerning the demographics of aging in South Korea, the extent of futile EOL treatment there, Korean familial and staff engagement with EOL issues, and the expansion of EOL services in Korea over time culminating in recent nationwide legislation. Then it examines the results of our Korean family caregivers' research, addressing topics including exclusion of patients from decisions, difficulties in decision-making, second-guessing prognosis and course of action, and confusion concerning life-sustaining treatments, comfort care, and hospice care. Next, it presents results of the hospice staff study, exploring staff perceptions of adequacy of their training and preparation for supporting patients and families through dying and for dealing with the stress of patient death. We conclude by putting these findings into regional context and recommending adaptations for building local hospice culture and structural supports for caregivers and staff.

Review of the Literature: Demographic, Policy, and Sociocultural Context

In examining scholarly literature on EOL care in South Korea, first we review the need for EOL services and evolution of government involvement in legislating senior service provisions. Then we address sociocultural issues related to EOL in Korean society and outline some key scholarly findings on the EOL experiences of Korean family caregivers and of EOL care staff.

South Korea has the most rapidly aging population in the world today (see also Introduction). The elderly there are living longer than ever before. Life expectancy at birth (UN 2017) in South Korea has risen for both genders to 82.44 years of age. Life expectancy at age sixty-five has also risen for both genders, such that those who make it to age sixty-five can expect on average to live until age 83.4 for males and age 87.6 for females (Organisation for Economic Co-Operation and Development 2019). In terms of healthy life expectancy at birth, the World Health Organization (2018) recently estimated that, as of 2016, on average South Koreans will be healthy until 73.0 years of age. Accelerated growth in the old-old population age eighty years and older, together with extremely low fertility rates accompanying economic development, is turning South Korea into a super-aging society set to surpass Japan in the next twenty-six years (UN 2017). Along with the blessing of rising longevity, increasing numbers of Koreans require many years of care in their last decade of life.

Due to these demographic changes, there is a large and growing need for services for the elderly in South Korea today. In health care and LTC, the nation has long been proactive (National Health Insurance Service [NHIS] 2019). In 1988 Korea established a national health-care plan to guarantee universal coverage for life-sustaining or health-enhancing medical treatment. In 2008 Korea rolled out a national LTC plan that now offers full coverage for LTC services with copayments of 20 percent to qualifying participants, regardless of patient income or assets. LTC facilities there provide physical therapy and nursing care to maintain or improve mental and physical functioning in elders who reside long term in nursing homes or senior congregate housing operated by an LTC institution.

Still, eldercare in Korea remains highly reliant on familial care due to reasons of cultural familism and lack of extensive nonfamilial LTC resources. The cultural value of filial piety (*hyo*) (see also Introduction) has long played a profound role in South Korea (Ikels 2004; Janelli and Yim 2004; Sorenson and Kim 2004). To the present, the family remains the backbone of eldercare, providing emotional, instrumental, and financial support for elderly kin (Kim and Han 2013). Most of those aged eighty and over who need daily assistance but do not qualify for LTC services remain in the care of their families, and recently a mere 5.9 percent of elderly citizens in South Korea were lodged in LTC facilities (LTC Insurance Act, Article 1, National Health *Insurance* Corporation 2019). Surveys show (Ministry of Health and Welfare [MHW] 2017), that about half of Korean elderly think that family members should be primarily responsible for meeting their daily needs (MHW 2017). Urban seniors expect more governmental support than rural seniors do, but many elders view receiving government aid, in lieu of family support, as a disgrace on the family (MHW 2017).

Despite enduring emphasis on familial home care, research shows that most deaths in South Korea do not take place at home. This relates to rapid growth over the past several decades in biomedical institutions and procedures, and to the idea that biomedical treatments represent "good care." Almost three-quarters (73 percent) of Korean seniors die in intensive care units, hospitals for acute or skilled nursing care, or LTC facilities (Korean Statistical Information Service 2013). Examining death records for more than 2 million older South Koreans from 2001 to 2014, Mai et al. (2018) found almost 58 percent of deaths took place in a hospital, with an increase in hospital deaths from a little over 31 percent in 2001 to over 75 percent in 2014. Over that time, about 32 percent of Korean seniors' deaths took place at home, falling from about 60 percent in 2001 to about 16 percent in 2014 (16). By contrast, recent U.S. figures show 40 percent of American seniors die at home (20 percent) or in nursing homes (20 percent) (Stanford School of Medicine 2019) rather than in hospitals.

Studies show a high rate of futile EOL procedures in South Korea, but low patient desire for such. A recent review by Cardona-Morrell et al. (2016) showed widespread use of futile treatments at EOL in Korea. Large-scale surveys examined by Yun et al. (2018) and Heo (2013) found that most Koreans are in favor of active pain control and comfort care and withdrawal of futile treatment aimed at prolonging life. One national survey found 88.9 percent of Korean elders hold such preferences (Kim 2015). Yet, many Korean elders stay far longer in acute care facilities than they had intended, enduring treatments they had not wanted. Research attributes this to a mixture of low sociocultural recognition of elderly patients' agency, family concerns about being seen as unfilial or uncaring, ideas that medical treatment represents "best care," insurance coverage for life-sustaining procedures, under-developed hospice infrastructure, and decades lacking adequate legislation or coverage for EOL care and decisions (EOLCD) (Han 2019b).

With regard to EOL services in South Korea, from the mid-1960s to 2002 they were sparse and were mainly provided by volunteers doing religious or community service. Australian nuns in a small Catholic old-folks home founded the first hospice in Korea in 1965, but the concept was slow to spread (Ro 2018). In early decades, the focus was largely on cancer deaths. From 2003 to 2005 the government began to take a more active role, sponsoring a small-scale inpatient hospital-based hospice pilot program "to develop a per-diem payment system" (Kwon 2013: 55). Gradually, EOL services have been gaining more structural presence; however, infrastructure remains underdeveloped. In 2008 the National Health Insurance Service (NHIS) began to cover EOL inpatient pain management and counseling (Rhee 2015). In 2012 the government made progress in designating forty-four palliative care centers, but demand outstripped supply (Kwon 2013). By 2014 hospice was offered by fifty-four facilities of various types in Korea, with 866 total hospice beds (table 12.1), with religious and charity organizations still the largest providers. Despite improvement, with a national population of more than 50 million, this meant that only 13.2 percent of end-stage cancer patients and only 3 percent of the total dying population in Korea had a chance at a hospice slot (An et al. 2014).

Further progress in EOL care has occurred from 2015 on. In 2015 Korea unveiled the Act on Decisions on Life-Sustaining Treatment for Patients in

TABLE 12.1. Status of Hospice Services in South Korea, 2014.

Administration	Number of Facilities	Number of Beds
Religious hospice organization	25	440
Public hospital	12	209
Regional cancer organization	12	154
Hospice unit in private medical center	3	32
Designated hospice organization	2	31

Source: National Hospice Palliative Association, Korea 2016.

Hospice and Palliative Care at the End of Life (Act 14013), hereafter the Act or the 2015 Act (Kim and Choi 2017; Korean Legislation Research Institute 2016). The Act expanded qualifying conditions beyond cancer.[1] In July 2015 Korea's NHI began to cover inpatient hospice care in medical or hospice facilities, with full or partial reimbursement (Economist Intelligence Unit [EIU] 2015; Rhee 2015). With that, some advance care planning, information on hospice and EOL care, and family caregiver counseling became available. In 2016 Korea enacted, and in mid-2017 began to partially enforce, the Act. Enactment of all parts began in February 2018, when amendments were added (Ministry of Government Legislation, Korea [MGL] 2018, MHW 2018d).[2] Stemming from the Act, since 2015 the number of hospice inpatient users has gradually increased (Lim et al. 2018). Today, eighty-one inpatient institutions, twenty counsel institutions, eleven inpatient institutions at geriatric hospitals, and twenty-five homecare agencies operate under the Act (National Hospice Center, Korea [NHC] 2018). Inpatient institutions may provide EOL care through doctors, nurses, health aides, social workers, therapists, clergy, and/or volunteers (MHW 2018a). Counsel institutions help hospital teams to cooperate with the attending physician and offer discharge services to link providers inside and outside network (MHW 2017; MHW 2018c). Homecare agencies may provide care in the patient's home with 24/7 on-call nurse service by phone or in person, although such home services are not covered by insurance (MHW 2018b). Current training requirements require all core staff for inpatient institutions to take certification courses of more than sixty hours of MHW-approved training. Staff for counsel institutions and homecare agencies need seventy-six hours of training (MHW 2018b).

This is progress, but there is still much room for improvement. Most hospice care in Korea is done inpatient in acute-care and geriatric hospitals. Home-based hospice, although available as of 2016, is not covered by insurance. Lack of coverage extends to patients in LTC residential facilities, which are considered "home-care" cases, not inpatient. In addition, patients in hospice facilities requiring acute or emergency care must transfer to a hospital, generally through the emergency department and acute care channels, risking futile medical procedures. This is so regardless of patients' prior care decisions. Furthermore, there are concerns about infrastructural adequacy, raising doubt about capacity to ramp up to accommodate the 14.2–19.0 percent old-old population age eighty and older projected for the period from 2050 to 2080, up from 3.6 percent in 2020 (UN 2017).

Beyond limits on government provisions, sociocultural considerations complicate EOL in Korea, conflicting with assumptions of patient agency and autonomy in international hospice discourse flowing from its UK birthplace. The strong family orientation of Korean culture leads to a collective approach to dying. End of life (*salm-ui kkeu*) in Korean refers to the shared EOL experiences of the dying patient and their family from life's end stage to the moment of death. Family caregivers in Korea tend to be heavily involved in EOLCD. Studies show that even when Korean seniors wish to make their own EOL decisions, their families often intervene because leaving things up to the patient can seem like abandoning the filial responsibility to beneficently make the best decisions for them (Kim and Han 2013; Park and Song 2013). Even when Korean seniors are mentally, emotionally, and physically capable of making their own decisions, Korean families often resist. Families fear that what seniors claim to want may not be what they really want. They want to shield their elders from the harsh realities of EOLCD. They fear that elderly patients may not have the knowledge or understanding to make the best choice. Often family members disagree over the best course, causing conflict. While studies show that most Korean seniors ideally would like to make their own EOL decisions and forgo life-prolonging treatment at the end of life, some Korean elders prefer in practice to delegate decisions to the family even if they themselves are capable of making decisions (Hong and Kim 2013). Finally, fear of family conflict over EOLCD has led some Korean seniors to commit suicide, finding that preferable to familial negotiations required to access palliative and hospice care services in the current system (Chang 2013).

At present, many studies on EOL issues conducted in South Korea have focused on the family caregivers' experiences in using intensive care (Kim et al. 2012; Kim, Kang, and Kim 2012), LTC facilities (Park and Song 2013), or hospice care units (Keam et al. 2014) for elderly kin. Some have described the difficulties of Korean family caregivers faced with the decision to withdraw life-sustaining treatments for terminally ill and unconscious patients (Kim, Kang, and Kim. 2012). A much smaller number of studies have focused on Korean patients' own experiences of EOL (Kim, June, and Son 2016; Kim et al. 2012; Yun et al 2018). A common finding is that Korean seniors and their families lack knowledge and understanding of EOL and related decision-making, complicating matters and adding stress and suffering (Han 2016; Hong and Kim 2013; Keam et al. 2014; Kim 2016).

Other scholarship has begun to examine experiences in providing EOL care of Korean medical and nonmedical hospice staff (Cho and Lim 2017; Han 2019a; Kim, Cho, and Kwon 2016; S. Shim 2016; Yi and Lee 2016; and Yun et al. 2018). Many such studies in Korea examine anxiety and stress in doctors, nurses, other hired hospice staff, or hospice volunteers (Lee and Park 2017; Yang and Kwon 2015). Some have pointed to lack of sufficient knowledge and skills concerning EOL care among professional staff tasked with such (e.g., Koh et al. 2018). Others have shown that, contrary to hospice ideals, Korean physicians have a tendency to avoid communicating with patients and their families about EOL in order to avoid the possibility of lawsuits from family (Heo 2013). It is hoped that full enactment of the Act in 2018 and increased training for hired staff and volunteers will help ease this problem in time.

Methods

Our data are derived from two original qualitative interview-based studies conducted by the first author and analyzed by both authors. The first is a pilot study with family caregivers, and the second is a study with hospice staff, all designed and conducted by the first author in South Korea. In the next section, we describe the methods for each of these studies.[3]

Methods for Family Caregiver Study on End-of-Life Decision-Making

The family caregiver study of EOLCD aimed to answer the following questions: What are family caregivers' experiences of EOLCD in South Korea? To what extent are the assumptions and practices of a hospice model a good fit? To answer these questions, qualitative interviews were conducted with Korean family caregivers concerning their experiences of EOLCD for elderly kin with end-stage cancer. Participants were recruited through one faith-based organization, which has a hospice volunteer program affiliated with an inpatient hospice facility in the community. The purposive sample sought family caregivers who were actively involved in EOLCD for an elderly family member in cases in which aggressive cancer treatment had been terminated. The study focused on caregivers' experiences of the process of deciding to reduce, shorten, or end life-sustaining treatments and to adopt hospice care.

The interviews were conducted with Korean family caregivers a year after their family member's passing. Interviews took place in the early 2010s before the Act. After an orientation, six caregivers each took part in an individual one-on-one semi-structured interview. Each of the family caregiver interviews took at least one and a half hours and was audiotaped and transcribed verbatim. While our emphasis was on hearing caregivers' stories, there were a few preset interview questions, including (1) When was the first time you engaged in the process of EOLCD for your elderly family member? (2) What was your role throughout the process of EOLCD? (3) What was your understanding about your decisions on behalf of your elderly relative? Participants were also asked about their age, relation to the patient, whether any patient-led advance planning was involved, who participated in EOLCD, the degree of mental acuity and physical

TABLE 12.2. Characteristics of Family Caregivers and Deceased Care Recipients.

	Family Caregiver			Deceased Elderly Care Recipient		
Case	Pseudonym	Age	Relation	Hospice care duration	Mental acuity	Pain
F1	Mi-sook	56	Daughter	6 months	4	4
F2	Kyung-ok	61	Daughter-in-law	2 months	4	6
F3	Jung-hee	53	Daughter-in-law	2 months	1	6
F4	Soon-ja	65	Wife	20 days	4	3

Source: Author data.

pain of the patient when EOLCD were made, and how long the patient received hospice care.

Following interview transcription, participants were given the opportunity to review their own transcripts, at which time two interviewees decided to withdraw from the study. That left us with four cases and six hours of interview material for analysis (table 12.2). We had hoped to include more participants, but the emotional intensity of the issues involved made recruiting and retention difficult. Although this is a small number of cases, we were able to glean some important information about Korean family caregivers' experiences with EOL care. Furthermore, the patterns of experience discovered in these interviews reflect patterns observed by the first author in her many years working as a social worker in the community with nongovernmental organizations (NGOs) and families in Korea on EOL issues. Qualitative data analysis was conducted following an iterative process of constant comparison to look for themes and for similarities and differences across cases.

In terms of characteristics of the final sample (table 12.2), the caregivers ranged in age from fifty-three to sixty-five years of age. All caregivers were female. With respect to their relation to the deceased, they included one spouse, one daughter, and two daughters-in-law. All caregivers were recruited through a religious organization and reported being religious. Duration of hospice care ranged from twenty days to six months. As described by the caregivers retrospectively, mental acuity of three of the four patients was quite good, as measured on a Likert scale with one representing little patient understanding of their prognosis and five full understanding of their prognosis. On a scale of one to ten, where one represents little pain and ten represents the worst possible pain, physical pain of the patients as judged by their caregivers was moderate.

Methods for Hospice Staff Study

The hospice staff study was aimed at answering the following questions: What are hospice staff experiences of providing hospice care and experiencing patient death in Korea? According to staff, how is the quality of hospice care in Korea, and how might it be improved? To what extent are the assumptions and practices of the hospice model a good fit? What requires more tailoring to fit this sociocultural context? To answer these questions, qualitative interviews were conducted with seventeen hospice staff. Participants included eight medical staff comprising four doctors and four nurses. It also included nine nonmedical staff comprising three social workers and two therapists, two clergy, and two volunteers. Recruitment was done via purposive sampling by contacting institutions involved in hospice care. The hospice staff interviews took place after the Act was unveiled but before full enactment and lasted one to one and a half hours per person. Interviews covered staffers' views of and attitudes toward death and their experiences of attending to dying patients and coping with patient death. If anything was unclear after transcription, interviewees were contacted by phone for clarification. Results were analyzed using qualitative coding.

Sample-wise, fourteen of the staff were female and three male (table 12.3). They ranged in age from their thirties to their seventies. Staff had worked in a variety of different hospice settings, including inpatient in acute care hospitals, inpatient in geriatric hospitals, counsel hospice (referrals in and out of institutions by an attending physician), and/or home hospice. Hospice experience ranged from less than a year to more than fifteen years. Twelve had experienced a death in their own family. All but three reported affiliation with religion, either Christianity or Buddhism.

Results: Korean Family Caregivers' Experiences of End-of-Life Care Decision-Making

The caregivers interviewed reported that families did not adhere to international hospice norms that stress the agency and wishes of the patient in facing death. The interviews showed that none of the patients had prepared an advance directive, and none participated in EOLCD at the time of end-stage cancer diagnosis, even though three of the four had a solid understanding of their prognosis. Instead, it was considered the role of filial family members to protect elders from the seriousness of their diagnosis and to free them from the burden of making medical decisions and EOLCD. Medical staff framed EOL matters as the decision of the family, not

TABLE 12.3. General Characteristics of Staff Participating in the Hospice Staff Study.

Case #	Hospice Staff	Age	Gender	Hospice Type	Profession	Experience of Death in Own Family	Career (years)	Religion
H1		60+	F	Inpatient hospital	Doctor	Y	<1	Catholicism
H2		30+	M	Counsel	Doctor	Y	5+	None
H3		30+	M	Inpatient hospital	Doctor	N	3+	Catholicism
H4	Medical staff	50+	F	Inpatient GH	Doctor	Y	2+	Buddhism
H5		40+	F	Counsel	Nurse	Y	5+	None
H6		50+	F	Inpatient hospital	Nurse	N	5+	Catholicism
H7		30+	F	Inpatient hospital	Nurse	N	2+	Protestantism
H8		50+	F	Home	Nurse	Y	5+	Protestantism
H9		70+	F	Inpatient hospital	Clergy	Y	15+	Catholicism
H10		40+	F	Inpatient GH	Clergy	Y	3+	Buddhism
H11		60+	F	Inpatient hospital	Volunteer	Y	15+	Catholicism
H12		40+	F	Inpatient hospital	Therapist	Y	8+	Catholicism
H13	Nonmedical staff	70+	F	Home	Therapist	Y	15+	Protestantism
H14		40+	F	Inpatient GH	Volunteer	N	1+	Buddhism
H15		40+	M	Inpatient hospital	Social worker	N	5+	None
H16		40+	F	Inpatient hospital	Social worker	Y	2+	Protestantism
H17		30+	F	Home	Social worker	Y	2+	Protestantism

Source: Author data. Note: GH = geriatric hospital.

the patient. Family members often thought themselves to be ill-equipped to make these decisions, because they did not understand what the physicians told them. Caregivers were uncertain about the correctness of forgoing life-prolonging procedures, but also felt regret for suffering resulting from steps to prolong life. With hospice facilities underdeveloped and even inpatient hospice services not yet fully funded by NHI at the time of this study, family members often thought that hospice was not providing adequate care. Lacking at-home hospice care, family members caring for their dying relative at home struggled with issues of safety. The first author is a gerontologist in Korea, and based on her observations all of these occurrences were typical at the time of this study, and remain common.

While EOLCD were framed by medical staff as the family's decision, interviews showed that family caregivers believed on many levels that they lacked the tools to be able to understand and weigh the options and make a truly informed decision. While caregivers did receive information about the patient's condition and treatment options, they often did not understand the medical terminology that the physician used to describe patients' condition and prognosis, the available medical options and their relative risks and potential benefits, and/or the palliative care options. Yet, caregivers were pressured to make a decision about next steps in a very short period, without room to ask the physician for sufficient clarification or to consult other sources. As a result, for the most part, family caregivers had to simply follow the doctor's judgment.

Kyung-ok: I heard that my mother in law had only two months or less left. The physician explained that the cancer had already spread to several organs, and he did not recommend surgery. He showed the numbers from the tumor marker test and computed tomography scan test. I did not understand what the numbers meant. I asked him how he would decide for his mother in the same situation. He shared his own story of choosing less aggressive treatment for his father, with only medications to control the pain. His medical opinion was critical. It was the only option for us. (F2)

Soon-ja: My husband deteriorated rapidly during the cancer therapy. His physician advised me to prepare his end and referred him to a hospice program. He [my husband] passed away just twenty days after admission to the hospice unit. The process went too fast to prepare for his end. It was a frightening moment. I had to depend on the physician's decision given the urgent situation. (F4)

As in Soon-ja's case, entering hospice too late to fully benefit is common, and is related to tendencies to isolate treatment and palliation, and the fear that hospice will hasten death.

However much caregivers relied on the attending physician's judgement, they also frequently found themselves questioning that same judgement. They were often uncertain about the accuracy of medical declarations that EOL had been reached. Caregivers often found themselves second-guessing. Especially when patients' abilities varied from one day to the next, caregivers were confused and worried that the physician had misjudged. This led caregivers to question their decision to withdraw life-sustaining treatment.

Mi-sook: I was confused by her condition. My mother was in good enough condition to attend my son's wedding ceremony and even to endure the long-distance trip with the family to get there, with an "end-stage" cancer diagnosis. I prayed for guidance about her end of life. I could not stop the questions that came into my head about "Was her physician misdiagnosing her?" or "Was I missing a critical time for surgery?" I could not sleep at all with all of the anxiety surrounding these questions. Finally, I brought her to try acupuncture therapy for twenty days. These ideas came up for me on and off during her last six months. Actually, I am still anxious about these questions. (F1)

The caregivers strongly believed that elderly patients would be highly distressed by participation in EOLCD. Caregivers said that being diagnosed with cancer, dementia, and/or other incurable diseases was stigmatized in Korean society. As a result, caregivers wanted to protect ailing kin from having to confront their diagnosis. Even though three of the four patients were clear about their condition and prognosis, family caregivers considered it taboo to discuss the patient's illness in front of them. They considered it their filial duty to try to shield the patient from exposure or re-exposure to bad news about their health, while at the same time having painful mixed feelings about doing so.

Mi-sook: My mother has devoted her life to raising her children without her husband. I do not want to let her confront her bad fortune again. I forced the physician to keep her out of the end-of-life care decision-making process. Sometimes I was curious what my mother's preference would be. She made a decision to surgically replace both of her knees around ten years ago regardless of my protests. But, regarding the EOLCD making process, my wish was to shield her this time. However, [it was hard to keep the decision-making to myself, because] I felt like I was all alone. (F1)

Kyung-ok: My husband and three brothers-in-law decided to keep my mother-in-law away from the end-of-life care decision-making process. They were deeply concerned that she might feel shame for being diagnosed with end-stage cancer. She always talked to us about and blessed God for her healthy and good life. They kept her condition a secret to maintain her confidence during her end stage. So we decided to extend her hospitalization [and life-sustaining treatment back] in her home town. But whenever she complained about the long hospitalization, I felt sorry for her that she was not able to have time to reconcile herself with her life and wrap things up for her end. (F2)

The one spousal caregiver, Soon-ja, talked about wanting to make the decision alone to spare both her dying husband and her children from the weight of the decision about withdrawing treatment. This mirrors the ideal circulating among aging parents in East Asia of not troubling the children (e.g., see chap. 2). This caregiver was influenced by the prior experience that she and her brother had with their own father's sickness.

Soon-ja: My husband's physician referred him to the hospice program. I thought, I have to be the only person to make this decision. I did not want to lay a painful emotional burden on my children. I experienced my father's long hospitalization and the related financial burden, and how my brother decided to discontinue treatment in the end. [Although my brother made the decision,] I still suffered mentally due to it. [So] I am glad to take this role for my husband instead of [burdening] my children. (F4)

Caregivers expressed mixed feelings about comfort care and confusion concerning other treatments. They had difficulty reconciling themselves with the hospice notion of letting go of disease treatment as "good care." All caregivers recounted times of deeply regretting giving up aggressive cancer therapy. While clear that they had decided to withdraw cancer therapy and pursue comfort care, they were unclear about how other treatments might fit into the picture. They had not been informed about the complications of choosing treatments such as cardiopulmonary resuscitation (CPR), artificial feeding, or respiratory ventilation. One daughter-in-law ended up requesting CPR on her mother-in-law hoping that she would get to see her son again before she passed. She had not expected the extreme pain that her mother-in-law would suffer as a result and how short a time she would live after CPR.

Jung-hee: My mother-in-law got CPR when she was hospitalized. I had asked the staff to do CPR on her. I had expected that she would be surrounded by family members, but I was the only person at her bedside at the time. I wish that she could have seen her son in her last moments. She suffered so much pain after the CPR [and died before her son could arrive]. I was embarrassed that my decision was futile. (F3)

Participants were dissatisfied with the material conditions of hospice facilities and perceived that staff could be neglectful and disrespectful. For example, the spousal caregiver said that staff acted as though they had given up on her husband and did not treat him with respect. Yet, she felt that she could not complain, because it had been she who had "given up" on his care by choosing hospice. The "comfort care" that she had chosen did not make her husband's last days comfortable, because the setting and care did not meet his expectations.

Soon-ja: I bitterly regretted my decision to transfer my husband to an in-patient hospice facility. It was shabby and in poor condition. I felt the staff treated us disrespectfully. This might not be the truth, but I felt like I was insulted. But I could not express any resentment for their attitudes since I had given up on his care, too. I wish that he could have been comfortable during his end stage of life. (F4)

Another participant, in trying to handle her mother's EOL care by herself at home, found herself lacking sufficient understanding of the effects of pain medications or how to toilet a patient on them. This was despite how she herself had been trained as a hospice volunteer. In focusing on using medications to control her mother's pain and not adequately balancing other considerations, she was concerned that she had inadvertently caused her more pain.

Mi-sook: I had trained as a hospice volunteer [in a program] administered by my church. I was pretty confident [that I could] . . . care for my mother by myself in my house. From the first day, I could not even manage to help her go to the toilet properly. She and I fell down on our knees on the floor. It was a laughably foolish moment. I had heard that pain medication could cause lethargy [but I didn't understand what that meant]. I was mostly anxious about controlling her pain. In the end, she was admitted to the emergency room with unbearable pain. (F1)

Others sometimes chose to forgo pain medication when their loved one was at home out of fear of bad side effects, later regretting the excruciating pain their loved one suffered and the resulting trip to the emergency room, which often resulted in painful and futile procedures. Despite this, however, only one of the participants (Soon-ja) ended up keeping their relative in a hospice facility. The others revolved between home and hospital, trying to manage hospice care largely on their own. With regard to dedicated inpatient hospice facilities, participants had trouble shaking the feeling that keeping their relative in such a facility was abandoning them and hastening death. Some even thought that it would increase their relative's pain, because they feared that staff, having given up on the patient, would skimp on pain medication.

Korean Hospice Staff Experiences of Hospice and Patient Death

Hospice staff of all types saw a large need for hospice in Korea. They noted heightened anxiety, pain, and suffering of patients without hospice support. They remarked on how hospice prepares the patient for a "dignified end" and helps to lessen family caregiver exhaustion. Hospice staff said that hospice services were a supportive supplement to, but not a substitute for, family care. They said that Korea needed a much larger, stronger hospice infrastructure, and needed to build up "hospice culture"—that is, the values, meanings, and practices associated with facing mortality and actively striving for quality of life in one's last months or days. They hoped that, with full implementation of the Act in 2018, both hospice infrastructure and culture would be strengthened in the future.

Staff recounted how they strived to implement some international hospice ideals, but how they struggled with others. The idea that death was a natural part of life was a hospice idea that staff were comfortable in conveying. However, patient agency was another matter. Although staff knew that international hospice norms stress the autonomy, agency, and wishes of patients, most Korean families were so used to the idea that family members should decide for the patient that staff found it indelicate to push the matter. So they said that, for the present, hospice practice needed to be adapted to the extant cultural norms of Korean hospitals and families.

> Doctor A: I know that I should explain the prognosis and the care plan to the patient directly. However, instead I do this [i.e., go over prognosis and care plan] with the family [rather than with the patient], because patients lack decision-making ability here.

> Doctor B: Families here are scared that patients will have a negative emotional response to their diagnosis and get psychologically distressed and depressed. So they usually want [everyone] to hide the truth from the patient.

In this sense, staff thought that in most cases it was not yet realistic to put the patient front and center in EOLCD in Korea, although they hoped that their work would stimulate culture change in time.

Focus on family as decision-maker extends to cases in which patients have informed staff and family of their desire to forgo life-sustaining treatment. Family members often disagree with the patient, and when a crisis occurs, they override the patient and request extreme measures.

> Nurse: Sometimes even though a patient here has made an advance medical decision to withhold life-sustaining treatment, they still get CPR, because without mutual agreement between the patient and the family, families will demand CPR.

Families did this out of a desire to provide good care, worrying that patients did not understand the situation or were trying to avoid being burdensome. At the time of this study, advance directives were not adequately supported by family education, hospital protocols, or legal measures.

Medical and nonmedical staff had different roles and tasks, as expected. Medical staff did hospice mainly through diagnosing problems and prescribing medications and palliative treatments to ease a patient's symptoms such as shortness of breath, physical pain, and anxiety. Nurses worked with family members to help keep the patient physically clean and comfortable, as well-rested as possible, hydrated as needed, in clean clothes and linens, and as free as possible of bedsores, constipation, and phlegm. Nurses did these tasks and/or taught family members to perform them. Physicians and nurses tried to help family members to assess how close to death the patient might be. Physicians also certified death. Nurses or social workers helped coordinate contacting morgue or funeral workers to remove the body when the family was ready. Nonmedical staff had other roles and tended to spend a longer amount of time with patients and their families and to extend their involvement more deeply into the time after death. Nonmedical staff assisted patients and families with last wishes, encouraged open communication about death, helped with gathering needed documents, and made referrals for funeral arrangements. Social workers and therapists offered counseling and legal consulting and participated in case conferences. Clergy provided spiritual counseling. Volunteers offered companionship, a listening ear, holding hands, playing music, massage, lotion, aromatherapy, adjusting bedding or lighting, reading aloud, getting favorite food or drink, fetching things, relaying messages, applying lip balm or mouth moistener, praying, keeping a watchful eye, and alerting professional staff if a need arose. After death, staff continued to assist families by offering or participating in family counseling and bereavement programs.

As the "Methods" section above showed, staff worked in several different types of hospice settings (table 12.3): nine in inpatient hospitals focused on acute care for patients of any age, three in inpatient geriatric hospitals, three in home hospice, and two in counsel hospice. The interviews showed that setting affected hospice practice in vital ways. Home and counsel hospice were more temporary. Counsel hospice was limited in that it only involved the patient's attending physician helping to transfer the patient in and out of networks, providing discharge education, and making referrals for family counseling. Home hospice was designed to provide 24/7 on-call support to the patient and family at home under the direction of a doctor working with a nurse and social worker as a team. The problem with both home and counsel hospice was limited staffing. In those forms, family often became overwhelmed by unexpected medical complications, gaps in service, and family limitations. Although global hospice discourse has idealized home hospice, staff observed that in their experience in Korea, home hospice, like counsel hospice, was more of a temporary stop-gap that lacked systematic proactive engagement with patient and family needs. They noted how patients in home hospice were more likely to end up dying in an emergency room. This was linked to the difference between already being in the hospital with a hospice plan and team in place, versus showing up at an emergency room. Compared with home, inpatient hospice was covered by insurance and had more skilled hands on deck and deeper benches for backup, reducing chances of panic. Thus far, the literature has tended to link hospital dying with more futile measures, but our findings indicate that hospital dying needs to be parsed more finely.

Staff found some dimensions of their hospice experience very valuable. Both medical and nonmedical staff said that they had developed the sentiment that with adequate preparation and planning, death could be very meaningful and beautiful. Medical staff said that they had become able to experience the death of hospice patients as a meaningful completion of life, and not as a failure of their medical abilities. Nonmedical staff said that they had learned to experience death in hospice as a beautiful ending. Both said that by observing the love and reconciliation between patient and family in the face of death, they themselves experienced personal growth.

Staff found other aspects of the hospice experience very stressful. Medical staff spoke of experiencing a sense of futility or helplessness watching patients decline and families grieving. Sometimes they avoided patients and/or family members due to unease about death. They knew that they needed to improve to provide good hospice care. Nonmedical staff spoke of negative reactions to certain kinds of death. These included watching a young patient die and seeing a patient's face in severe pain. Sometimes they became discouraged that their efforts were in vain since suffering was inevitable. Some became anxious about mortality and obsessed about their own or a family member's health. While bereavement programs did allow staff to join, which was helpful, the programs tended to be directed more at staff supporting families and less at staff recovery.

Another stressful aspect for staff was dealing with families who did not understand what hospice was about, or with family members who disagreed among themselves. Families who did not understand the palliative nature of hospice would complain about insufficient treatment and neglectful staff. Families who had not come to a common understanding with each other often got into arguments with each other or gave conflicting requests to staff.

> Social worker: Some family members who are not fully informed about the purpose of hospice care, they complain strongly about the care provided by the hospice team. When families do not understand hospice, they have many

complaints about the way in which staff is handling care of the patient. There are also often many conflicts among family members.

Hospice staff found some aspects of their hospice training, preparation, and/or support insufficient. Staff of both medical and nonmedical types believed that they needed improved training, preparation, and support to help them to provide better care for patients and families through the EOL care, dying, and bereavement process, and to avoid personal stress and professional burnout.

Overall, medical staff wished for Korea to establish detailed standards of care guidelines for hospice and palliative care to systematize best practice to both ease their deliberations and protect them from family accusations. Doctors and nurses often were torn between their role as providers of medical treatments to preserve life and their role in guiding patients and families on the path to acceptance, comfort care, and a good death. Some medical staff worried about lawsuits if family members perceived them to have given up on the patient, making them uneasy about steering patients away from treatment. However, they also felt compelled to guide families toward comfort care if that is what medical staff would have chosen had their own family member been sick. They said that all of these things could be helped by clearer guidelines. Medical personnel also noted the toll of patient death on them emotionally and how more coping support designed specifically for doctors and nurses would help them cope better with the stress.

Nonmedical staff talked about the importance of continuing education and professional supervision of hospice staff. They also noted needing more support to process patient deaths, especially young deaths and painful deaths. They thought that regular educational sessions and supervisory meetings were needed to prevent burnout. Both medical and nonmedical staff noted the need for more-comfortable hospice environments and for a robust hospice culture aimed at caring for everyone in the hospice ecosystem, including not only patients but also family and staff. Too much focus, they said, was often directed at the patient's symptoms, with too little focus on communication among patient, family members, and staff.

Limitations of the Studies and Recommendations for Future Research

The two studies described above were limited in terms of sample and being a snapshot in time. In sample size, the family caregiver study was particularly limited in including only four subjects, all of whom were women, although this is partially mitigated by the first author's extensive experience with families in her EOL social work practice. With seventeen subjects, the hospice staff study had a stronger sample; however, it was limited in its makeup. It did not include any doctors of traditional Korean medicine, and focused on staff in hospice institutions in large urban areas, including Seoul, Suwon, Sungnam, Daejeon, Pohang, and Ulsan. Future studies should work to fill these gaps. In addition, since these studies both took place before full implementation of the Act, things are likely to change quite a bit in the coming years.

Discussion and Comparison with Other East Asian Sites

Overall, we found a large need for improved and expanded EOL services in Korea, and both promise and challenges for implementing hospice in the Korean context. While hospice is a globally recognized standard of care, in some ways it is not translating easily to the Korean context, especially for family caregivers but also for hospice staff. For many family caregivers, the filiality involved in freeing seniors from the need to participate in EOLCD is more compelling than urging patients to be involved in such deliberations. Some family members worried that allowing their kin to die was a form of neglect or mercy killing. Both families and staff often prioritized family members' preferences over those of patients. Staff strived to achieve some international hospice ideals, but struggled with others. Some avoided seeing dying patients and families due to trouble coping. Families and staff wrestled with the idea of a "good death" as "good care."

These findings connect to at least three other chapters in this volume, including those by Kim (chap. 8) and Long and Campbell (chap. 9) for Japan, and by Shea (chap. 2) for China. Kim addressed distress about "lonely deaths" at home in Japan, in which the blame was pointed at declining social morals, but that can also be attributed to flaws in policy. Long and Campbell portrayed the caregiving careers of family caregivers, tracing their caregiving journey into the time after the death of their loved one. Shea demonstrated how meanings of spousal caregiving carried over into thoughts and practices related to dying and death.

It is useful to compare the situation in Korea with that of other East Asian societies. In doing so, we find both parallels and divergences in the emergence and configuration of hospice and palliative care services. To recap for South Korea, although the first hospice there emerged in the mid-1960s, it was slow to spread, and for decades involved small-scale interventions by volunteers, for the most part. Significant government involvement did not begin until 2003, when the state sponsored pilot hospice programs in hospitals. From there, things picked up in 2008 with NHI coverage of inpatient pain management and counseling at EOL, mainly for terminal cancer, and then government designation of palliative care centers in 2012. So far, usage has been low, however, even though surveys have shown hypothetical demand to be high. In 2015 the Act on Decisions on Life-Sustaining Treatment for Patients in Hospice and Palliative Care at the End of Life was unveiled, and partially put into effect in 2016, with NHI coverage for inpatient hospice launched in 2015. With this and full enactment of the Act in 2018, the numbers of hospice units and support for them has been increasing. However, factors slowing progress include lack of NHI coverage for home hospice, inadequate hospice infrastructure, insufficient education for families, inadequate training and support for staff, and difficulties with cultural fit of hospice for families and staff. Korea still has a high rate of futile medical procedures, with a majority of senior deaths occurring in a hospital.

To frame our East Asian comparison, it is helpful to reference the 2015 Quality of Death (QOD) index (EIU 2015), which placed the United Kingdom, hospice's birthplace, at the global peak for palliative care, followed by Australia, New Zealand, Ireland, and Belgium. South Korea came in eighteenth place (15). Based on the Act, the QOD report stated that Korea had a "well-defined government-led strategy" for palliative care, but that implementation mechanisms need work (23). Within East Asia, at eighteenth place worldwide South Korea ranked behind Taiwan (sixth), Singapore (twelfth), and Japan (fourteenth), but slightly ahead of Hong Kong (twenty-second), and far ahead of China (seventy-first) (Chu 2017; EIU 2015: 15). We will first look at Japan, on which the Korean system was partly based, then at Hong Kong at a rank similar to South Korea, then at China with the lowest ranking of the set, and finally at Taiwan and Singapore at the top of the group.

Ranked fourteenth on the QOD index, Japan has developed palliative care much more rapidly than South Korea, mainly due to earlier and broader state support. In Japan the first palliative care service was established in a hospital in 1973, and the first palliative care unit was formed in 1981. NHI in Japan started covering palliative care units in 1990, and home care palliative nursing services in 1992. Today Japan continues to offer and cover palliative care in both hospital and home settings (Mori and Morita 2016). The QOD report deemed Japan to have a "well-defined government-led strategy" for palliative care, but to fall short in some implementation mechanisms (EIU 2015: 23). For Japan, even though lonely home deaths are a social concern (chap. 8), Japan, like Korea, has a strong tendency for both home care and hospital death. With close to 80 percent of deaths in Japan in a hospital rather than at home or in nursing homes (chap. 9), even more hospital deaths occur in Japan than in Korea. So more-advanced palliative services, earlier hospice insurance coverage, and coverage of home-based services does not guarantee a low hospital death rate.

Ranked twenty-second on the QOD index, Hong Kong has developed palliative care more slowly than Korea. In 2002, the Hospital Authority of Hong Kong laid out ethical principles and guidelines for handling EOL decision-making and disputes (Kim and Choi 2017). Service availability is still limited, however. In recent years in Hong Kong, hospice or palliative care has been available on a very limited basis from fewer than two dozen public authority hospitals offering fewer than 400 beds, together with some private nursing homes and community organizations. Most insurance in Hong Kong does not cover hospice care (Lee 2018). This is curious since Hong Kong was a British colony for so long, and the United Kingdom ranks first for palliative care. The QOD judges Hong Kong to have a "well-defined government-led strategy" for palliative care, but a limited one thus far (EIU 2015: 23). Similar to Korea and Japan, studies show that in Hong Kong most deaths also take place in a hospital; for example, 90 percent of deaths occurred in the city's public hospitals in 2014 (Cheung 2016), even more than in Japan. This may reflect what Shum and Lum (chap. 4) noted about dependence on public institutions in Hong Kong. Low home death rates there are also linked to difficulties of certifying home deaths as non-suspicious (Cheung 2016) and to how advance directives have no formal legal footing (Lee 2018). Although institutionalization rates for seniors in Hong Kong are higher than locals would prefer, Hong Kong mixes emphasis on family caregiving at home, with a proclivity for hospital death, like Korea and Japan.

Ranked seventy-first on the QOD index, China's palliative care lags behind South Korea and the others, as would be expected based on its lower per capita income. Although the first two hospices in China opened in the mid-1980s in Beijing and Shanghai, palliative services are still uncommon there, with demand far outstripping supply (*Economist* 2018; Huang 2015). The World Health Organization (2006) reported that 70 percent of people in China died at home that year, and to this day many maintain that preference (Lu, Gu, and Yu 2018). Yet, in urban areas, there has been a rising trend toward hospital death for those with health insurance and some savings for the needed down payment for medical treatment. Palliative efforts have expanded since 2011, yielding more than 900 small pilot sites nationwide, offering some level of inpatient, outpatient, or home palliation (Lu et al. 2018). In 2017 five national model pilot hospice programs were instituted in top-tier cities, with Shanghai in the lead for community-based hospice. Urban nonprofits are active in promoting hospice. Still, however, the QOD observed no well-defined national strategy for EOL care (EIU

2015: 23). Due to lower means, rural dwellers in China are more likely than urban dwellers to have to give up medical treatment and have a home death without hospice assistance (EIU 2015). Many Chinese families still avoid talking about death with the patient or inviting palliative care due to a fear that it will hasten death itself (Lu et al. 2018) or seem unfilial (Huang 2015), an issue also raised for Korea. While pain medicines for terminal patients have been covered by health insurance in China since 2005 (Lu et al. 2018), hospice is not yet covered (Huang 2015).

Coming in sixth in the world and top for Asia on the QOD index, Taiwan did not have as early a start as Korea or Japan, but it made up for it by very early adoption of insurance coverage for home-based hospice services and development of a comprehensive national strategy for palliative care (EIU 2015: 23). As Ko et al. (2017) relate, palliative care in Taiwan was "introduced by local religious hospitals in the mid-1980s" (2). Then in 1996 Taiwan NHI began to cover home palliative care. In 2000 "Taiwan passed the 'The Hospice Palliative Medical Act' [Natural Death Act]," and Taiwan's NHI began to cover "inpatient palliative care. . . . [In] 2009, Taiwan NHI . . . expanded the indications of hospice care" to include more qualifying conditions (2). In 2015, the Patient Autonomy Act was passed, effective in 2018 (Kim and Choi 2017). The rate of hospital deaths in Taiwan is much lower than South Korea, Japan, or Hong Kong at 60 percent, with 40 percent of deaths occurring outside a hospital, at home (20 percent) or in nursing homes (20 percent) (Cheung 2016). This may relate to early first adoption of insurance coverage of home hospice before inpatient hospice.

Finally, ranked twelfth on the QOD index, like Taiwan although later up to the plate, Singapore also has a comprehensive national strategy for palliative care (EIU 2015: 23). The first hospice in Singapore was started by nuns in 1985 (Goh 2018) as part of a Catholic old folks' home. Influenced by the Japanese father of hospice, Dr. Kashiwagi, Singapore followed a path similar to Taiwan's in starting with home hospice. The first home hospice volunteer organization in Singapore was formed in 1987. Hospital-based palliative care was not introduced until 1996 (21–22). Since 1994, patients can use their defined-contribution Medisave accounts to cover hospice care, and recently first-degree relatives have been allowed to use their own Medisave accounts up to US$2,500 per year to cover familial hospice costs (23). Since 1996 home hospice care has been government-subsidized to reduce cost to patients by half, and means-testing was added later (23). Figures show that 61 percent of deaths in Singapore occur in the hospital, with 27 percent at home and 8.6 percent in nursing homes and the remainder in other locations (Lien Foundation 2014: 1–2, 21). This rate of hospital death is lower than South Korea, Japan, and Hong Kong, and similar to Taiwan. Cheung (2016) suggests that seniors in Singapore are more likely to die at home than are seniors in Hong Kong, in part due to Singaporean government subsidies for families to hire foreign domestic workers at home.

Concluding Remarks and Recommendations

Hospice in South Korea has made important steps forward in the past decade, and the 2018 Act is already helping to expand EOL care in South Korea, but there is still a long way to go. Overall, there is a large need for improved and expanded EOL services in Korea, and there are both promising developments and challenges for implementing the hospice model in the Korean context from family and hospice staff perspectives. Adjustments need to be made to allow insurance to cover home-based hospice at home and in residential LTC facilities, not just inpatient hospice, and to make hospice services and their presentation more compatible with local cultural sensibilities.[4] To help seniors realize wishes expressed in surveys to avoid futile life-prolonging procedures, much more support is needed to facilitate early and continuing communication with seniors and their families about EOL issues and to promote and support advance directives.[5] Instead of myopically focusing on patient symptom relief in the end stages, more attention should be paid to early and ongoing communication among patients, family members, and staff. In addition, more EOL education for patients and families and more training and support for hospice staff are needed in order to reduce stress and burnout. There also needs to be clearer guidelines for best practices and protocols for hospice staff. The Act provides clear criteria for education of doctors, nurses, and social workers, the latter of which just recently became a compulsory part of hospice teams, but does not provide clear certification standards for therapists, clergy, or volunteers, so that gap will need to be remedied in practice as hospice usage rises over time.[6] Given the current and rising need, more institutions need to be certified to be covered by insurance for EOL care.

The existence of hospice and palliative care services alone will not help much to move death out of the hospitals and back into homes and nursing homes unless government subsidies and insurance extend coverage to home hospice care, at least as generously as inpatient hospice care. Infrastructural and systemic approaches are needed, together with deepening hospice culture (Meier et al. 2016; Nakanishi et al. 2015). Indeed, many of the problems discussed in this chapter are not unique to South Korea, although they are very challenging there due to the rapid and extensive biomedicalization of EOL care and the continuing underdevelopment of hospice coverage, options, infrastructure, education, training, and support. South Korea has long looked toward Japan as a model for hospice care. Presently, it would be worthwhile to add more consideration of dimensions of Taiwan's and Singapore's approaches to the mix.

Acknowledgments

The National Research Foundation of Korea (NRF-2016S1A3A2925399) supported this research work. We are grateful to the families and hospice staff who participated in the project.

Sooyoun Han specializes in social work and end-of-life issues in South Korea. She is cofounder of the Care Rights NGO and a member of the Global Alliance for the Rights of Older Person (GAROP) steering group. Recently she was appointed executive director of the Well-Dying Civil Movement NPO NGO. Her work has been published in many journals and edited volumes, including *Asian Social Work and Policy*, *Hakjisa* (a Korean scholarly journal), *Development and Society, Health and Social Affairs Review*, and *Handbook of Social Work Ethic and Values* (MacKinney and Robert, eds.).

Jeanne Shea (邵镜虹) is associate professor of anthropology and director of the Health and Society Program at the University of Vermont in Burlington, Vermont, USA. Recipient of two Fulbright Awards, she has published on menopause and midlife, marital relationships, the family, spousal caregiving, senior volunteering, evidence-based medicine, and community supports for aging in place in China. Most recently, she has published several research articles in *Ageing International* (2016, 2017, 2018) and a chapter on China's Senior Companions Program for *The Cultural Context of Aging: Worldwide Perspectives* (Sokolovsky 2020).

Glossary

| *hyo* | 효 | Filial piety. |
| *salm-ui kkeu* | 삶의 끝 | End of life. |

Notes

1. Paragraph 6 of the 2018 amended Act defines hospice and palliative care as "the medical care provided to a patient at EOL, as well as to his/her family members, for

the purpose of comprehensive evaluation and provision of treatments in physical, psychosocial, and spiritual domains, including pain and symptom relief" (Korea Legislation Research Institute 2018).

2. The 2018 implementation of the Act expands the range of diagnoses beyond cancer to AIDS, chronic obstructive pulmonary disease, and chronic liver cirrhosis, and allows advance directives to patients aged nineteen and older.

3. The first author designed and conducted the research, reviewed relevant scholarly literature in Korean and English, and wrote drafts on relevant Korean policy and the two qualitative studies. The second author helped to construct the argument and to write the chapter in consonance with the themes and comparative vision of the volume, adding further analysis, evidence, and citations. The second author did both the research and the analysis for the section of the chapter on cross-national comparison of EOL care in East Asian contexts. In both studies, procedures were approved by the Institutional Review Board (IRB), and all interviewees participated voluntarily with informed consent. Names in this chapter are pseudonyms.

4. Existence of home hospice is insufficient. A study showed 77.4 percent of patients in Korean home hospice ended it in a month, and 65.9 percent in two weeks, going back to an acute care hospital; lack of insurance coverage for home hospice was a key reason (Kim, June, and Son 2016b).

5. One study found multiple reasons that lead people to decide on hospice service very late and/or to miss the opportunity for comfort care, including late referral by the attending physician, insufficient diligence in hospital discharge services, negative perception toward hospice, and lack of information (Han 2015). Lack of advance directives would be another. As of 2016 advance care planning, information on hospice and EOL care, and family caregiver counseling become available to some extent, but nowhere near enough to meet need.

6. In 2018 social workers became compulsory hospice staff, doing assessment, counseling, and interventions with doctors and nurses as partners (MHW 2018a, 2018b, 2018c).

References

An, Ah Reum, June-Koo Lee, Young Ho Yun, and Dae Heo. 2014. "Terminal Cancer Patients' and Their Primary Caregivers' Attitude toward Hospice and Palliative Care and Their Effects on Actual Utilization: A Prospective Cohort Study." *Palliative Medicine* 28 (7): 976–85.

Cardona-Morrell, Magnolia, J. C. H. Kim, R. M. Turner, M. Anstey, I. A. Mitchell, and K. Hillman. 2016. "Non-Beneficial Treatments in Hospital at the End of Life: A Systematic Review on Extent of the Problem." *International Journal for Quality in Health Care* 28 (4): 456–469.

Chang, Y. 2013. *A Status for Suicide and Policy Development.* Seoul: Korea Institute for Health and Social Affairs.

Cheung, Elizabeth. 2016. "Free Hong Kong Doctors to Help Dying Patients End Their Days at Home." *South China Morning Post,* 11 July. Retrieved 12 March 2020 from https://www.scmp.com/news/hong-kong/health-environment/article/1988078/free-hong-kong-doctors-help-dying-patients-end.

Cho, H., and H. Lim 2017. "Hospice-Palliative Care Activities of Personnel in a Long-Term Care Hospital: A Retrospective Chart Review." *Journal of the Korean Academia-Industrial Cooperation Society* 18 (4): 570–77.

Chu, Hayes. 2017. "Palliative Care in Hong Kong: An Option Outside Hospitals." *MIMS Today*, 1 June. Retrieved 1 January 2019 from https://today.mims.com/palliative-care-an-option-outside-hospitals.

Economist. 2018. "Loved to Death: Taboos Make It Hard to Discuss Mortality in China," 7 June. Retrieved 12 March 2020 from https://www.economist.com/china/2018/06/07/taboos-make-it-hard-to-discuss-mortality-in-china.

Economist Intelligence Unit (EIU). 2015. *The 2015 Quality of Death Index: Ranking Palliative Care across the World.* Retrieved 1 January 2019 from https://eiuper spectives.economist.com/sites/default/files/2015%20EIU%20Quality%20of%20 Death%20Index%20Oct%2029%20FINAL.pdf.

Foucault, Michel. 1991. "Governmentality," trans. Rosi Braidotti and revised by Colin Gordon. *The Foucault Effect: Studies in Governmentality*, ed. Graham Burchell, Colin Gordon, and Peter Miller, 87–104. Chicago: University of Chicago Press.

Goh, Stella Seow Lin. 2018. "Singapore Takes Six Steps Forward in 'The Quality of Death Index' Rankings." *Asia Pacific Journal of Oncology Nursing* 5 (1): 21–25.

Han, Sooyoun. 2015. "A Study of Social Workers' Understanding of Elderly Patients' and Family Caregivers' Rights to End of Life Care Decisions and of Their Own Roles in the Process." *The Korean Journal of Hospice and Palliative Care* 18 (1): 42–50.

———. 2016. "The Effects of South Korean Social Workers' Education and Knowledge of Advance Directives." *Development and Society* 45 (2): 255–74.

———. 2019a. "A Case Study of Hospice Team's Experience of the Decision of Hospice and Life Sustaining Treatments." *Health and Social Affairs Review* 39 (1): 453–84.

———. 2019b. "Social Workers' Dilemma in Patients' Rights on End of Life Care and Decision Making under the New Act of South Korea." In *The Handbook of Social Work Ethics and Values*, ed. B. MacKinney and S. Robert, 165–172. New York: Routledge.

Heo, Dae Seog. 2013. "Life-Sustaining Medical Treatment for Terminal Patients in Korea." *Journal of Korean Medical Science* 2013 (28): 1–3. Retrieved 1 July 2018 from https://www.ncbi.nlm.nih.gov/pmc/articles/PMC3546086/.

Hong, S., and S. Kim. 2013. "Knowledge Regarding Advance Directives among Community-Dwelling Elderly." *Korean Academy of Social Nursing Education* 19 (3): 330–40.

Huang, Qiu-Si. 2015. "A Review on Problems of China's Hospice Care and Analysis of Possible Solutions." *Chinese Medical Journal* (English) 128 (2): 279–281.

Ikels, Charlotte, ed. 2004. *Filial Piety: Practice and Discourse in Contemporary East Asia.* Stanford, CA: Stanford University Press.

Janelli, Roger L., and Dawnhee Yim. 2004. "The Transformation of Filial Piety in Contemporary South Korea." In Ikels, *Filial Piety*, 128–52.

Keam, Bhumsuk, Young Ho Yun, Dae Heo, Byeong Woo Park, Chi-Heum Cho, Sung Joo Kim, Dae Ho Lee, et al. 2014. "Attitude of Korean Cancer Patients, Family Caregivers, Oncologists, and Members of the General Public toward Advance Directives." *Supportive Care in Cancer* 21 (5): 1437–44.

Kim, Dong Joon, and Moon Seok Choi. 2017. "Life-Sustaining Treatment and Palliative Care in Patients with Liver Cirrhosis: Legal, Ethical, and Practical Issues" [South Korea]. *Clinical Molecular Hepatology* 23 (2): 115–22.

Kim, G. S. 2016. "A Phenomenological Study of Experiences of Family Caregivers for their Terminal Cancer Patients Receiving Hospice." *Korean Journal of Family Social Work* 52 (0): 35–66.

Kim, H. S., K. J. June, and Y. S. Son. 2016. "Home-Based Hospice Care Provided by a Free-Standing Hospice Center: Patients' Characteristics and Service Conditions." *Korean Journal of Hospice and Palliative Care* 19 (2): 145–53.

Kim, Ivo, Y. Kim, Y. Yun, S. Sin, D. Heo, and Z. Xiaomei. 2012. "A Survey of the Perspectives of Patients Who Are Seriously Ill Regarding EOL Decisions in Some Medical Institutions of Korea, China, and Japan." *Journal of Medical Ethics* 38: 301–16.

Kim, M., Kang, E., and Kim, M. 2012. "Family Decision-Making to Withdraw Life-Sustaining Treatment for Terminally-Ill Patients in an Unconscious State." *Korean Journal of Hospital Palliative Care* 15: 147–54.

Kim, T. H., and Han, S. 2013. "Family Life of Older Koreans." *Ageing in Korea*, 3rd ed., ed. S. J. Choi. Seoul, Korea: Med Inc.

Kim, W. S., H. H. Cho, and S. Kwon. 2016. "The Influence of Terminal Care Performance, Death Anxiety and Self-Esteem on Terminal Care Stress of Geriatric Hospital Nurses." *Korean Journal of Hospital Palliative Care* 19 (2): 154–62.

Kim, Yang-Jung. 2015. "89% of the Elderly Oppose Life-Sustaining Treatment." *Hani News*, 9 April. Retrieved on 24 March 2020 from http://www.hani.co.kr/arti/soci ety/health/686222.html.

Ko, Ming-Chung, Sheng-Jean Huang, Chu-Chieh Chen, Yu-Ping Chang, Hsin-Yi Lien, Jia-Yi Lin, Lin-Chung Woung, and Shang-Yih Chan. 2017. "Factors Predicting a Home Death among Home Palliative Care Recipients." *Medicine* 96 (41): e8210.

Koh, Su-Jin, Shinmi Kim, Jin Shil Kim, Bhumsuk Keam, Dae Seog Heo, Kyung Hee Lee, Bong Seog Kim, Jee Hyun Kim, Hye Jung Chang, and Sun Kyung Baek. 2018. "Experiences and Opinions Related to End-of-Life Discussion: From Oncologists' and Resident Physicians' Perspectives." *Cancer Research and Treatment* [Korea] 50 (2): 614–23.

Korea Legislation Research Institute. 2016. "Act on Decisions on Life-Sustaining Treatment for Patients in Hospice and Palliative Care or At the End of Life." Korean National Law Information Center, 3 February. Retrieved 24 March 2020 from http://www.law.go.kr/LSW/eng/engLsSc.do?menuId=2&query=ACT%20ON%20 DECISIONS%20ON%20LIFE-SUSTAINING%20TREATMENT%20FOR%20PA-TIENTS%20IN%20HOSPICE%20AND%20PALLIATIVE%20CARE%20OR%20 AT%20THE%20END.

———. 2018. "Enforcement Decree of the Act on Hospice and Palliative Care and Decisions on Life-Sustaining Treatment for Patients at the End of Life." Korean National Law Information Center, 2 February. Retrieved 24 March 2020 from http://www.law.go.kr/LSW/eng/engLsSc.do?menuId=2&query=ACT%20ON%20 DECISIONS%20ON%20LIFE-SUSTAINING%20TREATMENT%20FOR%20PA-TIENTS%20IN%20HOSPICE%20AND%20PALLIATIVE%20CARE%20OR%20 AT%20THE%20END%20OF%20LIFE#liBgcolor2.

Korean Statistical Information Service (KOSIS). 2013. *2013 Statistics for Korea.* Korean Statistical Information Service. Retrieved 1 June 2018 from http://kosis.kr/eng/.

———. 2018. *2018 Statistics for Korea.* Korean Statistical Information Service. Retrieved 1 April 2019 from http://kosis.kr/eng/.

Kwon, So-Hi. 2013. "End-of-Life Care in Korea: Issues and Trends." *Japanese Journal of Nursing and Health Sciences* 11: 54–60.

Lee, Joseph Kok-long. 2018. "Hong Kong Should Expedite Formulation of Hospice Care Policy." *EJInsight*, 3 April. Retrieved 12 March 2020 from http://www.ejinsight .com/20180403-hk-should-expedite-formulation-of-hospice-care-policy/.

Lee, L. J., and H. S. Park. 2017. "Death Anxiety and Terminal Care Performance of Nurses in Long-Term Care Hospital." *Korean Journal of Hospice and Palliative Care* 20 (1): 37–45.

Lien Foundation. 2014. *Death Attitudes Survey* (Singapore). 8 April. Retrieved 1 January 2019 from http://lienfoundation.org/sites/default/files/Death%20survey%20 Presser%20Final%20-%20Combined_0.pdf.

Lim, Kahyun, Jeong-Whun Kim, Sooyoung Yoo, Eunyoung Heo, Hyerim Ji, and Beodeul Kang. 2018. "Design of a Hospice Referral System for Terminally Ill Cancer Patients Using a Standards-Based Health Information Exchange System." *Healthcare Informatics Research* 24 (4): 317–26.

Long, Susan O. 2004. "Cultural Scripts for a Good Death in Japan and the United States: Similarities and Differences." *Social Science and Medicine* 58 (5): 913–28.

Lu, Yuhan, Youhui Gu, and Wenhua Yu. 2018. "Hospice and Palliative Care in China: Development and Challenges." *Asia Pacific Journal of Oncology Nursing* 5 (1): 26–32.

Mai, Tran Thi Xuan, Eunsook Lee, Hyunsoon Cho, and Yoon Jung Chang. 2018. "Increasing Trend in Hospital Deaths Consistent among Older Decedents in Korea: A Population-based Study Using Death Registration Database, 2001–2014." *BMC Palliative Care* 17 (1): 16.

Meier, E. A., J. V. Gallegos, L. P. M. Thomas, C. A. Depp, S. A. Irwin, and D. V. Jeste. 2016. "Defining a Good Death (Successful Dying): Literature Review and a Call for Research and Public Dialogue." *American Journal of Geriatric Psychiatry* 24 (4): 261–71.

Ministry of Government Legislation, Korea (MGL). 2018. "Act on Hospice and Palliative Care and Decisions on Life-Sustaining Treatment for Patients at the End of Life." Retrieved 12 March 20202 from https://elaw.klri.re.kr/eng_mobile/viewer .do?hseq=43945&type=sogan&key=10.

Ministry of Health and Welfare, Korea (MHW). 2017. *National Survey of Older Koreans: Findings and Implications*. Report by Kyong Hee Chung. Retrieved 24 March 2020 from https://www.kihasa.re.kr/web/publication/newbooks_pdsissue/view.do?me nuId=46&tid=71&bid=200&ano=1487.

———. 2018a. "In-Patient Hospice Institution Hospice Service Guidelines." Retrieved 24 March 2020 from http://hospice.cancer.go.kr/common/download.do? file_no=86091.

———. 2018b. "Guidelines for Home Hospice Pilot Service." Retrieved 24 March 2020 from http://hospice.cancer.go.kr/common/download.do?file_no=94949.

———. 2018c. "Guidelines for Counsel Hospice Pilot Service." Retrieved 24 March 2020 from http://www.hospice.go.kr/hospice/front/boardView.do?keykind=&keyword =&page_now&returl=/hospice/front/boardList.do&listurl=/hospice/front/board-List.do&brd_mgrno=181&menu_no=442&brd_no=88906.

———. 2018d. *Hospice and Palliative Care Medical Care Act*. Retrieved 1 January 2019 from http://law.go.kr/lsEfInfoP.do?lsiSeq=180823#.

Mori, Masanori, and Tatsuya Morita. 2016. "Advances in Hospice and Palliative Care in Japan: A Review Paper." *Korean Journal of Hospice and Palliative Care* 19 (4): 283–91.

Nakanishi, M., T. Nakashima, Y. Shindo, Y. Miyamoto, D. Gove, L. Radbruch, and J. T. van der Steen. 2015. "An Evaluation of Palliative Care Contents in National Dementia Strategies in Reference to the EU for Palliative Care." White Paper. *International Psychogeriatrics* 27 (9): 1551–61.

National Health Insurance Service (NHIS). 2019. "Long Term Care Insurance." National Health Insurance Service. Retrieved 24 March 2020 from https://www.nhis.or.kr/static/html/wbd/g/a/wbdga0503.html.

National Hospice Center, Korea (NHC). 2018. "The Status of and Statistics for Korean Hospice Palliative Care Services." Retrieved 24 March 2020 from http://hospice.cancer.go.kr/home/contentsInfo.do?menu_no=443&brd_mgrno.

National Hospice Palliative Association, Korea (NHPA). 2016. "Facts and Figures on Hospice Care 2015." Retrieved 24 March 2020 from http://hospice.go.kr/common/download.do?file_no=67412.

Organisation for Economic Co-operation and Development (OECD). 2019. "Life Expectancy at 65." Retrieved 1 April 2019 from https://data.oecd.org/healthstat/life-expectancy-at-65.htm, retrieved 7 April 2019 from doi:10.1787/0e9a3f00-en.

Park, J., and J. Song. 2013. "Knowledge, Experience and Preference on Advance Directives among Community and Facility-Dwelling Elderly." *Journal of the Korean Gerontological Society* 33: 581–600.

Rhee, Yong Joo. 2015. "Hospice and Palliative Care Services in South Korea Supported by the National Health Insurance (NHI) Program." *Health* 7 (6): 1–6.

Ro, Yu-Ja. 2018. *Hospice and Palliative Care: The Completion of a Meaning Life,* 1st ed. Seoul, Korea: Hyunmoon Co.

Sakhrani, Neetu. 2017. "Hospice and Palliative Care Services in Hong Kong: How To Access Them, and Why We Need to Talk More Openly About Death." *South China Morning Post,* 21 August. Retrieved 12 March 2020 from https://www.scmp.com/lifestyle/health-beauty/article/2107604/hospice-and-palliative-care-services-hong-kong-how-access.

Shim, S. H. 2016. "A Case Study on the Experience of Hospice Volunteers." *Korean Journal of Hospice and Palliative Care* 19 (1): 45–60.

Singapore Taskforce for Palliative Care Implementation. 2015. *National Guidelines for Palliative Care* (Singapore). Retrieved 12 March 2020 from https://singaporehospice.org.sg/site2019/wp-content/uploads/National-Guidelines-for-Palliative-Care-Revised-Ed.-Jan-2015.pdf.

Sorenson, Clark, and Sung-Chul Kim. 2004. "Filial Piety in Contemporary Urban Southeast Korea: Practices and Discourses." In Ikels, *Filial Piety,* 153–81.

Stanford School of Medicine. 2019. "Where Do Americans Die?" *Palliative Care Site.* Retrieved 1 March 2019 from https://palliative.stanford.edu/home-hospice-home-care-of-the-dying-patient/where-do-americans-die/.

United Nations (UN). 2017. 2017. *World Population Prospects: The 2017 Revision.* United Nations Department of Economic and Social Affairs, Population Division. Custom data queried by author Jeanne Shea for this chapter from website. Retrieved 1 June 2018 from https://population.un.org/wpp/DataQuery/.

World Health Organization (WHO). 2006. "Counting the Dead in China." *Bulletin of the World Health Organization* 84 (3): 161–256. Retrieved 1 August 2018 from https.who.int/bulletin/volumes/84/3/news30306/en/.

———. 2018. "Life Expectancy and Healthy Life Expectancy: Data by Country." Retrieved 1 February 2019 from http://apps.who.int/gho/data/node.main.688?lang=en.

Yang, K H., and S. I. Kwon. 2015. "The Effects of Attitude to Death in the Hospice and Palliative Professionals on Their Terminal Care Stress." *Korean Journal of Hospice and Palliative Care* 18 (4): 285–93.

Yi, M. J., and J. S. Lee. 2016. "Concept Analysis of Nurses' Acceptance of Patient Deaths." *Korean Journal of Hospice and Palliative Care* 19 (1): 34–44.

Yun, Young Ho, Kyoung-Nam Kim, Jin-Ah Sim, Shin Hye Yoo, Miso Kim, Young Ae Kim, and Beo Deul Kang et al. 2018. "Comparison of Attitudes towards Five End-of-Life Care Interventions: A Multicentred Cross-Sectional Survey of Korean Patients with Cancer, their Family Caregivers, Physicians and the General Korean Population." *BMJ Open* 8 (9): e020519. Retrieved 4 April 2019 from https.ncbi.nlm.nih .gov/pubmed/30206075.

●━●━●━●━●━●━●━●━●━●━●━●━●━●━●

CONCLUSION
Contemporary Trends in and Future Directions for Aging and Caregiving in East Asian Societies

Jeanne Shea, Katrina Moore, and Hong Zhang

Introduction

THE MATERIAL COVERED IN THIS volume is important not just for Asian Studies specialists, but also for anyone interested in global issues of population aging and varied human experiences of aging and caregiving. Taken together, the volume has brought together inquiry into social support for the aged and productive aging by seniors in East Asia by examining contemporary patterns of familial and/or nonfamilial care both for and by the elderly. This concluding chapter briefly places the aging of East Asian societies into global demographic context. It then recaps our key sociocultural findings on aging and caregiving in East Asian societies, arguing that, overall, these locales are more complex than being a paradise of reverence, support, and care for the elderly. The analysis emphasizes how filial piety in these locales today has a broader meaning and a wider range of practices associated with it than it did in past decades. It demonstrates how there is greater acceptance and practice of individual and situational flexibility with regard to aging and caregiving, including caregiving both for and by the elderly. The analysis then turns to issues of demographic projections and imagined futures of aging and care in relation to debates about whether population aging is a crisis or an opportunity. Finally, this chapter suggests some directions for future policy and research. Along the way, we illuminate some of the similarities and differences in how East Asian locales are responding to their rapidly aging societies.

Aging East Asian Societies in Global Perspective

Although other parts of the world such as Europe also have reached a high degree of population aging, East Asia is distinctive in its speed of population aging and modernization and in its shared Confucian heritage. As detailed in this volume's Introduction, based on United Nations (UN 2017) figures, the speed or "compression" of population aging in East Asia has entered uncharted territory. These locales took or will take fewer than two to two and a half decades to go from aging to aged societies (from 7 percent to 14 percent aged sixty-five and above), and only eight to seventeen years to go from aged to super-aging societies (from 14 percent to 21 percent age sixty-five and above). Japan was the first country worldwide to become a super-aging society in 2008, far ahead of Western countries. Starting in 2010 the populations of the four tigers (Korea, Singapore, Taiwan, and Hong Kong) began to age more quickly than that of Japan, and Korea is currently the most rapidly aging society on earth. By the 2020s the four tigers are expected to reach super-aging status, and by 2050 they are expected to nearly match Japan's level of 36.4 percent elderly and to be ahead of major Western nations. With its massive population, China already has the largest raw number of old people worldwide, and it is expected to be among the first developing countries to reach super-aging status, getting there in the 2030s. Three decades from now, all six East Asian locales are projected to have elderly population proportions above the predicted 2050 average for their national income level. In sum, East Asia is extraordinary in this regard.

In addition, as described in this volume's Introduction, a combination of dropping and sustained low fertility rates and rising life expectancies, each driven by swift modernization and economic development, has led to this degree and rapidity of population aging in these East Asian locales. By 1990–95 all six societies had fallen below 2.0 children per woman, following Japan whose fertility rate has been below 2.0 since 1975. By 2010–15 the fertility levels of South Korea, Taiwan, Hong Kong, and Singapore were hovering around 1.1 to 1.2, ranking among the lowest in the world. As of 2018 life expectancy at birth in the five high-income sites reached eighty to eighty-four years of age, and China, the one middle-income country, had a life expectancy older than seventy-six years old, not far behind the United States. In large part due to effective state interventions, East Asia has modernized and developed at a rate much faster than that experienced by Western societies, spurring speedier fertility decline and life expectancy increase. Dropping fertility has been driven by various aspects of rapid modernization, including industrialization, economic development, increasing female education and employment, rising gender equity, escalating lifestyle aspirations, improved contraceptive access, and various antinatalist family planning policies that were instituted during these locales' economic take-off stages. Rising life expectancies have stemmed from economic development, improved living conditions, better nutrition and preventive measures, and medical advances. If predictions hold, these low East Asian fertility levels may continue to fall or at least not rise much, and life expectancies are expected to continue to rise to age eighty-two to eighty-nine by 2050. As discussed below, recent pronatalist measures have failed to convince significant numbers of people to bear more children.

East Asia is also distinctive in its shared Confucian heritage and continuing social reference to filial piety (for definition, see Introduction) in relation to respecting, supporting, and caring for one's aging parents. As Ikels (2004) and Yan (2016) point out, however, another traditional dimension of filial piety much less articulated in relation to filiality in modern times is the obligation to produce and nurture descendants to successfully extend the family line. These two faces of filial piety lead to a strong tension between traditional injunctions to care for the elderly on the one hand, and to nurture the young on the other. This relates to not just the middle generations struggling to support old and young, but also to the elderly themselves who wish not only to be cared for but also to continue to foster descendants (chaps. 1–3, 9–11). While the focus on traditional ideals to respect, support, and care for the elderly acts as a social resource in lending moral weight to performing eldercare through both positive motivation to do the right thing and risk of guilt or shame (chaps. 6, 10), this legacy is also potentially a burden. While intended to spur positive behavior, it can add moral angst to young and old alike who find themselves living in a world of often-incompatible realities and competing priorities (chaps. 2–3, 6, 8–11). Often admired by observers from the outside, filial piety is thus both a valuable cultural resource and a heavy weight for East Asian societies to bear.

Key Findings on Aging and Caregiving in East Asian Societies

Neither in 2004 nor any time in the subsequent fifteen years would it be accurate to characterize any East Asian society as a paradise for the elderly (chap. 8). None of the East Asian locales studied in Ikels's (2004) volume nor this present volume have been able to live up in contemporary times to traditional standards for obeying, respecting, living with, supporting, and caring for the elderly. The chapters in the present volume depicted a complex landscape involving continuing attempts to respect, support, and care for the aged (chaps. 1–2, 4–7, 9–11), along with instances of devaluing, neglecting, or even taking advantage of elders (chaps. 2–3, 8, 10), often with the seniors' acquiescence (chaps. 1–2). Yet, in our volume, as in Ikels's before us, we also found that rather than being abandoned in the face of modernization, filial piety remains an important touchstone for both East Asian governments and the people alike.

While meanings and practices associated with filial piety, aging, and caregiving had already started to change and diversify in the decades prior to 2004, they have become even more varied since then. Unquestioning obedience to aging parents has become even less important than before. Mutual respect and talking things over between the generations has become the normative ideal. Coresidence of aging parents with adult children has become even less common, and less desirable not only for the younger generation, but also for the senior generation who increasingly wish to have their own living space. Emphasis on the marital bond has continued to strengthen, such that now not only is a high value placed on young people's conjugal ties and neo-locality, but also increasingly on those of seniors. Traditional notions of parents falling back on children for material or instrumental support in old age now meet even stronger competition from the notion that old people should ideally remain self-reliant and continue to provide support and care for younger generations well into old age. Not only is this often seen in terms of the need to avoid burdening younger generations, but also as a positive trend for senior "independence"; seniors today do not need to depend as much on adult children due to the rise of pensions and other state-sponsored entitlements. The trend toward increasing gender equity noted in Ikels's volume has also deepened, with rising insistence that daughters can not only be filial but also sometimes be just as or even more filial than sons. The idea that daughters should also be able to take care of their natal parents and not just their in-laws has also become much stronger. Many chapters in the present volume brought in the theme of the gendering of care (chaps. 2–3, 5, 7, 9–11), some noting a trend toward discursive gender neutrality (chaps. 2–3), with others also acknowledging some continuing gender inequity (chaps. 2, 5, 7, 9–10).

Overall, our volume has shown increasing individual and situational flexibility in terms of expectations and practices regarding filial piety. Already apparent in 2004, as of this writing fifteen years later there are even fewer set norms and clear lines of familial hierarchy. Even more than in 2004, now it is no longer the case that one necessarily needs to live with one's aging parents, support them financially, or take care of them personally in order to be considered filial. Today, adult children who outsource care to other relatives while they are at work or away are filial, as long as they check in regularly. Those who pay to place their parents in a nursing home or who hire in-home help are filial for covering the expenses for such care. Adult children who are too cash-strapped to support their parents are filial if they call or visit as often as they can. Those who focus on working hard in their jobs or careers to support themselves and to provide a good future for the grandchildren can also check off the filial box.

Our volume has also shown a growing flexibility concerning expectations and practices concerning aging and caregiving, whether caregiving for elders or by elders. There is increasing flexibility concerning who cares for whom, how they care, when they care, how care is shared or rotated, the degree to which direct versus indirect care is provided, and how forms of care are combined. This flexibility is not just due to increased individual choice and decreased moral adherence to traditional social norms, but also due to wider variation in the external constraints to which caregiving for and by elders has to respond. Nursing-home care is now both more available and also more acceptable than it was in the past, although the facilities are still not sufficient to meet demand in many places. Some seniors are seeing care by more-distant kin, nonfamilial hired help, community-based care, or nursing-home care as preferable to care by adult children. The reasons for this include not wanting to burden adult children or decrease the educational or career prospects of children or grandchildren and wanting to use market payment in order to not feel like a burden on others who are socially obligated to care.[1]

Within this theme of flexibility, variation, and change, our contributors have provided in-depth analyses of key scholarly literature and of their own original research to illuminate contemporary meanings, practices, and strategies related to aging and caregiving in the East Asian locales of China, Hong Kong, Taiwan, Singapore, Japan, and Korea. While showing certain commonalities, the volume has emphasized the plurality of East Asian experiences of aging, caregiving, and aging societies. Below we examine further some of the cross-cutting themes of the volume that were laid out in this volume's Introduction.

Tensions between Traditional Ideals and Contemporary Realities and Competing Values

All chapters engaged with the strong tensions between traditional ideals of Confucian filial piety versus contemporary realities or competing social values. They have shown that although these East Asian societies share filial piety as a reference point, there is variation in people's relationship to that value, including how they interpret it, and whether it is a priority in their lives in relation to competing values in what they say or do.

The chapters engaged filial piety in various ways. Some chapters examined how people mourn society's failure to uphold traditional ideals (chap. 8), express nostalgia for a primordial cultural identity (chap. 5), or explain current obstacles to fulfilling traditional ideals (chap. 2). Some illustrated how complex and multifaceted the concept of filial piety is (chap. 10) and how people are redefining what counts as being filial enough (chaps. 1, 10). Chapters also showed how elders and younger folks are reinterpreting which markers of filiality are critical, such as emotional caring versus pragmatic assistance, or warm interactions versus material support (chaps. 1, 4, 10). Some pieces traced how people are reinterpreting the timing and balance of reciprocity across generations (chaps. 1, 11) or how they are rethinking the relative importance of filial piety among other competing values (chaps. 2, 9, 11). Many chapters described how adult children may hold filiality as an ideal but lack capacity for follow-through (chaps. 2, 4–5, 11). They showed how optimal pragmatic achievement of filial tasks may involve delegating tasks to outsiders instead of providing personal care directly (chaps. 4, 6). They demonstrated how physical distance or household division can make achieving filial care more challenging (chaps. 6, 11), but make family relations more harmonious, another prized value (chap. 11). Many chapters showed how people may embrace alternative cultural ideals, including family harmony (chaps. 1, 11), self-reliance (chaps. 2, 7), and/or positive emotions (chaps. 1, 4). Chapters also observed how nurturing descendants often trumps support for elders (chaps. 2–3, 10).

This volume has also shown how other cultural values and social forces beyond filial piety are very important in shaping how contemporary East Asian people talk about and act in relation to aging and caregiving, be that care *of* the aged or care *by* the aged. Such competing cultural values include nurturance of descendants (chaps. 1–3, 9, 11), harmonious relationships (chaps. 1–3, 9, 11), and senior self-reliance, independence, or mutual aid (chaps. 1–3, 7, 11). Such competing social forces include the marketization of life (chaps. 3–4), societization of care (chaps. 1, 4, 6–7, 9–12), and increased geographic mobility (chaps. 3, 6, 11).

Most chapters engaged with the subtheme of the contemporary values of autonomy or self-reliance versus traditional values of dependence or interdependence in relation to elders and their relations with family, community, and/or the state. Many chapters explored the emergence of seniors desiring or needing to be self-reliant or independent, rather than depending on or "burdening" their children (chaps. 1–3, 6–7, 10–11). Two chapters examine spousal caregiving as a form of relative independence from children, while emphasizing interdependence among and/or dependence on spouses (chap. 2, chap. 9). Both of those chapters called for a rethinking of the notion of the "eldercare burden" on society, as well as on caregivers for whom caregiving is not always a "burden," and for whom "burdens" are not always bad. In one chapter filiality meant freeing seniors from the need to participate in decision-making in the case of end-of-life care (chap. 12), while in others filiality meant allowing seniors the autonomy to centrally participate in care decisions and arrangements (chaps. 2, 4). One chapter analyzed contemporary Japanese discourse on elders who die alone and the social perception of a negative social trend toward too many seniors living alone and insufficient intergenerational connection (chap. 8). Different framings of what constitutes senior independence versus dependence were also explored. In some contexts, self-reliance meant seniors relying on themselves rather than on their children (chaps. 2, 7), with government-derived benefits as a way to remain independent (chaps. 1–2, 7, 10). However, in another context self-reliance was read as reliance on family and filial behavior in order to avoid dependence on the state (chap. 4). Overall, these chapters traced shifting cultural discourses and social values and practices in relation to appropriate forms and levels of social intertwinement, reciprocity, dependence, and interdependence regarding seniors. As several chapters showed, this involves a trend away from a life-course ecosystem perspective toward more narrow short-term thinking in which youths' time has more value than seniors' time (chaps. 2, 7, 11).

Finally, many chapters also engaged additional ideals related to old age and care. Some addressed issues of what people think constitutes a "good old age" in today's society (chaps. 1, 3, 6–7, 11). Many chapters explored issues of personhood and perceptions of what it means to be a "good person" (chaps. 5–6, 9–10) or a "good old person" (chaps. 2–3, 6–7, 9, 11). All chapters had things to say about what people see as "good care," whether they were on the giving or the receiving end. A few chapters engaged what it means to have a "good death" (chaps. 2, 9, 12). In many pieces we found not a clear positive or negative orientation toward aging and caregiving but ambivalence (chaps. 2–3, 6–7, 9–12). With regard to failure to carry out ideals, some chapters addressed issues of the presence or absence of guilt or regrets (chaps. 1–2, 6, 10), and some chapters touched on issues of social reputation or "face" (chaps. 2, 9, 12).

Role of the State and Public Policy

The role of the state and public policy intersected in interesting ways with the filial piety theme above. Governments of these East Asian societies have continued to play a role in encouraging younger generations to be more filial (chaps. 1, 4–5, 8–9). All chapters showed how in recent decades such state promotion of filial piety has focused on cajoling adult children to support and care for their parents, rather than other traditional aspects

TABLE 13.1. Trends in Aging-Related Social Welfare in East Asian Societies.

TRENDS IN SOCIAL WELFARE	China	Hong Kong	Taiwan	Singapore	Japan	South Korea
Universal pensions	IP	N	√	N	√	√
Universal health-care coverage	IP	N	√	N	√	√
Long-term care insurance	P	RPO	√	√ ES	√	√
End-of-life palliative/ hospice care services	P	IP	√	√	√	IP
Health insurance coverage of hospice	N	RPO	√ NHI	√ MDS	√ NHI	√ NHI

Note: √ = developed, IP = process in-progress, P = pilot areas, N = no. NHI = covered by National Health Insurance. ES = covered by ElderShield. MDS = covered by defined-contribution Medisave. RPO = rare, a private pay option.

Source: Author data.

of filial piety related to obedience to parents or carrying on the family line. Some contributors described governmental attempts to promote filial piety in the face of perceived decline in social morality (chaps. 1, 5, 8). Two chapters indicated how some government policies to support the aged may be inadvertently contributing to weakening of filial behavior in families (chaps. 4, 10). Yet chapters also argued that more state support to shore up struggling family caregivers is sorely needed (chaps. 4, 12). Several pieces showed that many seniors see governmental benefits like pensions or health insurance as liberation from needing to rely on their children (chaps. 1–2, 4, 7, 11). Some chapters in part II (Japan) and part III (Korea) examined the effects of these countries' national long-term care policies on meanings and dynamics of filial piety or familial care (chaps. 7–8, 10, 12). At some sites there were concerns about not crowding out familial support or creating perverse incentives for overuse of state support (chap. 4), but also concerns about undershooting levels of state support (chap. 8). One chapter described how a local government program to support and house seniors in the village explicitly prioritized affective filiality and warm intergenerational interactions over material support (chap. 1). Another showed how seniors taking part in a Korean repatriation program prioritized lack of family conflict over geographic proximity or family support (chap. 11).

In addition, the chapters showed how different East Asian societies are taking varied policy responses to the issue of their aging societies; see table 13.1 with relation to pensions, health-care coverage, long-term care insurance, and end-of-life care. Japan, South Korea, and Taiwan have long-standing social pension systems and universal health-care coverage, while China is about a decade into the process of rolling these out, and Hong Kong and Singapore leave pensions and health-care coverage largely to the market. Japan, South Korea, and Taiwan also have established systems for publicly funded long-term care insurance. China is starting to pilot such systems in large wealthy cities like Shanghai. Singapore has a defined contribution system for long-term care insurance from which citizens may opt out. In Hong Kong, long-term care insurance is run through private insurance and is rarely purchased. Finally, regarding end-of-life care, Japan, Taiwan, and Singapore have well-developed palliative and hospice care services, all of which are covered by National Health Insurance. South Korea and Hong Kong are in the process of developing their end-of-life service infrastructure, and China is in the early pilot stages in some large cities. In Singapore end-of-life care can be covered by defined-contribution Medisave accounts. In Hong Kong it is left to private insurance, and is very rarely purchased. In China there is not yet formal coverage for these services.

"Models" for dealing with issues of aging and elder support and care were another governance theme found across the chapters. Traditional Confucian filial piety was one such model. In addition, Japan has often been seen as a model for social welfare policies and gerontechnological innovation, with South Korea following Japan in its aging policy in many respects. At other times, the West has been taken as a model, but one that needs to be modified to fit the local culture. Community- and program-level models, with promoters striving to be recognized as exemplary, also came into play. Whatever their level, models may be exemplary but not easily or wholly transferrable to other sites. Traditional standards for filial piety, for one example, while still admired by many, are often not practicable today, even in East Asian locales. The Jiangxiang village "model" (Tang and Shea in chap. 1), for another example, is an exemplary case unlikely to be feasible in many other villages. The hospice model, although a globally recognized standard of end-of-life care, in many ways was not translating easily to the Korean national context (chap. 12).

A final state-related theme in some chapters was that of surveillance. Kim (chap. 8) argued that the Japanese government is spending too much money on surveillance-type activities that track behavior, rather than on constructive activities to assist seniors and boost their quality of life. In China, provisions in the Law for the Protection of the Rights and Interests of the Elderly of 2013 that allow seniors to sue adult children for neglect have been seen by some as welcome enforcement of seniors' rights, however others have viewed the law as an attempt at populace control without adequate state recognition of their own responsibility for creating and thus rectifying the problem of population aging (Zhang 2017). Furthermore, few Chinese parents want to sue their children, with reluctance stemming from reasons of compassion or reputation (chap. 3).

Contemporary Patterns of Familial Care

All of the chapters in our volume addressed in some way contemporary patterns of familial care. Increased flexibility in who cares for whom, when, where, and how was a major theme therein. Earlier in this conclusion we discussed familial care issues in relation to decline in coresidence and rise in gender equity in parental care expectations, and in this volume's Introduction we noted how, with expanding longevity, many adult children caring for their aging parents are now in their sixties or seventies themselves (e.g., chaps. 8–9). Here we will underscore our volume's signature theme of eldercare by those other than immediate descendants, issues of familial reciprocity related to care for and by elders, and complexities of caregiving related to migration.

One of the features of our volume has been to highlight care by family other than adult children. With continuing increases in neolocal residence, empty-nest households, and state supports for seniors, there has been a slow increase in recognition of seniors' role in taking care of themselves and/or their spouses (chaps. 2, 9), which is a form of productive aging. While discourse on filial piety in East Asian populations has directed popular media and scholarly attention toward care of parents by adult children, a great deal of eldercare in the region is handled by older adults themselves, especially in spousal care (chaps. 2, 9). With longer life expectancies, the coexistence of multiple generations over long spans of time, and the flexibility sometimes offered in the schedules of students and unemployed youths, care by grandchildren is also emerging as an important supplementary source of eldercare, as Thang and Mehta discussed in their chapter (chap. 5) on attitudes and norms of filiality in grandchildren in Singapore.

Chapters also attended to issues of intergenerational and/or intragenerational reciprocity within families with regard to familial care both for and by seniors. Many chapters showed a strong tension between people's desire to support seniors, or to be supported as seniors, and people's wishes to nurture the younger generations (chaps. 1–3, 6, 9–11). Many discussed the idea of "burden" (chaps. 2–3, 7, 9–11) in various ways. These variations included seniors not wanting to be a burden, caregivers feeling or not feeling burdened, aging populations as burden or resource, living long as a burden on or boon to oneself, or being taken care of as a burden or not on the care recipient. In addition, there was a theme of children and grandchildren as burdens (chap. 3). At the same time, several chapters also showed how burdens were often chosen and even embraced as beneficial not just for the care recipient, but also for the care provider in terms of their own development as a person (chaps. 2, 3).

Reflecting on trends toward greater geographic mobility, some chapters examined how the meanings and patterns of care for and by elders are responding to domestic and international forms of migration by youths and/ or elders. One chapter examined international migration by adult children and its effect on support and care of left-behind elders (chap. 6). Another explored migration by older generations to care for adult children and grandchildren (chap. 3). A third analyzed migration by older adults in response to an offer of state-sponsored senior housing (chap. 11). Zhang's chapter (chap. 3) followed seniors in China who migrate domestically to assist their migrant worker children with housework and childcare, and found that grandchild care for the "floating elderly" was important as a normative experience of "good aging" for the young-old (sixty-five to seventy-nine) that later compromised their ability to age well as they crossed the threshold into old-old age (eighty and above). Sun's chapter (chap. 6) analyzed how Taiwanese immigrants to the United States remotely manage their aging parents' care back home in Taiwan and how they and their parents felt about it, finding both positive and negative sentiments about the arrangement on the part of both migrant children and left-behind parents. Szawarska's chapter (chap. 11) traced how in South Korea altruistic repatriation efforts to bring home seniors forcibly resettled in then-Japanese-occupied Sakhalin Island (now part of Russia) during World War II have led to complications for familial care, but have at the same time improved intergenerational relationships by reducing conflict.

Contemporary Patterns of Nonfamilial Care

Chapters also examined new social balances being forged between traditional dependence on family versus reliance on nonfamilial options for support or care (chaps. 2, 4, 6–7, 10–12). Some chapters found too much of certain kinds of nonfamilial care in their area (chap. 4 on over-institutionalization, chap. 8 on elder abandonment) and some too little (chap. 2 on institutional dementia care options in China, chap. 12 on hospice availability in Korea). Chapters showed how as the locus of responsibility widens beyond the family, nonfamilial options are emerging from a variety of sources, including government, community, nonprofit, and market sources (chaps. 1, 4, 6, 11–12). New or expanded nonfamilial services have appeared, including senior centers, adult day-care centers (chap. 2), domestic helper services (chap. 6), neighborhood volunteers (chap. 7), nursing homes (chaps. 4, 7, 10–11), hospital rehabilitation facilities, and end-of-life services (chaps. 2, 9, 12). These nonfamilial options have been variously framed as arising out of an unprecedented challenge in meeting eldercare needs or as presenting an excellent opportunity for social innovation.

Attitudes toward commercialization vary from seeing them as offering welcome new choices for those who can afford them, to allowing seniors to be more independent from their children, to serving as a last resort for those without children or without children willing or able to help. Whereas in some contexts market-based services may be seen as higher quality and more desirable (e.g., Zhang 2020 on new private luxury nursing homes in China), Shum and Lum (chap. 4) show how private nursing homes in Hong Kong are often viewed as less trusted and of lower quality than public institutions.

Some chapters raise the concept of the outsourcing of care or filial piety (chaps. 3, 6, 7). In one instantiation, adult children framed the purchase of eldercare services or products, such as hired home-helpers, high-end nursing homes, or private insurance packages, as a demonstration of their filial concern (Sun in chap. 6). While in some contexts nonfamilial care has been marketed as still homey, or traditional, in other contexts eldercare services are marketed as better than lay care, using terms like "professional," "modern," "scientific," "technological," "intelligent," "reliable," or "world class," whether in the case of technological tools or robotics (chap. 7) or a care facility. Another chapter (chap. 3) remarked on the advent of outsourcing grandparenting in which some "floating" Chinese grandparents with the means in a top-tier city would send their grandchildren to day care with professional teachers for some part of the day, easing their grandparenting burden and giving their descendants a head start in formal education.

In our volume, public, nonprofit, or community actors were shown doing a variety of things. They made home visits (chaps. 6–7), helped with tasks (chap. 6), created spaces for belonging (chap. 1) or for value reinforcement (chap. 5), filled the gap between government and family (chap. 4), and noticed a death next door (chap. 8). Several chapters provided a lay of the land of various emerging eldercare options, and in doing so addressed public, nonprofit, community, or volunteer services. Tang and Shea (chap. 1) provided a history of nonfamilial eldercare in rural China and an account of a reform-era collective model for old-age support. Shum and Lum (chap. 4) examined different forms of nonfamilial care offered in Hong Kong, with a focus on public eldercare. They observed how the Hong Kong system has involved perverse incentives leading to a high level of institutionalization relative to home- and community-based care, and how public institutions are far more trusted than private ones. They also noted neglect of the needs of family caregivers in Hong Kong due to the overemphasis on spending for frail elders. Moore (chap. 7) framed her analysis of elder self-reliance within the context of Japan's national policies guiding various nonfamilial options for eldercare and described the involvement of retired volunteers in Japanese neighborhoods and non-kin caregivers in a Buddhist nunnery. Lee and Chee (chap. 10) included an overview of emerging eldercare options in Korea especially concerning recent long-term care policy.

Social Stratification Issues

Some chapters brought attention to social stratification within elderly populations (chaps. 1–2, 4, 9–10, 12) or between older and younger generations (chaps. 1–4, 8–11). Many chapters mentioned expanding intergenerational inequity in which resources and care are funneled toward younger generations (chaps. 2–3, 7–8, 10). Several pieces showed how seniors with lower socioeconomic status have reduced access to familial and/or nonfamilial support and care (chaps. 1–2, 4, 8, 10, 12). Here we will comment on the one with the highest degree of social stratification within elderly populations. Despite recent attempts to reinstitute a safety net for basic subsistence and primary health-care coverage for the urban poor and rural dwellers (chap. 2), China has seen increasing social stratification over the past several decades of market reform. Tang and Shea's chapter (chap. 1) showed how even in rural China there can be a wide gap between "model" villages and more-typical, poor, rural areas. For urban China, Shea's chapter (chap. 2) depicts lower-middle-income seniors in the wealthy metropolis of Shanghai who did not have enough money to afford nursing-home care, had they wanted it. Another chapter shows how China's *hukou* system tying location of official domestic residence to social welfare benefits and health insurance constrains the ability of seniors to stay with migrant children for long periods (chap. 3).

Senior Voices, Agency, and Productive Aging

Many authors presented examples of senior subjectivity and agency (chaps. 2–3, 6–7, 9, 11), a perspective not often seen in scholarship on aging and caregiving. Several engaged issues of personhood (chaps. 2–3, 7, 9, 11), including what is involved in being a good caregiver and/or a good person in old age. Many authors also showed how seniors found meaning in later life through self-care, child and/or grandchild care, spousal care, participation in communities for mutual aid, and/or care of the ancestors (chaps. 1–3, 6–7, 9, 11). For example, the chapter by Tang and Shea (chap. 1) brings up how the elders in the Chinese village they studied prided themselves on continuing in old age to give money to their descendants. The chapter by

Shea (chap. 2) shows the deep sense of meaning and fulfillment that some elderly spouses in Shanghai attain by taking care of their ailing husband or wife. Moore's chapter (chap. 7) showed how contemporary Japanese elders are negotiating personhood within kin-based and non-kin-based care relationships, with self-reliance and independence as central values for being a good person in later life. M. Zhang's chapter (chap. 3) examines the caregiving that "floating grandparents" do by sojourning to larger cities in China to care for their grandchildren. In Sun's chapter (chap. 7), left-behind Taiwanese aging parents told of how, although they missed their emigrated child, those who received care from paid helpers said that they felt empowered by this care arrangement in that they did not have to worry about holding back the success of their children or grandchildren. Although not by their own will, the deceased seniors in Kim's chapter (chap. 8) provided for their descendants after death through non-discontinuance of pension flow.

Intersection of Aging, Caregiving, Life Courses, Dying, and Death

Three chapters examined the intersection of eldercare in life and death (chaps. 2, 9, 12), contrary to the sharp division common in most scholarly literature. Shea (chap. 2) showed how some widowed Shanghai spousal caregivers talked about how they continued to take care of their husband or wife, and how the deceased spouse extended care toward the family in dying and/or after death. Long and Campbell (chap. 9) showed important continuities in relationships and care work by Japanese family caregivers that crossed the threshold between life and death, as well as changes in caregiving roles as the care recipient transitioned from stage to stage. Shea and Han (chap. 11) revealed how most deaths in South Korea happen in hospitals due to a combination of factors, including families keeping prognoses from the dying and fears that enjoining hospice care will signal lack of filial effort.

Population Aging, Demographic Projections, and Imagined Futures

Throughout the volume, there exists a tension between the notion of population aging as a problem or crisis versus a blessing or opportunity. As Wen (2013) argued, demographic projections apropos aging societies can furnish pessimistic or optimistic visions of the future, depending on which demographic measures are the focus. Such measures and projections are themselves imbued with value judgments about aging and the aged and speculative social assumptions about future society and future seniors. In interaction with these projections are imagined social "futures" of a frail, sick, and draining geriatric dystopia (Shea and Zhang 2016), on the one hand, or an active healthy generative "gerontopia" (Sokolovsky 2009: 491), on the other. Some social commentators imagine a looming crisis of rising old-age dependency ratios, while others focus more on the boon of longevity and healthy aging and the promise of mature populations (HelpAge International 2015a). These two contrasting "imagined futures" (Wen 2013), one gloomy and one rosy, focus on different statistical measures and carry radically different assumptions about the value of old people and the repercussions of an aging society.

Population Aging as a Crisis

In some social commentaries, population aging in East Asia, as elsewhere, is viewed as a threat. From this perspective, rising proportions of elderly people are taken as the portent of a looming economic and social crisis. Figure 13.1 shows related terms used in policy, public, and media discourse, such as "the graying of society," "the gray doom," and "the silver tsunami." Such metaphors depict the elderly as a massive problem posing a hazard to the "social body" (Scheper-Hughes and Lock 1987).

This perspective emphasizes what Wen (2013) calls "prolongation of morbidity," that is that "increased life expectancy due to medical advances . . . means longer periods of disease" and aging is "prolonged suf-

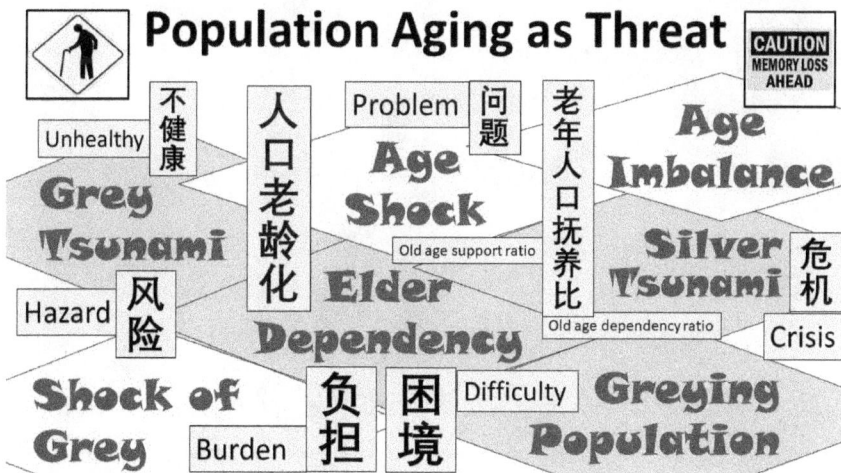

FIGURE 13.1. Population Aging as Threat. Created by author Jeanne Shea.

fering with no purpose," with "increased healthcare costs and burden on caregivers" (85). In this discourse, seniors are represented as a mass of chronic disease, ill health, addled minds, disability, dysfunction, dependency, and burden threatening to swallow the nation and its younger members, draining them of vitality. Replenishing funds to back pension and health-care systems is a key concern therein. These depictions create a public impression of population aging as an aberrant social imbalance, risking the health and future of the society by draining its resources and energies into the long decline of outmoded and unproductive people.

The old-age dependency ratio is a related measure (see figure 13.2), defined as the ratio of "the number of people older than 65 years per 100 people of working age (20–64)" (Organisation for Economic Co-operation and Development [OECD] 2017: 19). As illustrated in figure 13.2, UN (2017) data show that in 1950 this ratio in all six societies under comparison was very low. In Japan, the first country in the region to experience rapid aging, the ratio began a steep ascent around 1980. The others began a steep rise from 2010 onward. Whereas in 2015 China had 14.5 persons aged sixty-five and above for every 100 "working-age" people, Singapore 17.6, Taiwan 18.2, Korea 19.4, Hong Kong 22.2, and Japan 46.2, by 2050 China is expected to have 47.9 elderly persons per 100 "working-age" people, Singapore 65.6, Hong Kong 68.5, Taiwan 69.7, South Korea 72.4, and Japan 77.8.

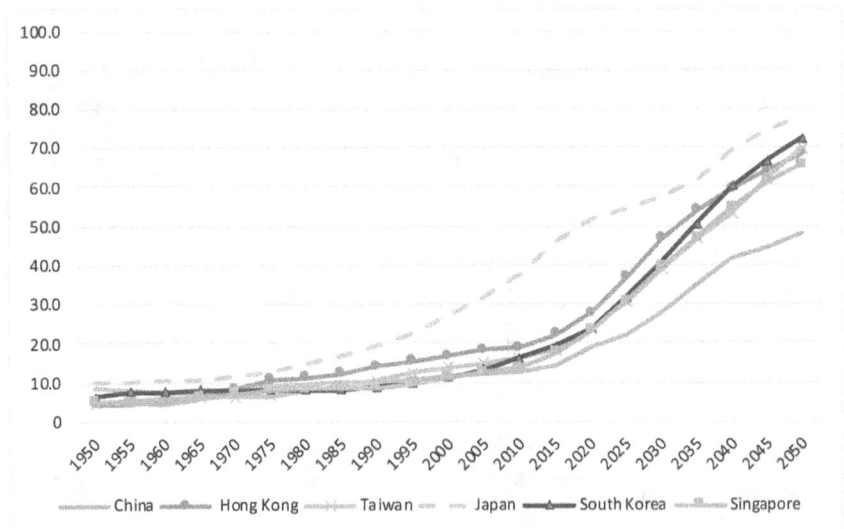

FIGURE 13.2. Old-Age Dependency Ratio. Created by the authors.

Due to this rapid and unparalleled level of population aging, East Asian societies are scrambling to adjust to the perceived moral and practical crisis of who will support the elderly and provide eldercare in the face of steep population aging. Morally, there is a deep concern in these societies that their people may have lost their moral bearings, and that modernization, individualization, Westernization, and marketization have gone too far (Kleinman et al. 2011; and chaps. 5, 8, 10). Practically, there are serious questions of who will provide support and care to the elderly in cases in which adult children are not willing or able to step in. With smaller family sizes and longer life expectancy, families are wondering how to manage. As longevity climbs and the population of the old-old (eighty years old and above) grows, an increasing number of adult children will find themselves faced with caring for elderly parents when they are already old themselves. These societies are also faced with rising numbers of seniors who decided not to marry or not to have children, or whose only child died, or who are widowed or divorced, and thus are living alone with few kin available to assist them. With a smaller proportion of working-age folks, governments are concerned about having enough revenue, hired helpers, day-care centers, and senior residential care openings to make up the shortfall. Increased need for extended intensive care measures for dementia is a particular concern.

Population Aging as an Opportunity

In other social commentaries, population aging is seen as an opportunity. This optimistic perspective argues that greater longevity is a cause for celebration, and with the proper structures in place many older adults can be healthy, active, and productive far later in life. In this sense, aging societies are seen as "mature" societies (Harper 2014). Such maturation, it is argued, can serve as an impetus for positive social innovation. Figure 13.3 shows terms used in scholarly, policy, and media discourse in relation to this theme.

This kind of discourse highlights compression of morbidity, that is "increased life expectancy with disease postponed until just before death" (Wen 2013: 85), through practices and programs to promote healthy, active, productive, or successful aging. This perspective focuses on notions of social progress and prosperity embodied in terms like "demographic transition," "epidemiological transition," and "demographic dividend." It emphasizes the positives of aging populations such as longevity, maturity, knowledge, experience, know-how, mastery, past and present contributions, generativity, wisdom, and transcendence. It conjures images of aging populations as presenting unprecedented opportunities for innovation, advancement, cooperation, and inclusiveness.

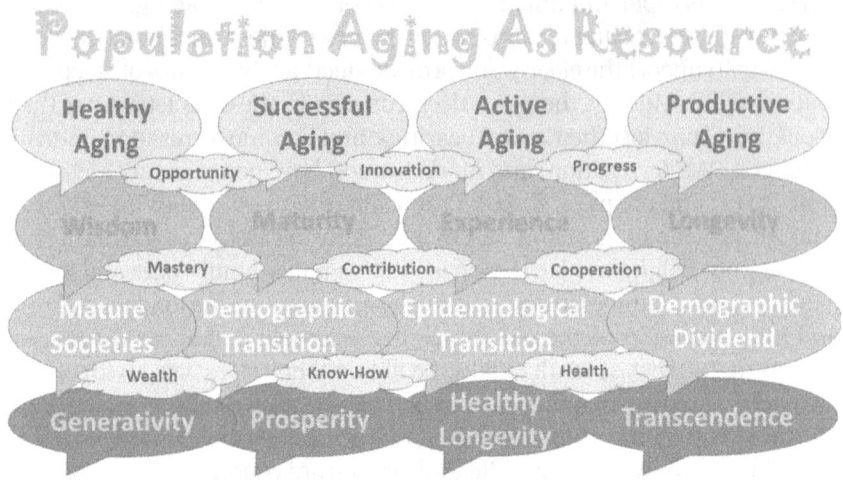

FIGURE 13.3. Population Aging as Resource. Created by author Jeanne Shea.

UN (2019) estimates for 2018 show remarkable longevity in these areas of East Asia, as described above. In the next three decades these societies are headed toward record life expectancies. The quest for long life has long been a desired goal, although concerns exist about preserving health and quality of life in old age. Recent calculations of healthy life expectancy at birth (HALE), a measure of the number of years people are expected on average to live in good health, show that under present conditions age sixty-five is too early to assume poor health in East Asian societies. World Health Organization (WHO; 2018) figures for 2000 to 2016 show that healthy life expectancies have been rising, albeit at a slower rate than plain life expectancies (see figure 13.4).

As shown below, healthy life expectancy at birth has reached unprecedented levels for East Asia, attaining 73.0 years or more of healthy longevity for the four locales measured. In 2016 Singapore at 76.2 years attained the highest healthy life expectancy in the world, surpassing Japan, which at 74.8 years, took second place globally. Not far behind, Korea reached 73.0 years. Worldwide, only nine other nations had 73.0 or more years of healthy life expectancy. China at 68.7 years was higher than both the world average of 63.3 years and the United States' 68.5 years (WHO 2018).

A large number of seniors in these societies are enjoying healthier and more productive years after the age of sixty-five, allowing many of them to continue to work and take care of themselves and others well into old age, rather than "needing to rely on" their children (HelpAge International

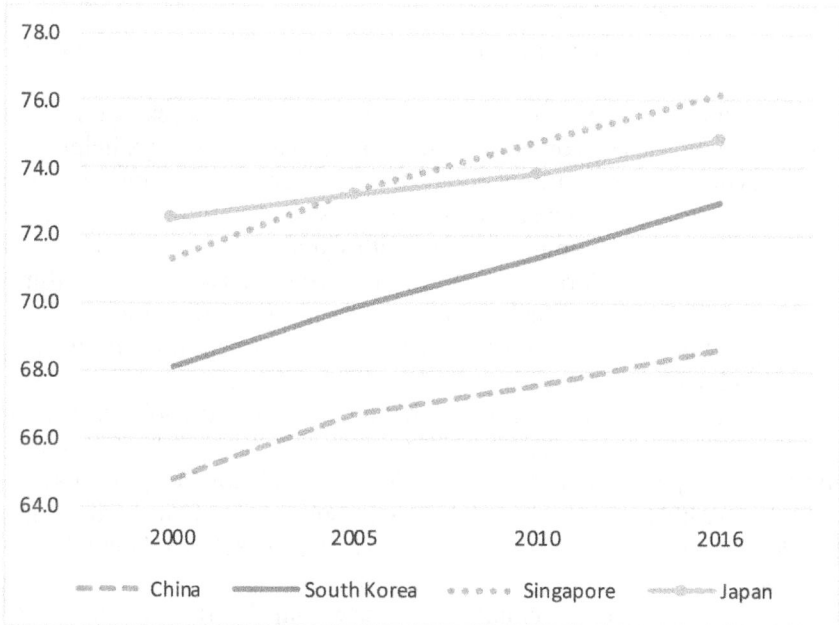

FIGURE 13.4. Healthy Life Expectancy at Birth, East Asian Societies, 2000–2016. Created by the authors.

2015a). Furthermore, were these trajectories to continue along roughly the same slopes, it is conceivable that by 2050 healthy life expectancy could approach seventy-nine years of age, at least for the high-income locales. These high healthy life expectancies raise questions about the old-age dependency ratio. Even if most seniors retire after age sixty-five, should we really be thinking of them as unproductive? Doing so means discounting the valuable informal labors that seniors do in their families and communities. In addition, given how most people at these sites are healthy into their seventies, East Asian nations are considering raising their minimum retirement age. If that occurs and retirement age is raised to higher than age sixty-five, then the idea of seniors not contributing to the pension system after age sixty-five will no longer be true. Another issue involves what is judged a "healthy life" in such statistics. As we saw, some senior caregivers have multiple chronic diseases, yet still make important productive contributions in their domestic labors (chap. 2).

If we instead look at numbers of old-old seniors who are much more likely to be no longer paying into pension systems and to need support and assistance than the young-old, the situation looks much more manageable. Based on UN (2017) figures, although the percentage of the total old-old population is rising, the population proportion of that group is still much lower than that of the young-old, both in 2015 figures and 2050 projections (see table 13.2).

If retirement ages were raised to be closer to healthy life expectancy for each location, the pension issue would not be nearly as severe, helping to compensate for higher numbers of old-old citizens. In addition, as some chapters have shown, there are old-old seniors who continue to make large contributions to their families, communities, and societies. Some chapters also showed how seniors tended to think of their pensions as something that they had already earned that allowed them to be independent in later life, not as them being dependent on society for their pensions. In this way, demographic logic and grassroots cultural logic diverge.

As our chapters demonstrate, in the face of increasing longevity, population aging, and social change, East Asian societies are also fashioning innovative responses at multiple levels. Families and individuals across East Asia are creating flexible, situation-specific solutions to family caregiving problems. Families are creatively adapting to incorporate nonfamilial measures as part of their caregiving strategies (chaps. 1, 3–7, 11–12). People are reframing kinship to emphasize elderly conjugal ties over intergenerational ones (chaps. 2, 7, 9). Families are re-creating kin relationships creatively over time to emphasize positive dimensions (chap. 9) and having grandchildren watch pro-filial media programs (chap. 5). Seniors and community members are putting together families of choice or neighborhood volunteerism for the purposes of eldercare (chap. 7). Grandparents are sojourning for grandchild care to accommodate their child's migration (chap. 3). Migrating adult children are managing transnational caregiving

TABLE 13.2. Comparison of Percentage of Young-Old vs. Old-Old, Selected East Asian Populations, 2015 and 2050.

	2015		2050	
	Age 65+	Age 80+	Age 65+	Age 80+
Japan	26.0%	7.6%	36.4%	15.0%
Hong Kong	15.2%	4.4%	33.9%	14.5%
South Korea	13.0%	2.6%	35.3%	14.3%
Taiwan	12.3%	3.1%	34.5%	12.9%
Singapore	11.7%	2.3%	33.6%	13.3%
China	9.7%	1.7%	26.3%	8.1%

Source: UN 2017.

networks comprising kin and non-kin (chap. 6), and resettled seniors and their families are creatively making the most of a limited repatriation program (chap. 11).

More broadly, governments, communities, markets, nongovernmental organizations (NGOs), and nonprofits are generating new options and strategies for addressing aging and caregiving through both novel forms of societal support for the elderly and enhanced options for continuing social contributions by seniors. Such creative societal solutions include a collectivized filial village (chap. 1), community volunteer programs (chaps. 2, 7), guest worker programs for foreign domestic workers (FDWs; chaps. 4–6), assistive technology and robotic care (chap. 7), long-term care insurance programs (chaps. 7, 9–10, 12), and, in Korea's case, family caregiver stipends (chap. 10). Not available at all sites and in many cases subject to stratified accessibility within sites (chaps. 1–2, 4, 10), these are nonetheless important innovations for aging and caregiving challenges. As responsibility for eldercare is diversifying and opportunities for productive aging are increasing, positive new patterns of intersectoral collaboration are emerging across families, communities, businesses, nonprofits, and local governments (chaps. 1–2, 4–12). Across sites, we see diversity in public policy, pension and health-care provisions, long-term care options, social programs, and nonprofit and market solutions and their interface with family and state agents.

Overall, this perspective sees aging, caregiving, and aging societies as positive stimuli, rather than as drains or burdens. Although Japan has been a super-aging society since 2008 (see Introduction), it is managing fairly well, without major catastrophe thus far (chaps. 7–9), which is a cause for hope. As Wen (2013) and others have argued, aging can be seen as an "opportunity to rethink current institutions, to question our basic paradigms of health, life and death" (Wen 2013: 85, quoting Inavatullah 2003: 11). Wen also points out how recent literature shows how care can be "a positive and empowering experience for" both recipients and caregivers (84).

Crisis and Opportunity

Moving forward, it is important to bring these utopic and dystopic visions together in policy and research. Such balance will help to develop more-realistic appraisals of likely futures in an aging East Asia and to advocate for policy directions and research agendas that address both sides in a more reflective and coordinated manner. We need to remember that demographic terms and statistics not only reflect reality, but also selectively reify attitudes and assumptions about aging persons and aging societies. A more complete picture requires many different kinds of statistical measures on both the rosy and cloudy sides, as well as ongoing qualitative data from a variety of perspectives and settings to establish their meaning in social and cultural context.

Directions for Future Policy and Research

As Wen (2013) has argued, policy responses to aging populations have tended to be predicated on value judgements and visions of the present and the future. Much policy meant to address the future has been "largely based on the assumption that the elderly of tomorrow will be similar to the elderly of today" (85). Most aging policy has also been based primarily on either a crisis model of aging as burden or a utopic model of aging as wealth or resource. Over the next several decades, societies in East Asia and beyond will face problems and opportunities in aging and caregiving that are uncharted, and it is difficult to predict what the future will bring, as the COVID-19 pandemic is illustrating. The needs and preferences of the elderly will likely change, as will the cultural, social, political, economic, and natural environment around them. The growing proportion of seniors and the likely changes in them and their surrounding environments will increase future need for fine-tuned research and responsive policymaking that is attentive to both the upsides and the downsides of aging societies.

Policy Directions

A number of different policy directions may help to mitigate matters in an aging society. These include policies encouraging childbearing; immigration or guest worker programs; later retirement age; reduction of ageism; healthy aging, active aging, and productive aging; increased state supports for the aged and caregivers; expanded eldercare services; age-friendly environments; medical developments; technological developments; and sustainability issues. Each policy is discussed in turn below with reference to East Asian settings.

Childbearing

With regard to encouraging childbearing, such policies have been tried, but so far have not been very effective. Singapore and Japan began pronatalist policies in 1987 and 1991, respectively, but with little impact on birth rates (Center for Public Impact [CPI] 2017; UN 2015). Later, Hong Kong, South Korea, and Taiwan offered some childbearing incentives, but again with little effect (E. Kim H-W. 2018; Poon 2018).[2] China loosened its family planning policy to two children per woman effective in 2016, but the expected baby bump did not materialize (World Bank 2018) and the number of live births nationwide fell by 2.5 million in 2018, contrary to a predicted increase (Weerasekara 2019). In 2021 China adopted a three-child policy whose likely effect is uncertain. What is needed are affordable quality childcare and less expensive childrearing costs so that parents need not choose between wage-earning and having children.

Immigration or Guest Worker Programs

While Japan and Korea have been reluctant to bring in outsiders and their long-term care insurance programs have discouraged use of FDWs (Peng 2017; and chap. 8), Singapore, Hong Kong, and Taiwan have encouraged large-scale use of FDWs (Wen 2013; and chap. 5–7). They have done so through guest worker visas and government incentives for families to hire FDWs, most of whom come from Indonesia, the Philippines, and Vietnam (Peng 2017). Japan is reported to be taking initial steps to allow more FDWs (Kajimoto 2019). In Korea, the numbers of Korean-Chinese migrant workers are growing, forming a low-cost alternative to certified Korea-born care workers (Y-S. Kim 2018). Problems with FDW use have included high turnover, poor working conditions, cultural and linguistic barriers, and inconsistent skill levels (Peng 2017).

Later Retirement Age

Given pension-provisioning challenges and longer healthy life expectancies, later retirement age is under consideration in many East Asian locales. Currently Japan requires employers to allow employees to work until age sixty-five, however, most companies have employees retire at age sixty and then reemploy them at a reduced wage; for the future its government is considering raising the retirement age from sixty-five to seventy or even seventy-five (Kajimoto 2019). South Korea's government is mulling raising the retirement age from sixty-five to seventy (Kim 2019). In Singapore age sixty-two is the official retirement age, with employers legally required to offer reemployment options to qualifying retirees up to age sixty-seven; recently government, trade unions, and employers there agreed to develop higher future cutoff ages for both (Geddie 2019). Taiwan's full pension eligibility age was raised from age sixty to sixty-one in 2018 and is set to gradually increase to age sixty-seven by 2027 (Taiwan Social Security Office of Retirement and Disability Policy 2019). In China, retirement has been set at age fifty to sixty, varying by gender and occupation. Recently, an official in China voiced governmental intent to gradually raise China's retirement to age sixty-five for both men and women by 2045; however, solid regulations have yet to materialize (China Labor Bulletin 2019). Hong Kong has no universal mandatory retirement age, but retirement for civil servants has been set at age sixty, the same age that is set by many companies (Chiu 2019). Recently, Hong Kong's government raised civil servant retirement to age sixty-five, and announced that it will raise "elderly welfare payments from the Comprehensive Social Security Assistance [CSSA] scheme" from age sixty to sixty-five. Hong Kong's Elderly Commission also called for a voluntary rise in the retirement ages set by publicly funded organizations, lest the government need to legislate (Chiu 2019). Yet, this can conflict with youths' employment and with the pull for the healthy young-old to care for the sick young-old or the old-old in their families or for children or grandchildren.

Reduction of Ageism

Reduction of ageism is another way to improve matters in aging societies (Featherstone and Hepworth 2009). In workplaces, families, and communities, promotion of positive views and treatment of the aged can help increase younger people's level of understanding and appreciation of older folks and promote seniors' mental health and functioning. Ironically, despite the Confucian tradition of filial piety, ageism is a large problem in many East Asian contexts, as some of our chapters (chaps. 2–3, 5, 8, 10) have shown. There is a continuing need for greater legal protections to protect seniors from abuse and neglect not just on paper but also with effective enforcement mechanisms. With regard to employment, reduction of age discrimination in hiring, training, job assignment, pay rates, workplace interactions, and retention is a necessary complement to extension of retirement age limits (OECD 2018). To accommodate long productive lives, continuing education and retraining of older workers and instrumental accommodations for emerging disabilities are also needed. Facing population decline and a labor shortage, Japan's Public Employment Service is helping workers age sixty-five and older with job placement, finding employers who are seeking older workers to find matches; it has a long way to go, however, to meet the further criteria recommended by the OECD (2018).

Healthy Aging, Active Aging, and Productive Aging

Policies promoting healthy aging, active aging, or productive aging are another means to improve aging societies. Each of the East Asian locales we have examined has some form of government policy promoting healthy, active, and/or productive aging (HelpAge International 2015b; Lum 2013; Morrow-Howell and Mui 2012; Wen 2013). All of them formed in response to earlier deficit-based visions of aging, these three frameworks overlap but also have some distinctions. The WHO (2019) defines healthy aging as "the process of developing and maintaining the functional ability that enables wellbeing in older age." Policies promoting healthy aging encourage older adults to take good care of their health and societies to create health-promoting environments, supporting proper diet, exercise, social engagement, medical checkups, fall prevention, and other preventive measures. The WHO (2002: 12) defines active aging as "the process of optimizing opportunities for health, participation and security in order to enhance quality of life as people age." Policies promoting active aging encourage seniors to stay physically, socially, and civically active, and encourage societies to create environments that allow them to do so safely. Productive aging experts Morrow-Howell and Mui (2012: i) define productive aging as "the involvement of older adults in society through employment, volunteering, caregiving, education and skill building." Policies focusing on productive aging encourage seniors to contribute to their families and communities through prosocial efforts such as housework, caregiving, volunteer work, continuing paid labor, community service, lifelong learning, and/or civic engagement. While policies aligned with these frameworks are present in East Asian settings, more effort will be needed in this regard as population aging increases.[3] Service to family, leisure activities, and community volunteering have emerged as important forms of positive aging in all of these locales. In addition, HelpAge International (2015b) reports that Japan, Korea, and Singapore have policies to support senior employment (152–53). Such policies are not a good fit for labor-rich China, so its focus has been on providing retirees with universities for senior citizens, free public transportation, free public park admission, free or low-cost senior recreational activities, and, more recently, volunteer opportunities. Yet, there is a danger that overemphasis on productive aging may turn into a neoliberal devolution of responsibility from government and younger family members onto the elderly.

Increased State Supports for the Aged and Caregivers

Increased state supports for the aged and family elder caregivers are another way to address the challenges involved in an aging society. As Kim's chapter (chap. 8) showed, even in high-income Japan with its generous pension system, pension amounts are sometimes inadequate. It will likely be necessary to raise pensions across East Asia in the future, especially in rural China where the pension system started late and very modestly (chap. 1). Even if retirement and pension ages are raised as described above, a major increase in the number of people of pensionable age is anticipated due to population aging (Introduction). Likewise, even with longer healthy life expectancies, there will be higher numbers and proportions of elders in need of health insurance coverage. Fortunately, all six locales now have widespread health insurance coverage (chaps. 1, 4–6, 9–10), even though the amount of covered in rural China is very low (chap. 1). There will also be a higher number and proportion of elders requiring long-term care, with fewer family members available to provide it. Japan and Korea can provide lessons if the other four locales consider instituting long-term care insurance (chaps. 7–12). Family caregiver stipends such as those in South Korea may be worthwhile to pursue in other locales, such as in Japan where labor shortage is acute and the reluctance to hire FDWs strong. While Singapore, Hong Kong, and Taiwan have made extensive use of FDWs (chaps. 4–6), there have been concerns about turnover and fit as described above, so a complementary family caregiver stipend program may be useful, especially because these locales plan to raise retirement and pension age. Nationally, China does not have the labor shortage problem that Japan does; however, because rural areas in China are often gutted of young people due to urban labor migration, a family caregiver stipend for rural family care might be useful there, although finding funding for it would be unlikely in the foreseeable future. Any paid family caregiver program needs strong quality oversight to avoid the problem that Korea has encountered, with some family caregivers doing a bad job and getting paid for it (chap. 10). For any such government benefits, there are concerns about intergenerational and intragenerational equity to manage. A life course, family-system-based, and social-justice approach to government benefits is needed to balance the interests of different age cohorts and socioeconomic groups. If senior pensions and health-care benefits are too low, adult children may deplete savings that would otherwise go to their own retirement years. If current senior pensions and benefits are too high, however, it may be difficult to provide sufficient pensions to the old of the future. Pension-wise, East Asian women's historical disadvantage in the paid workforce and their disparate contribution to informal, unpaid, volunteer, or low-paid labor and to domestic duties and caregiving is also important to take into account. If family caregiver stipends are impracticable, perhaps time banks could be used, in which caregiving service hours are tracked with logged hours later redeemable by the caregiver for nonmonetary assistance. Given the mobility of young and old, however, banked time should be made transferable geographically.

Expanded Eldercare Services

Another way to meet the tasks required in aging societies is to expand the amount and kinds of eldercare services available through government programs, nonprofits, NGOs, volunteer programs, for-profit companies, community-based mutual-aid initiatives, and public–private partnerships. These include a variety of services to support and prolong independent living, such as meal and grocery delivery services, housekeeping and home repair services, emergency services, and so on, while acknowledging that some seniors prefer and are able to do things themselves (chap. 3). At higher levels of need, services include assisted living, adult day-care centers, outpatient clinics, and respite care, and then nursing-home, inpatient hospital, rehabilitation, and dementia care services. Since up to a third of adults older than age eighty-five in many populations have some degree of dementia, the latter service need will likely become acute over time. Finally, there is a rising need for hospice and palliative care (chap. 12). All these avenues are being pursued in each of the studied locales, but with greater availability in the high-income locales and in the urban and wealthier regions within locales. Caregiver workforce training, development, and monitoring, together with monitoring and oversight, will be critical to ensure quality and fidelity of services. As these chapters have shown, tailoring such services to local cultural preferences and socioeconomic needs is key, while at the same time learning what one can from national or international models (chap. 12).

Age-Friendly Environments

Creating age-friendly public and private environments and disability accommodations will be another critical area for development. Taking a disabilities studies perspective (e.g., Rice et al. 2017), the quality of our aging future may be less about the demographic proportions of old people and more about our value interpretations about "good people," "good lives," and "good societies," and about the future fit between the built environment and seniors and persons with various impairments. Useful accommodations include things like accessible public bathrooms, public benches, large-type signs and menus, good lighting, quality sound systems, elevators and curb cuts for wheelchairs, entryway ramps, slip-proof home interiors, home visits by community volunteers, and neighborhood watch systems for mutual protection. Consulting with a variety of senior groups with different repertoires of ability and impairment and sociocultural sensibilities will be important to make accommodations that will suit their priorities and be both user-friendly and cost-efficient. Again, high-income locales and urban and wealthier areas are far ahead therein. How to make environmental accommodations more accessible and affordable is the next hurdle.

Medical Developments

Medical developments can be helpful or harmful in the context of aging societies. Better prevention guidelines, screening, diagnosis, medicine, treatment, surgery, rehabilitation, and physical therapy can help to compress morbidity, improving quality of life and generating more healthy years of life with shorter periods of sickness (chap. 9). For example, development of an effective vaccine against emerging infectious diseases would help to reduce disease severity and mortality in older populations, who in the case of

COVID-19 have been found to be at a significantly higher risk of case fatality than younger populations. Medical interventions can also contribute, however, to years of suffering and expense for an elderly person and their family, often related to patient and family misunderstanding of the situation, poor communication between family and doctors, and structural incentives for doctors to prolong life at all costs (chap. 12). As a result, in the interest of quality of life, it will be important to develop better guidelines for families and individuals as they weigh various medical procedures and to better protect health professionals from lawsuits when following patient or family wishes to allow someone to die. Advance directives for medical choice, palliative care, hospice, and death with dignity may be useful, but at present they are also culturally and logistically tricky to administer in many East Asian settings (chap. 12).

Technological Developments

There is also great hope placed on technological developments in the form of assistive devices, memory prompts, monitoring devices, and artificial intelligence (chap. 7). These may help seniors themselves and/or their caregivers, although there are pros and cons (chap. 7). Japan has taken the lead in this regard, and is often portrayed as a glimpse of the global future. For the most part, Japanese society has embraced coexistence with robots, which are viewed as useful tools rather than as a mode of surveillance. Japan has exported some care-related robots to other parts of East Asia (Foster 2018), and recently the Chinese government has begun promoting a Smart and Healthy Aging Industry Development and Action Plan (State Council of the People's Republic of China 2017), as well as developing its own robotic applications including assistive and companion devices (Chen 2019).

Sustainability Issues

Finally, sustainability issues are a major consideration for aging societies (Stephenson et al. 2013). Climbing temperatures, increasing air pollution, more severe and more unpredictable weather events, and sea level rise associated with global warming and climate change could lessen the health of the elderly (Span 2019; Stephenson et al. 2013). The considerable overall population decline projected for aging East Asia between now and 2100 (UN 2017) may be a helpful carbon offset against the population rise expected in other high-fertility parts of the globe.[4] However, retirees in East Asia will also need to moderate their rising consumption levels to reduce their footprint (Span 2019). Senior environmental activism in Japan is one example of such efforts. The key will be to balance provisions for today's seniors with the needs of younger generations.

Directions for Future Research

Aging and caregiving for and by the elderly and the phenomenon of aging societies in East Asian locales are vitally important topics for future research. All of the topics explored by the chapters in this volume will continue to be highly significant into the future. Any of these chapters can be taken as a point of comparison for research in a different sociocultural setting or social group, or as a baseline from which to conduct future research in the same sociocultural setting.

All of the policy directions discussed above are important areas for new research as well. Since care work is increasingly distributed across different social actors, more in-depth research is needed on interactions of policy and grassroots action, familial and nonfamilial care, and nonprofit and marketized forms of care. Researchers with a deep understanding of the language, culture, society, and history of East Asian societies should be an integral part of research design and data analysis. We need mixed methods research to monitor and assess the diverse effects of social change and societal interventions on these aging societies from multiple social and generational perspectives. It is important to bring a historical and cross-culturally comparative eye to understand baselines, trajectories, and complex interactions of factors and to learn from other sites while assessing sociocultural fit. In the 2020s to 2030s, when more East Asian locales than just Japan will have reached the super-aging level, it will be important to study and compare how they each deal with related challenges. As the situation unfolds, it will also be important to consider whether and how the COVID-19 pandemic may dampen the global population aging curve in some locales.

Another area for future research is investigation of these issues in other Confucian-influenced localities like Macao and Vietnam and eventually North Korea, if feasible, since population aging is accelerating there as well. In 2015 the elderly proportion (age sixty-five and above) of their populations were North Korea 9.7 percent, Macao 8.6 percent, and Vietnam 6.7 percent (UN 2017). By 2050 it is predicted that Macao and Vietnam will reach super-aging status at 28.0 percent and 21.5 percent elderly, respectively; North Korea will be close at 19.8 percent. North and South Korea would form an interesting intracultural comparison, as would Macao and Hong Kong. Since they are developing countries also slated to become old before getting rich ("Destitute Dotage" 2018), Vietnam and North Korea would lend a valuable comparison with China.

An additional area of limitation of this volume is that it does not address the full range of diversity within the East Asian locales studied. Future research should pay more attention to aging and caregiving in relation to lesbian, gay, bisexual, transgender, queer or questioning, and intersex (LGBTQI) and minority ethnic groups within these societies.

Concluding Remarks

Aging affects individuals and societies that are fortunate enough to get there. Long lives and aging societies are both a blessing and a challenge. East Asia is one important site from which to examine these issues due to the rapidity of its aging and modernization and its continuing concern with Confucian ideals of filial piety. We have strived to provide data and analysis useful for rethinking the intersection of aging and caregiving in East Asian societies, with reference to but going beyond traditional filial piety. We hope that our chapters help both to illuminate social changes that have taken place since Ikels's (2004) groundbreaking volume and to provide a new baseline for future comparative research.

Aging and caregiving by and for the elderly will only become more important with time, in East Asian societies and other places, as life expectancies continue to rise and more locales enter super-aging territory. We need well-designed research and well-informed policy to analyze the past and present, and to forecast, forge, and monitor the road ahead. More-innovative responses will be required to meet the eldercare challenges and productive aging opportunities of the coming decades. We look ahead to the future with curiosity, concern, and hope.

Acknowledgments

We are grateful to our mentors and families and to series editor Jay Sokolovsky and assistant editor Tom Bonnington.

Jeanne Shea (邵镜虹) is associate professor of anthropology and director of the Health and Society Program at the University of Vermont in Burlington, Vermont. USA. Recipient of two Fulbright Awards, she has published on menopause and midlife, marital relationships, the family, spousal caregiving, senior volunteering, evidence-based medicine, and community supports for aging in place in China. Most recently, she has published several research articles in *Ageing International* (2016, 2017, 2018) and a chapter on China's Senior Companions Program for *The Cultural Context of Aging: Worldwide Perspectives* (Sokolovsky 2020).

Katrina Moore is an honorary associate in Japanese Studies, Faculty of Arts and Social Sciences, the University of Sydney. She is the author of *Joy of Noh: Embodied Learning and Discipline in Urban Japan* (SUNY Press 2014). She contributed chapters to Vera Mackie and Mark McLelland (eds.), *Routledge Handbook of Sexuality Studies in East Asia* (Routledge 2015); Maren Godzik (ed.), *Altern in Japan* (Verlag 2009); and articles in *Aging and Anthropology* (2017), *Japanese Studies* (2013), *Asian Anthropology* (2010), and *Journal of Cross-Cultural Gerontology* (2010). She currently researches conservation practices as well as family and household relationships.

Hong Zhang is associate professor of East Asian Studies at Colby College in Waterville, Maine, USA. Her research interests include family and marriage, one-child policy, intergenerational relations, population aging, new eldercare patterns, urbanization, and rural-urban migration in contemporary China. She has published in numerous edited volumes, including recent chapters in *Transformation of Chinese Patriarchy* (Santos and Harrell, eds. 2017) and *Cultural Context of Aging: Worldwide Perspectives* (Sokolovsky 2020). Her work has also appeared in academic journals such as *Ageing International, Journal of Contemporary China, China Quarterly, Signs, the China Journal*, and *Asian Anthropology*.

Appendix 1

Historical Trends Noted in Ikels's Volume (2004) and This Volume

HISTORICAL TRENDS	Similar in 2004 and 2020	Similar but Trend Deepening 2004–20
DEMOGRAPHIC CHANGE		
Rising life expectancy		X
Falling fertility rate		X
Degree of population aging increasing		X
Accelerating speed of population aging, compression		X
Old-age dependency ratio rising		X
Number and proportion of old and old-old rising		X
Healthy life expectancy rising		X

HISTORICAL TRENDS	Similar in 2004 and 2020	Similar but Trend Deepening 2004–20
MODERNIZATION		
Not deculturating convergence with West	X	
Not total resistance of tradition to modernization	X	
Increasing modernization		X
Increasing industrialization		X
Increasing urbanization		X
Increasing globalization		X
ECONOMIC DEVELOPMENT		
Rising prosperity		X
More personal savings		X
Increasing social stratification in society		X
ROLE OF THE STATE/PUBLIC POLICY		
Continuing state encouragement of filial piety	X	
Some government policies undermining filial piety	X	
Growing state involvement in elder support and care issues		X
More resources for pensions		X
More resources for health services or coverage		X
More state support for nonfamilial services		X
ROLE OF THE MARKET		
Role of the market		X
As undermining filial piety		X
As providing more options for elder support and care		X
CHANGES IN THE FAMILY		
Smaller families		X

HISTORICAL TRENDS	Similar in 2004 and 2020	Similar but Trend Deepening 2004–20
Less coresidence, more neolocality		X
More geographic mobility and longer distances		X
Greater ability to communicate over long distances		X
Conjugal bond strengthened	X For younger couples	X For not just younger but also older couples
Intergenerational independence with reciprocity		X
Growing individualism but with continuing familism	X	
Ascending familism declining relative to descending familism	X	
Combining bilateral kinship with patrilineal tradition		X
Continuing gender inequity	X	
More gender equity than before		X
Discursive gender neutrality		X
Intergenerational stratification		X
AGING		
Not paradise for the elderly	X	
Greater longevity		X
Healthy longevity into later old age		X
Longer periods of late-life chronic illness		X
FILIAL PIETY		
Remains an important touchstone, not rejected	X	
Majority continue to hold filial piety as a value or ideal	X	
Difficult to realize traditional form in practice	X	
Reinterpretation of filial piety		X

HISTORICAL TRENDS	Similar in 2004 and 2020	Similar but Trend Deepening 2004–20
Greater diversity in practices counted as filial piety		X
Greater flexibility in how to enact filial piety		X
DIMENSIONS OF FILIAL PIETY		
Continuance and success of family line	X Reduced state focus on this	X More family focus on this
Obedience toward aging parents		X Reduced focus
Coresidence of adult children with elders		X Reduced focus
Living apart can enhance filial piety		X Enhancing affective bonds and interactions, reducing conflict
Material support from adult children		X Reduced focus
Declining respect of elders by younger generations in family		X More about mutual intergenerational respect
Affection between aging parents and their adult children		X
Warm interpersonal interactions in family		X
Harmony and reduction of conflict		X
Hands-on direct care		X Reduced focus
Managing indirect care done by others		X
Filial state		X
Filial village	X	
Filial community, volunteer, nonprofit, or business		X

Appendix 2

Topical/Thematic Coverage in Ikels's Volume (2004) and This Volume

TOPICS/THEMES	Ikels's Volume (2004)	This Volume
LOCALES		
China	X	X
Hong Kong		X
Japan	X	X
Korea	X	X
Singapore		X
Taiwan	X	X
Urban areas	X	X
Rural areas	X More rural coverage	X
DEMOGRAPHIC THEMES		
Compression of speed of population aging		X
Healthy life expectancy rising		X
MODERNIZATION		
Compression of modernization		X
FILIAL PIETY DIMENSIONS		
Continuance and success of family line	X Reduced state attention to this as element of filial piety	X Reduced state attention and more family attention in some instances
Obedience toward aging parents	X As declining	X As displaced by value of mutual negotiation
Coresidence of adult children with elders	X As declining	X As declining even further
Living apart can enhance filial piety	X Mentioned briefly in Zhang 2004: 73	X Enhancing affective bonds, warming interpersonal interactions, reducing conflict

TOPICS/THEMES	Ikels's Volume (2004)	This Volume
Material support from adult children or elders	X As declining	X As declining
Declining respect of elders by younger generations in family	X More about mutual intergenerational respect	X More about mutual intergenerational respect
Affection between aging parents and their adult children		X Increasing emphasis
Warm interpersonal interactions in family		X Increasing emphasis
Harmony and reduction of conflict		X Increasing emphasis
Hands-on direct care	X As declining	X As declining further
Seniors encouraging filiality by contributing and being self-reliant as long as possible	X	X
Outsourcing eldercare to other kin, hired help, or even nursing home can be seen as filial		X
Managing indirect care done by others from afar		X
Filial state	X	X
Filial community, nonprofit, or business	X As in filial village	X As in all of these
CONTEMPORARY REALITIES		
Contemporary realities in conflict with traditional filial ideals	X	X
Filial ideals being modified to fit with current realities	X	X
COMPETING VALUES		
Individualization	X	X
Descending familism (versus ascending familism)	X Mentioned although not using those terms	X Covered in more depth

TOPICS/THEMES	Ikels's Volume (2004)	This Volume
Nurturance of descendants as a competing value (rather than part of filial piety)	X	X
Harmonious relationships, avoidance of conflict (rather than part of filial piety)	X	X
Senior self-reliance, independence, mutual aid	X Mentioned	X Covered in more depth
COMPETING SOCIAL FORCES		
Societization of care	X Mentioned although not using those terms	X Covered in more depth
Marketization of life	X Mentioned although not using those terms	X Covered in more depth
Increasing geographic mobility	X Mentioned	X Covered in more depth
Globalization	X Mentioned	X Covered in more depth
FLEXIBILITY		
Less strict adherence to traditional social norms	X	X
Situational flexibility	X Mentioned	X Covered in more depth
Mutual negotiation of what works for all concerned	X Mentioned	X Covered in more depth
CAREGIVING FOR ELDERS		
Caregiving for elders	X	X Extended periods of time due to prolonged morbidity
Good care	X	X

TOPICS/THEMES	Ikels's Volume (2004)	This Volume
CAREGIVING BY ELDERS		
Caregiving by elders for themselves, spouses, and other old people	X Mentioned care by selves and spouses	X Covered all and in more depth
Caregiving by elders for children or grandchildren	X Mentioned	X Covered in more depth
Good care		X
Migrant grandparenting		X
FAMILIAL ELDERCARE		
Elder support and care by adult children	X	X
Care by seniors: see "Productive Aging" below	X Mentioned	X Covered in more depth
Grandchildren caring for elders	X Mentioned	X Covered in more depth
NONFAMILIAL ELDERCARE		
Nonfamilial eldercare	X Mentioned	X Covered in more depth
Nonfamilial eldercare by seniors: See "Productive Aging" below		X
Collectivist model of care	X In past years	X In past and present
Community-based care	X	X Covered in more depth
Nonfamilial caregivers becoming family-like		X
MIXED MODELS OF ELDERCARE		
Combining familial and nonfamilial forms of care	X Mentioned	X Covered in more depth
New balance of family, society, market, and state responsibility for eldercare	X Mentioned	X Covered in more depth
GERONTECHNOLOGY		
Use of technology in eldercare		X Robots, assistive devices, communication technologies

TOPICS/THEMES	Ikels's Volume (2004)	This Volume
SENIOR VOICES/AGENCY		
Senior subjectivity/voices	X Mentioned	X Covered in more depth
Senior agency	X Mentioned	X Covered in more depth
Intragenerational reciprocity, senior mutual aid		X
Seniors finding meaning in later life		X
Seniors finding meaning in caregiving for others		X
Seniors finding meaning in being cared for	X	X
Seniors finding meaning in dying, death, or grieving		X
PRODUCTIVE AGING		
Senior self-care	X Mentioned	X Covered in more depth
Senior care for spouses or other elderly kin	X Mentioned	X Covered in more depth
Seniors caring for non-kin elders		X
Elders caring for their children or grandchildren	X Mentioned	X Covered in more depth
PERSONHOOD		
Good person, good old person		X
Good caregiver	X	X
Good life		X
DEATH AND DYING		
Care in dying		X
Care after death		X
Death rituals	X	X
Dying or dead person as caring for others		X
End-of-life care		X

TOPICS/THEMES	Ikels's Volume (2004)	This Volume
Grieving process		X
Good death		X
Hospice care		X
DEVALUING ELDERS		
Devaluation of elders	X	X
Neglect of elders	X	X
Taking advantage of elders	X	X
Elders devaluing themselves	X	X
SENIOR EMPOWERMENT		
Pensions promoting elder independence from children	X Mentioned	X Covered in more depth
OTHER TOPICS/THEMES		
Ascending versus descending familism		X
Burden of the old on the young	X	X
Burden of the young on the old		X
Caregiving as trajectory		X
Centenarians		X
Dependence of elders	X	X
Disempowerment of younger generations	X	X
Division of family household	X	
Elder suicide	X Mentioned	
Face or shame	X	X
Globalization and transnational eldercare networks		X
Great grandparenthood	X	
Guilt		X
Imagined futures		X
Inheritance issues	X Covered in more depth	X Mentioned
Interdependence of generations	X	X

TOPICS/THEMES	Ikels's Volume (2004)	This Volume
Long-term care		X
Meal rotation	X Jing 2004	
Media portrayals	X	X
Models for eldercare, how well they travel		X
Neglect	X	X
Pension fraud		X
Repatriation of seniors		X

Notes

1. For a more detailed outline of similarities and differences between the findings in the present volume and Ikels's edited collection, the reader is directed to the appendixes for this chapter. Those tables lay out two kinds of differences between the volumes. In appendix 1, the table involves those differences that are clearly related to social change over time. Appendix 2 involves those differences that are more tied to the particular analytical foci of the chapters in each volume. In addition, of course, the present volume contains material from Hong Kong and Singapore that were not within the scope of the earlier collection.
2. Yet, Japan's birth rate has not fallen quite as low as that of the four tigers, perhaps due to a slightly more effective pronatalist policy.
3. While such definitions include societal obligation to provide salutary conditions, some regard active, healthy, or productive aging campaigns as a neoliberal tactic to shift responsibility from families and government onto individuals, premising seniors' value on personal responsibility, societal productivity, and successful acquisition of capabilities and resources (Wen 2013: 83).
4. Whereas global population is expected to rise to more than 9.7 billion by 2050 and more than 11 billion by 2100, East Asia's expected overall population decline could help mitigate global warming. Based on UN figures (2017), between 2015 and 2100, Japan's population is expected to fall from almost 128 million to under 85 million, China's from just under 1.4 billion to 1.02 billion, South Korea's from 50.6 million to 38.7 million, and Taiwan's from 23.5 million to 16.9 million. Hong Kong and Singapore's populations are predicted to hover between a little over 5 million and a bit over 8 million over the same period.

References

Center for Public Impact (CPI). 2017. "Tackling the Declining Birth Rate in Japan." *Center for Public Impact Case Study,* 7 April. Retrieved 1 May 2019 from https://www.centreforpublicimpact.org/case-study/tackling-declining-birth-rate-japan/.

Chen, Siyi. 2019. "China Is Developing Care Robots to Provide Companionship to Elderly." *Quartz*, 28 May. Retrieved 3 June 2019 from https://classic.qz.com/machines-with-brains/1016249/china-is-developing-care-robots-to-provide-companionship-to-elderly-nursing-home-residents/.

China Labor Bulletin (CLB). 2019. "China's Social Security System." *China Labor Bulletin*, 1 March. Retrieved 1 May 2019 from https://clb.org.hk/content/china%E2%80%99s-social-security-system.

Chiu, Peace. 2019. "Hong Kong Retirement Age Must Rise or Legislation May Be Needed, Elderly Commission Chief Says." *South China Morning Post*, 17 February. Retrieved 1 May 2019 from https://www.scmp.com/news/hong-kong/hong-kong-economy/article/2186518/hong-kong-retirement-age-must-rise-or-legislation.

"Destitute Dotage: Vietnam Is Getting Old Before It Gets Rich." 2018. *The Economist*, 8 November. Retrieved 1 May 2019 from https://www.economist.com/asia/2018/11/08/vietnam-is-getting-old-before-it-gets-rich.

Featherstone, Mike, and Hepworth, Mike. 2009. "Images of Aging: Cultural Representations of Late Life." In Sokolovsky, *The Cultural Context of Aging*, 3rd ed., 134–44.

Foster, Malcolm. 2018. "Aging Japan: Robots May Have Role in Future of Elder Care." *Reuters News Service*, 27 March. Retrieved 3 June 2019 from https://www.reuters.com/article/us-japan-ageing-robots-widerimage/aging-japan-robots-may-have-role-in-future-of-elder-care-idUSKBN1H33AB.

Geddie, John. 2019. "Gray Matter: Singapore, Unions Agree to Raise Retirement Age." *Reuters News Service*, 5 March. Retrieved 1 May 2019 from https://www.reuters.com/article/us-singapore-ageing/gray-matter-singapore-unions-agree-to-raise-retirement-age-idUSKCN1QM12O.

Harper, Sarah. 2014. *Aging Societies.* New York: Routledge.

HelpAge International. 2015a. "Older People in Ageing Societies: Burden or Resource?" *HelpAge Network Asia/ Pacific Regional Conference 2014*, 1–20. Retrieved 12 December 2015 from http://envejecimiento.csic.es/documentos/documentos/HelpAge-personasmayores-sociedadesenvejecen-Carga-recursos-05-2015.pdf.

———. 2015b. *Policy Mapping on Ageing in Asia and the Pacific Analytical Report.* Retrieved 1 May 2019 from https://www.refworld.org/pdfid/55c9e6664.pd.

Ikels, Charlotte, ed. 2004. *Filial Piety: Practice and Discourse in Contemporary East Asia.* Stanford, CA: Stanford University Press.

Inavatullah, Sohail. 2003. "Aging: Alternative Futures and Policy Choices." *Foresight* 5 (6): 8–17.

Jing, Jun. 2004. "Meal Rotation and Filial Piety." In Ikels, *Filial Piety*, 53–62.

Kajimoto, Tetsushi. 2019. "Retiring Late: As Pensions Underwhelm, More Japanese Opt to Prolong Employment." *Reuters News Service*, 10 April. Retrieved 1 May 2019 from https.reuters.com/article/us-japan-economy-retirement/retiring-late-as-pensions-underwhelm-more-japanese-opt-to-prolong-employment-idUSKCN-1RM0GP.

Kim, Erin Hye-Won. 2018. "Low Fertility and Gender Inequity in Developed Asian Countries." *Asian Population Studies* 14 (2): 113–15.

Kim, Hyun-bin. 2019. "From 65 to 70: Government Mulls Revising Legal Age of Seniors to Delay Arrival of Aged Society." *Korea Times*, 25 January. Retrieved 1 May 2019 from http.koreatimes.co.kr/www/nation/2019/01/371_262688.html.

Kim, Yang-Sook. 2018. "Care Work and Ethnic Boundary Marking in South Korea." *Critical Sociology* 44 (7–8): 1045–59.

Kleinman, Arthur, Yunxiang Yan, Jing Jun, Sing Lee, Everett Zhang, Pan Tianshu, Wu Fei, and Jinhua Guo. 2011. *Deep China: The Moral Life of the Person, What Anthropology and Psychiatry Tell Us about China Today.* Berkeley: University of California Press.

Lum, Terry Yat-sang. 2013. "Advancing Research on Productive Aging Activities in Greater Chinese Societies." *Ageing International* 38 (2): 171–178.

Morrow-Howell, Nancy, and Ada C. Mui, eds. 2012. *Productive Engagement in Later Life: A Global Perspective.* New York: Routledge.

National Statistics Republic of China (Taiwan) [Taiwan Department of Statistics]. 2018. "Life Expectancy and Death Rates." Retrieved 24 March 2020 from https://eng.stat.gov.tw/public/data/dgbas03/bs2/yearbook_eng/y006.pdf.

Organisation for Economic Co-operation and Development [OECD. 2017. "Old-Age Dependency Ratio." *Pensions at a Glance 2017: OECD and G20 Indicators,* ed. Organisation for Economic Co-operation and Development, 122–24. Paris: Organisation for Economic Co-operation and Development. Retrieved 1 March 2019 from https://doi.org/10.1787/pension_glance-2017-22-en.

———. 2018. "Working Better with Age: Executive Summary and Assessments ad Recommendations." Extract from *Working Better with Age: Japan, Ageing and Employment Policies.* Paris: Organisation for Economic Co-operation and Development. Retrieved 1 May 2019 from http://www.oecd.org/els/emp/Brochure%20OW%2028-08.pdf.

Peng, Ito. 2017. "Elderly Care Work and Migration: East and Southeast Asian Contexts." Paper for Expert Group Meeting on Care and Older Persons: Links to Decent Work, Migration and Gender. United Nations Headquarters, New York, 5–7 December. Retrieved 1 May 2019 from https://www.un.org/development/desa/ageing/wp-content/uploads/sites/24/2017/11/Peng-UN-Expert-Group-Meeting_Dec-5-7-final-Paper_4Dec.pdf.

Poon, Linda. 2018. "South Korea Is Trying to Boost Its Birth Rate: It's Not Working." *City Lab,* 3 August. Retrieved 1 May 2019 from https://www.citylab.com/life/2018/08/south-korea-needs-more-babies/565169/.

Rice, Carla, Eliza Chandler, Jen Rinaldi, Nadine Changfoot, Kirsty Liddiard, Roxanne Mykitiuk, and Ingrid Mündel. 2017. "Imagining Disability Futurities." *Hypatia: A Journal of Feminist Philosophy* 32 (2): 213–29.

Scheper-Hughes, Nancy, and Margaret Lock. 1987. "The Mindful Body: A Prolegomenon to Future Work in Medical Anthropology." *Medical Anthropology Quarterly* 1 (1): 6–41.

Shea, Jeanne, and Hong Zhang 2017. "Introduction to Aging and Caregiving in Chinese Populations." *Ageing International.* 42 (2): 137–41.

Sokolovsky, Jay. 2009. *The Cultural Context of Aging. Worldwide Perspectives.* 3rd ed. Westport, CT: Praeger.

———. 2020. *The Cultural Context of Aging: Worldwide Perspectives.* 4th ed. Westport, CT: Praeger.

Span, Paula. 2019. "Older People Are Contributing to Climate Change, and Suffering from It." *New York Times,* 24 May. Retrieved 31 May 2019 from https://www.nytimes.com/2019/05/24/health/climate-change-elderly.html.

State Council of the People's Republic of China. 2017. "China Plans Smart and Healthy Eldercare." Retrieved 24 March 2020 from http://english.www.gov.cn/policies/latest_releases/2017/02/17/content_281475569998024.htm.

Stephenson, Judith, Susan Crane, Caren Levy, and Mark Maslin. 2013. "Population, Development, Climate Change: Links and Effects on Human Health." *Lancet* 383 (9905): 1665–73.

Taiwan Social Security Office of Retirement and Disability Policy (TSS). 2019. "Old Age, Disability, and Survivors." *Social Security Programs, Taiwan.* Retrieved 24 March 2020 from https://www.ssa.gov/policy/docs/progdesc/ssptw/2010-2011/asia/taiwan.html.

United Nations (UN). 2015. "Do Pro-Fertility Policies in Singapore Offer a Model for Other Low-Fertility Countries in Asia?" United Nations Expert Group Meeting on Policy Responses for Low Fertility, New York, 2–3 November. *East-West Policy Center Policy Brief,* no. 15. Retrieved 1 November 2019 from https://www.un.org/en/development/desa/population/events/pdf/expert/24/Policy_Briefs/PB_Singapore.pdf.

———. 2017. *World Population Prospects: The 2017 Revision, DVD Edition.* Department of Economic and Social Affairs, Population Division. New York: United Nations. Custom data for original charts developed by author for this chapter acquired via website Retrieved 1 July 2018 from https://population.un.org/wpp/DataQuery/.

———. 2019. *World Population Prospects: The 2019 Revision.* Department of Economic and Social Affairs, Population Division. Custom data for original charts developed by author for this chapter acquired via website. Retrieved 15 May 2019 from https://population.un.org/wpp/DataQuery/.

Weerasekara, Poornima. 2019. "China's Population Shrinks Despite Two-Child Policy." *Mail and Guardian,* 3 January. Retrieved 3 June 2019 from https://mg.co.za/article/2019-01-03-chinas-population-shrinks-despite-two-child-policy-experts.

Wen, Wong Kai. 2013. "Futures of Ageing in Singapore." *Journal of Futures Studies* 17 (3): 81–102.

World Bank. 2018. "Total Fertility Rate, Births Per Woman, China." Retrieved 1 May 2019 from https://data.worldbank.org/indicator/SP.DYN.TFRT.IN?locations=CN.

World Health Organization (WHO). 2002. "Active Ageing: A Policy Framework." Retrieved 1 May 2019 from https://extranet.who.int/agefriendlyworld/wp-content/uploads/2014/06/WHO-Active-Ageing-Framework.pdf.

———. 2018. "Life Expectancy and Healthy Life Expectancy, Data by Country." *Global Health Observatory Data Repository.* Retrieved 1 August 2019 from https://apps.who.int/gho/data/node.main.688?lang=en.

———. 2019. "What Is Healthy Ageing?" Retrieved 1 May 2019 from https://www.who.int/ageing/healthy-ageing/en/.

Yan, Yunxiang. 2016. "Intergenerational Intimacy and Descending Familism in Rural North China." *American Anthropologist* 118 (2): 244–57.

Zhang, Hong. 2004. "'Living Alone' and the Rural Elderly: Strategy and Agency in Post-Mao Rural China." In Ikels, *Filial Piety,* 63–87.

———. 2017. "Recalibrating Filial Piety: Realigning the State, Family, and Market Interests in China." In *Transforming Patriarchy: Chinese Families in the Twenty-First Century,* ed. Goncalo Santos and Stevan Harrell, 234–55. Seattle: University of Washington Press.

———. 2020. "Globalizing Late Life in China and Realigning the State, Family and Market Interests for Eldercare." In Sokolovsky, *The Cultural Context of Aging,* 4th ed..

INDEX

www.ingramcontent.com/pod-product-compliance
Lightning Source LLC
Chambersburg PA
CBHW062106040426
42336CB00042B/2255